£1.25

D1582039

Rosie Lipsts
14 Thornton Court
Cambridge

R

HESSIAN TAPESTRY

Also by David Duff:

BIOGRAPHIES:

MOTHER OF THE QUEEN

THE SHY PRINCESS

EDWARD OF KENT

PRINCESS LOUISE, DUCHESS OF ARGYLL

THE DUKE OF CAMBRIDGE (WITH E. M. DUFF)

NOVELS:

LOCH SPY

CASTLE FELL

TRAITORS PASS

ESSAY:

MAN OF GOD—THE STORY OF A NORFOLK PARSON

Alice, Princess of Great Britain and Ireland
Wife of Grand Duke Louis IV of Hesse and the Rhine
Wearing the Orders of Victoria and Albert and the Crown of India

HESSIAN TAPESTRY

DAVID DUFF

FREDERICK MULLER

First published in Great Britain 1967
by Frederick Muller Ltd., Fleet Street, London, E.C.4

The main text is Copyright © 1967 by David Duff

The extracts from the memoirs of the Marquess and Marchioness
of Milford Haven are Copyright © 1967 by the Broadlands
Archives Settlement

Printed in Great Britain
by Ebenezer Baylis and Son, Limited
The Trinity Press, Worcester, and London

CONTENTS

5

CONTENTS

ILLUSTRATIONS

7

Genealogical Tables

AUTHOR'S NOTE

THE foundation of this book is Earl Mountbatten of Burma's comprehensive work, *The Mountbatten Lineage*, prepared for private circulation in 1958. By courtesy of Lord Mountbatten I have been able to study the Reminiscences of his parents, Prince and Princess Louis of Battenberg, the first Marquess and Marchioness of Milford Haven, and with his permission, and that of Lord Brabourne and the Broadlands Archives Settlement, to make extracts from these Reminiscences.

Prince Louis of Hesse and the Rhine has allowed me to make use of information in the Hessian Grand Ducal Archives at Wolfsgarten. I am indebted to him for his detailed amendments and suggestions, and for steering me away from certain widely believed and accepted theories which have no foundation in fact.

I have dealt in considerable detail with the life and work of Princess Alice, Grand Duchess of Hesse, second daughter of Queen Victoria, as to date scarce tribute has been paid to this forward-thinking Princess who was foremost in furthering the cause of emancipation of women in Germany, and in organising welfare and hospital services there. Although a memoir by her sister, Princess Christian, was published in 1885, in the main this consisted of letters to Queen Victoria, and, in the words of Lady Milford Haven, the Queen was "some one whom my mother regarded with respect and almost awe". Consequently there were sides to Princess Alice's character which did not show in these letters.

Among the many volumes of biography and reminiscence which I have studied, special mention must be made of the following: *The Life and Tragedy of Alexandra Feodorovna, Empress of Russia*, by Baroness Sophie Buxhoeveden; *Dearest Child—Letters between Queen Victoria and the Princess Royal, 1858–1861*, edited by Roger Fulford; *"My Dear Duchess"—Social and Political Letters to the Duchess of Manchester, 1858–1861*, edited by A. L. Kennedy; *An Unbroken Unity—A Memoir of Grand-Duchess Serge of Russia, 1864–1918*, by E. M. Almedingen; *Memoirs of H.R.H. Prince Christopher of Greece*;

A*

9

and *Towards Disaster—The Greek Army in Asia Minor in 1921*, by Prince Andrew of Greece. I am grateful to Lord Rennell of Rodd for permission to quote from the Reminiscences of his father; to Mr. John Terraine for permission to quote from his documented statement on the part played by Prince Andrew of Greece in the Asia Minor campaign of 1921–22; and to Mr. Michael Llewellyn Smith, of St. Antony's College, Oxford, for advice on the chapter dealing with this campaign.

The portrait of Prince Andrew of Greece, which hangs at Buckingham Palace, is reproduced by permission of His Royal Highness Prince Philip, Duke of Edinburgh; the portrait of the Princess of Battenberg by permission of Her Majesty Queen Victoria Eugenia; the portrait of the Grand Duchess Eleonore of Hesse and the Rhine by permission of His Royal Highness Prince Louis of Hesse and the Rhine; and the portraits of Empress Marie of Russia, of Prince and Princess Louis of Battenberg (Marquess and Marchioness of Milford Haven), and of Princess Alice, Grand Duchess of Hesse and the Rhine, which hang at Broadlands, by permission of Earl Mountbatten of Burma.

By permission of Prince Louis of Hesse and the Rhine I have selected certain pictures from the family photograph albums at Wolfsgarten. Of particular interest is Princess Alice's own album, covering, as it does, the first years of camera studies.

The Arms on the cover are those of the Grand Duke of Hesse, reproduced by permission of Prince Louis of Hesse and the Rhine, and of Earl Mountbatten of Burma and the Marquess of Milford Haven, by their permission. Although I do not deal, except for passing reference, with Lord Milford Haven or Lord Mountbatten of Burma, I use their Arms as they embody those of so many people dealt with in this book.

My thanks are due to Mr. Arnold McNaughton for compiling the genealogical tables; to my wife and Mrs. Fenella Baines for advice and assistance with the manuscript; and to Mrs. J. M. Rochester for typing, and patiently retyping, and for help with proof reading and indexing.

DAVID DUFF

Weybread, September 1965—March 1967

ACKNOWLEDGMENTS

The author wishes to thank the following publishers for permission to quote from books published by them: John Murray for *From Whippingham to Westminster*, the Reminiscences of Lord Ernle; *A Victorian Diarist*, edited by the Hon. E. C. F. Collier; *My Dearest Duchess*, edited by A. L. Kennedy, and *Letters of Queen Victoria* (various series); Evans Brothers Limited for *Dearest Child*, edited by Roger Fulford; The Bodley Head for *An Unbroken Unity* by E. M. Almedingen; George Allen & Unwin Ltd. for *Queen Mary* by James Pope-Hennessy; Cassell & Company Ltd. and D. C. Benson & Campbell Thomson Ltd. for *Queen Victoria's Relations* by Meriel Buchanan; and Cassell & Company Ltd. and A. P. Watt & Son for *The Daughters of Queen Victoria* by E. F. Benson.

I

Alice in Nurseryland

QUEEN VICTORIA HAD NINE CHILDREN. SHE WISHED TO make it ten, but, after the birth of Princess Beatrice in 1857, Sir James Clark, the royal physician, told her that she had had enough.

The third child's name was Alice. When she arrived in the Buckingham Palace nursery, that closely guarded wing was firmly under the sway of two important little people, Victoria, Princess Royal of England, known as "Vicky", in her third year, and Albert Edward, Prince of Wales, known as "Bertie", in his second.

The early hours of 25th April 1843. Only those concerned with the beginnings of life and its end, and the watchmen and the bakers, were astir. As the first streaks of dawn outlined the City of London, the Queen was delivered of a girl child. Prince Albert fussed around, too concerned with the present to dream that the great-grandchild of his new daughter would play a similar role to his own in that same Palace a century of years ahead.

Of all the official personages whose duty it was to be present only the Earl of Liverpool, Lord Steward of the Household, was on parade. The others arrived late, as the first bulletin was being posted.[1] Relieved that they had been saved the tedium of a long

13

wait, and that mother and child were well, they hurried home to breakfast.

The Queen suffered severely during the birth, but only for a short time. There was no repetition of the nightmares through which she had passed on previous occasions, particularly with "Bertie". In 1858, as she prepared to become a grandmother, she wrote to her eldest daughter: ". . . my first two confinements—for want of order—and from disputes and squabbles (chiefly owing to my poor old governess* who would meddle) were far from comfortable or convenient. . . ."[2]

The Queen kept notes of her experiences during all her pregnancies and thus had a store cupboard full of hints to pass on to her daughters when their turn came. She considered that it was best that the first child should be a girl, as they were less trouble than boys. She was of the opinion that only a year between births was too short a time, and that the Prince of Wales would always suffer from arriving so soon after the Princess Royal, a point which may have influenced her attitude towards him. She was a great believer in keeping calm and doing what she was bid. A natural revulsion for the intimacies upset her deeply at first, but when Alice was born she was able to tell her Uncle Leopold, King of the Belgians, that for the first time she was independent of nerves.[3] By the time her last children arrived she was in fact guiding the doctors and nurses as to what to do next. In the case of her youngest son and daughter she experienced the comfort of "that blessed Chloroform".[4]

Alice was a fat and forward baby. Her father, whose firm belief it was that, to be popular with the British, one had to crack little jokes, nicknamed her Fatima. He considered that she would be the beauty of the family. Even her mother, who admitted that she was "no admirer of babies generally", also agreed that she was pretty, and was very proud of her. She was not always so complimentary. She thought that the Prince of Wales in infancy looked "too frightful".[5]

As a young mother Queen Victoria did not often make the journey down the corridor to the nursery. She liked to have her

* Baroness Lehzen.

children around her when she walked in the gardens or to the farm at Windsor, calling to them, "Come along, my chicks."[6] But there was no desire in her to see them bathed in the evenings, and it was not until she was thirty-eight and had had her last baby that she insisted on doing this duty herself. The wet nurse therefore reigned unchallenged. There were many applicants for this regal post, "some being from ladies of wealth and position". To those in the lower stratas the fee was an added attraction. The £500 paid in the case of the Princess Royal was doubled for the Prince of Wales.[7] But on this occasion the honour and the reward led to tragedy. The lady in question ended her career by murdering her own six children.

Victoria was only twenty-three when Alice was born. After her girlhood in seclusion she was tasting still the thrill of dancing far into the early hours, of going in state to the theatre, of visiting great houses. In the evenings alone with Albert she demanded *égoïsme à deux*, not wishing a baby's chuckle to steal the glitter from her role. Ten years later she wrote to Princess Augusta of Prussia:

> ... I find no especial pleasure or compensation in the company of the elder children ... only very occasionally do I find the rather intimate intercourse with them either agreeable or easy. You will not understand this, but it is caused by various factors. Firstly, I only feel properly *à mon aise* & quite happy when Albert is with me; secondly, I am used to carrying on my many affairs quite alone; & then I have grown up all alone, accustomed to the society of adult (& never with younger) people ...[8]

That Queen Victoria could not bridge this gap in intimacy was in the main due to the fact that she did not feed her children herself. And she had very definite views on the subject. When her two eldest daughters married and, after experience with wet nurses, took on the task themselves (on occasion, the one helping the other out),[9] their mother was frantic and accused them of making "cows of themselves".[10] There was soon to be a black Angus heifer in the byre at Balmoral, which answered to the name of "Princess Alice".[11]

The root cause why Queen Victoria had so large a brood was because she wished to keep the love of Albert at a high peak.

Although she disliked the operation of childbirth, put the responsibility for it square on man's desire for pleasure, and was of the opinion that, if men had to go through it, they would not be able to stand the pain for a minute, it had its recompense. During her pregnancies and while she recovered from the birth, all was peace between husband and wife. After the arrival of Princess Alice she wrote: "Albert has been, as usual, all kindness and goodness."[12]

Prince Albert was German through and through. His ideas on marriage fitted in with the national constant, supplemented by that which he had seen in his father's house. In addition he and his wife were first cousins. Often such a relationship restricts romantic extravaganzas. "There is not the same stimulus for those masculine and feminine feelings that novelists like to write about as when there is no relationship. Social graces languish, *sans gêne* taking their place."[13] In the romantic sense, their courtship was short. Their real love grew stronger with the passing of the years, based on a mutual admiration of the other's qualities, aided by the loneliness at the top. Yet she was for ever asking for more than he could give. Tormented by jealousy, she insured herself with the policy of babies.

Albert loved his babies. They did not have opinions of their own or answer him back. They laughed naturally with him. He was in complete sympathy with them until the time when they developed minds of their own. Then he lost his magic touch.

In his early years as a father, while his State duties were still light, he was a far more frequent caller at the nursery apartments than the Queen. Ever since the Boy Jones (known by the royal staff as In-I-go Jones) had been found under a sofa there, Albert had nightly checked the windows of the wing, locked the outer door and kept the key on his person. He would appear again at eight in the morning and often take the children along to see "Mama".

The absence of the Queen from the nursery allowed the Prince to prepare a surprise present for her birthday on 24th May. He smuggled Landseer into the Palace, and, under a veil of secrecy, set him to work to paint "Fatima", lying in a cradle, with Dandie, the black terrier, keeping guard over her. She saw the result, wreathed with flowers, as she came into her breakfast room on the great day. Albert's stock soared still higher.[14]

The christening was fixed for 2nd June. The Queen wrote to King Leopold:

> Our little baby . . . is to be called *Alice*, an old English name, and the other names are to be *Maud* (another old English name and the same as Matilda) and Mary, as she was born on Aunt Gloucester's birthday.* The Sponsors are to be: The King of Hanover—Ernestus the Pious; poor Princess Sophia Matilda,† and Feodore‡ . . .[15]

In her selection of invited guests, the Queen was trying to patch up relations with the older members of her family. The Duke of Sussex had died four days before the birth of Princess Alice, and she considered it time that the jealousies and bitterness that had clouded her younger years should be finally put aside. It was for this reason that she asked the Duchess of Cambridge, who had on one occasion refused to drink the health of Prince Albert. Her son, George, had been the Tory selection for Victoria's husband, but had taken refuge in the Mediterranean until Albert was safely installed, and had now set up an establishment with an actress from Drury Lane.

Yet the ogre of the occasion was Ernest, King of Hanover— Duke of Cumberland until the salic law entitled him to take over British responsibilities in Germany in 1837. This most terrifying son of George III was responsible for introducing into English vernacular the phrase "To Hell or Hanover". Despite the court verdict, many people still believed that it was the Duke who was responsible when his valet Sellis was found dead on his bed with his throat cut in 1810. Furious at the thought of no longer being heir-presumptive, he had refused to attend his niece's wedding. He referred to Albert as "that paper Royal Highness", to which Albert replied with "Ernestus the Pious". It seemed that sparks might fly again on that happy day of 2nd June.

Ernest played true to form. He drove up to Buckingham Palace

---

* Princess Mary, Duchess of Gloucester.
† Princess Sophia Matilda of Gloucester.
‡ Princess of Leiningen, the Queen's half-sister.

after the christening and the luncheon were over. He then made a scene because the proceedings had not been held up until his arrival. But for the Queen there was relief and she was able to report: "Our christening went off very brilliantly . . .: nothing could be more *anständig*, and little *Alice* behaved extremely well."[16] But Ernest was not done with yet. Three weeks later, at the wedding of Princess Augusta of Cambridge,* he played his hand. As the royal procession neared the altar, he pushed his way quickly forward and took his place by the Queen. Whereat Albert punched him, knocking him down the steps. The Master of Ceremonies led "the Ogre" away.

When she was ten months old Princess Alice underwent the ordeal of vaccination. The first instance of this preventive step had taken place seventy years earlier, when Edward Jenner inoculated a boy with matter from the cow-pox vesicles on a milkmaid's hands. Early in the nineteenth century he was introduced to the Royal Family and described his theories. It was through the patronage of the Palaces that vaccination spread through Britain.

"A magnificent baby" was produced for the occasion and seated before Alice. "Such a duet of shrieks as the two kept up, staring and terrified at each other, and ascribing the cuts, no doubt, to each other, instead of Mr. Brown."†[17]

Quickly the halcyon days of Victoria and Albert slipped away. The elder children moved on to the schoolroom, yielding place in the cots to new arrivals. "Fatima" was renamed "Alee". Alfred, alias "Affie", was born in 1844, Helena, alias "Lenchen", in 1846, and Louise, who was burdened with the sobriquet of "Loo-loo", in 1848. Then the spacing opened out, nine years covering the birthdays of the three youngest, Arthur, Leopold and Beatrice. The prophecy made in the much publicised cartoon published in 1841, entitled "*1855; or a Scene in Perspective*", had so nearly come true. Then a rotund Albert and a dumpy Victoria had been depicted with a crocodile of fourteen children behind them. They are addressing a lean and tattered Mr. Bull. Victoria coos: "Our

---

* To Frederick William, Grand Duke of Mecklenburg-Strelitz.
† Dr. Brown, who for many years attended the Royal Family.

little family, Mr. Bull! I quite envy the *pleasure* you *must have* in *contemplating* them. What a happy man you must be!!!" Albert is saying: "Ah, ah, Mistare Pull, I tell you one, two, three fouten year ago, I come to your country for your *Goots!*" The dismayed Mr. Bull replies: "Goods indeed! you have had Money and Goods with a vengeance!"[18]

To cope with the domestic and educational needs of the increasing royal brood, an army of carefully chosen attendants moved into the Palace. At their head was the famous governess, Lady Lyttleton, whose reign lasted until 1851, when she was succeeded by Lady Caroline Barrington, sister of Earl Grey. The nurses were Mrs. Packer, whose real name was Augusta Gow, a Scottish student at the Royal Academy of Music; Mrs. Ratsey, who, to the annoyance of Prince Albert, *would* gurgle "boo-boo" at the babies; Mrs. Hull, known as "Old May"; and Mrs. Thurston, who played her part until 1865 and spent her evening days in a cottage in the grounds of Kensington Palace. Miss Hildyard taught the children English; Madame Rollande de Sange, French; Fräulein Gruner, German; Mrs. Anderson, music; and Mr. Corbould, music. To this number were added tutors for the boys. Then there was Miss Skerret to look after clothes and Monsieur Nestor to care for hair. It was as she was having her locks adjusted that Princess Alice lost her heart for the first time.

The apartments of Buckingham Palace began to bulge with the pressure. The Queen and Prince Albert decided that something must be done, and called in Mr. Blore, the architect. He reported that the nursery department was confined to a few rooms in the attics, into which the smell of oil and glue permeated from a basement workshop. He asked for £150,000 to make "a new east front to the Palace, clear out and rearrange rooms in the south wing, make alterations in the north wing, new kitchen and offices with ballroom over, take down the Marble Arch, decorate, paint and alter the drains."*[19] As George IV had squandered over

---

* The Palace, as it was then, surrounded only three sides of the quadrangle, the fourth, facing the Mall, being open, the Marble Arch standing as a detached gateway. The Marble Arch was moved to its present site in 1851.

£1,000,000 on remodelling the Palace only twenty years earlier, the British public viewed the further expense with horror. Albert once again got the blame. *Punch* depicted him standing before his home, his family about him, addressing an audience of ragamuffins. "Such is our distress," he pleads, "that we should be truly grateful for the blessing of a comfortable two-pair back, with commonly decent sleeping rooms for our children and domestics. . . ."[20]

Among the brothers and sisters of Alice, "Vicky", the first born, reigned supreme. She was precocious. By the time she was three she was fluent in French, and spoke English with a German accent and German with an English. Driving in Windsor Park she announced: "*Voilà le tableau qui se déroule à mes pieds.*"[21] On another drive, in company with her mother, she considered that insufficient attention was being paid to her. She said: "There's a cat under the trees." Everyone turned to look at the non-existent animal. "Cat come out to look at the Queen, I suppose," she commented quietly. She referred to ladies-in-waiting as "those girls" and demanded that they run her errands.[22] She was her father's pride and joy.

"Bertie", after a bad start, found favour with his parents until the time for lessons came along. At the age of three he was described by Lady Lyttleton as "altogether backward in language, very intelligent, and generous and good-tempered, with a few passions and *stampings* occasionally. . . ."[23] The trouble was that Albert was trying to pump too much learning of an unpalatable kind into his son's head. This was the creed of Baron Stockmar, Albert's mentor. The result was that the boy blew off steam that he could no longer control, and often in a manner that hurt others. Mrs. Lilly, the monthly nurse, passed down the story of his treatment of a housemaid who was about to be married. She left her bridal gown lying across her bed. The Heir to the Throne crept in and smeared it all over with blacklead. In the frightful domestic scene which followed Prince Albert used a horsewhip, but he never cured his son. He ran amuck among a flock of sheep, and the shepherdess boxed his ears. He was well into his 'teens when he threw a bottle of ink over his valet. Causing discomfiture seems to have amused him. At the end of the century he was staying at Chatsworth. He sent a mince-pie, with special recommendation, down the table to Midshipman Pat Acheson,* Lord Gosford's younger son. As "middies" were unaccustomed to receiving such high royal favour, Acheson bit into it with relish. It was full of mustard.[24]

Of those junior to Alice, Alfred was the most mischievous of the family, and so resentful of his elder brother's inheritance that eventually the two had to be separated; Helena was a hearty tomboy, and rather plain; Louise was pert and artistic, and so independent that in later years she was seldom seen in her mother's house. Arthur was the Queen's favourite, a normal boy who liked to play with soldiers, the only one who could give advice to his mother without retaliation; Leopold was delicate, suffering from haemophilia; and Beatrice, upon whom the sun shone brightly for four years, moved under the dark shadow cast by the umbrella of her mother's gloom in 1861, and never managed to escape from it.

Alice herself was the problem child of the family. Her father began by describing her as the undoubted beauty of his brood, then changed to the pointed "poor dear Alice" and by the time she was twelve wrote of her as "still very delicate and nervous".[25] In 1876, two years before her death, the Princess told her mother that her childhood days had been the happiest of her life, but, judging by the experiences that she underwent in Germany, this is not surprising. There was no reason why she should not have been happy. At Osborne, in the Isle of Wight, there was a brand-new mansion, with grounds sweeping down to the sea, at which she spent the summer days. There was a splendid new castle in Scotland for the autumn-tinted times. At Windsor there was the park to ride in and all the fun of the farms. There was not the pressure on her that daily was applied to "Vicky", who was being groomed as the consort of the future King of Prussia from the time that she could toddle. Sentimental, hating to see pain inflicted, seldom naughty yet shy and wild as a fawn, loving animals and never happier than when on her pony, her teachers

* Hon. Patrick Acheson, D.S.O.; Captain, R.N.

soon noted the embryo of strange thoughts and powers. But on her fourth birthday she was still the happy "Fatima", and this was the scene, from the pen of her governess.

> Dear Alice is too pretty, in her low frock and pearl necklace, tripping about and blushing and smiling at her honours. . . . *One* present I think we shall all wish to live further off: a live lamb, all over pink ribbons and bells. He is already the greatest pet, as one may suppose. Princess Alice's pet lamb is the cause of many tears. He will not take to his mistress, but runs away lustily, and will soon butt at her, though she is most coaxy, and said to him in her sweetest tones, after kissing his nose often: "Milly, *dear* Milly! *do* you like me?"[26]

Early the parents, the nurses and the teachers noted the deep bond of understanding that existed between the Prince of Wales and Alice. Hers was the balm that melted away the passion and the stampings. She was watchful over him, then and always, as if she felt responsibility for him. When he made hurtful remarks, she would follow with some sweet saying that would take the sting away. "Bertie & Alice are the greatest friends & always playing together," the Queen wrote in her *Journal*.

She brought the best out in him. Alice was not often naughty, but on one occasion she disgraced herself by some breach of etiquette and was sentenced to solitary confinement in her bedroom. "Bertie" grieved for her and decided to take her comfort. Silently he crept up the stairs and along the corridor towards her door, darting from shadow's pool to shadow's pool between the oil lamps. He was nearing his goal when a hand came out of the darkness and gripped him by the hair. The Heir to the Throne, thus pinioned, made the sad excuse that he was "only going to give Alee a morsel of news".

Sheltered as she was, Alice underwent the horror and strain of two assaults on the Royal Family before she was eight. On 19th May 1849 she was driving down Constitution Hill with her mother when William Hamilton, an Irishman, fired a blank round from a home-made pistol at the carriage. Back at the Palace the Princess was asked to describe what she had seen and her mother commented: "Alice gives a very good account of it."[27] On 27th

22

June of the following year Alice was again with her mother when she was attacked, this time with a cane, handled by a deranged ex-officer of the Hussars named Robert Pate. As the blow fell and the children screamed, the crowd seized the attacker and gave him rough treatment. The Queen wrote to the King of the Belgians:

> I have not suffered except from my head, which is still very tender, the blow having been extremely violent, and the brass *end* of the stick fell on my head so as to make a considerable noise. I own it makes me nervous out driving, and I start at any person coming near the carriage. . . .[28]

Such excitements apart, girlhood proceeded on its unruffled way. The Princess grew tall and thin. She had measles in 1853 and scarlet fever two years later. She was painted by Thorburn, Landseer, Winterhalter, Moira and Queen Victoria. There were no holidays from learning except on fête days, Christmas, birthdays and anniversaries, particularly of the royal wedding. Then the children, in honour of the occasion, would make some theatrical offering. Baroness Bunsen was at Windsor for the wedding anniversary in 1855:

> We followed the Queen and Prince Albert a long way, through one large room after another, till we came to one where hung a red curtain, which was presently drawn aside for a representation of the four seasons, studied and contrived by the royal children as a surprise to the Queen, in celebration of the day. First appeared Princess Alice as the Spring, scattering flowers, and reciting verses which were taken from Thomson's *Seasons*. She moved gracefully and spoke in a distinct and pleasing manner, with excellent modulation, and a tone of voice sweet and penetrating like that of the Queen. . . .[29]

To the younger children Alice acted the role of aunt. She was also banker. She lent young Arthur threepence. For some time she heard nothing about repayment. Then a letter arrived for her, addressed, "Princess Alice, Windsor Castle." Inside were three pennies and this note: "My Dear Princess Alice, Here's the threepence, Yours affectionately, Arthur."

2

Orange Sauce

Lthough Queen Victoria often expressed her deep
concern for, and horror at, the fate of young brides on
entering the nuptial chamber, she was not slow at propelling her own daughters towards its door. The only exception came
in the case of her youngest, whom, in the fashion of widows of the
last century, she looked upon to devote her life to the care and
support of a lonely mother. When Princess Beatrice excitedly
blurted out the secret of her love, the Queen did not speak to her
for six months, all communications being pushed across the
breakfast table in note form.[1]

To Victoria the choice of mates for her brood was in the nature
of a parlour game, the cards being confidential messages passed
round the courts of Europe. She began early—in the case of the
Princess Royal when she was only two. Prince Arthur's bride was
picked on the day of her birth and although, of his own account,
he inspected many other possibilities, it was his mother's choice
whom he eventually led down the aisle. The Queen was expert
at drawing red herrings across the trail, and few at Court could
guess her real aims. Prince Christian of Schleswig-Holstein arrived
in Britain believing that he was destined to be the husband of
Queen Victoria, instead of Princess Helena, as the plan proved to be.

The Queen was guided in her choice of candidates by the political situation in Europe and by family ties, both of herself and Albert, the whole being subject to the approval of Baron Stockmar. The Coburg seed was to be planted in many palaces. But these plans sometimes came into conflict with those of other members of the family of George III, in particular the Cambridges. Duke Adolphus had married Princess Augusta of Hesse-Cassel and the family network had ideas of its own. Already its members had been twice foiled of the great prize. In 1819 young George* had for a few weeks been the leader in the Royal Marriage Race, only to be relegated by the birth of Victoria† to the Kents. Twenty years later George had failed to marry his cousin. The Cambridges had much ground to make up. They eventually found their prize in Queen Mary. Meantime the cards were being shuffled again.

The early choice of the Queen and Prince Albert for their eldest daughter was Prince Frederick William of Prussia, born in 1831. His father was Prince William, Prince of Prussia, brother of the childless King Frederick William IV. His mother, Princess Augusta,‡ was a close friend of Queen Victoria.

Prince Frederick William first met his future in-laws at the opening of the Great Exhibition in 1851. With the children he saw the sights of London and played on the Osborne shore. He clearly knew his part, for thereafter a correspondence began between ten-year-old "Vicky" and himself. She ended her letters with ". . . from your ever loving and devoted Vicky".

Frederick William's next visit was in September 1855, when he received an invitation to stay with the Royal Family in Scotland. These were exciting times. On their arrival on Deeside on the 7th the Queen and Prince Albert had led their children into the wonders of the new Balmoral Castle. Three days later a telegram arrived from General Simpson—"*Sevastopol is in the hands of the Allies.*" The Crimean war was over. It was late and Alice and her brothers and sisters were abed. But soon they were mixed

---

* Born 26th March 1819. Succeeded to the Dukedom on the death of his father in 1850. Commander-in-Chief 1856–95. Died 1904.

† 24th May 1819.

‡ Princess Augusta of Saxe-Weimar, daughter of Karl Frederick of Saxe-Weimar and Grand Duchess Maria Paulowna of Russia.

in the wild excitement which swept through the tartaned house. From the windows they watched the flames leap from the great bonfire on the top of the hill, listening to the cheering and the singing of the men around it, which grew louder as the whisky flowed. Balmoral had got away to a start that no child could ever forget.[2]

On the 14th Prince Frederick William travelled up from London. Strolling along the platform at a stopping place, he thought he saw through a carriage window a man whom he recognised. He spoke to him. By coincidence strange indeed, it was none other than George of Cambridge, now the Duke, convalescing after his experiences in the Crimean campaign. That evening the Duke wrote to his mother: "To my astonishment it was the young Prince of Prussia *en route* to Balmoral, so evidently that marriage is to be. . . ."[3] The cat had escaped from the bag and jumped right on to a Cambridge knee.

Yet other eyes were also watching the movements of the Prussian Prince. *Punch* reported: "A very suspicious-looking eagle has been observed hovering about the Royal palace of Balmoral. It is supposed that the bird of ill-omen has an eye towards HER MAJESTY'S dove-cote."[4]

The Royal Family gathered at the Castle gate to receive the Prince. He kissed the Queen's hand, shook Prince Albert's, and then turned to the Princess Royal and Princess Alice. A fortnight later, during a ride up Craig-na-Ban, Frederick William seized the opportunity of being out of earshot of the rest of the party to press a piece of white heather into the hand of "Vicky", as a preamble to making "an allusion to his hopes and wishes".[5] As the hopes and wishes of the two were coincident, the fourteen-year-old Princess Royal became unofficially engaged. The parental idea was that the engagement should remain hidden from the public eye until "Vicky" was seventeen, but such was not to be and soon it was common knowledge. *The Times* had some trenchant opinions on the subject, many of which, in the event, proved true.

To Alice, apart from the matrimonial magic which now enlightened the schoolroom, the marriage had two particular meanings. Firstly, she would soon be exalted to the important position of being the Queen's eldest daughter at home. Secondly, there was the exciting question, had Papa and Mama a Prince up their sleeve for her?

They had, though the secret was of course kept from Alice. On 1st April 1856 Queen Victoria wrote to the King of the Belgians: "May I beg to remind you to make enquiries, *quietly*, about the young Prince of Orange*—as to his education, *entourage*, and disposition?"[6]

Alice sat in the restful shadows of the schoolroom, whilst her elder brother and sister, in their emblematical role, travelled round with their father and mother on their journeys, both at home and abroad. She was not very quick at her lessons. She lacked "Vicky's" power of speedy reception of parental teaching, and the retention of it, without query as to its logic. After a period of obsession with ponies, and a liking for games with her younger brothers, she began to show an interest in music and the arts. She drew well. There was always in her a strong desire to help others, to be in touch with ordinary people. On a Sunday morning at Windsor she escaped her governesses and worshipped from the public pews, just so that she could experience the feeling of having people unknown to her on either side. She was happiest at Balmoral because she had the most freedom there and could come and go as she pleased. She was usually to be found in some tenant's cottage, helping to solve some problem, learning how others lived.

She took her first step out of the schoolroom set on 27th July 1857. It was the day that Princess Charlotte of Belgium, "Uncle" Leopold's daughter, married the Archduke Ferdinand Maximilian,† and there was a half-holiday from lessons. That evening Alice was allowed to dine with her parents and their guests for the first time. There may well have been a motive behind the elevation. A few days later the Queen of Holland,‡ mother of two sons, arrived to stay at Osborne. Alice's presence at dinner showed that she was no longer looked upon as a child.

---

* Prince William Nicholas, elder son of King William III of Holland. Born 1840.
† Emperor of Mexico. Shot at Queretaro, 1867.
‡ Sophia Frederica, daughter of King William I of Wurtemberg.

Soon the interests of the Royal Family were concentrated on one subject alone, the forthcoming marriage of the Princess Royal. On the night of 24th January 1858 "Vicky" and Alice shared a bedroom for the last time.

On the insistence of Queen Victoria the wedding took place in the Chapel Royal, although it was far too small to accommodate in comfort all those invited to attend. The authorities tried to solve the problem by allotting twenty inches for male backsides, and twenty-four for female. In the event these measurements did not meet the requirements, and considerable damage was done to wardrobes.[7]

In the procession Alice walked behind her mother, a sister on either side. She was wearing white lace over pink satin. Now the eldest unmarried daughter, she was privileged to carry a wreath, but Helena and Louise "had only bouquets in their hair". It was her most important public appearance to date. She did not seem to be a child any more, and there was a dawn of loveliness about her. There was much speculation as to who would be her groom when the time came.

When the ceremony was over emotions exploded. The bride "gave way to her pent-up feelings, and threw herself upon her mother's bosom, her whole form heaving with agitation. The Queen, whose feelings now became uncontrollable, warmly embraced her daughter again and again."[8] Off went "Vicky" and "Fritz" for a brief two days of seclusion at Windsor. On arrival they sat down on a sofa, one at either end, and the minutes passed in silence, for they knew not what to say.[9]

The population of the royal schoolroom, which had begun the year at nine, was reduced to six by its close. The Prince of Wales was studying under his tutor at White Lodge, Richmond. Prince Alfred joined the Navy. More and more often was Princess Alice sent for to spend the free hours with her mother. She was a more restful companion than "Vicky" had been, with her imperiousness, her back answers, her assuredness. Nagging at the back of the Queen's mind was the knowledge that the Princess Royal had been better educated than she had been, and in addition there was a touch of jealousy over the firm hold that the girl had on her father's affections. She admitted that she found her "trying" at times. But there were none of these drawbacks about Alice. She was not stirred to controversial level by the little problems of everyday life. Her mother wrote of her: "She is really very good, so amiable, so gentle, so obliging and so humble."[10] By the time of her sixteenth birthday Alice had become so useful, with a poise well beyond her age, that her mother decided that she would keep her services for at least two more years. The Queen of Holland was informed that, for the present at least, marriage plans were to be shelved. Victoria kept her interest in this direction stoked by planning a union for the Prince of Wales, a list of seven possibles having been prepared.

The Queen's summing up of her daughter's character was not, in full part, correct. Although deeply dutiful, Alice was in fact humouring her mother, intent on avoiding the scenes that could so easily blow up if the Sovereign considered that she was being crossed and not getting her way. Alice always handled her mother, treating her sometimes as if she was a child. In later years there were to be many secrets that she withheld from her. Already inside of her there was a spring bubbling with mischief and modern thinking, and doubts intermingled with artistic yearnings.

The parents noted a strong similarity between Alice and "Bertie". Yet there was a great difference between them. While Alice was studious and amenable, her brother was lazy and rebellious. Even at this time the Queen on occasion became so angry with her eldest son that she could hardly write his name, referring to him as "you know who". Then the parents were grateful indeed to Alice, for she alone could influence him.

Gradually she was allowed to feel her wings. In the summer she sparkled at an Osborne dance. In September she was with her mother at the opening of Leeds Town Hall.

Meantime the Queen was undergoing the emotional travails of being separated from her first-born. Having carefully planned her early departure to Prussia, she was now doing everything in her power to retain as firm a hold over the Princess as she had been able to do when she was in the schoolroom. Several times a week letters full of the grief at parting, of advice about sex, draughts, fresh air, cough medicines and lavatories, of instructions as to how to behave to whom and how to toe the Coburg party line, of accusation and remorse for non-compliance with previous instructions, were despatched to Berlin. As the only wish there was that the Princess Frederick William should forget all about England and, with complete loyalty and submission, become a German wife, the strain on the young bride soon reached near to breaking point. When she became pregnant, the danger to her health became very real.

Baron Stockmar saw what was happening and spoke thus to Lord Clarendon,* whom he met on a visit to Germany:

> I want to talk to you on a very important matter, and to invoke your aid. It relates to this poor child here. Her mother is behaving abominably to her, and unless a stop can be put to her conduct I know not what may be the consequences, for she is not in good health, and she is worried and frightened to death. The Queen wishes to exercise the same control and authority over her that she did before her marriage, and she writes her constant letters full of anger and reproaches, desiring all sorts of things to be done that it is neither right nor desirable that she should do, and complaining of her remissness in writing to her sisters or to Miss Hildyard† and her forgetting what is due to her own family and country. . . .[11]

In truth the point had become abundantly plain to Victoria that she was not Queen of both Prussia and Britain and that she had lost a daughter, and a very richly endowed one at that. But she would never acknowledge defeat and the propaganda and reproaches flowed on. In the event she nearly lost her daughter, and her first grandchild was born with a withered arm and other defects which eventually were unified in Kaiser William. But one lesson Queen Victoria did learn. Under no circumstances would Alice be allowed to marry into a Court where the wishes and powers of the British Sovereign took second place to nationalistic customs and ambitions. A prince from some poor and peaceful state was envisaged.

Alice was taking lessons from her father now. She would go to his study at six o'clock, but often she would wait for him in vain.

* 4th Earl of. Secretary of State for Foreign Affairs, 1853–58, 1865–66, 1868–70.
† Royal governess.

Gone was the dedicated enthusiasm with which he had instilled into "Vicky" on past evenings the absolute importance of working towards a liberal-minded, unified Germany. He had tried so hard to ensure that the apostle of Coburg, whom he had despatched to Potsdam, was fully briefed. Now he found that his teachings and beliefs were unwanted at the receiving end. He also found that the loss of his eldest daughter had left a gaping hole in his heart, a hole that was never to be filled. He was tired, and his eyes were dull. Often he complained of feeling unwell. Now that he had been elevated to Prince Consort, and had proved himself, higher and higher piled the papers on his desk. He rose early and in silence worked upon them by the light of his little green lamp.

Alice saw the change, and was kind, laying the foundations of the nurse role that she was later to play. The Queen was puzzled. Having terrific reserves of physical strength herself, she could not appreciate that her husband was weary and fatigued. Thinking that he pined for Coburg, in the evenings at Osborne she would take him by the hand and walk with him in the gardens, to listen to the nightingales. She knew that their song reminded him of his boyhood days.

In April 1859 Alice was confirmed. It was conducted according to the Coburg ritual and was a considerable ordeal. First she had to convince the Prince Consort and the Dean of Windsor that she was fully versed and ready. Then the Archbishop of Canterbury arrived and conducted his examination before the Princess's parents and her governess. After which she retired in solitude to her room to wait until the moment came. But there was the solace of many presents. From her mother and father came the Family Order, a cameo with diamonds, a gift upon which Roger Fulford makes an interesting observation: "This is possibly the earliest example of the gift of the Queen's private, family order."[12]

A few days later came her sixteenth birthday. Her mother saw that the child had gone, giving place to a pretty young lady, with perfect manners, able to move around among the Palace guests with easy grace. But, nevertheless, she wrote to King Leopold: "I shall not let her marry as long as I can reasonably delay her doing so."[13]

But the Prince Consort had other ideas. He let it be signalled to the Queen of Holland, by a tactful word in the right quarter, that he considered that an alliance between his daughter, Alice, and her eldest son, William (known as "the Orange Boy" and, later, "Citron") would be desirable, and T.R.H. would be glad to receive him and look him over should he visit England. Albert had apparently received information from his own private sources (in this case probably the Princess Royal) that young William was shaping well. It was an erroneous assessment, and one that he was deeply to regret having received.

In considering the proposal the Prince Consort made the mistake of ignoring the strong possibility that part of the father might be in the son. The King of Holland's marriage had been unhappy, ending in complete estrangement. There had been other ladies in his life. In addition he was addicted to strong spirits, Baron James de Rothschild being of the opinion that he could put back more undiluted spirits than any man he had ever met.[14]

Such dangers apart, there were obvious political advantages in Alice moving into the Dutch Palace. Uncle Leopold reigned in Belgium. There was a plan afoot to marry the Prince of Wales to Princess Alexandra of Denmark. What could be more cosy than installing Alice in between, in a peaceful country not far from home? The Prussians might not be too pleased about it, but they had already had the first slice of cake. Princess Frederick William was urged to produce more information. This she was able to do when she visited England in May. Of all the changes in her family, that in Alice struck her most. She had left behind a shy girl of fifteen. Now she was able to describe her sister as being "extremely elegant, well dressed and well coiffed".[15]

During the months which followed, the Queens of Britain and Holland put their heads together, and the news reached Alice, who had her own sources through her mother's Ladies, that a Prince was in the offing. Then she learned something else. The mothers considered that it should be the younger sister, Helena, who should make the trip to Holland. Whereat there was a scene. Princess Alice confided in Lady Ely* that "she shd: die no other

* Marchioness of, Lady-in-Waiting to Queen Victoria.

death than her sister being preferred to her & that she wanted
to be Queen of Holland".[16] The matter was resolved and Alice
took up her rightful position.

Yet with the autumn disquieting rumours began to reach the
Prince Consort about "the Orange Boy". It was said that, even
at this early age, he was both drinking and gambling. Although
such indulgence might be attributed to the high spirits of youth,
Lord Clarendon thought that he would have a word with the
well informed Madame B. He heard disquieting news, which he
passed on to the Duchess of Manchester:*

> ... she thought him thoroly ungentlemanlike & lowlived and that
> he evidently had no sense of what was decent or proper. She had
> had a very disagreeable letter about him from her husband since
> she left Baden & unless he mends very much she does not think
> it wd: be at all safe for the little duck Alice to marry him. ...[17]

By now the same information had reached Victoria and Albert,
one source being Princess Frederick William, who had been on a
visit to Baden. But she was less severe on "the Orange Boy". She
found him shy, and the fact that he was plain was not his fault.
He had good hair and complexion, and his teeth were white.
She thought that he was being led astray. To which her mother
tartly replied that if his teeth were white now, they could not be
his own, as they were anything but that when she had last seen
him three years before.

Fortunately Alice had put aside all thoughts of marriage in the
beauty of the present. The Royal Family was at Balmoral and
each day they went out for picnics and expeditions in the autumn
sunshine. The Princess put on four inches across the shoulders and
became quite plump.[18] As their ponies scrambled up Ben Muich
Dhui she told her mother that she could not bear the thought of
leaving her family and dear Balmoral. Four thousand feet up
Alice dismounted and ran with her father to look down over a
view where the Dee rises among the mountain walls. The Queen
stayed on her pony, John Brown at its head. "It is good," the

---

* Louise Frederika Augusta, daughter of Count von Alten, of Hanover. Married,
1st, 1852, 7th Duke of Manchester; 2nd, 1892, 8th Duke of Devonshire. Died 1911.

ghillie said, looking towards Prince Albert, "to walk with a person who is always content."[19]

The contentment was not to last long. Back at Windsor news was received that "the Orange Boy" had set his cap at the daughter of the Archduke Albrecht, a Catholic Princess. This was unfortunate, not only because it looked like a snub for Princess Alice, but also because anything to do with Papacy, at least at this stage in her life, gave the Queen the shivers. The feeling would doubtless be shared by the people of Holland. The Queen grieved for the Dutch mother, for whom the sun rose and fell in her elder son. Princess Frederick William arrived from Germany on a short visit and received stern instructions that she was not to mention "the P. of O." to Alice. Albert would do the talking in due season.

The season arrived quickly. In December "the Orange Boy" announced that he would be visiting England at the end of the following month. Alice was called to her father's study and warned, in careful words, of the dangers ahead. The Queen's immediate preoccupation was to ensure that "Bertie" was well out of the way when the visitor arrived, as he was near enough to Beelzebub as it was without receiving further assistance. She was also seized by the fear that the arrival of "the P. of O." might be construed that he was being accepted as a husband for Alice, and thus other suitors, more eligible than he, might be frightened away.

He arrived at Windsor. To everyone's surprise he made a favourable impression. This was undoubtedly due to priming, as Lord Clarendon had sent stern warning to the Queen of Holland. He played his cards well, his ace of trumps being that he listened intently to the Prince Consort's political diatribe at breakfast. With the Queen the line that he took was one of fatigue and melancholy, fatigue as a result of the strenuous educational pro-gramme that he had been set, and melancholy because he had never known a real home and at the loss of a dear brother—always a sure way to Victoria's sympathy.[20] He sat next to Princess Alice at dinner but suddenly shyness overcame him, and he turned his back on her.[21] He apparently found the position regarding her awkward. But the shyness came strange from a young man who, on the way to England, had paused in Paris and dipped deep into the pleasures there.

He visited, too, the other marriage mart—that of the Cambridges. The Duchess had an unmarried daughter, Mary.* The Duchess took him to the theatre. There was a pulchritude of ballet dancers upon the stage, but "the Orange Boy" did not stare at them and remained quiet. Lord Clarendon commented that she said this with surprise, as if she had expected him to leap from the box.[22]

The newspapers were now in full cry on the scent of a royal romance. All the details were blazed forth, even down to the date of the wedding and visits to be paid on the honeymoon. Princess Alice was furious. "The Orange Boy" was due to make a farewell visit before he returned home, and she just did not know what she was to say to him.[23]

A large dinner party was given in his honour at Buckingham Palace on 2nd March. It was to prove the end of the hopes of the House of Orange. Either "the Orange Boy" had forgotten the warnings that he had been given before he left home or he had found another attraction during his stay in England. That evening he was positively dull. In addition, he was rude to Princess Alice. All desires of being Queen of Holland faded away. Queen Victoria parted with him with the fear that one day he might return in pursuit of one of her younger daughters. Her fears were well founded.

What, then, of the future of "the Orange Boy", who, of man's age, became "Citron" of the Paris boulevards? Not long after the débâcle with Princess Alice, he pondered on the possibilities of Princess Mary of Cambridge, with whom he had been at the theatre on the night when he had no eyes for the ballet girls. He prepared another onslaught on London.

The thought of such an alliance filled Napoleon III with many misgivings. Princess Mary's brother was British Commander-in-Chief. Her family was, on her mother's side, strongly entrenched in Germany. He decided that the marriage should not take place.

* Married, 1866, Francis, Duke of Teck.

But he shelved the customary high level methods of rulers, and employed more subtle means. His plan was made easier when he learned that "Citron" was travelling to London via Paris.

There was laid across his route, as if by accident, one Elizabeth Cookson, a strumpet of great renown, who had once served in a New York whisky dive. The trap proved even more successful than the Emperor had dared to hope. Not only did the Prince of Orange delay his journey to England so that he might dally with Elizabeth, but he openly drove around with her in an orange-coloured landau bearing on its panels the Royal Arms of Holland. The news was flashed to London and, when the Prince finally arrived there, he found all doors firmly closed.

Apparently unconcerned, the Prince returned to Paris and continued his love life with Miss Cookson. The idyll was broken by the furious King of Holland, who cut off financial supplies. The couple were quickly in debt. It was Elizabeth who suggested the plan that she should go to The Hague and appeal to the King for help to relieve them of their most pressing needs. "Citron" agreed, and she took the train to Holland.

At The Hague the unbelievable happened. The King of Holland lost his heart to Elizabeth Cookson, and set up his son's mistress in her own establishment. For a time he managed to visit her in secret, but when, after a few months, the Dutch people came to know of the liaison, there was a scandal of mammoth proportions. The King had no alternative but to tell Elizabeth to leave. To help her on her way he presented her with the title deeds of a lead mine, which he thought was worthless. It turned out to be the opposite. The King tried to get those deeds back, but failed. Elizabeth returned to Paris a rich woman.[24]

She did not forget her "Citron". In August 1861 they were together in Wiesbaden. By this time Elizabeth had been dubbed *La Reine d'Hollande*, and the sight of the two walking about together openly in public caused a sensation[25] and was considered one of the blackest pages in the Prince's book.

Elizabeth eventually married a musical director in Paris and was thereafter always very kind to young men, particularly those in debt.

"Citron" continued his search for a bride. He put out feelers about Princess Louise, Queen Victoria's fourth daughter, but the Queen was ready for that one, and quickly blocked it. Overcome by an American heiress, he placed his heart and his Crown (when it came to him) at her feet. Unaccustomed as she was to such proposals, she turned him down, but kept his letters as souvenirs. He stayed with Corah Pearl for "quite a long time".[26] At the house of Sir George Arthur he became engaged to Diana, daughter of the Duke of St. Albans.[27] But the betrothal was broken off. It was at a performance at the Tuileries in 1869, given in honour of Queen Sophie of Holland, that "Citron" became entranced with Sarah Bernhardt. But the immortal actress would have no play with the butterfly of the Boulevards and, like a butterfly, she brushed him aside.[28]

In 1877 "Citron", suffering from diabetes, was told that he had not long to live, five years if he reformed and one if he did not. He told a specialist that he had no intention of reforming. Rather was he going to increase his excesses in the time left to him. The specialist gave him eighteen months on condition that he visited his surgery every day. "Citron" agreed to this. Within two years he was dead. Even so, he survived by a few months the British Princess whom two Queens had planned should be his bride. In the words of Sir George Arthur, he died with no real enemy in the world except himself.[29]

3

⚜

Alice in Wonderland

QUEEN VICTORIA ALLOWED HERSELF TO DRIFT INTO A STATE
of emotional perturbation over the question of the marriage of her second daughter. Once again, after an oasis
of comparative peace since the birth of her last child, she chivvied
her husband round the corridors, accusing, beseeching. She raised
her cudgel against her eldest daughter. She was convinced that the
two of them were in league against her, aiming to thwart her plans.
An additional cause may well have been that she saw in Alice some
of the gay, wayward tendencies that were so obvious in "Bertie".
Although Victoria was apt to exaggerate until true proportion was
left far behind, she was seldom completely wrong.

As she came up to the beginning of her eighteenth year Princess
Alice was proving a very pert and forward young lady, ever
anxious, when the chance came, to slip the royal apron strings.
"A good, dear amiable child", her mother described her on her
birthday,[1] but that was not quite the impression of others. In May
Lord Clarendon wrote of her: "Our *little friend* is so full of lark
that she admits *she doesn't know what to do with herself. . . .*"[2]

The Princess went to the House of Lords to hear Lord Lynd-
hurst* speak. When he had finished she turned to Lady Clarendon

* Lord Chancellor.

and said: "Now let's go off to your house and take the girls by surprise."* Having first checked that this was in order with the Queen, Lady Clarendon complied. On arrival the Princess told the servant to take her straight to the girls' room, and not to announce her. They were about to dress for dinner. She stayed there chatting until long after she was due home. She revealed to her hostess the secrets of her little loves and discussed whether she should marry the Prince of Orange (whom she said was ready at any time), although she knew full well that her parents would not now accept "the Orange Boy" at any price. Lord Clarendon (who only remained safe from royal attention by hiding, undressed, in his dressing-room) commented: "I think that damsel will give trouble before she has done."[3]

It was being said that if a husband was not found for her soon, she would be off on her own to Germany to find one for herself. The possibility that she might find one among the great houses of Britain was, at this stage, apparently not even being considered.

Yet the Queen had been giving the matter a great deal of thought since the time of the marriage of "Vicky", looking beyond the Dutch suitor. She had in mind "a good, kind husband—*no* brilliant position (which there is not to be got), but a quiet, comfortable position".[4] She had clearly had enough of the stranglehold that a court such as Berlin put on a married daughter. It was her wish, not to lose a daughter, but to gain a son. The two other people most directly concerned, the Prince Consort and Princess Frederick William, had differing views. Albert had to hold the balance of commonsense and take regard of politics. He also had to consider the financial angle. Being an astute business-man, he naturally wished his children to receive as much in the way of annuities and dowries as Parliament could be persuaded to confer. For a Princess to depart into the distant obscurity of a minor continental Duchy, bearing with her a large slice of public money, was hardly likely to find favour with the British people, many of whom considered themselves fortunate if they were able to buy a piece of fat pork once a week. "Here in this country," the Prince Consort remarked, "such a choice for Alice would not be

* Lord Clarendon had three daughters, Constance, Alice and Emily Theresa.

popular . . . the small German Courts are not held in any great esteem. . . ."⁵

Nor were the small German Courts held in much esteem in Berlin. Princess Frederick William, although at loggerheads with many of those around her, had already absorbed much of the superiority complex surrounding the Prussian eagle. She would have liked her sister to join her at Potsdam, or at least share some minor throne. She in fact produced a likely Prussian, but, as in the case of the Dutch candidate, family failings ruled him out.

It was in 1858 that Queen Victoria had first turned her gaze upon Darmstadt, a quaint, sleepy town, with narrow, cobbled streets, lying by the flat lands which lead westward to the Rhine. There dwelt Grand Duke Louis III of Hesse and the Rhine,* six

---

* Grand Duke Louis was head of one of the oldest Houses in Europe. Earl Mountbatten of Burma has traced the story of the Brabant/Hessian/Mountbatten family with great detail in his private published work, *The Mountbatten Lineage*. Beginning in the fourth century, he covers the lives of forty-four generations, ending with the children of Queen Elizabeth II and Prince Philip, Duke of Edinburgh, but points out the dangers of compiling a pedigree which goes back 1600 years, adding that it is not until the ninth century that the ground becomes sure and well documented. The first person known definitely, by documentary evidence, to be an ancestor of the House of Brabant is GISELBERT, who lived in that century, and thus Prince Charles of Wales is in the thirty-fifth generation of known descendants.

Among the Hessian ancestors was Charles the Great, King of the Franks. Called Charlemagne, he lived from 747–814. On Christmas day in the year 800 Charlemagne was crowned as Holy Roman Emperor in Rome by Pope Leo III.

A forbear of interest to the British was Prince George of Hesse-Darmstadt (1669–1705), a roving soldier who fought in many campaigns. In 1704 he sailed with the Hapsburg claimant King of Spain, Charles III, to Portugal and was appointed Captain-General in command of the Allied Army being assembled there for the invasion of Spain. The British placed their fleet at his disposal and he embarked on Admiral Rooke's flagship. Foiled by lack of support in his attack on Barcelona, Prince George decided to capture Gibraltar. He personally led the Marines who successfully took the Fortress on 5th August. Although he was the life and soul of the enterprise, and responsible for its success, full credit was never given to him. But, as commander of the expedition, Prince George assumed the office of Governor of Gibraltar, and the shield bearing his Coat of Arms hangs in the senior position of all the Governor's Shields in "the Convent", the present residence of the Governor.

Prince George was the second member of the Hessian family to play an important part in the history of British possessions in the Mediterranean. Frederick of Hesse-Darmstadt (1616–1682) matriculated at Sienna University, became a Roman Catholic in 1637 and entered the Order of St. John as a Knight of Malta. He served in the galleys of the Knights of Malta, of which he became Captain-General. In 1640 he commanded the galleys which defeated the Turks off Malta. A portrait of Frederick of Hesse-Darmstadt hangs in the Yellow Drawing Room of the Palace of the Grand Masters in Valletta.

feet and ten inches tall and the quintessence of Grand Dukery. He had six homes in the town and eighteen in the countryside. His chief claim to fame was that his sister was Empress of Russia, the ill-fated Marie. In 1841 she had married the Grand Duke Cesarevitch Alexander Nicholaievitch,* the same dashing young man who had taught the young Queen Victoria to dance the *Mazurka* and set her heart a-flutter.

Although twice married, the Grand Duke had no children. The heir presumptive was the brother next to him in age, Prince Charles. The third, and youngest, brother was Prince Alexander, who became the founder of the House of Battenberg/Mountbatten.

In 1836 Charles had married Princess Elizabeth of Prussia who, having been born on the day of the battle of Waterloo, had the Duke of Wellington and Prince Blucher as godparents. They had four children—Louis born in 1837, Henry† in 1838, Anna‡ in 1843 and William § in 1845. It was towards the eldest three that Queen Victoria turned her matrimonial sights.

It was to Princess Frederick William that the Queen looked for the necessary background material on the Hesse family. The girl she had in mind for the Prince of Wales, one of the boys for Alice. Therefore the necessary queries were included in her epistles to Berlin. To her annoyance no information came. Reminder followed reminder. Surely six weeks was long enough for basic enquiries? By the beginning of 1860 the Queen became convinced that "Vicky" was firmly on the side of the Prince of Orange.[6] But at last there came from the harassed Princess Frederick William an excellent report on the Princes of Hesse, complete with photographs. The Queen picked out that of Prince Louis, and from him her choice never wavered.

"Uncle" Leopold was now drawn into the net. He was ever a powerful ally of the Queen. He was invited to join the royal party for Ascot races, the precedent for attendance having been set by King William IV and Queen Adelaide. The King of the Belgians was asked to bring with him the two Princes of Hesse.

* Emperor Alexander II, died 1881.
† Married 1st, Baroness zu Nidda; 2nd, Baroness von Dornberg. Died 1900.
‡ Married Frederick Francis II, Grand Duke of Mecklenburg-Schwerin. Died 1865.
§ Married Josephine von Lichtenberg. Died 1900.

They duly presented themselves, rather shyly, at Buckingham Palace. The Queen thought that they were two of the nicest young men that she had met for a long time, and could not resist comparing them with "the P. of O.", to the latter's detriment. She poured over them a spate of pleasant adjectives. She liked their figures (she once vetoed a marriage because she considered the suitor had feminine hips), but did not consider them exactly handsome. Louis was the more robust of the two, taking after his Prussian mother. Henry looked delicate and had a strong look of his father.[7]

Alice moved towards Louis as a moth does to a flame. Completely at her ease, she circled close. She needed no brilliant ball or lilting tune to stir her heart, for on the evening that the two met the Yorkshire Choral Union was performing at the Palace. It was at Ascot that the knot was finally tied. Now Louis was her squire, and the pelting rain could not rob the days of their magic. Others did not find the experience so exhilarating. Her father commented: "We returned yesterday from the Ascot races, which unfortunately were made more tedious than usual by incessant rain."[8] Other royalties since that time have experienced the same feelings.

Before the sad farewell came on 9th June, Louis asked Alice for her photograph. She replied that she did not have one, as they were all in the possession of her mother. So off the Prince went to the Queen and asked for all the photographs, a point which the Queen considered indicative.[9] She was watching every point now, every sign of budding affection. It was her little plan and she was determined that it should succeed.

To some, at least, Princess Alice was making no secret of her love. She drove Constance Villiers around for two hours and chatted of nothing else. Lord Clarendon duly reported to the Duchess of Manchester:

> . . . She talked almost exclusively of her own anxieties and sufferings from excessive love for Pce: Louis; he is now the "*one* being" the only man she ever did, shall, can or will love and Mama knows from his Mother that she (A) is the only girl he could ever bring himself to marry. . . . She is just like a bird in a cage beating its' wings agst: the bars and if she could get out *wouldn't she go it*!![10]

The next step, as the Prince Consort wrote to Stockmar, was an approach from the young gentleman's family. The matter was handled by Princess Frederick William, prompted by her father, and in due course the vital letter arrived from Princess Charles of Hesse. The Queen had to tell someone and wrote to the King of the Belgians: "I venture now to confide a *secret* to you. . . . It is that *our* surmises respecting Louis of Hesse have turned out to be true, and that we have *reason* to *hope* that this *affair* will be in due time realised. . . . The feelings are very reciprocal on both sides. . . . Please do not say anything about it to any one. Your very great kindness and affection for our children has induced me to mention this to *you*, who moreover *saw the first dawning of these prospects.*"[11]

Meantime Princess Frederick William had given birth to a second child, a daughter, whom she named Charlotte. The choice was not to the liking of the Queen, who wished to perpetuate her own name as soon and as often as possible. But to her own younger children the news brought both delight and stature. When asked to conform with nursery routine, three-year-old Princess Beatrice would reply: "I have no time. I must write a letter to my niece."[12]

Now that the foundations had been laid for a marriage between Princess Alice and Prince Louis, the timely arrival of Princess Charlotte gave the Prince Consort a splendid opportunity to explain the facts of life to his second daughter. Once again she went to his study and "Papa told her all". The Queen commented that the news was joyfully received,[13] but whether she was referring to the biological data or that Princess Frederick William had, on this occasion, had an easier time, remains clouded. Nevertheless Princess Alice was later to profess horror at the thought of having children, a like feeling being expressed by the Prince of Wales during his engagement. Considering that, upon once reaching schoolroom age, the brothers and sisters were never allowed to be alone together in a room for a minute, the fact that fear and mystery hung over sex is not surprising.

The Queen made other preparations for the marriage. If the country was to provide generously for the financial security

43

of Princess Alice, it was advantageous that she be seen as much as possible in public. Thus she accompanied her mother to the opening of Parliament and to the first great volunteer reviews in Hyde Park and at Edinburgh. So that her outlook should be widened, it was decided that she should accompany her parents on a visit to Germany at the end of September.

This was to be the greatest adventure in Alice's life to date. In Belgium they were to stay with Uncle Leopold and see the beauties of Laeken. At Aix-la-Chapelle they were to be met by the Prince of Prussia, now acting Regent as the King was ill and dying. At Frankfurt the Grand Duke and Duchess of Baden would be waiting for them. At Coburg she would see the boyhood home and haunts of her father, and also "Vicky" and her son would be staying with them. Everything was set for a memorable holiday. For the Princess the only disappointment was that she would not be seeing Louis of Hesse, his home and his family. But her mother had decreed that this should not be, deeming that the matter should not be hurried.

For the Prince Consort the dual pleasure lay in seeing Coburg again and in meeting his grandson. He had tried so often to persuade "Vicky" to bring the boy to England, but each time she had pleaded some excuse. The truth was that she was hoping for some miraculous cure for young William's arm before he was inspected by his grandparents. But no miracle had come, and now the moment could be postponed no longer.

Yet from the moment that the royal holiday makers embarked on the *Victoria and Albert* at Gravesend, bound to see the boy who was one day to be Kaiser and Britain's foremost enemy, it seemed as if a curse descended on Albert the Consort. During the journey news reached them that the Dowager Duchess of Coburg* was seriously ill. She was dead by the time they reached Coburg, and a pall of gloom hung over the town. Bowed and pale, the Consort attended the funeral service.

Some light relief was afforded by the meeting with Prince William, who, wearing a white dress with black bows, was led into the presence by Mrs. Hobbs, his English nurse. The Queen

---

* The Prince Consort's stepmother, formerly Princess Marie of Wurtemberg.

enthused, saying how good he was. She was not to be able to say this for long, for within a few years he had referred to his British relations as "a pug-nosed lot"[14] and bitten one of his uncles in the calf.

The next blow followed quickly. On 1st October the Queen and Princess Alice went into the countryside to sketch. The Prince Consort was going about his business in Coburg, driving in a four-horse carriage. The road ahead was blocked by closed level crossing gates. An engine whistled, a leader took fright, and bolted. The carriage careered towards the gates. Albert flung himself clear, landing face down in the road. As he raised himself, wiping the blood and dust from his face, he saw the wrecked carriage and horses struggling wildly in their traces. One of them was dead. The coachman was seriously injured.

A messenger was sent to find the Queen and her daughter, and they raced back. To their great relief they found that the Prince Consort had only superficial injuries. What they did not guess was that his nerves were shattered. But when Baron Stockmar arrived, he saw the truth. "God have mercy on us!" he exclaimed. "If anything serious should ever happen to him, he will die."[15]

When out for a last walk with his brother, Duke Ernest noted that he was dabbing his face with his handkerchief. He thought that Albert was attending to his scratches, but then saw that he was crying. Albert then broke down and sobbed that he would never see his native land again.[16]

There were other troubles. The Queen was taken ill in Belgium, feeling more unwell than at any time since her marriage. The row over Captain Macdonald, a British tourist who had refused to give up a seat in a German train and had been ejected by fellow travellers, flared up to heights far above its real importance. *The Times* seemed to place the blame on the royal marriage ties with Germany, which incensed and saddened the Consort.

From this time forward blow after blow descended upon his tired brain. It was as if a curse . . . The word "curse" had a particular meaning to the Coburg family, for the generation before Albert and for two generations after him. In moments of travail

they heard the clear echo of the words that the Kohary* monk
had spoken in a churchyard at midnight: "Then verily shall I
pray to the Lord Almighty to visit the sins of the fathers upon the
children to the third and fourth generation of the Coburg line."
Already, in a superstitious age, there had been many happenings,
strange and sad, which had given the family reason to believe
that there was something more behind the bitter words than mere
hate. The fate of the Prince Consort, of Princess Alice and her
children after her, strengthened that belief. The curse pursued
the Coburg seed into the palaces of Portugal, Spain, Bulgaria,
Greece, Germany, Austria and Russia.

Yet, at sweet seventeen, Princess Alice saw none of these things.
Her father was only forty-one, and all fathers lived to become old
men like Uncle Leopold and Baron Stockmar. Her heart was full
of Louis and, as she correctly guessed, his of her. In November he
obtained leave from his regiment and made his joyful way to
Windsor.

* Prince Ferdinand of Coburg (1785–1851), brother of King Leopold of the
Belgians, married Antoinette de Kohary. She was the only child of Prince Joseph
Kohary, Chancellor of the Austrian Emperor, and a member of one of the richest
families in Hungary. The estate was entailed in favour of the male line, but Prince
Joseph persuaded the Emperor to issue a "filiation" order, which bestowed on
Antoinette the benefits of a son. The male members of the Kohary family, deprived
of their inheritance, resisted in vain, and one of them, Brother Emericus Kohary,
called down a curse on the Coburgs, according to the ritual detailed in the *Manuale
Exorcisorum*.

4

"Up the Airy Mountain"

IN STAGE-MANAGING THE DELIVERY OF PROPOSALS TO HER
daughters, Queen Victoria employed strange and devious
means, meticulously prepared. It was as if she was arranging
her own engagement all over again, she the star and the man
concerned uttering words of a suitable nature at a predestined
moment. Princess Frederick William commented that, in this
case, it was obviously not only the future bride who was in love,
but the bride's mother also.[1]

The time allowed for the exchange of the vital question and
answer was strictly limited, and the advantage of solitude was not
considered essential. On a later occasion the Queen allowed a
Princess to get well out of her orbit while the proposal was made,
and was thereafter filled with terror that the worst had happened.
Her fears proved ungrounded.

On 30th November the Queen and Prince Albert drove to
Aldershot to inspect troops. On their return the Prince blandly
informed Louis of Hesse that it had been arranged that he should
be given the opportunity of speaking to Alice.

After dinner, when the guests were occupied in conversation,
Louis and Alice gravitated towards the fire. Those in that comfortable area melted away. The Queen chatted gaily on, so posed

47

that she could watch the couple. She noted an earnest air creep into the conversation. After a suitable interval she made towards the door. The guests fell back. She, of design, passed close to Alice. The Princess whispered that she had received a proposal. Louis begged for her blessing. The Queen squeezed his hand and said "Certainly", adding that they would see him later.[2] She then went to her own room to do her evening work. This included the writing of a letter to Princess Augusta of Prussia in which she said that, although she was certain that "Vicky" would already have given her the glad news of Alice's engagement, she, the Queen, felt now she must do it herself.[3] So, if the Princess had that night answered the proposal in the negative, her mother would indeed have been in a dilemma.

Immediate matters of state settled, the Prince Consort summoned Louis to his study. Alice went to her mother's room, "agitated but quiet". Soon a message came from the study, the Queen and her daughter repaired there, and with joyous tears the fate of another Princess was settled.[4]

Lord Campbell was a guest at Windsor. He reported: "My stay at Windsor was rather dull, but was a little enhanced by the loves of Prince Louis of Hesse and the Princess Alice. . . . They reminded me of Ferdinand and Miranda in *The Tempest*, and I looked on like old Prospero."[5]

It had been laid down that the couple must wait for at least a year before they could be married. This upset the German Prince considerably and he pleaded for a remission. "Such a man!" Albert wrote to "Vicky". "He desires to see the fairest moments of his life curtailed, because he knows the issue and longs to leap towards it at once. How wisely is it ordained that in general we do not know our destiny and end; but for this, no one would wish to live."[6] It was indeed fortunate that he himself could not know of his destiny in the year ahead. Already he was victim of gastric trouble, his gums were swollen and the nerves jumped in his cheeks. At an age when many men were at the outset of their careers, he was weary of life.

In contrast, for his wife the flame of young love brought perpetual sunshine into the winter gloom of the Castle. The second stage of her planning was now revealed. She confided in her uncle in Belgium that Alice and Louis would spend much of their time with her after they were married, "Louis not having any duties to detain him much at home at present".[7] The monopoly exercised over "Vicky" by Berlin was not to be repeated in the case of Alice. This young wife would have her babies in the rightful place, her mother's home, and once again Albert would be able to walk down the corridor to the nursery and find relaxation by the same cot in which his own children had lain.

Prince Louis stayed on with the Royal Family for Christmas. His second experience of British weather was as unfortunate as the first. For the first half of December the rain pelted down, until the Queen thought that she would be marooned on the island of Windsor. Then the cold set in. It was the coldest Christmas for half a century. Twenty-two degrees of frost gripped the Thames hard and frozen white fog hung over the Park.[8] If the draughts in the Castle chilled to the marrow, at least there was skating to warm the blood. Albert sat at his desk, trying to fill the hole in his heart by writing to his adored "Vicky", telling her how the birds missed her and her supply of crumbs, expressing his love through the medium of treatises on the political future of Germany, while to his ears came the roars of delight as some royal backside hit the ice. But he was delighted with his presents from Berlin—a bust of young William's head, a boar's head, and an album of photographs.[9]

Among other guests at Windsor were the Prime Minister, Lord Palmerston, and the Leader of the Opposition, Mr. Disraeli, with his wife. Disraeli told the Queen that his wife was an excellent woman, but could never remember which came first, the Greeks or the Romans.[10] There was an ulterior motive behind the invitations. In the glow of the Yuletide cheer the Queen hoped to be able to make smooth the path for the passing through Parliament of an annuity of £6,000 and a dowry of £30,000 for Alice on her marriage. She knew that there might be opposition from the rank and file of the Tory Party, and she relied on Disraeli to quieten it. Her distrust of the clever Jew had faded. His personal loyalty was so touching and, in addition, he always said such nice things, particularly about Albert. Now she received his pledge that he would support the motion. So all went well when, on 14th February, the Queen opened Parliament and announced the happy event. Yet, in the light of future happenings, there was to be a touch of sadness about the day. It was to be the last occasion that she delivered the speech from the throne with her own voice.

The time came for Louis to return to Germany. Alice gave him her handkerchief, wet with tears. He pressed his upon her. It was equally wet. He had presented her with a little miniature of himself. She put it on a band of velvet. It hung round her neck, night and day, and she caressed it so often that there were fears as to how long it would last.[11] Yet, in certain circles, doubts were being expressed at the inadvisability of this marriage to a comparatively junior German princeling, and the opinion that someone more suitable might turn up if the ceremony was long delayed.

The year 1861, which should have been such a happy one for Princess Alice, was stained by death. It began on 1st January with the dying of the incurably mad King of Prussia. At two o'clock in the morning poor "Vicky" had to hurry through the frozen streets to the death chamber and there, in the shadows, she was kept for twelve hours until the old man died.* The experience made her physically ill.

At Frogmore the seventy-five-year-old Duchess of Kent, who had been suffering from cancer for the past six years, was weakening. Her eyesight was failing and her fingers were stiff. Alice went over almost every evening, playing the piano to her, sometimes attempting a duet, and reading to her. On 15th March the Royal Family were at Buckingham Palace when the call came that the Duchess was dying. The royal train was ordered, and off to Windsor hurried the Queen and Prince Consort, taking Princess Alice with them. The Duchess was too far gone to recognise her daughter, but all through the night the Queen kept watch, tiptoeing down from her room by the light of her little white lamp. At nine in the morning Prince Albert and Princess Alice were called in. They knelt by the bedside. Half an hour later the woman

---

* On the death of King Frederick William IV, Princess Frederick William became Crown Princess.

who gave Britain Victoria, died. Albert, in floods of tears, half carried his wife to a sofa in the colonnade. Then he turned to his daughter and said: "Comfort Mama." They were words that were to ring in her ears through the years to come.[12] At seventeen, she was the strength.

The intensity of the Queen's grief bordered on derangement. She made little effort to control it. She cried all day. Each morning and evening she made a pilgrimage to Frogmore. She recorded on paper every detail of the last hours. She penned extravaganzas about her grief to her relations, in particular to Uncle Leopold, who was not noted for his reticence. With the exception of Alice, she could not bear her children around her. The Crown Princess arrived from Germany and was told that her voice was too shrill. The Prince of Wales got into trouble because he did not cry, and the sound of him bickering with the younger children nearly drove the Queen mad. The rumour that she had, in fact, gone mad spread through the country. There had always been the danger that the mental weakness of George III would come out in his granddaughter. If so, what then would be the fate of Britain?

The Prince Consort, trying with all his might to soothe his wife, kept the rumour from her. But he was feeling the strain himself. Not only had he now to do much of the Sovereign's work, but in addition he had sole charge of the affairs of the Duchess of Kent. There were a number of skeletons in her cupboard that needed careful handling. These included the aftermath of her husband's mammoth debts and his long affair with Madame Julie de St. Laurent.

This first meeting of the Queen with death set the pattern for a nation's mourning during the remainder of her reign. She ordered that the Duchess of Kent's room should be left exactly as it was when she died. She was to do the same in the case of her husband, and today his room at Osborne is as it was when he walked from it on a summer's day in 1861. Queen Alexandra, then Princess of Wales, followed the same pattern when her eldest son, Prince Albert Victor, died at Sandringham. In so many homes, unknown, unnumbered, there was a room in a corridor, the door of which was kept locked, and the blinds drawn. Many were to remain so until far into the twentieth century.

Part of Queen Victoria's grief was due to remorse, remorse over the quarrels with her mother twenty years before. Part was frustration. To her Jehovah was a ruler, like herself, of a vast area, with headquarters probably somewhere out past Australia. The frustration came in her rival's totally unfair powers of disposal. Without having to account for it, and without recriminations, he could simply put people out of the way, often at the most inconvenient moments. So she floated on her sea of tears, unheeding the burden that she was placing on the shoulders of a tired husband and a young daughter. She needed a John Brown to tell her, direct to her face, to pull herself together. But he was still only a ghillie at Balmoral, earning his few shillings a week.

Fortunately for Princess Alice, Louis of Hesse came over for a visit in May. He had a tonic effect on the Queen, who always liked men who were full of fun and did not contradict. She was so delighted with him that she conceived the plan of making him a Royal Highness. After all the troubles that she had gone through to achieve the same status for her husband, it was hard to understand why she wished to tackle an even greater problem over this minor German Prince, whom Lord Clarendon described as "*un petit galopin*". He would only be able to use the title when he was in Britain, where no one would care. It would certainly not be accepted in the German courts.[13] Fortunately the Queen was persuaded to drop the matter before it developed into a storm.

Yet in the garden of the Queen the Prince from Hesse flourished. Not even his developing measles, which he passed on to delicate Prince Leopold, who suffered severely, and with permanent ill effects,[14] diminished the pleasure of his presence either to his fiancée or her mother.

After a summer stay at Osborne, Princess Alice accompanied her parents on a visit to Ireland. The underlying reason for this visit was that the Prince Consort wished to check on the progress and behaviour of the Prince of Wales, who was at the Curragh Camp, attached to the 2nd battalion of the Grenadier Guards.

Life for poor "Bertie" had been hard of late. After a triumphal tour of Canada and America the previous year, he had returned only to be told that the success was entirely due to his being his mother's son and the fine work of his staff. There was no parental bouquet for the Heir. The Prince Consort wrote sarcastically to Stockmar about "our Hero". To "Vicky" he referred to her brother as the most thorough and cunning lazybones that he had met in his life.

With the echo of the cheers and laughter of New York and Boston still in his ears, "Bertie" was hustled off to Oxford, to study under conditions which amounted almost to imprisonment, ever under the steely eye of his governor, General Bruce. On one occasion he did manage to escape those eyes and was quickly on a train for London, pleasure bent. He reckoned without the electric telegraph. On dismounting from his carriage, he found a grim reception committee awaiting him.[15]

In the New Year the Prince of Wales was sent on to Cambridge, living with General Bruce and his wife in a large house at Madingley and insulated against the pleasures of the town by four miles of countryside. His temper grew worse. But now there began to veer towards him, when the opportunity arose, a few young men hell bent on the pleasures of life. Admiring him for his outstanding performance in America, they saw in him a companion who might well join them in their jaunts, and in the future prove useful to them in the fields of influence and finance. In addition there was fun in showing the apple to one so sternly controlled by the Queen, the Prince Consort and General Bruce. They smuggled to him books in paper covers and tobacco. Soon they were to smuggle more compromising goods. They were the kind of aristocratic young gentlemen whom the Consort considered to be among the worst elements in Britain.

The Prince of Wales had long wished to undertake military training. This had been vetoed. But in the spring General Bruce unaccountably changed his views as to the evil influences of the society of soldiers, and "Bertie" was allowed to join the Guards in camp. The experience was to have considerable effect on him. Even his usually reticent biographer, Sir Sidney Lee, remarked on it.

Colonel Percy saw that the Prince was kept hard at work, but he found opportunities for relaxations free from the supervision of his middle-aged guardians. At the Headquarters hut he exercised private hospitality. Under the influence of comrades in camp near his own age his outlook on life widened, and he was introduced to dissipations which were new to him. He learned for the first time something of the meaning of unimpeded liberty.[16]

Suspicions that too much liberty and levity were being indulged in urged the Prince Consort to see for himself. The presence of Princess Alice was advantageous, as it was in her, and her alone, that "Bertie" would confide. However secret such confidences might be, the Queen was expert in wheedling them out. There was particular reason for the Prince's good behaviour at the moment as, unbeknown to him, a bride had been chosen for him, and the knot all but tied. Princess Alice openly told her parents that she would not appreciate a mate being chosen for her without her knowledge, but she was informed that "Bertie" was different and incapable of making the selection himself.

On 22nd August the royal party reached Viceregal Lodge in Phoenix Park, Dublin. Two days later the Queen inspected 10,000 men at the Curragh, including her son, and was glad to see he did not look so very small.[17] Both she and his father seemed pleased with him, but at lunch in Headquarters hut afterwards the Prince Consort held forth on "the idle tendencies of British youth" and deplored the fact that officers discussed hunting and shooting in the mess, instead of concentrating on military tactics.[18]

Then off they went to the lakes of Killarney. There all was peace. The Prince Consort wandered about repeating, "This is sublime! This is sublime!"[19] The Queen loved the noisy reception of the country crowds and the way that the women picked up their skirts and waded into the water to get a closer view of her. "The Irish always give that peculiar shrill shriek—unlike anything one ever hears anywhere else."[20] Princess Alice wrote to the Duchess of Manchester: "You ask me how I like Killarney. This is the place I admire most of any I have ever seen. It is so beautiful. . . ."[21]

On the 31st the Queen's party departed on its way to Balmoral. The Prince of Wales stayed in Ireland until 12th September. He then proceeded to Germany, where, in the cathedral at Speyer, he was to meet, as if by accident, the bride of his parents' choosing.

Of established custom the ending of a camp, or the departure of one who had shared its rigours and its pleasures, called for celebration of a boisterous nature. At the close of such merry-making the Prince of Wales, retiring to his hut, found there installed one Nellie Clifden, an actress,[22] fair of face and form.

In the stories of the Princes in his family before him, there had been little resistance to the sudden flash of female beauty. Young George III had caught a glimpse of Hannah Lightfoot at an upstairs window while on his way to Covent Garden and the child born of this royal infatuation for a Quakeress upset the British Government considerably.* In 1787, George III's son, William, had been chased down Mountain Street, Quebec, by an irate father who was not impressed by the royal prerogative to enslave his daughter.[23] Polly Finch, "Perdita" Robinson and Dorothea Jordan had all left their names on the royal escutcheon. Only twenty years before George of Cambridge had sat night after night in Drury Lane, entranced by the beauty of Louisa Fair-brother as she moved about the stage. As in the case of those who had trod the princely path before him, now Albert Edward, Prince of Wales, succumbed to the temptation of Nellie Clifden. It was therefore a somewhat disturbed young man who, under the watchful eye of his elder sister, made his slow and silent way into the cathedral to meet, as if by accident, the demure virgin from Copenhagen.

The seven-week stay on Deeside was like unto a last oasis on the life's journey of the Prince Consort. Ahead lay a few steep crags to climb, and beyond the endless sands of time into which he would stagger and be lost. As in the case of King George VI, it might have been kinder if the journey had ended there amid the heather and the mists and the music of the burns.

* George Rex, as the son was known, proved an embarrassment to the Government of Pitt. He was sent out to Africa under the escort of an Admiral. The story of George, the first town founded after the Cape came into British possession, is full of the doings of George Rex, who assumed royal airs in the Colony. His offspring entertained Prince Alfred, Duke of Edinburgh, when he visited the Cape in 1860. In 1947 George was visited by King George VI, Queen Elizabeth and their daughters. See *The Royal Family in Africa*, by Dermot Morrah, p. 49.

Victoria was recovering from her sorrow. Now only sights that reminded her of her mother, such as the carriage which she had used at Abergeldie, began the flow of tears. Her mind was full of speculation as to how "Bertie" would behave when he returned from his tryst in Germany. She dreamed of a changed young man, fired with the desire to set up home with Alexandra and give an example of happy family life to the nation. In this she was to be disappointed.

As for Princess Alice, she was delirious with delight. Her Prince Louis arrived, and the day long they could roam together. The Queen was allowing this Prince and her second daughter far more freedom and familiarity than had been the case with Frederick William and the Princess Royal, a point which "Fritz"* was quick to make. The only fly in the Hessian ointment was where the young couple were to live in Darmstadt after they were married. Queen Victoria had sent a demand to the Grand Duke of Hesse that they should be allowed to live in the Palace for two years or so while a suitable house was built for them, for which she was prepared to contribute to the cost. But the Grand Duke turned the idea down flat, which the Queen considered was both rude and stupid. The idea that they might live with Louis's parents, the Prince and Princess Charles, was dismissed with disgust. The only other accommodation available was the small house which Louis had been sharing with his brother, Henry. The Queen did not consider this fitting for a British Princess. She therefore came to the conclusion, which in reality exactly fitted her book, that for some time at least Louis and Alice should live with her.[24] But she was learning fast the disadvantages of marrying off her daughters into Germany.

Before going back to his studies at Cambridge, the Prince of Wales reported at Balmoral. He shuffled in somewhat shyly and with very little evident enthusiasm about Alexandra. The only point upon which he was definite was an expression of horror at the thought of becoming a father, which the Queen thought most unnatural. It was obvious to her that he was not in love. As she could extract no emotional data from him, she decided for the

* The family name for Crown Prince Frederick William of Prussia.

present to leave the matter in the hands of Alice, to whom he was certain to open his heart. But in this she was again to be disappointed, and for good reason. "Bertie" chatted away about the private affairs of his friends, but left out Alexandra. The Queen commented: "This tells volumes—I knew it would be so!"[25] She admitted that she did not understand the boy, but, as her wish would be law in the end, she did not worry unduly about it.

The highlights of the 1861 autumn holiday at Balmoral were the Great Expeditions, the Second, and the Third, and the Last. Prince Louis took part in all of them, and thus his name was intertwined in the Queen's memories of her last happy times with her husband. And the Hessian Prince, who was a fount of fun, and Alice's love for him, helped to make those memories as happy as indeed they were.

The Second Great Expedition began on 20th September and took the royal trekkers south-east over the mountains to Fettercairn, lying on the edge of the flatter lands which stretch out to the sea. Eighty-two miles, on foot, by pony and by carriage, were covered, in two days. The Queen and Prince Consort, Alice and Louis, attended only by Lady Jane Churchill* and General Grey,† drove to the Bridge of Muich, where six ponies and five ghillies were waiting. They crossed the Tanar Water and, after a steep ascent, reached the shoulder of Mount Keen. Then the way led through the lonely Glens of Mark and Esk. They came upon a group of women shearers, smoking their pipes; upon a well of pure water from which they must drink; they lunched in a Highland cabin and sketched the view from its door; they peered into the ivy-covered ruins of a castle, the erstwhile inhabitants of which would have cut their Germanic throats in a trice if life's resurgence had come to them. Evening found them in the silent village of Fettercairn, the Queen, her husband, Alice and Lady Jane Churchill installed in "the Ramsay Arms", and Louis and General Grey, as luck or the Prince Consort ordained, in "the Temperance Hotel" opposite.

No one but the landlord and his wife knew the identity of the

* Lady of the Bedchamber.
† Equerry to the Queen and Private Secretary to Prince Albert.

travellers, who supped in the room usually occupied by "commercials". The Queen told John Brown to wait at table. Instead he sent in a village girl. The Queen upbraided him. He replied that he feared he might not do it right. Brown had come far since the days, ten years before, when he had first held the head of the Queen's pony. He had never been caught for an answer, whether it be lighting a fire in a strong wind, finding the way home in the fog, or producing a drop of whisky to lace the tea. He had become the right hand of Victoria in the Highlands. But at last she had found something that he could not do! She stuck in the needle and insisted that he take away the plates. He also had to brush her skirt and clean her shoes. Princess Alice, Brown's favourite among the royal children, noted the ever-increasing dependence of her mother upon her "particular" ghillie.

The evening was still and the moon was shining. Arm in arm, the party walked through the deserted streets. In the square Louis climbed the steps to the market cross* and read out the notices posted there. "We walked on along a lane a short way, hearing nothing whatever—not a leaf moving—but the distant barking of a dog." Suddenly the night was filled with the beating of a drum and the music of the fifes. They turned towards one another, the spell broken. The secret was out—the Queen was discovered! They began to retrace their steps back to the inn. The music became louder, and six men marched by. Not a bit of notice did they take of the strollers so late in the street. Albert asked the serving-girl the meaning of it all. She replied: "Och, it's just a band."

Victoria lay close to her husband, in the tiny room no larger than that of Alice's next door. She was at peace, but she did not sleep. She could see, through the open window, the moonlit patchwork of the countryside beyond. No sound, and the blessed freedom of anonymity. These were the moments that she loved best in all her life. These were the moments that she was best to remember. She did not know the time. May be it was two o'clock, may be three, when she dozed off.[26]

The Third Great Expedition was the toughest and most exciting

---

* This originally belonged to the extinct town of Kincardine.

of those undertaken by the four hardened trekkers, Victoria and Albert, Alice and Louis. They set out on the morning of 8th October and in two days covered 129 miles, by way of Glen Fishie, Dalwhinnie and Blair Castle, the historic home of the Dukes of Atholl. The weather was bad, and often they were drenched by the rain and sodden from the fords in spate. The paths they followed were narrow, steep and slippery, making it necessary to dismount from the ponies. Yet this was the adventure that they cherished most of all.

They drove westwards along the Braemar road to the Geldie Water, where the ponies were waiting. There was a new one for Alice, grey, ugly, and said to be safe, but before the day was through it was to have given the Princess some anxious moments. An hour out it began to rain, slanting on the wind, and to add to their trials a ghillie let the bundle of dry cloaks slip into a burn. The paths through Glen Fishie were treacherous now, and progress was slow. The luncheon stop was cut to the minimum, but they were an hour late at the rendezvous with the carriages near Loch Inch, and already the light was going. At Kingussie, long and straggling, rumour had come of their passing and people were standing at the cottage doors. Those who asked Brown in which carriage the Queen was travelling were directed to the one containing the maids, but one old gentleman, crowned with a high wide-awake hat, was not fooled and became very inquisitive. Then on along the rough road to Dalwhinnie, which was reached just before nine.

Here something must have gone astray on the quartermaster's side, for the reception at the inn was definitely not fitting for a Queen. For supper there was only tea and two starved chickens. There was no serving-girl, and the two maids travelling with the party had had enough and were too busy drying their own and other people's clothes to play parlourmaid to anybody. The ghillies helped as best they could, and then retired to pick the chicken bones. The Queen summed up the situation: "No pudding and no *fun*."

From the ridiculous to the sublime. Next morning the party sipped coffee with the Duke and Duchess of Atholl amid the baroque grandeur of the dining-room of Blair Castle. The nightmare of the chickens' skeletons faded before the beauty of the stucco ceiling, Bardwell's corner roundels of the Seasons, and the carved marble chimney-piece.[27] Then, refreshed, to pony again and off up Glen Tilt, the Duke with them.

The water was deep at the Poll Tarf, and the Duke offered to lead the Queen's pony through. But she laughingly declined, saying that she liked to be led by the person she was accustomed to. Brown held fast to her bridle. Away they went into the ford, two pipers, the water up to their waists, in the van, the Queen and the Duke next, Alice and the Prince Consort close behind.

At the edge of the Atholl land, the Duke proposed the Queen's health, ending his short speech with "Nis! nis! nis! Sit air a-nis! A-ris! a-ris! a-ris!" Then whisky was drunk and off they rode again, the pipers playing *The Atholl Highlanders*. At Bainoch Lady Fife had tea ready for them, and the carriages were waiting. That evening the Queen and Princess Alice dined in their riding clothes, and then pored over maps, tracing the route which they had followed. Later the Queen wrote in her diary: "Was so glad dear Louis (who is a charming companion) was with us."[28]

A week later the Last Expedition took place. They rode high to the south-west. Looking around they could see Ben Muich Dhui, Ben Nevis, the Lomond hills and Perth. "We sat on a very precipitous place, which made one dread any one's moving backwards; and here, at a little before two o'clock, we lunched. The lights were charmingly soft, and, as I said before, like the bloom on a plum." The Queen ended her description of this expedition with the words: "Alas! I fear our *last* great one!"*[29]

Now the day was over and shadows of the evening crept across the sky. It was all departures. Louis said goodbye to the ghillies and the ponies, to his hostess and to Alice, and drove away.

Alone, the Princess moved around the cottages as Balmoral prepared for the winter. The tenants and the servants, who were nearest to her, Duncan, John Brown of course, and the Grants, were making their plans to travel south for her wedding. Mrs.

* Six years later Queen Victoria was to add this note: "IT WAS OUR LAST ONE!"

Grant had never been further than Aberdeen and was in a dither because she thought that everyone would stare at her in London.

On the morning of 22nd October the Princess was standing by her mother when Brown approached to say his goodbye. He wished them a winter without ills and a safe return to Deeside in the spring. He ended with another wish. It was that there would be no deaths in the Family.[30]

The words rang strange on that bright autumn morning at Balmoral. Before many weeks were out the echo of them seemed to come from beyond the border of the world they knew.

5

The Angel of Windsor

T HE PRINCE CONSORT LAY PEACEFULLY IN THE TRAIN WHICH bore the royal party from Scotland to ancient Windsor through the late October night. He seemed better in health than he had been for some time past. For two months he had allowed his brain to rest. Now there seemed few clouds on the horizon. Alice had chosen a good man with whom she was deeply in love and one whom both the Queen and he found restful and amusing as a companion. "Vicky" was expecting a third child. A suitable and charming bride had been chosen for "Bertie" and that affair would doubtless move quietly towards its conclusion. The threat of the Curse on the Coburgs was far from his mind. Yet it hung low over the cold walls of the Castle of Windsor.

On arrival there domestic relations were exacerbated by a return bout of grieving by the Queen over the death of her mother. Such emotional display upset her husband considerably.

There came trouble over Prussia. At his coronation at Königsberg King William proclaimed that he received his Crown from the hand of God. This return to the belief in the Divine Right of Kings incensed Mr. John Delane, editor of *The Times*, and he castigated everything Prussian. The Queen protested to Lord Palmerston, but Delane proved unrepentant. The Prince Consort wrote to Stockmar: "The difficulty of establishing united action between Prussia and England has been again infinitely augmented by this royal programme."[1] Relations with France were also strained, this time by the news that the flamboyant Napoleon had ordered twelve more armed frigates.

On the family front worries piled up. The Crown Princess caught a severe chill from exposure to the weather during the crowning of the King of Prussia. She retired to bed, to the surprise of her mother who considered one should remain on one's feet whilst there was life in the body. Worries hindered the Princess's recovery. Her son's withered arm showed no signs of improvement and was now sometimes blue. In addition, she was at loggerheads with the King and Queen, particularly the Queen. She wrote home: "Nothing pleases, nothing satisfies her, there are quarrels without end."[2]

Then there was anxiety over seven-year-old Prince Leopold. He suffered from haemophilia and had had a bad attack of bleeding during the summer. It was decided that he should spend the winter months in the South of France. He was despatched in the care of a gentleman of seventy-four, who retired to his bed on reaching Cannes and died shortly afterwards.

The next blow toppled the branch of the Coburgs in Portugal. This branch was most directly affected by the curse put on the family by the Kohary monk. Ferdinand, uncle of both Queen Victoria and Prince Albert, had married Antoinette de Kohary. Their eldest son, Ferdinand, had married Maria da Gloria, Queen of Portugal, who had died in 1853. They had five sons, of whom, Pedro, the eldest, succeeded to the throne.

Two of the younger boys had been on a visit to Windsor and were on their way home when the news was received that one of the brothers, Ferdinand, had died of typhoid fever. Five days later, on 11th November, King Pedro V died of the same disease.*

The swiftness of the tragedy upset the Prince Consort very deeply. He was tied close to the members of his family and he had held great hopes that young King Pedro "might contribute towards setting on its legs a State and a nation which had fallen

---

* A third brother, John, died from the same cause in December.

low. It has shaken me in an extraordinary way," he told the King of Prussia.[3]

To the Queen and Princess Alice there was a strange significance in the tragedy. They recalled now the last words which John Brown had spoken before they left Balmoral. *"And above all, that you may have no deaths in the family."* Brown, himself, had lost three brothers and a sister from typhoid fever within a few weeks. How could he have foreseen this repetition in the Coburg line? How could he ever have known?

On the morning of Tuesday, 12th November, the Prince Consort, badly shaken by the news telegraphed from Lisbon, opened a letter from Baron Stockmar. The blood drained from his face, his hands trembled. The Baron reported that a rumour was running round Europe that the Prince of Wales was having an affair with an actress. So Nellie had bragged of her conquest at the Curragh![4]

With the letter clenched in his hand, Albert went to his wife's room. The look on his face shocked her. Later she was to say that it was this letter which broke her Angel's heart.[5] For four days the couple retired to their sanctums to lick their wounds in privacy. They ate alone. No one was told of the contents of the letter from Coburg, with the possible exception of Princess Alice, who was becoming more and more the confidante of her father and could not help noticing that something was amiss. "Vicky" was simply told that there had been bad news, but was not to ask what it was.

Albert lay sleepless through the nights. He flogged his brain to decide on what the next step should be. Corroboration of the story seemed the first essential, and in this he was lucky.

There had just come into waiting George Byng, 7th Viscount Torrington, a man for whom the Prince Consort had no great esteem but one who had his uses. "Witty and indiscreet, he gorged himself on royal chat and gossip which he retailed to his fashionable friends in London, and later made a habit of sending regular private letters to the editor of *The Times* about Court events allocating to himself the title of 'Your Windsor Special'."[6] It was therefore to Lord Torrington that the Consort turned in his hour of need. Not only did he obtain confirmation of the story from this

Princess Alice in 1857

Marie, Princess of Hesse and the Rhine
Daughter of Grand Duke Louis II of Hesse and the Rhine
Wife of Emperor Alexander II of Russia

gay courtier, but enlargement as well.[7] Further alarmed now by the knowledge that the escapade was being retailed in the London clubs, he wrote a letter of reproach and warning to the Prince of Wales.

The overwhelming importance which the Prince Consort placed upon the aberration of his son, an aberration stemming from a high-spirited farewell party at a military camp, had four root causes.

The first was fear of the damage that might be done to the emblem of the Throne. For twenty years Victoria and Albert had striven to set an example in married life that would outweigh, and cause to be forgotten, the moral laxity of the sons of George III. The old order had not died easily and there had been several awkward cases with which to deal. Yet, by the coming of age of their marriage, they had revolutionised the public's idea of domestic life in the palaces. The Prince Consort had before his eyes the examples of his father and his brother. All that he and the Queen had built up could now so easily be thrown away if "Bertie" yielded further to temptation. He had been well aware of the possibility of such temptation before he heard the news and had written to Stockmar before he left Balmoral that everyone in England said, "You must marry the Prince of Wales soon, unless you do so he is lost."[8]

Secondly there was the danger that, if the news reached the ears of the parents of Princess Alexandra, they would proceed no further with the engagement. Princess Christian was very strict and strait-laced on such matters and had told her daughter, in front of the Crown Princess, that if ever she became such a coquette as Princess Mary of Cambridge she would get a box on the ears.[9]

Thirdly came the matter of the Prince Consort's health. It would appear that the very beginnings of his last illness came in the hours when he received both the news of the death of King Pedro and the scandal about his son. Always prone to worry, the state of his health exaggerated this failing. Also, he was working much too hard. In an age when mental concentration was often side-tracked by leading figures, when reliance was laid on preconceived notions, on position, power and confidence, the Prince Consort found no greater pleasure than in a long and closely connected train of reasoning. His knowledge of Government matters was immense and few Heads of Departments could further enlighten him. He handled financial matters with the greatest acumen and detail. He was an expert on military tactics and equipment, and had even turned his mind to the problem of powered flight. There is a note in the Introduction to the published *Speeches of the Prince Consort* which is indicative of the views of his widow. "The Prince had very good health. At any rate he had begun with a fine constitution. Every one of the chief organs of life was well developed in him, with the exception of a heart that was not quite equal to the work put upon it; so that he mostly had but a feeble pulse. It was upon the nervous energy that this constant stress of work, and this striving after excellence in everything, must have told. . . ."[10] In the same Introduction his epitaph was written: "He cared too much about too many things."[11]

The fourth cause, and the one that now hit him the hardest, was a horror and an abhorrence of extra-marital sexual relations between males and females. Any such activity he put under the general heading of vice, and the depression that it caused him came in strange contrast with the attitude of many men of his age. Back in his childhood days the terror had been born. Then his father had erred, his mother had followed suit, and been divorced. As a young man he had said that there was no temptation for him in women, as "that species of vice disgusted him".[12] Those placed near to the Throne are, of natural course, opened to greater temptations than those in humbler station. Yet, with one exception, throughout his twenty years there, no woman received more than the touch of a cold and lifeless hand and no woman pierced behind his eyes. The exception was the lovely Empress Eugenie, and she, of her own admission, had little use for men.

Meantime, outside his sanctum, the Prince Consort kept up the façade that all was well with the world. On the 22nd he went to Sandhurst to inspect the buildings for the new Staff College and Military Academy. The day was one of incessant rain and he was wet through and shivering by the time that he returned to

66

Windsor. Yet he wrote to the King of Prussia: "Both privately and politically we are in complete calm. The potatoes have failed in Ireland, and here there will be unemployment in the cotton industry. . . ."[13]

On Sunday, the 24th, he complained of rheumatic pains and wrote in his diary that he had scarcely closed his eyes for the past fortnight.[14] Nellie Clifden danced through all the nightmare hours, and he decided that he must get to grips with his problem. Accordingly the next day he journeyed to Cambridge. He had a frank talk with his son, and appeared relieved by the response. In making his revelations the Prince of Wales begged that the intimacies should be kept from his mother. To this the Prince Consort agreed. But, in his weak state, he underestimated both the depth of the morbid curiosity of his wife and the power of her steam-roller tactics in wheedling out "the ghastly details". She found out all she wanted to know, just as she was to do when another of her sons erred a few years later. Fortunately the Prince of Wales was to remain in ignorance of the fact that his mother had been told. But it was because she knew that a few weeks later she was to say that she would never again be able to look at her eldest son without a shudder.[15]

Back at Windsor the Prince Consort staggered through the days, leaving his meals untouched. He reviewed the Eton College Volunteers and attended chapel. His last written work was the re-drafting of the despatch on the *Trent*, which went far to avert the danger of war breaking out between America and Britain. When he had finished he told the Queen that he was so tired that he could scarcely lift his pen.[16]

For a week the sick man refused to retire to bed. He shuffled from room to room in his dressing-gown, fretting over current affairs. His coughing and restlessness made the nights horrible for the Queen. The doctors hesitated to insist that he keep permanently to his bed for fear of his assuming that he had fever, which he dreaded, and also because of frightening the Queen. But on the 7th December gastric fever was diagnosed and on the next day the Court Circular announced that he was confined to his room with a feverish cold. Once the conditions surrounding a serious illness had been established a leading figure moved in upon the scene. It was eighteen-year-old Princess Alice.

Throughout her husband's illness the Queen appears to have been unable to appreciate the seriousness of it, despite the obvious signs. On his despondency, she commented that all men were so when unwell. As late as 9th December she wrote to the King of the Belgians: "Every day, however, is bringing us nearer the end of this tiresome business, which is much what I had at Ramsgate, only that I was much worse, and not at first well attended to."*[17]

From the moment that he moved under the jurisdiction of the doctors, Albert knew that he was going to die. He could not tell his wife, or leave instructions for her for completion after he was gone. She would not listen to such talk, would shut her eyes, and turn away. So he told Princess Alice. As he spoke the girl disappeared and a woman was born. With the recent experience of her grandmother's death to guide her, the truth came to her that it was upon her firmness that her father's will to live and her mother's control of her feelings, depended. The immediate exhibition of adult fortitude amazed those whose duties took them to the royal apartments. A member of the Queen's Household was later to pen a description of that courage.[18] Occupying the position of chief nurse, never once did the Princess show any trace of emotion in the sickroom. If she felt that she could bear no more, she would tidy the bed, calmly leave the room on an excuse, and seek the shelter of her own room for a while. There was no sign of agitation on her face when she returned, nor did she allow her mother to see such traces.

The Prince Consort was a difficult patient, restless, irritable. He wandered round the corridors, undecided as to which room to occupy next. He finally chose the Blue Room, in which both George IV and William IV had breathed their last. He asked for a piano to be brought in. Alice played chosen pieces to him. Sometimes he would lose interest and say, "That is enough." She read to him for hours on end. He would decide on one book, and then change his mind and ask for another.

Tired out by worry and lack of sleep, the Queen was also

---

* Queen Victoria had suffered from typhoid fever early in 1835.

handicapped by having to deal with State affairs, many of which had previously been cared for by her husband. The task of writing to relations and close friends, with progress reports on the patient, fell largely on Princess Alice. She wrote tactfully to the Prince of Wales. She kept the Crown Princess constantly informed. Her father asked what she had told "Vicky". She replied that she had said that he was very ill. "You did wrong," he replied. "You should have told her I was dying."[19] Knowing that a sight of "Vicky" would be the best medicine her father could have, Alice had asked her sister to hurry to England, but the German doctors decreed that the Crown Princess's health was not up to the winter journey.

All manner of well-intentioned people were now calling at the Castle to make enquiries. Princess Alice saw many of them, although it added to the strain of the day. Some arrived at awkward hours. The Duke of Cambridge chose 7.15 in the morning. All were full of praise for the Princess, as was her mother. The Duke wrote: "Alice has behaved most beautifully throughout."[20] Lady Lyttleton described her as "the angel in the house".[21]

On the afternoon of Sunday, 8th December, Alice was alone with her father, the rest of the family being in church. He asked her to draw his sofa near to the window, so that he might watch the sky and the clouds sailing by. She began to play to him, choosing the tunes that he loved best. He did not move or speak. She turned, to see him lying with his eyes shut and his hands clasped in prayer, as soon, in death, in stone, he was to be portrayed. "Were you asleep, Papa?" she asked. He smiled at her. "Oh no, only I have had such sweet thoughts."[22]

In the last stages of his illness the doctors did their utmost to keep the Princess from his room. But suddenly he would call her name, looking wildly round for her, and they could not refuse him. His daughter was always waiting by the door.[23]

Meantime no step, or apparent consideration of such step, had been made for summoning the Heir to the Throne. On the evening of Friday the 13th Princess Alice took matters into her own hands. It was on her decision that a telegram was sent to the Prince of

Wales telling him to come at once. He caught the last train and reached Windsor at three in the morning.

It was during the afternoon that the Queen noted:

> Albert folded his arms and began arranging his hair just as he used to do when well and dressing. These were said to be bad signs. Strange! As though he were preparing for another and greater journey.[24]

One by one his younger children, and the members of the Household who had been close to him, came in to say goodbye. Towards half past nine the Queen's grief overcame her and she left the room to speak with the Dean of Windsor. Princess Alice was comforting her sister Helena, who had broken down. Suddenly she looked towards the bed. She turned to Lady Augusta Bruce* and whispered in perfect calm, "That is the death rattle." She then left to give the warning to her mother, and led the Queen back to the room. They knelt at either side of him.[25]

At ten minutes to eleven Albert, the Prince Consort, died. Princess Alice ordered her bed to be placed in her mother's room. She obtained a sedative from Dr. Jenner and sat in vigil hour after hour until the tears and tiredness at length bore Queen Victoria to sleep on the first dread night of her loneliness. "Suddenly," Lady Augusta Bruce noted, "Princess Alice . . . seemed to be a different creature."[26]

---

* Lady Augusta Bruce, who had been living with the Duchess of Kent at the time of her death, had been appointed by Queen Victoria to be her resident Bedchamber Woman.

6

Alice in the Wilderness

IN AN OVERCOAT OF BLUE, ALBERT THE GOOD LAY IN THE Blue Room at Windsor. The rings were still upon his fingers and his stiff hands held a photograph of Victoria his wife, her hair loose about her shoulders.[1] Into this chapel, draped in black, his widow led those who were dearest to her. She had been told that now she must kiss him no more. Instead she grasped convulsively at his clothes.[2]

Those first, few endless nights were a nightmare and an ordeal of such intensity that Princess Alice was later to say that she wondered how her mother and herself came through them with their reasons intact.[3] Their beds lay close. In the Queen's, clasped tight to her, were her husband's nightshirt and his red dressing-gown, and his likeness and a cast of his hand were on the pillow beside her. It was only in the early hours that sheer fatigue brought them short oblivion. These were the crisis times for the widowed Queen, and that she survived them without mental and physical collapse was widely attributed to the amazing fortitude of Princess Alice, a girl herself heart-broken over the loss of a father whom she adored.

From all the courts of Europe the mourners began their journeys towards the Channel ports. Among them were King Leopold of the Belgians, the Crown Prince of Prussia, and Prince Louis of Hesse.

The doctors and the Household wished the Queen to leave Windsor and rest in the peace and privacy of Osborne. The Queen at first refused, deeming it her duty to stay close to her husband to the end, and in this she was backed by Princess Alice. It was pointed out that there was a risk of the fever spreading to other members of the Royal Family. The Princess then changed her stand, and it was she who at last persuaded her mother to move to the Isle of Wight.[4]

Before she left, the Queen had one duty to perform. On the afternoon of the 18th she drove with Princess Alice to Frogmore. There Sir Charles Phipps, Sir James Clark and Prince Louis were waiting to receive them. On the arm of her daughter she walked around the gardens, selecting a spot where the mausoleum of the Prince Consort should be built. She had determined that he should lie in a garden, and she, in due season, beside him.

For Prince Louis, on arrival, there was a shock beyond the utter grief which encompassed his future mother-in-law. He looked at the girl he was to marry, and he hardly recognised her. He had left behind in October a radiant creature, plumpish, full of endless fun, ready to run to a hill-top to snatch a view, finding delight in the hardships of a Highland inn. Now he found a nurse, an organiser, lifeless of hand and unseeing of eye, her pale cheeks emphasising the length of her nose, a feature which she had often described as a calamity.[5] He who should have been the star in her life, was only a bit-player now. His marriage had, in any case, to be postponed. He was soon to fear that it might never take place, for there was little thought of it in the Princess's mind. In the aftermath of shock she had become imbued with the belief that it was her duty to spend the rest of her life as the other right hand of the Queen, filling, as best she could, the gap left by her father.[6]

On the 23rd unbroken silence hung over the Isle of Wight. By the Queen's direct order to the Commander-in-Chief no gun was to be fired that could possibly be heard at Osborne.[7] Morning at Windsor. The bells of St. George's Chapel and of the parish churches were ringing single and double knells at intervals. The artillery were firing minute guns in the Long Walk. Then the clock struck twelve.

Six columns wide, black-leaded, the *Daily Telegraph* traced the final scene of the foreign Prince who had been, in all but name, king for twenty years.

> The deepest and most awful silence prevailed. A sort of shivering presentiment chilled every heart that the Hearse was at the door, and that It was coming. All at once was heard the sharp, ringing word of command, as the Grenadiers presented arms outside. Then the heavy curtains of the southern door were gathered into black festoons, and the body of ALBERT THE PRINCE CONSORT was brought in to be buried in peace. . . . Anon came Garter with his sceptre, swiftly passing through a crowd of foreign princes and officers of state; and he was soon seen to make a profound reverence as a slight young man, with fair hair, walked with a slow but firm step towards his appointed place. Then the bier, pushed by invisible hands and bearing its august burden, began slowly toiling up the southern aisle of the nave. The procession fell into rank and moved sadly forward. For the Chief Mourner was there, so close to the coffin of his father that he could touch it; that slight, fair-haired young man, with his blue Garter ribbon just peeping from beneath his closely-buttoned mourning garment, was the Hope of England, the Heir of immeasurable power, the present inheritor of un-utterable woe.[8]

No fragment of the scene, ceremonial or human, was missed. It was remarked that the resolute demeanour of the Prince of Wales, who did not resort to a handkerchief, might well have shocked a few. On the other hand the tearful affliction of his Grand Ducal Highness Prince Louis of Hesse was noted with satisfaction. The comment on poor little Prince Arthur who, dressed "in a black dress of Highland fashion", was sobbing his heart out, was: "It is good for children to weep thus." The decision that the coffin was to remain at the gates of the royal tombhouse until the mausoleum was ready was attributed to repugnance on the part of the Queen to have her loved one near "that huge, dingy coffin, wherein lies in gloomy unlamented state all that remains of him who was once George the Fourth, King of England".[9]

For ten days the Queen moved as if in a trance, obedient of the suggestions made to her. Her grief was absolute. She had come to look towards him for everything, from the morning until the evening. He had even helped her to choose her clothes. He had been a man aware of his knowledge and happy in the giving of advice. It was as if she had an ever open encyclopaedia on the desk beside her. She groped for him in the lonely mists of sorrow that hid the splendours of the room at the top. There had been in him that same prop of essentiality that later caused her grandson, George V, to call—"May"—each time he returned home, as if he feared that she had been spirited away.

There was the other loneliness, the loneliness of the nights. Now came the absolute certainty that her great wish for another child could never come to pass. She was a young woman, only forty-two. She was a woman who could put seventy hard Highland miles, by pony, carriage and on foot, in a day, sleep off the effects and do the same thing the next. She was ten years younger than her father when he had married. She was eight years younger than her mother when the familiarities between the Duchess of Kent and her major-domo, Sir John Conroy, had come to light. She was left with a nightshirt and a red dressing-gown, wet with tears.

With the coming of 1862 a germ of new life was born in her. Strength came from the obvious grief of the country at the passing of the Prince Consort, and the tributes that were being paid to his memory by leading figures, even those who had disagreed with him in life. He had led Britain by the hand through the intricate paths of change that linked the stage coach with the express train. He had cleaned out the Augean stables of the Georgian palaces and set a new standard of morality. There was satisfaction in knowing that his work had been recognised at last.

With the resurrection of Victoria came a trinity of determinations. The first was that everything that *he* had planned, dreamed, ordered, should come to pass. The second was that the memory of *him* should be perpetuated, in brick and stone, in oils and iron, beyond her vision of the years, and as *he* had left the little things of his life, his pens, his walking-sticks, his handkerchiefs, so should they remain untouched, until she joined *him*, and out beyond that time. The third determination was that no person should dictate to her and the creed that *he* had written for her should be inviolate. *Égoïsme à deux* was to become *égoïsme à l'une*, when one has the power of two. She wrote to King Leopold:

> I am also anxious to repeat *one* thing, and *that one* is *my firm* resolve, my *irrevocable decision*, viz. that *his* wishes, *his* plans about everything, *his* views about *every* thing are to be *my* law. And *no human power* will make me swerve from what *he* decided and wished, and I look to *you* to *support* and *help* me in this. I apply this particularly as regards our children—Bertie, etc.—for whose future he has traced everything so carefully. I am *also determined* that *no one* person, may *he* be ever so good, ever so devoted among my servants—is to lead or guide or dictate to *me*. . . .[10]

This plan she put into immediate action. Only those who said "Yes ma'am", and kept on saying "Yes ma'am", were tolerated in her presence.[11] Towards persons who queried she would slowly turn her face, as if she was a stone statue and a rod allowed the head to swivel on the body. They were seen no more.

Of the members of her family who might tend to lead or influence her, or usurp any of the powers that belonged to her and the ghost of Albert, the number was limited to her three eldest children. Foxy Uncle Leopold, be-wigged now, was too senile to grasp again at the powers that had been within his reach almost half a century before. Duke Ernest of Coburg was too poor and too immoral. George of Cambridge lived in a house of glass, and anyway was well content at the War Office. The younger children, from Alfred downwards, offered no problem, and she had already decided that in the future her relations with them would be more intimate than heretofore.

"Vicky" had been imperious since her nursery days. The court at Berlin had tamed her, but there might be a dictatorial resurgence if King William died and she became Queen of Prussia, without the restraining hand of her father to guide her steps.

"Bertie" was the chief danger, not so much from his own aspirations but from a possible desire and expectation on the part of the country that he should relieve his mother of some of her duties and take over a piece of the mantle of Prince Albert. That, Queen Victoria determined, would never happen. She was now fully convinced that the incident at the Curragh and the visit to Cambridge were the underlying reasons for her husband's death. The doctors had affirmed that his fever could be traced back to 22nd November, the day on which he travelled to Madingley to talk with the Prince of Wales. Fortunately, as regards the Queen, plans had been made for him to visit the Near East and the Holy Land in February. This had been arranged by the Consort, and was therefore law. The Prince departed on the 5th, leaving his mother, free and undisturbed, to take such steps as she thought necessary to ensure that the Heir's role remained as minor as before.

Her suspicion that the public would now expect the Prince to play a greater part in State affairs was quickly confirmed. *The Times* drew attention to his hereditary place in the State and took it for granted that more public duties would fall on his shoulders, so that he might "earn the confidence of the country".[12] King Leopold tried to patch up relations between the two, but found in the Queen "an antipathy that is quite incurable". When he told her that the Prince would be happy to forego his foreign tour so that he might comfort her, she not only would not hear of it, but seemed only anxious to be rid of him.[13] Lord Clarendon tried and was told: "It quite irritates me to see him in the room."[14] So it was that "Bertie" was condemned to play second fiddle softly for the best years of his life.

The third danger, Alice, was drawn into the danger zone through no fault of her own. For six months, except for a short recuperative rest with the Van de Weyers at New Lodge in February, she was the visual representation of the Sovereign.[15] Through her all communications passed between the Queen and her ministers. It was, to the elder among the latter, as if the clock had been turned back a quarter of a century and Britain had a girl Queen once again.

In the dark smoke of grief and mourning which poured from the Windsor tragedy, people looked for some light that might pierce its gloom. They found it in the Princess, a Princess in love postponing her marriage, the nurse to her father, the comforter of her mother, the visible sign that royal authority continued. In

76

days when far greater demands were put on a daughter's devotion and loyalty, she became the paragon in countless homes.

In the columns of *The Times* Mr. Delane wrote extravagantly in praise of the Princess, a monument both to her bravery and her goodness.[16] Biographers of last century, and this, have added their bouquets.

> Throughout his (the Prince Consort's) illness Princess Alice had been her mother's chief support, and now she took upon herself the whole burden of the tragedy. She slept in the Queen's room, she saw the Ministers of the Crown, she made herself responsible for all immediate arrangements, and, most difficult of all, she managed to reach, by the mere force of love and sympathy, that stricken heart. She put aside her own grief for the father whom she adored, and devoted herself body and soul to her mother. . . . During those first days, had it not been for her, the Queen might have irretrievably collapsed.[17]

Those few who crossed the narrow water to Osborne brought back brave tales of Alice. Among them was the Duchess of Manchester. She confided in Lord Clarendon, who replied: "I need not say how entirely I agree with you about Pss. Alice— there is not such a girl in a 1000. I never met one who at her age had such sound principles so great judgment & such knowledge of the world, yet she has been boxed up in a gilt cage all her life & has not had the advantage of interchanging ideas as other girls have." But this favoured adviser of Queen Victoria was none too sure about the Prince whom she was to marry, fearing that he might not give her enough in life and that she might not be happy.[18]

Strangely enough, the expected reaction of a woman plunged into such a situation, that she would turn for love and comfort to her children, did not apply in the case of Queen Victoria. There was to be no substitute for Albert. She wrote to the Queen of Prussia: "The longing for intercourse, the desire to see and hear him, to throw myself into his arms and find peace and security there . . . all this is too frightful and galls me day and night! . . . The children are good and loving, but I do not find their company the same and it is no support."[19] This even applied

77

to Princess Alice, who had piloted her through the storm. The thought of the daughter sacrificing her life for her mother was not to be considered. Just as Albert had planned that the Prince of Wales should tour the Near East, so had he planned Alice's wedding. Therefore it would take place. The date was fixed for as early as 1st July. This not only gave the Princess no chance to regain her health after the harrowing experience through which she had passed, but also meant that the ceremony would be held in an atmosphere of funereal gloom.

If it had been postponed until the autumn, time would have been given a chance to heal some of the wounds, the trappings of mourning could have been put aside, and the Princess could have started her married life with the accustomed ceremonial. But, as in the case of her eldest daughter, whom she allowed to marry out of the schoolroom and then moaned that she had lost her, the Queen seemed anxious to see Alice married.

The reason was that she was looking forward to having a man in the close family circle. She was always more at ease with men than women. She was devoted to her elder son-in-law, Frederick William, and he had been a great support to her, but his duties did not allow of frequent visits to England. There were no such urgent duties to occupy Louis, and she was determined to have him with her.

The wedding was to be held in the dining-room at Osborne, under conditions of complete privacy. This meant that the eight bridesmaids, selected and briefed prior to the Prince Consort's death, would not now be able to play their part. There arose the awkward point of wedding presents. While the damsels would have been quite happy to sacrifice a substantial slice of their allowances, and their parents to dig into the family coffers, if the reward was to be a secondary role in the magnificent ceremonial of a royal marriage, they did not feel the same about it if all they were to know about the nuptials was what they read in the newspapers. Neither had any of these girls been allowed long enough in the gilded cage in which the Princess lived, to be able to come to know her well. The mothers were not at all happy about the situation. Then the Duchess of Buccleuch, without consulting the other mothers, took the initiative. She asked the Princess what she would like, and was told—a gilt breakfast service. The Duchess then passed the word round that £50 each should meet the requirements.

This announcement caused much whispering and fluttering among the mothers, some of whom considered they had just as much right as the Duchess of Buccleuch to have a say in the matter. So a little rebellion was born. Lady Mount Edgecombe drew the line at £25, and Lady Elgin said her limit was £30.[20] At length £335 was collected and deposited with Messrs. Garrard, who produced "a magnificent tea and coffee service of silver gilt and embossed, each piece bearing the monogram of the donors".[21]

A suggestion that the Lords-in-waiting should combine in a present was defeated by comment from above that H.R.H. would appreciate individual presents. Lord Clarendon considered this "a dodge, of course, to get them more valuable".[22]

Meantime the Princess was given none of the peace and privacy usual in the case of brides. For her there was no happy concentration on her trousseau. After two months in retirement at Osborne, the Queen began the journeys that she was to follow with routine throughout the next forty years. From Osborne she moved to Windsor, and then back to Osborne again. In May she went to Balmoral. Then she retraced her steps back through Windsor to the Isle of Wight.

The return to Balmoral was a considerable shock both to the Queen and Princess Alice. Only the few short months, between the falling of the gold leaves and the coming of the green, separated them from the happiest days of their lives. The ghost of Albert walked every path and track, haunted every tartaned room. His voice came from the river and his gun cracked on the hill-tops.

The Minister-in-attendance was the Duke of Argyll.* On his arrival Dr. Robertson, the factor, asked if he could speak to him. He told the Duke that the Queen had "had a day of the deepest waters to go through", and that Princess Alice was "quite knocked up". Even so the Duke was surprised at the low ebb at which he

* George Douglas, 8th Duke. 1823–1900.

79

found the Queen. She was hardly able to speak, and merely shook her head. Yet Scotsmen had always a tonic effect upon her, and soon she was smiling at his tales of the countryside.[23] But hopes that some weak rays of sunshine might break through the dark clouds by the time of the Princess's wedding were quickly quashed. On 26th May the Queen wrote: "The Angel of Death still follows us. The Grand Duchess of Hesse* has just died and so now Alice's marriage will be even more gloomy."[24]

The Press, which was taking a great interest in the forthcoming marriage, even though it was to take place in privacy, now hazarded that it would be postponed once more. But the Queen had no such intention, even if it did entail her daughter moving from one house in mourning to another in a like state. On the contrary, she awoke to a sudden interest in the ceremonial to be observed, minor though it was. In the three weeks before the wedding she sent more orders to the Lord Chamberlain's Office than she had done in the previous six months.[25]

In the middle of June Prince Louis came over for a few days, to acquaint himself with the matrimonial arrangements and to visit the Second Great International Exhibition with the Princess. The Queen could scarce bear to dwell upon the substantiation of this second dream child of the Prince Consort, and could not bring herself to visit it. But to her daughters it represented a heaven-sent chance to escape from the Windsor gloom into the outside world, and throughout a week they were present every day.

Princess Alice was also busy with a secret. She arranged with Charles Martin to draw her, in crayons, with her wedding wreath and veil. This entailed Martin hiding at Windsor and making the best of rush sittings when the Queen was unlikely to call for Alice, which was not often. It was to be presented to the Queen just before the ceremony.[26]

Prince Louis and his brother Henry reached England on the 24th, in good time for the wedding. They stayed in London, which gave the public at least a chance of seeing the kind of man their Princess was marrying. Their every movement was news—"Their Grand Ducal Highnesses" lending a touch of romance. "Their

* Grand Duchess Mathilde, wife of Grand Duke Louis III.

Grand Ducal Highnesses" arrived in the John Penn steam-packet from Ostend, at two o'clock on Monday afternoon, at Dover. . . . "Their Grand Ducal Highnesses" landed at the Admiralty pier, where a guard of honour was drawn up. . . . "Their Grand Ducal Highnesses" left by the South-Eastern Railway for town, and arrived at the Palace Hotel at six p.m. . . . "Their Grand Ducal Highnesses" visited the International Exhibition. . . . "Their Grand Ducal Highnesses" visited the Royal Agricultural Society's show. . . . "Their Grand Ducal Highnesses" met the Prince of Wales and Prince Arthur in Battersea Park. . . .[27]

Over the weekend a small group of selected royal relations were ferried from Portsmouth to Ryde to await, in the silence and the shadows, the saddest wedding of the nineteenth century.

7

No Cake at the Wedding

HROUGH THE EARLY HOURS OF 1ST JULY 1862 QUEEN
Victoria tossed fretfully in her bed at Osborne. Then, with
the light, came a deep rumble as the great table was moved
from the dining-room. Hammering followed. The night was no
longer for sleeping. In the bed beside her, Princess Alice stirred
and woke. Rising, she went over to her mother, smiled down at
her and kissed her. "I gave her my blessing and a Prayer Book,
like one dear Mama gave me on *our* happy wedding morning."[1]

It was a dull day and the wind was strong. Grey clouds rolled
in from the sea and white horses chased one another across
Osborne bay. The relations breakfasted at nine, without their
hostess, who kept to her room except for a sally down to the
dining-room to see how the transformation into a chapel was
proceeding.

The Cambridges were present in force. Good trenchermen, they
were always punctual for meals and recorded prandial details in
their diaries. The tribe consisted of the old Duchess, widow of
Adolphus;* her son, George, the Commander-in-Chief (without
his wife† and sons, who were supposed not to exist); and her two

* Seventh son of George III.
† Louisa Fairbrother (Mrs. Fitzgeorge).

daughters, Augusta, the Grand Duchess of Mecklenburg-Strelitz, and Mary,* powerful both in form and character. "Fritz", the Crown Prince of Prussia, was alone as his wife was expecting her third child† in August. The senior representative on the paternal side was Prince Albert's brother, Ernest, Duke of Saxe-Coburg and Gotha, who was to give the bride away.

Two children of King Louis Philippe were present. Both had married into the family of Ferdinand of Coburg and Antoinette de Kohary. The Duc de Nemours had lost his wife, Victoria, five years before. Clementine had married Prince Augustus of Coburg. Queen Victoria's half-sister, Feodore, Princess of Hohenlohe, her son, Count Gleichen, Prince Edward of Saxe-Weimar‡ and the Hessian family completed the party.

After breakfast, as a means of finding relaxation from the increasing air of tension, George of Cambridge, Duke Ernest, and Prince Augustus strolled out on to the terrace and lit cigars.[2] Windy or no, it was essential that they went outside, for if the scent of tobacco had wafted down the corridors of Osborne, Cousin Victoria would be sure to have noticed, and war would have been declared. No trouble was wanted that day, particularly in the case of George and Ernest, both of whom had eyes for the ladies. The C.-in-C. was in the throes of a liaison, and "the Fairbrother" had discovered it. She had threatened, if he did not bring it to a close, to tell the Queen about her husband's rude and lewd collection of drawings of herself and Prince Albert, which George had secretly collected over the past twenty-five years.

The morning was enlivened by the arrival of Ministers and guests from London, and the officiating clergy. In the absence of the Archbishop of Canterbury§ through illness, the service was to be conducted by the Archbishop of York,‖ assisted by the Dean of Windsor¶ and Mr. Prothero,$ Rector of St. Mildred's, Whippingham. When all were present the men went upstairs to change

* Later Duchess of Teck, and mother of Queen Mary.
† Prince Henry.
‡ A nephew of Queen Adelaide. He had married Lady Augusta Gordon-Lennox.
§ Dr. Thomson.
‖ Dr. Longley.
¶ Dr. Gerald Wellesley.
$ Afterwards Canon of Westminster.

into black evening coats, white waistcoats, grey trousers and black neckcloths, and the ladies into morning dresses of grey or violet, with grey or white gloves.[3] Zero hour was one o'clock.

The room was empty except for the Archbishop, the Dean and the Rector when the Queen entered. "The time had come, and I, in my 'sad cap', as baby* calls it, most sad on such a day, went down with our four boys. . . ."[4] She took her place in an armchair, and there she was to sit, sombre, still, throughout the service. Her two sons, the Prince of Wales and Prince Alfred, stood beside her, so positioned that they hid their mother from the inquisitive eyes of the guests.

The arrangement of the room, the altar, the chairs, the blue cushions, all was the same as it had been at her own wedding. Above the altar hung Winterhalter's picture of the Royal Family painted fifteen years before. Prince Albert's outstretched hand pointed towards the Queen's chair. Her eyes were fixed firm upon him.

The Lord Chamberlain† and the Vice-Chamberlain now led the guests to their allotted places. The Lord Chamberlain then withdrew and silence fell. To those who waited, hearing only their own breath, it seems as if this was more a funeral service for Albert than the wedding of his daughter. His likeness stood out above the candles on the altar. If a coffin had come through the dining-room door, the scene for it was set, was fitting. The tension was broken by the arrival of Prince Louis, and his brother Henry, who were led to the right of the altar.

Again the Lord Chamberlain retired, this time bound for Her Majesty's apartments to fetch the bride. The wait seemed an eternity. The Queen was not the only one to struggle to restrain her tears. Then the door opened and in came the bride on the arm of her uncle, the four bridesmaids, sisters Helena, Louise and Beatrice, and Anna of Hesse, close behind her. Her full dress was covered with flounces of Honiton lace, and the veil that hung from the wreath round her hair was of the same pattern. It had been designed by her father. She was completely calm and com-

---

* Princess Beatrice.
† Lord Sydney.

posed, serious and dignified. It was left to her baby sister to let a ray of sunlight into the hymeneal hour. Five-year-old, irrepressible Beatrice was playing bridesmaid for the first time, and she thought it the greatest fun.

Alice and Louis were married. The Lord Chamberlain led them to an adjoining room. The Archbishop and his supporters bowed and faded away. The Family retired to the Horn room. The other guests moved towards the marquee where *déjeuner* was to be served. The Queen sat alone in her chair, before the candles which burned below the likeness of Albert.

After a suitable and impressive interval she rose and joined her relations. Here, under the antlers of the stags which Albert had shot, the weeping began. "Alfred had been crying bitterly all through the service, and now the Queen clasped him in her arms and broke down herself, and the younger boys joined in. The bridegroom's parents were admitted and told the Queen how deeply they felt for her, and tears rolled down the Archbishop's cheeks."[5] After a series of embracings, the Queen withdrew to lunch alone with the bride and bridegroom.

The day was over now for the relations and the guests and, after they had eaten, they left to catch the special train which was to carry them back to London.

Alice and Louis prepared to depart on their three-day honeymoon, which was to be spent at St. Clare, Spring Vale, some three miles from Ryde. For them no confetti or old shoes, no cake and no fun. Yet Louis was to leave with a gift of more lasting value. Quietly, and with little comment from anybody, the Queen had conferred upon him the dignity of His Royal Highness. She was accustomed to having her own way.

A four-horse brougham came up to the doors of Osborne House. There was an outrider before it, and two mounted gentlemen behind. The trousseau, in black, was stowed away. Then, in an apozem of smiles and tears, the mother, the brothers and the sisters waved their goodbyes. It was as the carriage drove away that young Prince Arthur made the following announcement: "When I marry, I shall bring my wife home to live with us all, and we shall eat our own cake."[6]

Apart from its delightful situation and grounds, the Queen had chosen the home of Colonel and Lady Katherine Vernon Harcourt for the honeymoon, for two reasons. Firstly, St. Clare had been one of the houses which she and Prince Albert had inspected when they were looking for a retreat in the Isle of Wight. Secondly, Lady Harcourt was a daughter of the Earl of Liverpool, who had been a great favourite of the Queen. Yet this vast, castellated mansion, in which "the Tudor style of Gothic" predominated, with its keep-tower, mammoth conservatory, and lodge by the sea, seemed a strange choice for a stay lasting only three days. But, to the Queen, its great advantage was its handiness. Having allowed Alice and Louis one day of peace, on Thursday she drove over to tea at St. Clare,[7] having made a detour so that she should not be seen by the people of Ryde. The next evening the couple returned to Osborne. The Queen then presented, privately, the insignia of the Order of the Garter to Prince Louis. For four days she had the pleasure of having a man who was dear to her again about the house.

At five o'clock on the afternoon of the following Tuesday the Prince and Princess embarked on the Royal yacht *Victoria and Albert* at Osborne pier, and began their journey to Antwerp. "I strove," wrote the Queen, "to cheer her up by the prospect of an early return."[8] The Queen and her younger children sailed with them in the yacht *Fairy* as far as the Nab light. The Channel fleet, at anchor in the Spithead roadstead, *Revenge*, *Trafalgar*, *St. George*, *Emerald*, and *Chanticleer*, fired a twenty-one gun salute, and a second of the current series of British Princesses slipped over the horizon bound for the melting pot of Germany. Bismarck was already lighting the fire beneath that pot.

The Prince Consort had been correct when he confided in Stockmar that the British public did not take kindly to the marriages of Princesses to minor German princes,[9] and their subsequent disappearance with substantial dowries. The Queen was not to appreciate this to the full until later. Six months earlier she had written to the Crown Princess: "Oh dear, how dreadfully I long for everything that is German! Both my husband and my mother were Germans from the same place and now both are gone."[10] But in the case of Princess Alice the public did not realise that they were to lose her, an impression fostered by the Queen who was determined that her needs and wishes should override those of Darmstadt. It was even announced in the Press that Her Majesty had allocated Clarence House as the London residence of the Prince and Princess, and Frogmore as their country home.[11] *Punch*[12] published a full-page picture of the couple leaving Osborne for the honeymoon. Mr. Punch bows to Alice and says: "Bless your Royal Highness! I am glad we are not going to lose YOU!" This was a hit at the fate which had overtaken "Vicky".

Punch was obviously delighted with the nineteen-year-old Princess and full of praise for the role that she had fulfilled since the previous autumn. Its treatment of her was in striking contrast to the lambasting that the editorial staff had meted out to her father in years past. He had been attacked for his slaughter of stags, particularly when they were driven past him; for his financial dealings, with special mention of railway shares; for the royal demand for more public money to improve Buckingham Palace; for his education of the Prince of Wales; and, of course, over the Great International Exhibition. But now as the Princess sailed away, *Punch*'s readers perused these loving lines:

> Dear to us all by those calm earnest eyes,
> And early thought upon that fair young brow;
> Dearer for that where grief was heaviest, thou
> Wert sunshine, till He passed where suns shall rise
> And set no more: then, in affection wise
> And strong, wert strength to Her who even but now
> In the soft accents of thy bridal vow,
> Heard music of her own heart's memories.[13]

There were other blessings, of a more substantial nature, carried away on the Royal yacht *Victoria and Albert*. These were the wedding presents. In the latter half of the nineteenth century a wedding, a marked anniversary of the same, or an important birthday, were looked upon to provide a considerable slice of capital by the members of the Royal Houses, particularly if such royalties were on friendly terms with the imperial House of Russia or the potentates of the East. In one day more capital gain could be accrued than many worthy citizens accumulated in a life-time. Despite the fact that in the years to come Alice was to be called "the Princess with the second best pearls" and much play was to be made of the financial stress in which she struggled, on that summer's day in 1862 the royal yacht carried below her decks a treasure trove that would excite world-wide interest if offered in a sale room of today.

Outstanding among the chief presents* were the extravaganza

* The following articles of jewels and plate were presented to Princess Alice:
By the Queen—A tiara of diamonds, composed of a rich bandeau, with foliage spires, etc., and a pearl and diamond brooch, with pearl pendant.
Jointly by the Queen and the Prince Consort—A set of three ornaments for the table, in silver, consisting of a candelabrum composed of a group of boys supporting branches for nine lights, and two side candelabra composed of a group of boys supporting branches for nine lights, and two side candelabra for four lights each; the branches being so arranged as to be substituted by baskets for flowers or fruit if required.
By the Prince Consort—A cross, two brooches, and a pair of ear-rings, all in very fine opals and diamonds.
By the Prince of Wales—A parure of sapphires and diamonds, consisting of a necklace and brooch, a pair of ear-rings, and a bracelet.
By Prince Alfred, Prince Arthur, and Prince Leopold—Three keeprings, diamond, ruby, and emerald.
By Princess Helena, Princess Louise, and Princess Beatrice—A locket and pair of ear-rings in turquoise and diamonds.
A diamond rose sprig bouquet which had belonged to the Duchess of Kent.
By the Duke of Saxe Coburg and Gotha—A bracelet of gold, with diamonds and enamel snap, containing a painting of the Duke's eye.
By the Duchess of Saxe Coburg and Gotha—A gold emerald tiara, with emeralds.
By the Queen of Bavaria—A gold band bracelet with emerald and diamond snap.
By Prince Augustus of Saxe Coburg and Gotha—A bracelet, with circle of turquoise, and in the centre "A.E.I." in rubies, and a diamond horseshoe.
By Princess Augustus of Saxe Coburg and Gotha—A four-row garnet necklace and bracelets, with diamond and garnet snaps.
By the Empress of Russia—A bandeau of thirty-five collets of large and fine diamonds.
By Prince and Princess Charles of Hesse—A large and very fine diamond stomacher.
By Prince Louis of Hesse—A pair of very fine top and drop diamond ear-rings.
By Prince Henry, Princess Anna, and Prince William—A blue enamel bracelet, with three pearl and diamond stars.
By the Maharajah Dhuleep Singh—A magnificent white silk fan, mounted in carved mother-of-pearl and gold sticks, the two outsides ornamented with pearls and emeralds, and Princess Alice's cipher in rubies and diamonds.
By the King of the Belgians—A diamond and emerald linked bracelet.
By the Grand Duchess Alexander of Russia—A gold heart-shaped locket, suspended by a gold chain, on one side the miniature of the Grand Duchess Alexander (Constantine) of Russia, set in diamonds, on the reverse the arms of the Grand Duchess.
By the Grand Duchess of Mecklenburg-Strelitz—Twenty-four silver-gilt worked spoons, a pair of sugar-tongs to match, and a sugar-sifter.

of diamonds from the Empress of Russia and the magnificent jewelled fan from the Maharajah Dhuleep Singh.* This was in gold, one of its features being the rose of England carved from a large ruby, with emerald leaves surrounded by pearls, with the Princess's initials in diamonds, rubies and emeralds blended. To remind her always of happy days in Scotland was the silver-gilt jewel casket from the Countess of Fife, which was surmounted with a Cairngorm from Mar Forest, set in gold. To remind her that the eye of Coburg was ever upon her the Duke of Coburg had included a painting of his own eye in his bracelet of gold. There were also many gifts from the public, including a Bible and casket from "The Maidens of England", five thousand of them in all, limited to a donation of one shilling each.[14]

The couple made their leisurely way across Europe, part by rail and part by river, the journey taking five days. From Bingen onwards the people of Hesse gathered to wave to them and catch a glimpse of the pretty Princess who would one day be their Grand Duchess. The Grand Ducal family joined the train at the station before Darmstadt.

It was half past five, the bells were ringing and bands playing, as they drove in a six-horse carriage, with mounted escort, along the Wilhelminenstrasse, gay with flags. The roar of "Welcome" greeted them and flowers rained down from the upstairs windows. There was not to be such a day again until Princess Alice of Battenberg married Prince Andrew of Greece† forty years later.

Along the Rheinstrasse and into the Luisenplatz, dominated by the Grand Ducal Palace and the statue of Duke Louis I on its

---

By the Duchess of Cambridge and Princess Mary—A pair of engraved crystal claret-jugs, set in silver-gilt ornamental work.

By the King and Queen of Prussia—A gold bracelet with a centre of sapphires and diamonds.

By the Crown Princess of Prussia—A handsome dressing-case with gold fittings.

By the Marquis of Breadalbane—A gold band bracelet, the centre composed of diamonds and rubies, with a large Oriental pearl in the centre; pendants to the bracelets of Scotch pearls and rubies to correspond.

By the Countess of Fife—A large silver-gilt engraved casket; four angels in the corners; on the top a large cairngorm from Mar Forest.

* Of Lahore. Deposed in 1849, he had made his home in England and became a Christian.

† The parents of Prince Philip, Duke of Edinburgh.

Doric column. Here they alighted at the palace of Prince and Princess Charles. Time and time again, until after darkness had fallen, the crowds, which had come in from all over Hesse, called them out on to the balcony, to see the bride who was sister of the Crown Princess of Prussia.

Meantime the British newspaper correspondents, who had followed the Princess to Germany, were looking around for tit-bits of information that would interest their readers at home. Having followed her to church next morning and watched her drive round the town, they turned to topographical and statistical information to fatten their reports. They discovered that the Grand Duke stood ninth in the list of Princes represented in the German Diet and that the population of his State was half that of Norway. They reported that there were 30,000 inhabitants of the capital and that Liebig, the chemist, had been born there. With the town itself they could raise little enthusiasm. In fact they found it gloomy, with little architectural merit. They discovered that the garden of the old Palace had once been an old dry ditch, and remarked that it was indifferently kept. They liked the idea of a covered-in drilling ground for the garrison, but thought the Town Hall most depressing.[15] They then packed up and took the train for Frankfurt, leaving their Princess somewhat in the position of the rich girl from the marble halls who is deposited in a boarding school where strange rules apply and even the food is different. In the event, it was over the food that she was to stage her first rebellion.

8

Of Darmstadt and a Child

PRINCESS ALICE HAD NEVER BEEN AWAY FROM HER MOTHER for more than a few days at a time. Her travels had been limited to single journeys to Ireland and Germany. Her concepts of life were confined to the routine at Windsor and Buckingham Palace, Osborne and Balmoral. Queen Victoria's stern adherence to her code made deviation from that code appear strange, funny or plain blasphemous to her daughters and grand-daughters, when they married. Princess Ena of Battenberg dissolved into fits of surprised laughter when, after her wedding to King Alfonso of Spain, she saw him dip his toast into his tea.

The Princess now found herself in a court the members of which were equally determined that the Hessian way of life was the only way, where women were repressed and the old order carefully conserved by the Grand Duke. She was therefore in a position which was in part parallel with that of her sister in Berlin. The words which Lord Rennell of Rodd was later to use concerning the lot of the Empress Frederick, applied in the main to Alice.

She had brilliant intellectual gifts. But fate had willed that she should labour in a soil which was inevitably unreceptive of the seed she had to sow. Her qualities of mind and character met with little appreciation in the Germany of those days which looked for other virtues in women.[1]

One of the first reactions of the Princess was a determination that she would retain her status as a Princess of Great Britain and Ireland, and to this determination she vigorously adhered throughout her years at Darmstadt. When she dined at the Legation the British Chef de Mission always carried his gibus hat under his arm, thus making clear to the Princess that she was on her own soil and that he was only her guest.[2]

At receptions on Hessian ground, once the first enthusiasm of welcome had waned, the Princess found herself in difficulties. She soon realised that her every action was open to criticism and that no latitude was to be allowed to her if she deviated off the narrow path of Darmstadt etiquette. She was at a loss as to how to cope with people who, when presented to her, merely stood and looked at her; who, when asked some innocuous question, would answer with a monosyllable and then return to their passive gazing. The Princess had been trained from the schoolroom to *"cerclé"*. This had entailed walking round the room addressing remarks to pieces of furniture as if they were people, passing on with a smile and asking some chair, as if she meant it, how its aunt was recovering from her long illness. By the age of sixteen she was accomplished at the art and had been complimented by her mother. She could switch from English to German to French in a trice. But in England she had known of the people whom she was going to meet, and any gaps in her information could easily be filled in by her parents or the Household. In the main these people were stars in the worlds of politics and diplomacy, or visitors from foreign Courts. They understood the art of *"cerclé-ing"** and would give the kind of replies that allowed a Princess to smile. Now she was faced with bunches of minor officials and their wives who grunted *ja* or *nein* and returned to their Teutonic surveillance. At nineteen, she found it most disconcerting.

In reaction, she quickly turned for company to people who were considered "not eligible" for presentation, people of the middle classes, particularly to British families whose calling necessitated stays in Germany. This inevitably led to criticism, yet she let a breeze into the Old Palace which was to grow fresher with the years.

* The description used by Queen Victoria.

Marie, Princess of Battenberg, thus commented on the stranger Princess:

> She was a foreigner, came from distant England, and, as I soon remarked, did not fit in at all with the Darmstadt connections. I often felt sorry for her. . . . In our circle but little was known, in those days, of England and English customs; of its luxury and practical, solid enjoyment of life; and it was a long while before the really very great difference between the modest little house in Darmstadt and the castle at Windsor was appreciated. . . . For me, Alice was a most attractive and arresting personality; her voice particularly, and her pretty mouth, with its even teeth, aroused my admiration; as did her clothes, which had a distinctive, and to me an unfamiliar, style.[3]

Against one practice of Darmstadt domestic life the Princess went into immediate rebellion. It was "four o'clock dinner". In royal circles this entailed everyone changing into evening dress. The meal was so gargantuan that the hours following it were spent in a state of stupor, from which the partakers were aroused at eight to take their places at tea. To the Princess, this bordered on the barbaric. She accordingly ordered that, in her own house, lunch should be served at two and tea follow at the hour customary in England. This vexed the Grand Duke considerably.

In her Reminiscences, Lady Milford Haven recalls her first impressions of her great-uncle:

> The Grand Duke Louïs III was immensely tall and stooped very much when I knew him. He had two little stiff curls over his ears. Uncle Louis and my grandfather were most severely brought up. When as children they refused spinach and it was not all eaten up for dinner it was served for supper cold, and if some remained, it reappeared at breakfast the next day. To go to their rooms at night they had to walk unaccompanied down a long unlit passage and suffered agonies of terror from a tame raven which sometimes popped out on them.
>
> Uncle Louis still used the old-fashioned mode of address to the lower orders in the third person "Er".
>
> An amusing incident was told me in connection with this custom which occurred to the Grand Duke of Saxe Weimar, the son of Goethe's patron. He was driving from one of his castles to another and, on coming to crossroads, his coachman did not know which was the right turning. The Grand Duke, seeing a man standing by,

addressed him: "Which is the way to Eisenach?" "You must take the turning to the right and drive straight ahead." "Muss, muss," the old Prince fumed. "Er glaubt wohl er ist der Grossherzog— dumm genug ist er dazu." (Must! must!—he thinks he is the Grand Duke—he is stupid enough for it.)

Lord Milford Haven enlarged the picture of the Grand Duke in his own Recollections:

Uncle Louis was somewhat of a "Recluse" and had many odd habits. He lived alone in the Schloss, from where he made frequent excursions for the day, which included the midday meal, to one of his numerous small country houses and shooting boxes within driving distance. He used a barouche and four, with postillions and outriders. This was preceded by a "Fourgon" with cooks and food, and by a Kalesche containing the three brothers Fleck, his personal attendants. One was valet, the other his hairdresser, whose principal duty was to restore with hot irons the curls which Uncle Louis wore on each side of his bald head. The third attended to the pipes, or rather Meerschaum cigar holders of which there was an enormous collection, all numbered and catalogued, and used in strict rotation to colour them. These holders were carved in every conceivable shape and were attached to long stems. This collection, which was added to by family and friends at every birthday and Christmas, was eventually constituted as an Heirloom, together with a far more interesting collection of watches of all periods, which were all placed together on stands on a huge table in Uncle Louis' study; they were kept going and carefully set and, as many of them struck the hours, the effect was disturbing.

Uncle Louis never carried a handkerchief and when he wanted to blow his nose he rang a handbell, which stood on a small table by the side of his high-legged armchair, when Fleck the valet at once appeared with a clean handkerchief on a salver, to which it was returned after use. Whenever a letter or telegram arrived for him it was brought in by Fleck on a salver together with an enormously long pair of scissors with which Uncle Louis carefully cut off the top edge of the envelope. After being read the sheet was replaced in the envelope and taken to the Private Secretary to be dealt with after registration. Nothing in the way of paper was ever destroyed and after uncle's death tons of these envelopes, with their often trivial contents, were found in the archives.

Lady Milford Haven continued:

Besides the *Schloss* at Darmstadt, where he lived, and the *Alte Palais*, there was *the Pavillion* in the *Prinz Emil Garten*, the *Braunshart*, some miles from the town (which was sold by my brother), the *Palace at Mayence* which had belonged to the Teutonic order, the big shooting box at *Wolfsgarten*, the *Schloss* at *Friedberg*, a shooting box called *Konradsdorf*, which my father pulled down, *Kranichstein*, the *Fürstenlager* at Seeheim and the *Fürstenlager* at Auerbach, also the old castle at Romrod. In all these houses, except the latter which my father restored, Uncle Louis arranged a little apartment for himself which he never allowed anyone else to occupy, the bedrooms of which were identical in every house—dark green wallpaper, mahogany furniture upholstered in green rep. A small collection of novels and memoirs bound in black, as well as a musical stand for cigars, and a packet of papyrus—stale tobacco wrapped in rice paper. By the time I took to smoking as a girl, and tried them, they tasted as if made of dust. All these places were visited by the Grand Duke in turn, usually for one night, and in summer he gave his Sunday family dinners in those that were not too far distant from Darmstadt. These dinners my mother was greatly bored by. They took place at 4.30 p.m. and spoilt the Sunday, when my father was free of his military duties and we of our lessons. We often had to appear at the end of them, beautifully got up, and were presented with finger biscuits by the old gentleman, my mother having protested against the free distribution of sweets.

We were amused, but also rather terrified by a series of grimaces our great uncle produced for our benefit.

In his latter years he married his housemaid, who was kept discreetly out of sight. She was an unassuming, kindly body and my mother befriended her after his death. I remember her coming to tea and speaking of the Grand Duke as "Der gute Herr". She had received the title of Frau von Hochstätten. Louis III was popular in the country and a good, honest Constitutional Sovereign. He was a firm believer in Kaspar Hauser being the lost Prince of Baden.

The first home of Prince and Princess Louis was a small house in the old part of the town. Carts rumbled over the cobbled street outside the windows, and to the Princess there was an atmosphere of nearness to the everyday world that she had never experienced before. In the midsummer months the rooms were hot and airless, but she could always escape to ride in the woods or drive in the parks. The Prince's military duties were not arduous, and much of the day they could spend together. They were very much in love. English tea in the garden—still evenings when he read to her as she sewed. Then, when she was alone, the letter-writing.

95

There were so many relations to write to, but priority was always to her mother.

Alice had a conscience about leaving the Queen. She had, since the previous December, been the nurse and constant companion of a woman who was apparently beaten down to the ground, a woman who said that she wanted to die, a woman who tapped her head and cried, "My reason, my reason". At eighteen she had had to take the lead. In the circumstances it was not unnatural that the Princess should see too much of her mother's weaknesses and not enough of her strength. Queen Victoria had no intention, or desire, either to die early or to go mad. She had a job to do, and a man's memory to immortalise. She possessed what she termed "pluck", inherited from her mother and her father, whom George III had called "the bravest of my sons". She herself admitted that it was through lack of pluck that her husband had died.[4] She badly needed, for company's sake, a married daughter and her husband about the house, but under the surface she had no intention of being dependent on anybody. She eventually found exactly what she wanted in quiet Princess Beatrice and her gay husband, Prince Henry of Battenberg.

Alice, herself missing sorely the advice that her father could have given in the new role, struggled in her letters to give her mother all the support that she could muster. "Take courage, dear Mama, and feel strong in the thought that you require all your moral and physical strength to continue the journey which brings you nearer to *Home* and to *Him*. I know how weary you feel, how you long to rest your head on his dear shoulder, to have him to soothe your aching heart. You will find this rest again, and how blessed will it not be! Bear patiently and courageously your heavy burden, and it will lighten imperceptibly as you near him, and God's love and mercy will support you. . . ."[5] But soon a new note was entering her letters. She began to urge her mother to be seen more in public. "Try and gather in the few bright things you have remaining." She ended: "Forgive me, darling Mama, if I speak so openly."

The two were not to be long separated. The rendezvous was to be Gotha, in September. There would then be two important

Prince and Princess Louis of Hesse—Balmoral, 1863

Above, the Hesse family at Heiligenberg in 1864. From left to right: (standing) Julie, Princess of Battenberg; Prince Charles of Hesse; Prince William of Hesse; Prince Louis of Hesse; Prince Gustav Wasa; Prince Alexander of Hesse; (seated) Elizabeth, Princess Charles of Hesse; Empress Marie of Russia; Alice, Princess Louis of Hesse

Below, Heiligenberg Castle in 1891

subjects to discuss. The first was the engagement of the Prince of Wales. The second was that Princess Alice was going to have a baby.

Queen Victoria, anxious as she was to see her eldest son married, was spurred into even faster action by the news that the Emperor of Russia, Alexander II, was thinking of one of the Danish Princesses for his heir. Accordingly she arranged with King Leopold of the Belgians that a meeting of those concerned should take place at Laeken. There she met Prince and Princess Christian and their daughters, Alexandra and Dagmar. The two mothers, closeted together, sealed the arrangement. Then off went the Queen with her brood of younger children, to Rheinhardtsbrunn, a picturesque castle near Gotha. "Bertie" arrived at Laeken. He took Alexandra, the girl whom he had met but briefly a year before, into a grotto, proposed to her, was accepted, and then remarked that he hoped now that everybody would be satisfied.[6] Having inspected the field of Waterloo with his bride-to-be, he joined his family in Gotha. Here he was quickly to learn that the Anglo-Danish alliance was not universally popular, his Uncle Ernest describing it as "a thunder-clap for Germany".[7]

The Royal Family gathered in strength at the castle in the Thuringian mountains. The Crown Prince and Princess arrived, seething with anger over the strong line being adopted by the King of Prussia and Bismarck. A relieving note was provided by their son, William, who rode into his grandmother's presence on a donkey, with a parasol held over his head. Alice and Louis came from Darmstadt, and spoke their secret. The Queen thought Alice "most delightfully happy, so quietly and peacefully so, finding Louis so pleasant and companionable a companion, and so willing to share his pursuits and to let him share hers".[8] Then they went their individual ways. The Queen made for Osborne, to await the arrival of Princess Alexandra who was to undergo a period of indoctrination there. The Prince of Wales, with "Vicky" and "Fritz", headed south for a Mediterranean cruise, Lord Clarendon presuming that the Queen must consider the Continental temptations less strong than the British.[9] Alice and Louis returned to their Hessian home to prepare for a long visit to England. It had been

D

decreed that their child should be born at the castle of Windsor.

Princess Alexandra arrived at Osborne on 5th November. She was very, very good, and pretty in the dresses that had been made specially for the visit. Prince Alfred, always covetous of his elder brother's lot, said that he would marry her immediately if "Bertie" changed his mind.

The Princess found life at Osborne a striking contrast with the simple existence to which she was accustomed at the shabby Yellow Palace in Denmark. There, her father struggled to make ends meet on £800 a year. Daily he gave his children instruction in gymnastics, and their mother looked after their education. When there were guests the two girls waited at table. After their afternoon walk they immediately took off their best clothes, so as not to wear them out. One advantage she now had over the British Princesses. She could turn cartwheels, an accomplishment which she demonstrated behind closed doors.[10, 11]

The Queen was entranced by her future daughter-in-law. "This jewel! *She is one* of those sweet creatures who seem to come from the skies to help and bless poor mortals and lighten for a time their path!"[12] But she was firm with the jewel. She told Alexandra that, once she was married, she must leave her country and family behind, and not use her influence to make the Prince a partisan in any political question.[13] She was angry with "Bertie" because he wrote to his fiancée in English. She said:

> It grieves and pains me as the German element is the one I wish to be cherished and kept up in our beloved Home now more than ever. . . . The very thing dear Papa and I disliked so much in this connection is the Danish Element.[14]

It was to inculcate further the German element that the Queen arranged that Princess Alice and Prince Louis should arrive at Osborne half-way through Princess Alexandra's stay.

For Alice there was another reason for being at her mother's side at this time. She feared that the first anniversary of the Prince Consort's death, coinciding with the moving of his coffin to the completed Mausoleum, might bring about another state of crisis and collapse. Through the prayers on the 14th in the bedroom, untouched except for fresh flowers on the beds, and the service of

Consecration four days later, Alice stood by the Queen's side, the strength that she had been one year before. Louis was of endless comfort. More and more determined grew the Queen that these two should live with her.

Interest now centred round the wedding of the Prince of Wales and the arrival of Princess Alice's baby, general priority being on the former. But to the two Princesses still in the schoolroom, Helena and Louise, their sister's interesting condition was somewhat of an education. True they had become aware of the general outline when Beatrice was born, but a sister was very different to a mother. And as their knowledge grew, the truth became more and more apparent to them that the Queen was grieving that she was in the sad position where she could not herself have another child, and even jealous of Alice's condition. The night clothes laid out on the bed, the dressing-gown clasped close, these things became problems to the younger Princesses.

The Queen first stipulated that the wedding should take place on 10th February,[15] the anniversary of her own marriage. It was feared that this might lead to a funereal ceremony similar to that through which Princess Alice had passed, and she was persuaded to postpone the date to 10th March. But, Lent or no, it must be then, as she wanted Windsor clear for Alice's baby. From her decision that it should be held at St. George's Chapel, Windsor, she would not stir, as the thought of taking part in a procession through London appalled her. As only nine hundred guests could be accommodated, the jealousies engendered were sufficient to start a civil war.

The interest in the wedding, and in all things royal, was intense throughout the country. The magazines carried page after page of solid type about the Danish Family, the heritage of the Prince of Wales, Windsor Castle, the grief of the Queen, and Princess Alice, the mother to be. The full-length portrait of Alice by E. H. Corbould appeared frequently, and with it fitting lines:

> And when, a bride, you left our English palace,
> There was a void that none like you could fill:
> Let him, who wed, well guard our darling Alice
> Whom we could spare so ill![16]

The enthusiasm was fanned by the recent lack of any royal ceremonial, the beauty of the bride, and the fact that this was the first wedding to benefit from the full stimulus of photography. For weeks past the shops and public places had been full of camera studies of Alexandra. It was within the Queen's grasp, at this moment, to do much to consolidate the popularity of the Throne, but, despite the advice of her daughters, she hid away in the dark shadow of Albert. Thus she set in train the wave of Republicanism that was to sweep the country seven years later.

Princess Alexandra arrived at Gravesend on 7th March and was met by the Prince of Wales. While London's decorations and illuminations were splendid, the organisation of the procession and the policing of the route were appalling. The crowds were prodigious. Early in the morning a correspondent reported: "In all the main roads leading from suburban to central London, the roar of wheels increases, and four abreast in the carriageway a host of vehicles seems tossed together in one tumultuous sea . . . five great armies bearing down upon the City and the West End."[17] Those who were lucky enough to reach the route saw a line of shabby old carriages, horses without trappings, and no outriders.[18]

For the next three days Alexandra lived with her future sisters-in-law, all five of them. There were awkward moments. She told one of them: "You perhaps think that I like marrying your Brother for his position, but if he was a cowboy I should love him just the same and would marry no one else."[19]

The Queen sat in the Royal Closet of St. George's during the wedding. At first she appeared as if in a trance, but soon curiosity overcame her, and she began to look for the members of her brood below. She picked out Alice, "looking extremely well in a violet dress, covered with her wedding lace, and a violet velvet train, from the shoulders trimmed with the miniver beloved Mama had worn at Vicky's wedding, Louis in the Garter robes leading her".[20]

But for the bride keeping the groom waiting ten minutes at the altar and young Prince William of Prussia biting his uncle Leopold in the calf, the ceremony passed off without incident. Then away went the Prince and Princess of Wales to Osborne, Marlborough House and the wide park of Sandringham.

At Windsor the aftermath of the reception in the State Apartments was cleared away and attention switched to the nurseries. There five-year-old Princess Beatrice dwelt with Nanny Thurston. So short a time ago that she had lain there as an infant . . . so short a time since Victoria had given her last child to Albert. The shift that Victoria had worn at all her lyings-in was made ready again, for Alice was now to wear it. Oh, cried Victoria, if it could be I who was to wear that shift, that it could be I who was to undergo the trial, that I could be giving another child to Albert.

Yet for Victoria, in her longings and her grief, there were blessings. For the first time a grandchild was to be born in her home. She was in a position to help a daughter with her love and experience. For the first time a grandchild was to be named after her.

On 5th April Princess Alice was delivered of a girl child. The wet nurse was a pretty Irish peasant girl, who had to be bathed before she could go into service.[21] Queen Victoria always feared the appearance of a lymphatic tendency in her family. The Irish girl was the antidote.

Lady Milford Haven wrote:

> The bedroom I was born in was in the Lancaster Tower, alongside the "Tapestry" room—looking straight on to the Long Walk. I remember my grandmother sitting with me in the latter after Alice's* birth and saying: "I detest this room." She told me that in it she had been terribly scolded by her mother, who had accused her of making up to King William IV at the dinner he had given for her birthday, when he had drunk her health and had insulted the Duchess of Kent.

The baby was christened at Windsor on the 27th, a clergyman coming from Darmstadt to take the service. He was assisted by Mr. Walbaum, Pastor at the German Chapel, St. James's Palace. Lady Milford Haven continued:

> I had a heap of godparents. I was given the names of Victoria Alberta (after the Prince Consort) Elizabeth (after my German grandmother) Matilda (in memory of the old Grand Duchess of Hesse) and Marie—one of my godmothers being Queen Marie Amelie, widow of Louis Philippe, King of the French, who died a

* Princess Andrew of Greece.

short time after my birth.* She gave me a locket—a little round one with a pavé of pearls, separated by little brilliants, which contained a lock of her hair. The interesting thing is that Queen Marie Amelie was the real niece of Queen Marie Antoinette, being the daughter of her sister, Queen Caroline of Naples, who was the friend of Nelson and Lady Hamilton.

Among the relations present at the christening was Prince Alexander of Hesse and the Rhine. He was most impressed by Prince Louis's adoption of English ways. He told the Empress of Russia:

> He wears a Norfolk jacket, short breeches and multi-coloured garters, is very fond of sherry and horses, reads as little as possible, and never writes at all. He is the Queen's confidant, and is popular in England.[22]

Prince Louis had been filling in his days, while the Princess awaited her child, by visiting industrial cities in the North and various military establishments. He was much sought after in London and on 2nd May made his maiden speech at the Royal Academy Dinner, and did it exceedingly well.[23]

So that the Princess might have the benefit of sea air before returning to Germany, the Queen now moved to Osborne. A guest there was Sir Charles Lyell.† In his letters[24] home to his family he gave a clear and simple picture of life on the Isle of Wight, free of the wit and cynicism of statesmen such as Clarendon and Granville, avoiding the subservience of observers of lesser stature. As he wandered along the beach looking for geological specimens, he saw the Queen and Alice drive down to the shore alone, and, calling up a rowing-boat, row far out, Princes Louis and Alfred following and trying to race them. He saw Beatrice shut her governess into the fort which Arthur had built, roaring with laughter as her teacher barked like a dog and pretended to be in a kennel. In the evenings they discussed the Darwinian theory, or Sir Benjamin Brodie's ideas on death, the latter causing the Queen to comment that, if we knew the exact time of our own death, it would alter the complexion of our lives, and probably

* Died 1866.

† British geologist (1797–1875), author of *The Principles of Geology, Elements of Geology*, and *The Antiquity of Man*, upon which last he was working at this time.

make us perform our duties less well in this life. Alice posed to him the problem of how long it would take for all the races of the world to have come from one original pair. She was happiest now when talking with men such as Lyell or his friend, and hers, Dean Stanley, with whom she would delve deep into religious matters. Only two years before fears had been expressed as to the mischief into which she would get if she could escape the palace walls. Highly intelligent as the Princess was, she had suffered, and seen too much, too young. Already the mental storms, which were to blow her on to the shore of Strauss, were building up. Two interests were to dominate her, the religious, and the care of the sick and wounded.

The latter interest was fanned when the Princess accompanied her mother to the military hospital at Netley, the Queen's first public appearance since the Prince Consort's death. The wards were full of wounded brought back from India. It was a harrowing experience. A dying soldier told them that he thanked God that he had lived long enough to see his Queen. It was an inoculation which was to stand Princess Alice in good stead in the years to come.[25, 26]

Prince Louis's duties now demanded his return to Germany. The couple, with their baby, set off for Darmstadt, and the Queen journeyed north to Balmoral. The parting was not without its altercations. On arrival in Scotland Victoria wrote to King Leopold:

> Alice's departure is a *great* loss and adds to my loneliness and desolation! She is a most dear, good child, and there is *not* a thing I cannot tell her; she knows everything and is the best element one can have in the family! Louis, too, is *quite* excellent; *un coeur d'or.* The baby a great love. The good children have no duties at present to perform at home, no house to live in, and ought to be as much with me as possible.

She went on to say that, "unless Alice lived constantly with me, which she won't," a husband must be found for Princess Helena, a man content to make his permanent home with his mother-in-law.[27]

Upbraided upon thus leaving her mother in loneliness, Princess

Alice replied from Darmstadt: "You mention again your wish that we should soon be with you again. Out of the months of our married life, five have been spent under your roof, so you see how ready we are to be with you. Before next year Louis does not think we shall be able to come. . . ."[28]

But the maternal pressure was such that they were soon to leave Darmstadt again. Princess Alice now decided that, if she and her husband were to be able to lead a life of their own, something would have to be done about filling the gap left in that of Queen Victoria.

9

The Gathering Storm

SOON AFTER PRINCESS ALICE'S MARRIAGE, THE GRAND DUKE, seeing that she felt somewhat cramped in the little house in Darmstadt, had taken her to see the old castle of Kranichstein, lying in the low, wooded hills a few miles out to the north-east. The castle had not been lived in for almost a century, but she fell in love with its grey stone, its big rooms, its lake and the park around, reserved for the shooting of wild boar. She told the Grand Duke that she would love to spend the summers there, and he accordingly put in hand the necessary repairs and modernisation.

Now, when Prince and Princess Louis returned from Osborne with their baby, Kranichstein was ready for them. It was to be one of the happiest summers of their life together. Although, to the north, the clouds of war were beginning to drift over Berlin, and the Crown Prince and Princess were at loggerheads with the King of Prussia and Bismarck, as yet no signs of the gathering storm showed in the Hessian skies. Alice bathed in the lake, rode in the glades in the woods, played with little Victoria in the gardens. There were expeditions, too, into the countryside that was still new to her. They visited the castles of Marburg and Mainz and it was while staying at the latter that they commissioned Konrad

Krauss to build the New Palace for them in Darmstadt.[1]

Many visitors came to Kranichstein, among them the Emperor of Austria, the King of Bavaria and the Empress of Russia, all curious to see how the young British Princess was fitting into the German picture. There were old friends from England, including George, Duke of Cambridge. He was at Frankfurt to keep an eye on what happened at the Congress of the German princes, summoned together by the Emperor of Austria to determine upon a scheme of reform for their common country. But as the chair reserved for the King of Prussia remained empty, in the event little happened. One evening the Duke took the train to Darmstadt and drove out with the Prince and Princess to Kranichstein to dine. He thought it "a very nice old place which they have managed to make very comfortable".[2] His trigger finger itched when he saw the large numbers of wild boar and red deer in the woods.

Then, in September, hectic preparations began for the reception of Queen Victoria, her younger children and her suite.

More troubles had come into the life of the lonely Queen. In July Baron Stockmar had died. It was to her as if one more stone from the bridge of her old life had fallen into the river of death. She wrote to the Queen of Prussia:

> With every loss I grow poorer, my poor heart more broken, and must withdraw once more into its inmost recesses, where it languishes with grief. Oh, how bitter, how hot are the tears that I often pour forth in the evening in his room, kneeling beside his chair! How fervently do I implore his aid, and how I wring my hands towards heaven and cry aloud: "Oh God have pity, let me go soon! Albert, Albert, where art thou?"[3]

One of the reasons for her plan to visit Coburg had been to talk with the Baron and seek his advice. But there was an underlying reason. Disturbed by the worsening relations between Prussia and Austria, deeply upset by the quarrels between King William and Bismarck on the one hand, and the Crown Prince and Princess on the other, she was determined to talk with the King and the Emperor on their own ground. The prospect alarmed her, but her strength was such that she never turned aside from a task which she considered that it was her duty to perform. Her safety valve was the alarming display of grief over the death of Albert, now showing more obviously than before.

It was worry over the Queen's depression that influenced her two elder daughters to agree to visit Balmoral in October with their families. For the German in-laws, who were becoming exasperated with the frequent visits of their Princesses to Britain, this time there was an excellent excuse. A statue of the Prince Consort was to be unveiled in Aberdeen.

Kranichstein could not hold Queen Victoria, Princesses Helena, Louise, Beatrice, Prince Alfred and the retinue which accompanied them. There took place a hectic moving round of furniture and reassortment of beds, but even after this it was obvious that some members of the suite would have to be lodged in Darmstadt. It was perhaps fortunate that the Queen, battered down after her struggles with King William and Emperor Franz Joseph, only stayed one night. She longed for the tranquillity of Balmoral, the sturdy support of Brown and Grant and the song of the river. It was there that she was joined at the end of September by Alice, Louis and Victoria, who stayed with her, and a few days later by "Vicky" and "Fritz", with their young children, who lodged at nearby Abergeldie.

Balmoral regained some of its erstwhile spirit. The Prince and Princess of Wales were at Birkhall. Mr. Gladstone was the Minister in attendance, enlightening the evening conversations and delighting in his daily walks through the hills. His room was under that of baby Victoria and he feared nocturnal interruptions, but, to his relief, heard nothing. She paid him a visit and he was entranced. Not so well behaved was Prince William of Prussia, now approaching his fifth birthday. On his first meeting with his British relations on their own ground, he eyed them carefully and dismissed them as a pug-nosed lot.[4]

Another young diversion was a Malay boy, named Willem, whom Princess Alice had acquired in Darmstadt as a servant. Lady Milford Haven wrote of him:

> He wore a fez, a blue embroidered zouave jacket and wide trousers. He served at table and sat on the seat behind my mother's

pony-carriage when she drove herself. Willem was taught by the master Herr Geyer, who gave me lessons. As the boy was quite illiterate, he had composed a book of simple Bible stories for his benefit which was passed on to me. Poor Willem died of consumption before 1870.

Black skins were a complete novelty on Deeside. "A woman, and an intelligent one, cried out in amazement on seeing him, and said she would certainly have fallen down but for the Queen's presence. She said nothing would induce her to wash his clothes as the black would come off!"[5]

Some amusement was caused when Prince Louis wore the kilt for the first time.[6] Frankly, the dress of Scotland did not suit him. The men of Hesse were tall and slender, but with disproportionately broad hips, upon which the kilt hung ill—"the Hesse hips" as the family called them.[7] In addition, German officers were prone to adopt the erect, *stramm* attitude, which further upset the hang.[8]

Conversation and interest centred round religious matters, Gladstone keeping careful note of who attended what services. He saw Prince and Princess Louis heading for the parish church. The Queen was at this time waging her own private war against the Romans. Relying, as usual, on the views of her husband, she had been further fired by a visit to a convent when in Belgium the previous year. She had then written to her eldest daughter: "Oh, I feel now in my terrible grief as if that terrible Catholic religion was quite hateful to me (I never disliked it so much as now) as beloved Papa had such a horror of the priestly dominion."[9] She became intrigued with a book entitled *The Female Jesuit; or the Spy in the Family*, which purported to reveal the enormities practised by Roman Catholic priests. She admitted that she could hardly put it down.[10]

On 7th October Princess Alice decided that her mother needed some outdoor exercise and persuaded her to make an expedition to Glen Clova. Princess Helena with them, they drove to the shiel of Altnagiuthasach. There they lunched, heating up some broth and boiling potatoes. Then, mounting their ponies, they headed south towards the Capel Mount.

Snow showers drifted like white smoke across the water from Lochnagar, until the brilliant sun succeeded, then showers came again. White were the crests of the green Clova hills and sweet the views as they climbed towards the glen. Oh, the Queen sighed, for the touch of a vanished hand and the sound of a voice that was still.

The setting sun was garbing Loch Muick in dark green and gold as they came back to the shiel for tea. The Queen lingered, for it was always the early evening hours which she found the loneliest. It was twenty minutes to seven when they boarded the carriage for home. It was now quite dark and the lamps were lit. Willem, the little Malay boy, climbed up behind. Brown and Smith, the coachmen, were on the box.

From the start Smith, who had been having trouble with his eyes, seemed confused and found difficulty in seeing the road. Several times the wheels bumped along the verge, on one occasion at a most dangerous spot. Alice called out in alarm. Brown dismounted, lit a lantern, and started to walk ahead. This settled the Queen's qualms, but not those of her daughter, who was convinced that Smith had no idea where he was driving. She was right.

Twenty minutes out from the shiel, the carriage began to keel over, slowly at first. To the Queen's demand, "What's the matter?", Alice replied that they were upsetting. Higher and higher rose the off-side wheel. Steeper grew the angle of the Queen and the Princesses. The moments passed slowly. There was time for the Queen to reflect on whether she would be killed and to hope that she would not, as there were things she had not settled and wanted to do. Then her face hit the gravel, hard. Her hand hurt. Her daughters struggled beside her. She heard a voice say: "The Lord have mercy on us! I thought you were all killed." It was the reassuring voice of John Brown.

The Queen, with his help, struggled to her feet. Willem had jumped clear and was unhurt, but the Princesses were still on the ground, their long riding clothes entangled with the wreck of the carriage. Brown freed Alice by ripping all her clothes, with scant respect for the material or her person. Helena, more firmly trapped, was crying out piteously. Brown's strength soon freed her and the two Princesses, tattered but unharmed, turned to their mother. Her face was bleeding where the grit had cut deep, and she was nursing a sprained thumb.

Alice, completely calm, and Brown, went to the horses, which were lying as if dead. Smith was about, unhurt but of little use. The Princess held the lantern while Brown cut the traces. They got the horses to their feet, apparently none the worse for the accident.

A conference was held to decide the next step. As a result, Smith was sent off with the two horses to fetch help, Princess Alice deciding that, until such help arrived, they would sit in the up-turned carriage. So they made themselves as comfortable as possible, leaning against the bottom of the vehicle, with a plaid over them to keep out the cold. Willem squatted before them, holding a lantern and with his *burnous* over his head. No stranger setting has ever come the way of a British Sovereign. The Queen was most upset that she could not tell Albert about it.

Brown fussed round like a nursemaid. The contusion on the Queen's forehead ought to be bathed. As the only liquid available was a bottle of claret in the picnic basket, this was opened and used for the purpose. Then the light of the lantern showed blood coming from Brown's knee. He had cut it when jumping from the box. The Princess attended to that. The remainder of the wine was available for its prescribed purpose.

Meantime, Kennedy, the ghillie who had gone ahead with the ponies, became worried that he had not been overtaken by the carriage. Listening, he heard the sound of hooves in the still night, but no rumble of wheels. Then he picked out specks of light. He turned and rode back with the ponies, coming across Smith and hearing of the accident. Fortunate indeed it was that he acted as he did, or the stranded royalties might have had to sit it out until ten o'clock. The staff at the Castle was hesitant to interfere with the movements of Her Majesty, especially when she was in the care of Brown.

Brown was taking no chances now. Helping the Queen on to one pony and Princess Alice on to another, he walked between them, the two particular women in his life, holding a bridle in either hand. On the way, by the distillery, they passed Smith with a carriage, but they had had enough of him for one day, and rode on to the Castle doors.[11]

There the Crown Prince and Prince Louis were waiting, in a state of considerable upset. People, said the Queen, were "foolishly alarmed" and made "a great fuss". Dr. Jenner told her that she should go to bed. She said that she would not. Contrariwise, she went to bed late. The details of the accident were kept secret. When Gladstone informed Lord Palmerston, he was reprimanded by the Queen. He felt it incumbent upon himself to warn her against the dangers of such night drives. She replied that all her habits were formed on her husband's wishes and directions, and she could not alter them.[12] But the tell-tale scratches on her face entailed the postponement of the unveiling of the Prince Consort's statue.

On the 13th Princess Alice, in a blue silk dress, white bonnet and grey cloak, journeyed with her mother to Aberdeen. There, in the rain-washed, silent streets, her family and the lairds of Scotland around her, the Queen watched the unveiling of the first of the Albert memorials begin its long fight against the British weather.[13]

Winter came to Darmstadt. The Princess donned her skates and found, to her delight, that she could outshine the German women on the ice. She made ready for Christmas. There were decorated trees all over the house, including a tiny one for baby Victoria. It was a custom that her father had introduced to England, and she had known from childhood days. A turkey came from the Windsor farm. She learned of a poor woman who had just given birth to a child and had no money for Christmas fare. In secret, she visited her with a maid. Together they tidied the house, helped with the cooking and gave much needed presents. She was only doing the same as had been her custom at Balmoral, but in Darmstadt such expeditions were looked upon as strange on the part of a future Grand Duchess.

With the New Year Princess Alice had her taste of the bitterness of war and the sadness of divided loyalties. The squabble over the Baltic Duchies of Schleswig and Holstein is well remembered on account of the remark of Lord Palmerston that only three people had ever understood the real causes, the Prince Consort, who was dead, a German professor, who had gone mad, and himself, who had forgotten them. Yet the reason for the eventual attack on the Duchies by the Prussians was simple enough to comprehend. Bismarck was set upon a policy of annexation, he wanted the port of Kiel, he was annoyed over the marriage of the Prince of Wales to Princess Alexandra of Denmark, and, in addition, he required a nice simple military exercise, so that he could rehearse the army for more difficult campaigns ahead.

There were three claimants. Princess Alexandra's father, who had succeeded to the Throne of Denmark as Christian IX on the death of King Frederick in November, was adamant that the Duchies were Danish. Duke Frederick of Augustenberg was equally certain of his family right to the territories, and declared himself Frederick VIII of Schleswig-Holstein. Prussia was of the opinion that, as the population was mostly German speaking, rule should come from Berlin. The Prince and Princess of Wales, and the majority of the British public, were pro-Danish. The Queen backed Prussia. The smaller German states, including Hesse-Darmstadt and Coburg, were solid behind Duke Frederick. So, in the preliminary stages, was the Crown Princess, although she later gave her loyalty to the country of her adoption. Thus the British Royal Family found itself divided, and Alice, for the first time, in disagreement with "Bertie". Family meetings ended in rows, until the Queen forbade the very words "Schleswig-Holstein" being used in her presence.

Bismarck then persuaded Austria to join with Prussia in attacking the Duchies, anticipating that the British Government would not resort to armed intervention against the two powers. Into action against the forces of Princess Alexandra's father went two of Princess Alice's brothers-in-law, the Crown Prince and Prince Henry of Hesse, who was in the Prussian army. By June the war was over, Denmark humbled, and a bias against Berlin firmly planted in the hearts of the Prince and Princess of Wales.

Prince and Princess Louis again made a long stay with Queen Victoria in the summer of 1864. The Princess, who was expecting her second child in the autumn, watched her mother carefully.

There was little sign of the abatement of the grief or loneliness. Rather did it seem to grow exaggerated as she realised that the increasing family ties of her daughters lowered her in the scale of their importances. Alice realised that her mother's reliance on herself and Louis for companionship, and the lengthy visits to England, would have to cease. When their new house in Darmstadt was finished, they would be expected to live in it. There had been much talk in Hesse of suspected Anglicisation, and the Princess had been criticised because she had a British lady-in-waiting and that her private secretary, Dr. Becker, had been librarian to the Prince Consort. There were other considerations. The Schleswig-Holstein war had split Europe apart, and further troubles could be expected, bringing with them the heartache of divided loyalties. She was intent upon having a large family, and her first duty must be to her children. Yet the Queen still slept with her husband's coat over her, his red dressing-gown beside her and some of his night clothes in the bed.

No tame husband had yet been found for Helena. Prince Albrecht of Prussia had been considered, but discarded as a result of the war. Louise was independent, artistic, and of little help as a companion. Alice talked with her sisters, and then she talked with Dr. Jenner. A cleric suggested that the Queen should consider herself as a "bride" of Christ, but, on hearing this, she dismissed it as absolute twaddle. Something more mundane must be introduced to the Palace. Alice selected John Brown. There was little choice.

Alice was modern in her thinking, had political leanings towards Socialism and from childhood had always been anxious to help others and to smooth the path. She had no time for criticism of others. "She was not interested in their failings and futilities: she was alert only for admiration and the instinctive ministries of love; that was the way her mind worked."[14]

This was not a question that could be solved by "Vicky", who had married straight from the schoolroom. She was too imperious, egotistical, to solve a problem that demanded deep humanity, and, in addition, she had too many problems of her own. "Vicky" had not seen the Queen and Brown together, as if alone, on the

Balmoral outings. Alice had, on countless days of spring and autumn. She had seen her mother's complete dependence on the ghillie, her complete trust that no harm would come to her if he was there. She had noted all the little familiarities that must of nature come when a small party of people is alone amid the empty hills and glens, when the difference between a monarch and servant becomes of little account. Scratches to be bathed, wet clothes to be changed, potatoes to be boiled, the helping hand when an ankle was strained, the attention to an insect's sting, the pick-a-back across the burn, the steadying touch when a tired rider slipped from her pony, in the stillness of a snowbound morning on Lochnagar, in the twilight's magic down by the loch— these little things. Princess Alice had noted them all. She, too, felt the same ease and peace when with Brown. She was the ghillie's favourite among the royal children. Her signed photograph hung in his bedroom.

The relationship of the Queen and John Brown was, in the years ahead, to blow up into the greatest scandal of the nineteenth century. The cause, as the Marquis of Huntly was to point out,[15] was a general misunderstanding of the character and tradition of the "retainer class" in Scotland. To the Cockneys, in their tight-crammed bedrooms, the answer was obvious. To the gossips in the West End clubs it was a source of laughs over the port. The French thought they understood very well and gave the pair adjoining rooms. The Germans despatched Brown to a remote end of the servants' wing.[16] It was easy to draw a conclusion. That Queen Victoria loved Brown, in her own peculiar way, is beyond doubt. She had to have a full-time male interest in her life. She had filled it with Melbourne, and with Albert. She longed to fight in love, to fight, to master and then be mastered. Albert found the fight too fierce, prolonged. After a like interval Brown, too, was to tire and die. Queen Victoria never lost a fight with any man, not even with Bismarck. But with Brown she was always the Queen and he the ghillie. She missed him, when he had gone, with pangs of loneliness little less than she had felt for Albert.

Princess Alice's second child, a daughter, was born at Bessungen on 1st November.[17] She was christened Elizabeth Alexandra Louise Alice. The second name was a pretty compliment to the Princess of Wales, by this time herself a mother.*

In the nursery the baby was known as Ella. The Princess wrote to her mother: "I forgot to tell you, in answer to your letter about Ella's name, that of course she must be called Elizabeth; only *entre nous* Ella."[18]

It was in December that John Brown arrived at Osborne,[19] his role to lead the Queen's pony when she rode and drove. She found riding good for her nerves. Brown knew her requirements, and her fads. He had been holding her bridle for thirteen years.

Excitedly, the Queen wrote to her daughter, telling her of the new arrangement. Alice replied that she was delighted to hear about it, that now the monotony would be taken from the daily exercise. She sent her kind remembrances to Brown, adding what a lucky man he was to serve so kind a mistress. Shortly she was to tell her mother, "What you tell me of Brown is most interesting."[20]

The Queen's demands that she must have a married daughter about the house came to an abrupt end.

* Prince Albert Victor had been born, prematurely, at Frogmore on 8th January 1864.

10

Seven Weeks of War

FROM THE TIME OF THE APPOINTMENT OF JOHN BROWN TO BE personal servant of the Queen, a marked change came over the relationship between Princess Alice and her mother. The demands that the Hessian couple should spend much of their time in England ceased, giving place to a temporary reluctance on the part of the Queen to ask them to her homes. Such was the price to be paid by a daughter who took an independent line. In due season the same fate was to overtake Princess Louise.

The first departure from the rule book of the Queen came when Princess Alice began to feed her own child. This new-fangled and unladylike practice drove Victoria frantic. She fumed that Alice was making a cow of herself.[1]

The next disagreement arose over the question of Drawing Rooms. These were entertainments that the Queen did not wish to attend. She accordingly fobbed off the responsibility on to the Princess of Wales and Princess Helena. To bolster up the latter, she demanded the assistance of Princess Alice.

It was not until the end of her reign that Queen Victoria came to terms with, and to understand, the British aristocracy. In the sixties, still clinging tight to the coat tails of Albert, she was imbued with the social superiority of Germany. She automatically turned there to find husbands for her daughters. The idea of such superiority was not shared in the great dining-rooms of Britain, where as often as not the royal toast was still drunk over the finger bowls.

The point that, in Germany, Dukes had "Grand" before their titles and kept their peasants, and their women, well to heel, did not impress English and Scottish Milords and Ladies, who had a thousand years of history behind them, often more wealth and, in some cases, more land. The basic difference between their cases was not fully appreciated by the British. That difference was that the Grand Dukes had sovereign powers, with rights over life and death, powers which had hastened the fall of the Holy Roman Empire. So the rivalry between the upper strata of the two nations continued throughout the century. To the British, it was just unfortunate that their own great families had spent the centuries fighting among themselves and omitted to find a ruler from their own ranks. As Lord Lorne was to say to Queen Victoria when Berlin took exception to his engagement to Princess Louise: "Ma'am, my ancestors were Kings when the Hohenzollerns were parvenus."[2] Lord Lonsdale also made the position clear. The Kaiser was to visit him, travelling by train. The local station-master rang up on the newly installed telephone: "My Lord, His Imperial Highness is five minutes early at the junction. What shall I do?" To which Lonsdale made the laconic reply: "Shunt him."[3]

While those fortunate enough to be invited to Drawing Rooms were well content to bow to the Sovereign, they were not eager to be received by young girls or continental imports. The point had penetrated to Princess Alice, and she accordingly refused to come over for the occasion. "This," commented Lord Clarendon, "is probably about the wisest thing that the said Alice ever did, for the freeborn Britisher wd: have no fancy for putting him or herself into fine clothes & a fine coach in order to do hommage to the smallest of German Princesses."[4]

The Princess was in disgrace, the position exacerbated by the angry correspondence which passed between Windsor and Darmstadt. One letter from Germany was considered so disrespectful that it was immediately consigned to the fire.

A reaction of the Drawing Room row was that Alice and her eldest brother grew closer in their sympathies. Once more they were "in the corner" together. The Prince had visited Darmstadt and Kranichstein and found peace there. He liked the easy way of life, the lack of formality, Louis falling asleep before the fire. He contrasted it with the military clatter in Berlin. There the sight of his brother-in-law wearing medals, awarded for valour in the Schleswig-Holstein war, made him stamp his feet in rage.

When the second son of the Prince and Princess of Wales was christened in July 1865, Princess Alice was asked to be a sponsor.[5] Thereafter she held a special place in the life of "Georgy", who was to become King George V.

The next difference of opinion between the Queen and Princess Alice came over the choice of a husband for Princess Helena. The Princess's objection was not only to the man in question, but also to the method of selection. She strongly disapproved of arranged marriages, particularly when the two persons involved were kept in ignorance of planning behind the scenes. Now the procedure which had been adopted in the case of "Bertie" was being used to decide the future of Helena. The planners were the Queen and the Crown Princess.

The man involved was a strange choice, from a number of directions. He was bald, poor, and fifteen years older than Helena. He smoked cigars from breakfast to bedtime, an obvious indication that, now that Brown was around the house, the Queen would not be sharing a sitting-room with the proposed son-in-law. His political background was dynamite. He was the younger brother of Duke Frederick of Augustenburg whose claim to the Duchies of Schleswig-Holstein had been so brutally crushed by Prussia. His name was Prince Christian of Schleswig-Holstein-Sonderburg-Augustenburg.

At the end of hostilities Bismarck had dealt hardly with the Duke and his brother. He had deprived them of their commissions, their property and their status, making it abundantly clear that there was to be little mercy for those who stood in the way of the Iron Chancellor.

Prince Christian was now hanging about the house of his

friends, the Crown Prince and Princess, time heavy on his hands. Happily he was very fond of children, and spoke English. "Vicky" wrote to her mother: "You know he is our *Hausfreund*. He comes and goes when he likes, walks and breakfasts and dines with us, when he is here and we are alone. He is the best creature in the world. . . ."[6]

Unfortunately the opinion of the Crown Princess carried little weight in Germany. In the case of both Bismarck and the King, any opinion of hers was regarded in the light of unwarranted interference. The marriage of the Queen of England's daughter to the brother of a rival claimant to the Duchies would only be regarded as a slap in the face for the Prussians, as Princess Alice saw quite clearly. She was intent on avoiding trouble with Berlin, not seeking it.

Once again vitriol was mixed with the ink on the letters which flowed between Windsor and Darmstadt. By the time the year was out, when the engagement had been finalised, the Queen had referred to her second daughter's behaviour as "jealous, sly and abominable". Alice had been told that when " 'Your Parent & Your Sovereign' settled something for a sister's good . . . it was sheer selfishness to object".[7] Such rebuke could have but one effect on the Princess who had supported and led her mother through the slough of despond only four years earlier, and a long time was to pass before the breach between the two, concealed but deep, was to be closed.

Meantime the ghost of Albert was to bring the Royal Family together in unity. In August the Queen again made the journey to Coburg. There, on the 26th, her husband's birthday, she unveiled his statue. It stood at a spot where, as a student, he had eaten his lunches of bread and sausage.[8] Around her were twenty-four relations, including all of her nine children.[9]

A subsidiary reason for the visit was to meet Prince Christian, and allow Helena to get to know him. All went off satisfactorily and the details were fixed in the minimum of time. There was also the possibility of meeting the King of Prussia. This the Queen wished to avoid if possible. Prussia and Austria were already squabbling over the administration of the Duchies of Schleswig-

Holstein, a possible preliminary to a decisive bout to decide the headship of the German States. The Queen wished to remain free of involvement.

But it was not to be. King William expressed his desire to see her. Kranichstein, Princess Alice's summer home, was suggested as the rendezvous. There the Queen repaired, and waited. Then there was a change of plan, and she was called to the Palace in Darmstadt. In the broiling heat she drove to the town. The Prussian King kept her waiting for half an hour. When he at last arrived, escorted by the Crown Prince and Prince and Princess Louis, he tactfully restricted the conversation to remarks about the weather, and soon departed.[10] The point that he was accompanied by the Queen's daughter and son-in-law was duly noted.

The last year of the Old Europe, the Europe of Prince Albert and Baron Stockmar, moved sadly towards its close. Lord Palmerston died. In the first week of December news came from Laeken that King Leopold of the Belgians was sinking. He died on the 10th, so near to the "dreaded anniversary". The Queen felt that she had lost a father, and Alice's comment that she was now head of the family[11] was of little consolation to her.

The building of the New Palace in Darmstadt was completed in March 1866, and the Princess had at last a home that she could really call her own. Yet it was to prove her greatest mistake, and the costliest. It was in the style of a Victorian Piccadilly mansion, and completely unsuited to its surroundings. The bill was far beyond that which had been expected and bit deep into the savings of herself and her husband and, although Queen Victoria made a contribution, that contribution was not as big as had been hoped for. Yet it was she who had been the driving force behind the extravagant enterprise.* Although the upkeep of the New Palace was, in the years ahead, to prove a permanent drain on the finances of her children and grandchildren, in the thrill of the moment the drawbacks were hidden from Princess Alice. The rooms were large and airy, and bright with chintzes from London. She fashioned on the homes which she had known in girlhood,

---

* The New Palace was sold in 1943 and was destroyed by the Royal Air Force the following year.

and she wrote to her mother that the decoration and domestic arrangements were so English that it was hard to realise one was in Germany. There was also an atmosphere of deep luxury that came strange to Hessian visitors. Portraits and photographs of her family were everywhere, those of her father predominating. There were sketches of Osborne and Balmoral, Windsor and Frogmore, some of which she had executed herself. A much prized picture was of Loch Katrine. It had been presented to her by two hundred and fifty women, members of a Darmstadt organisation in which the Princess had taken an interest. The German artist had been sent, in secret, to Scotland.[12]

Yet, as the Princess lazed through the spring days, playing with her two children in the big garden, and preparing herself for her third child, due in July, Bismarck was completing his plans for Prussia's hegemony in Germany. By the Convention of Gastein, of the previous year, the administration of the Duchies of Schleswig and Holstein had been handed respectively to Austria and Prussia. Now Austria, realising that she had been ill advised to join the incursion into Denmark, suggested that the Duchies should become a separate state, under the leadership of the Duke of Augustenburg. This was in direct opposition to Bismarck's wishes, although he had seen the move coming, and welcomed it as it fitted in with his machinations. The matter was referred to the Frankfurt Diet, and the claims of the Duke were supported. Bismarck saw the chance of putting an end to Austrian influence, and took it. He arranged with King Victor Emmanuel that Italy should attack Austria as soon as Prussia fired the first shot.

Queen Victoria looked around in apprehension. The Crown Prince and Princess were indelibly tied to Prussia, and Prince Henry of Hesse was serving in the Prussian army. The Grand Duke of Hesse, Prince and Princess Louis, her cousin, the blind King of Hanover, and her brother-in-law, Duke Ernest of Coburg,* all backed Austria. She offered to act as mediator. In return Bismarck heaped terms of contumely on her head, accusing her of trying to rob Prussia of rightful supremacy in Central Europe on purely domestic grounds. Nothing could stop it now.

* In the ensuing war Coburg remained neutral.

On 14th June the Frankfurt Diet voted for the mobilisation of the Federal Army. The Grand Duke's brother, Prince Alexander, was recalled from retirement and given command of the hastily formed Eighth Confederate Army Corps. Prince Louis's brother, William, joined his uncle's staff. Prince Louis himself, promoted Major-General, was given command of the Hessian Cavalry Brigade. The third brother, Henry, on the opposing side, was in command of the 2nd Prussian Lancers, fortunately despatched to a distant front where he would not find himself facing members of his own family.[13]

Bismarck interpreted the mobilisation as a declaration of war. He marched. On Saturday, 16th June, Princess Marie of Battenberg wrote in her diary: "A sad day, full of fear! News came the Prussians have occupied Hanover, Saxony, Kurhesse, Nassau, and Oberhesse. Papa* has gone to Darmstadt; when he will return, and what will happen now God alone knows!"[14] Then the hair of the Army Corps Commander was dark. When he came back, seven weeks later, it was grey.

Next day Princess Alice took her two children to the station and sent them off to the care of their grandmother in England. She wanted, once her baby was born, to be free to follow her husband, if necessary, and to be able to help in the hospitals. Trains were still running, but confusion reigned in the Darmstadt streets. Soldiers were pouring in, and there was fear of an insurrection. Louis had already left. She hid his standard in her bedroom.[15]

Hesse-Darmstadt was unprepared for war. The field hospitals were ill equipped. The Princess spent her days tearing up sheets to make bandages. She sent an urgent message to her mother asking for any linen that she could spare from Osborne. Rumours poured in. The Elector of Hesse had been taken prisoner and carted away by night in a waggon. The Prussians were at Coblenz and heading for Frankfurt. The 4th Hessian Regiment had been cut to pieces! The King of Hanover had been driven from his throne and had disappeared. It was impossible to tell of the true course of the war. Then, on 3rd July, the blood-red name of Königgrätz was written into history. For eight hours the two main

* Prince Alexander.

armies, each near a quarter of a million strong, duelled for the mastery of Germany. When evening came to the village of Sadowa, the Austrians had suffered 45,000 casualties, the Prussians less than 10,000. The Duke of Cambridge wrote in his diary:

> The Needle Musket of the Prussians, it appears, is so offensive, that all the gallantry of the Austrians cannot stand up against it. The slaughter seems to have been terrific. . . .[16]

Now the fate of the minor German States was sealed. No longer was it a question of whether the Federal Army would be victorious. It was a question of how severely Bismarck would deal with those who had opposed his plans. It became a war of nerves.

On 11th July a third daughter was born to Princess Alice. Three days later the Bavarians and the Eighth Federal Corps were defeated at Aschaffenburg. A great transport of wounded came back to Darmstadt and the military gymnasium was converted into an emergency hospital. The Prussians entered Frankfurt. To avoid further bloodshed, Princess Alice begged the Grand Duke to accept terms that they offered. For this, Prince Alexander, the trained soldier with a hatred of Bismarck, never forgave her. He wrote to his sister, the Empress of Russia: "These foreigners who want to barter the country to Prussia, and cherish the incredible illusion that the King of Prussia may prove generous to Hesse."[17]

Yet further resistance would have been futile. There was too much of Ruritania about the Palace in Darmstadt. Tales of the Grand Duke are still told there. When he was asked by a Minister how many cannon should be sent against the enemy, he asked how many there were. On being told that there were two, he replied: "Send them all." A few days later, on being informed that the Prussians were in the Treasury, he remarked: "Impossible. I have the key in my pocket."[18]

The trains stopped. There were no newspapers and no mail. The only hope of getting a letter to the outside world was by carriage or horseback. On the 21st Princess Alice wrote to her mother:

> The Prussians marched in this morning, their bands playing and making as great a demonstration as they could. . . . I do not know

where dear Louis is now. Please God he is safe, but the anxiety is fearful. I am well, baby too. . . . We must get the gracious permission of the Prussians for anything we want, we smuggle people with our things with difficulty out of the town, if we wish anything, but the Prussians watch so well, to prevent our communicating with our troops or with anywhere outside, that we are complete prisoners. This goes so far, we have difficulty in getting any decent meat, or the common luxuries of life, for the Prussians devour everything. . . .[19]

The occupying troops went through the barracks and the arsenal and took away everything left there, including the sheets of the officers' wives. Princess Marie of Battenberg lamented:

They have demanded thirty-one million thalers, beside the contribution money, and ever so much more besides. And if the thirty-one millions are not forthcoming by the stipulated time people are to be punished by having men billeted on them, the lesser people fifty men, and the richer ones one hundred to two hundred and fifty men.[20]

In Frankfurt the Prussians were driving round in cabs and refusing to pay, ordering jewellery and clothing and putting them down to the Hesse Government account. In despair the Burgomaster hanged himself.

An armistice was signed on 3rd September. Louis came back from the field of operations. Victoria and Ella returned from England. The new baby was christened Irene.*

It was fortunate indeed for the Grand Duke of Hesse and the Rhine that his sister was the Empress of Russia, for Alexander II had spoken privately with the King of Prussia and insisted that his brother-in-law should retain his sovereignty and most of his land.[21] Fortunate also was it that the Crown Prince, whose reputation stood high as a result of the war, was a close friend of Louis and Alice.[22] Although the Grand Duke was spared the fate of other rulers, such as the King of Hanover whose territory was incorporated into Prussia, he suffered an adjustment of his boundaries, and the Landgraviate of Hesse-Homburg was taken away from him. This was a grave loss, and Princess Alice was upset and

* Irene Marie Louisa Anna. Irene is the Greek for Peace; Anna was after Prince Louis's sister, who had married Frederick Francis II, Grand Duke of Mecklenburg-Schwerin in 1864, and died the following year, aged twenty-two.

angry when her sister, the Crown Princess, paid a visit to Homburg shortly after its seizure.[23]

Yet it was in the fields of economy and finance that the Grand Duchy was most severely hit. Prussian soldiers had been billeted in Darmstadt for six weeks, and when they left the cupboards were bare. The railway, telegraph and postal revenues were taken over. There was an indemnity of three million florins to be found.[24] The members of the Grand Ducal family had to dig deep into their pockets, and the last of the dowry which the British people had given to Princess Alice faded away.

The Princess was paying the price for the anxiety through which she had passed during the weeks surrounding the birth of her third child. She began to suffer from rheumatism and neuralgia.[25] She was tired, and in the evenings, as she sewed away at her daughters' dresses, she would fall asleep. She longed to get away for a change, but could not afford it. Yet she was not bitter—she wanted only peace. She had no brief for the conquered rulers who still tried to resist Prussia. She told her mother that they should concentrate now on the welfare of their people, and ensure that such a tragedy did not occur again. She knew full well, from what she had seen, the fate that would overcome Hesse-Darmstadt if Bismarck's plans were crossed on another occasion.[26] The policy which she and her husband adopted found critics, both in their own land and in Britain, where anti-Prussian feeling ran high.[27]

From one direction from which it was anticipated sympathy would flow, little came. In reply to her mother's plea that all possible leniency should be shown to the conquered states, the Crown Princess replied:

> At this sad time one *must* separate one's *feelings* for one's relations quite from one's *judgment* of political necessities. . . . Those who are now in such precarious positions might have *quite well* foreseen what danger they were running into; *they were told beforehand what they would have to expect.* . . .[28]

The prowess of her husband on the field of battle, the medal that the King had pinned there upon his breast, had filled her with the glory of the eagle's strike. The warlike blood of her Kent grandfather ran strong in her, but not in Alice. Like him, she would tilt at any windmill. She herself admitted that her heart and her head were set at right angles. And as she showed the iron to others, she asked for sympathy for herself. In the summer her twenty-one-month-old son, Sigismund, had died of meningitis. She was never to recover from the blow, and the letters which poured back to England might have been written by Victoria in the dark days after the death of Albert:

> I have to bear this awful trial alone, without my poor Fritz. My little darling, graciously lent me for a short time, to be my pride, my joy, my hope, is gone; gone where my passionate devotion cannot follow, from where my love cannot recall him. . . .[29]

The aftermath of the war fanned Princess Alice's interest in the nursing of the sick and the workings of the human body. She had already become patroness of a home for pregnant women, helped the blind and backed a scheme for the better care of the mentally defective. Now she founded the Women's Union, the members of which were trained to assist in the hospitals and how to treat the wounded in time of war. The need for such an organisation had been most tragically clear. The Princess was in constant attendance at lectures and learned things, and saw things, which her mother thought were indelicate and outside the scope of a Princess.[30] Again the two differed. As a result Alice kept silent about her hospital experiences and the biological knowledge that she devoured so eagerly.

It was a sad Christmas for Darmstadt. There were few gifts to be bought in the shops and little money for festivities. There were still many wounded in the hospitals and the Princess took her daughter, Victoria, round the wards to amuse them.[31] She thought of "Vicky the victorious" in Berlin; of Helena in the peace of Frogmore, secure with her dowry and the income that came to her husband from the Queen. She thought of herself as the Princess "with the second-best pearls", although the famous Hessian jewels graced her neck.

Purse-Strings and Prussians

FULL COMPREHENSION OF THE MEANING OF MONEY WAS singularly lacking among members of the Royal Family from the days of the four Georges to those of the fifth. The leanings were towards the spendthrift on the one hand, and the miser on the other. Few trod the central path. Child differed from parent and brother from sister. Edward, Duke of Kent, considered that the Royal Mint existed for the benefit of royalties. On borrowed money, he built a palace at Ealing which rivalled pre-revolutionary Paris. Guests were received by a powdered porter, the head gardener, six footmen and a French steward. They climbed into bed up velvet-covered ladders. Hidden doors led to the toilets, where artificial streams rippled and fountains played.[1] His daughter, Victoria, paid the bill. George IV spent a vast fortune on alterations to Buckingham Palace, in which he never lived. The Duchess of Teck, the amusing "fat Mary", was so liberal in her spending that she had to retire to Florence to lick her financial wounds.[2] Among her creditors was John Barker. On the platform at a Kensington church affair, she said: "And now I must propose a vote of thanks to Mr. Barker, to whom we all owe so much."

Her brother, the Duke of Cambridge, on the other hand, was most canny. He had seven toothbrushes, one for each day of the week, because he considered that they lasted longer that way.[3] As he lay dying, he looked out of the window and saw that it was raining. He instructed his valet that, if it was wet on the day of his funeral, his second-best pair of boots was to be put on the saddle of his charger.[4] He rivalled George V, who had his collar stud mended when it broke and whose small bets on the turf had to be made on credit, as he could not bring himself to part with silver pieces bearing his likeness.

The exception to the lack of financial comprehension was Prince Albert, upon whose acumen the royal fortune was built. He raised the revenues of the Duchy of Cornwall from £16,000 to £60,000, cut the internal expenses of the Palaces to ribbons, made the royal farms pay, and set in train large capital gains by the purchase of Balmoral for £31,000 and Sandringham for £220,000. Yet even he was careful with the silver. When he won a half-crown prize at an agricultural show, he put the money in his pocket, to the disgust of the assembled gentry.

It was over finance that, in 1867, Princess Alice came to differences with her mother.

There had been little opportunity for Alice to handle, or learn about, money to this date. While her father was alive, such matters did not concern her. He handled everything. After his death the grief tended to obliterate so mundane a matter. On her marriage, she had her dowry of £30,000, the Grand Ducal family was financially comfortable, although not rich, and she spent much of each year living as a guest with her mother. The Seven Weeks War altered all that. Not only was Hesse reduced to near penury by the Prussian demands, but now invitations to stay in Britain were slow in coming.

The Princess could not bear to look upon suffering or hardship. There was in her the same love for people as that which radiated from the Princess of Wales. If anyone came to her for help, that help was forthcoming, even if her own finances could not bear the burden. If word of tragic cases came to her ears, she would hurry off at once to help.

Some days ago I went with Christa* to a poor sick woman in the old town, and what a trouble we had to find the house! At last we

Grand Duke Louis IV and the Grand Duchess with their family at Kranichstein, summer, 1878. Prince Ernest Louis is seated opposite to his mother. The Princesses are (left to right) Victoria, Irene, Alix, Elizabeth and Marie (on pony)

Julie of Hauke, created
Princess of Battenberg,
wife of Prince Alexander
of Hesse and the Rhine

Princess Alix of Hesse on
holiday at Eastbourne in
the summer of 1878

went through a little dirty court, up a dark ladder, into a small room, where the poor woman and her baby were lying in bed. There were four other children in the small room, the husband, two other beds, and a stove. I sent Christa downstairs with the children; then I cooked something for the woman with her husband's help, arranged the bed a little, took the baby from her, bathed its eyes, which were very sore—poor little thing—and put everything in order. They did not know at all who I was.[5]

Suddenly she found that she could not give all that she would like to the wounded, could not help the poor, could not be patroness of welfare societies. She could not even afford a governess for her own daughter.

Queen Victoria had been brought up in a household where money was scarce, and ever before her was the example of her father's extravagance. Shortly after her marriage Prince Albert relieved her of all worry over financial matters. In 1852 John Camden Nield left her a sum estimated to be near half a million pounds, and the Queen was a rich woman. Another half-million came to her from her husband's estate. Yet the widow did not realise the extent of her fortune.

By 1867, as the Republican spirit spread through Britain and greater and greater grew the clamour against the Sovereign's seclusion, more and more questions were asked about her finances. She received in all £385,000 annually from the country. What did she do with it? She was accused of hoarding moneys which were intended to be spent on royal ceremonial. It was not only the public who queried, but her daughters also.

True, in her widowhood, in the daily company of John Brown, the Queen spent little on herself. She took pleasure in little things, such as the egg cup that he had given her. She wore her clothes until they were frayed. Even then, they were never thrown away, but stored away in drawers, labelled with details of the service that they had given.[6] The silversmith at Windsor was beginning to think that his journeys to the Castle were a waste of time. It was only after he had entertained Brown to lunch that orders recommenced.[7] A lady-in-waiting was much surprised when the Queen

* Baroness Christa Schenck, Lady-in-Waiting.

stopped the carriage on Windsor bridge and handed two florins to a beggar who was rendering *Rock of Ages.*

Victoria was a firm believer in the rule that members of her family should live within their incomes. She did all in her power to see that they were provided for, even agreeing to open Parliament to ensure that Princess Helena received her dowry and annuity, but, once the settlement was made, it was up to them to care for themselves. This rule she now applied to Alice. Always with a strong appreciation for a solid bankroll, there was in her a tendency, and one not uncommon in the nineteenth century, to retain the power of financial superiority over those not so well equipped.

Princess Alice, looking around at the peace and plenty of Sandringham, at the unruffled life at Frogmore, where Prince Christian held the sinecure of Ranger of Windsor Park, pondering on the £15,000 a year which the country handed out to Prince Alfred, who had few responsibilities, noting the generosity of the Queen to Prince Arthur, her favourite son, now began to submit demands on her own account. They became so frequent, and so pressing, that the Keeper of the Privy Purse regarded their arrival with feelings akin to horror.[8] The Queen grew very wide awake to the opening gambits to such demands, such as appeared in letters from Darmstadt, "If, in your great kindness, you could see your way . . ."[9] On a later occasion, at dinner at Osborne, the Princess began to talk loudly about her husband's requirement for a horse. Her mother smartly switched the conversation to the beef and cutlets.[10] The Queen turned to her eldest daughter for help, and it was left to "Vicky" to point out that pearls did not grow on the bushes at Windsor.

The Queen had another bone to pick with her daughter. She was convinced that, not only was Alice behind a scheme to make her appear more in public, but also that she was set on injecting a dose of levity and gaiety into the domestic scene at Windsor, Osborne and Balmoral. And, to this aim, she was corrupting Louise and Alfred.

On the first suspicion, the Queen was quite correct. The Princess considered that it was essential, both for her mother's mental outlook and the good of the country and the Throne, that the Sovereign should appear more in public. In a long talk with Sir Henry Ponsonby, she stressed the danger of all the talk about the royal hermit on the Continent.[11] She said to Lady Ponsonby: "I daresay Royalty is nonsense and it may be better if it is swept away. But as long as it exists, we must have certain rules to guide us." The same sentiments were to be expressed by her eldest daughter fifteen years later.[12]

When the Queen steeled herself to the ordeal of opening Parliament in 1866, Alice wrote to her:

> It was noble of you, my darling Mama, and the great effort will bring compensation. Think of the pride and pleasure it would have given dear Papa—the brave example to others not to shrink from their duty; and it has shown that you felt the intense sympathy which the English people evinced, and still evince, in your great misfortune.[13]

It was such subtle propaganda which now antagonised the Queen against her daughter. She had made it abundantly clear to her Ministers, and to her people through the columns of *The Times*, that she was not going "to appear as before at Court balls, concerts, etc.",[14] and she had no intention of accepting promptings from Alice as to what she should and should not do.

On the accusation that Alice was trying to bring levity into the domestic life at Windsor and Osborne, and planning with her younger brothers and sisters to this end, the Queen was not being just. Louise and Alfred were at an age when they wished to enjoy themselves, and they considered that the gloom over their father's death should now be put aside. Of natural course they confided their views to Alice. In the case of Alfred, she was being used as a scapegoat. The young sailor Prince had erred from the straight and narrow path at Malta, a not infrequent fate for visitors to the naval base. His mother decided that such aberration must stem from the free and easy way of life that he enjoyed at Darmstadt, where he spent his weekends while a student at Bonn university. He had helped his sister with one of her bazaars, and actually sold goods at a stall.

So it was decided that Alice should not be invited to stay in

England that summer. Having made her decision, the Queen knew full well that efforts would be made to dissuade her. They were. She gracefully gave in. She had no intention of doing otherwise, as a most important guest, in the person of the Sultan of Turkey, was due, and she was relying on Alice for support. But she made stipulations.

> It must be understood, however, that Alice would not try to alter "the sad way of life" she had worked out for herself. Alice must neither give orders to the servants, nor grumble about rooms and hours and Mama's being read aloud to after dinner (which sent Louis to sleep) and Mama not doing this and that—in short about everything.[15]

That Alice looked for fun and company when she visited England can be readily understood. Her husband's duties kept him much away, and she thus described her life in 1867:

> I am often for several hours consecutively quite by myself; and for my meals and walks only a lady, as she is the only person in the house beside ourselves. It is during these hours, when one cannot be always reading or at work, that I should wish to have someone to go to, or to come to me to sit and speak with . . . accustomed as I was to a house full of people, with brothers and sisters. . . .[16]

She experimented with amateur theatricals, but the sight of a daughter of Queen Victoria playing a coquettish widow found little favour in Darmstadt.[17]

So it was that Princess Alice was in trouble both in the land of her birth and the land of her adoption. In England she was accused of being bored by "the sad way of life" there. In Hesse she was accused of being intolerant with the people around the Palace and making no effort to hide her boredom when she returned from London. Here the chief critic was her uncle Alexander. Both he and the Queen had one common point of criticism. They had both noted that Alice smiled and shone in the presence of the King of Prussia, and that he flattered her.[18] He promoted Prince Louis to Major-General in the Prussian army. In the event this meant that the Princess gravitated more and more towards Berlin. She had learned her lesson in two wars. If "Vicky" and

Alice had changed husbands, the story of the royal relationship in Europe might have been very different.

In June 1867 Prince and Princess Louis set out for London, stopping in Paris on the way. There Emperor Napoleon was entertaining Heads of State, the Emperor of Russia, the King and Queen of Prussia, the Prince of Wales (in the place of his mother), the Sultan of Turkey, the Khedive of Egypt, with a series of fêtes and balls to mark the opening of the International Exhibition. Half-way through the festivities, the Crown Princess, still grieving for her baby son, packed up and went home, to the annoyance of the Prussian King. Alice, on the other hand, glittered in gaiety such as she had never known, and, when the time for departure came, the Emperor and Empress begged her to stay on for a few more days.

The Ministers had persuaded the Queen to invite the royal visitors to Paris to continue their jaunt and be her guests in London, but she had stipulated that she could not bring herself to entertain Sovereigns who were not her personal friends. In the event she took as small a part as possible in the festivities, leaving Princess Alice to play the star role. This was the first occasion that a Sultan of Turkey had set foot on British soil, and he was the lion of the London season. Everyone wanted to meet him, the handicap being that he did not speak English. The Princess sat beside him at a State luncheon at Windsor, and he intimated that her attentions were greatly appreciated.[19] The climax was the great ball given by the Secretary of State for India at the India office, the courtyard being roofed over to make a ballroom. Princess Alice led in the procession on the arm of the Sultan, and then opened the dancing. A few minutes later, Madame Musurus, the wife of the Turkish Ambassador, fell dead as she walked towards the supper room.[20]

Back went Alice to the quiet streets of Darmstadt, the taste of banquets in her mouth and the flash of diamonds before her eyes. She was richer by one horse, from a grateful Sultan. Back to the quiet evenings making clothes for little girls and the endless routine of nursery meals. The mere thought of rice pudding and baked apples revolted her children in later life.[21] By the following spring she was longing for the Osborne sea again and the appearance of meals as if by magic from some place unknown. She wrote to her mother:

> I long so very much to see you, my own precious Mama, this summer, for I cling to you with a love and gratitude, the depth of which I know I can never find words or means to express. After a year's absence I wish so intensely to behold your dear, sweet, loving face again, and to press my lips on your dear hands.[22]

She added that Louis's leave extended from 11th June to 11th August. Accordingly the family again travelled to the Isle of Wight, the rest being particularly appreciated by the Princess, who was expecting another child. She gave birth to a son and heir, Ernest Louis Charles Albert William, on 25th November 1868.

Meantime the Princess was planning, and looking forward to, a visit to her sister in Berlin. She had first suggested such a trip only a few months after the end of the Seven Weeks War, although her husband was still being accompanied by a Prussian soldier when he rode out. But at the time she was suffering from a severe attack of neuralgia, and her doctor, tactfully, insisted that she take a cure at Wiesbaden instead.

Alice did not see the Prussian problem in the same light as the indigenous die-hards at the Grand Ducal Palace. The latter considered that they had been attacked by enemy forces, overrun, and were now being treated like a vanquished people. For ample reason, Prussians were unpopular in Darmstadt. The Princess had been imbued with her father's dream of a unified and liberal-minded Germany under the leadership of Prussia. She had grown up with Prussian affairs. In 1848 the King, then Prince of Prussia, had sought refuge in England when revolution upset his own land. There had followed the engagement of "Fritz" and "Vicky". Always hating ill-feeling and nursed grudges, she now considered that the immediate past should be forgotten, and she did her best to persuade her family and her in-laws to forget their differences. Thus it was that, when the Prince and Princess of Wales called in upon her in October 1867, when the hospitals were still overflowing with wounded, who should walk into the New Palace but the

King of Prussia! It was a bold experiment, and one that apparently succeeded. But, deep in her heart, Alexandra of Denmark had not forgiven King William, and never did. When he died, she refused to cancel the party arranged for her twenty-fifth wedding anniversary.

It was in June 1869 that Prince and Princess Louis and their children set off for the pomp of Potsdam and Berlin. Their departure did not escape criticism. The Empress of Russia, who was dead set against conciliation with Prussia, told her brother, Alexander: "Louis and Alice are, with all due respect, possessed of the devil, in their mania for inappropriate visits."[23]

Once again they found themselves in the midst of a galaxy of Kings and Heads of State. At the Potsdam Palace a French comedy was staged for their entertainment. To her great delight, little Victoria was allowed to attend.

> Behind the Crown Princess sat the Princess Charlotte and the Princess of Hesse, two little girls of six or seven years old, and between them they had the son of the Khedive. The two girls were very intimate with their playfellow with his red tarboosh and his impassive Turkish face. The little Princess of Hesse arranged the silken tassel on his tarboosh for him, and when the representation was over and she went away, she gave him a kiss, at which he was very much astonished. She asked him, too, where his mamma was, but he could give her no information on this point.[24]

Lady Milford Haven's own impressions of the occasion appeared in her Reminiscences:

> The Emperor William II was then 11, Charlotte 9, Henry $7\frac{1}{2}$. I remember a parade of the I Garde Regiment in which William appeared in the complete uniform of a lieutenant. He was so short, that his hand was held by a tall sergeant during the march past to keep in pace with the men.
> Dr. Hinzpeter, the boys' Tutor, we were very much in awe of. All his interest was in the heir and Henry was rather shoved aside. However, as Henry was destined for the Navy, in the afternoon he climbed a full sized mast erected in the grounds under the supervision of a sailor and I was much disappointed at not being allowed to do so too. There was much formality at the Prussian court and we were always followed by footmen in livery wherever we went.

Whilst we were there the Khedive of Egypt came to Berlin with his small son and Charlotte and I attended a ballet in their honour. The Khedive's son was dressed in a little frock coat with a grand cross and star, and wore a fez on his head. He was about 9. He sat between Charlotte and me. As we could not talk to him (he only spoke his own language) to show our goodwill, we took turns in kissing his little yellow cheeks.

There was to be further close contact with the Prussians. In the autumn the Crown Prince was due to make a lengthy tour of the Near East and, on Princess Alice's idea, it was arranged that her husband should accompany him. She wrote to her mother: ". . . Travelling in new countries is so good for a man, and Louis may never find so good a chance again."[25] So one of the principals concerned in the victory at Sadowa set off in company with a Brigade Commander of the defeated army.

The arrangement for the deserted wives was equally amiable. They were to spend two months at the Grand Hotel at Cannes. The Crown Princess sallied south with a retinue of twenty-five. Princess Alice, leaving her daughters in the care of her mother-in-law, followed in more humble fashion, attended by a lady-in-waiting, a secretary, a steward, and Mrs. Orchard, the English nurse of baby Ernest.

In the sunshine the ills of Alice, the rheumatism and the neuralgia, faded away. "The heavenly blue sea, stretching so far and wide, is in accordance with one's feelings. . . ."[26]

I2

The House of Battenberg

O
F THE FAMILIES WITH WHICH PRINCESS ALICE CAME INTO
constant contact in Hesse, that of her uncle Alexander
was the most interesting. He and his charming Polish
wife, the Princess of Battenberg, were much travelled and together
had undergone experiences which had bequeathed to them a
broadness of vision unusual in the narrow confines of the Hessian
borders. They had five children, older than Alice's but merging
with the age group of her own young brothers and sister, Arthur,
Leopold and Beatrice. In their household the mother spoke French
to her children, the servants were English, Swiss and German, the
governess was English,[1] and Russian and Italian could also be
heard. Yet, because of her conciliatory policy towards Prussia,
Prince Alexander did not approve of his English niece by marriage.

During the winter months the Battenbergs lived in the Alexander Palace, but with the spring moved to the castle of Heiligenberg,
by the village of Jugenheim, some ten miles south of Darmstadt.
Originally a simple farmstead, Heiligenberg had been bought by
Wilhelmine, Grand Duchess of Hesse, in 1820.

In the 1860s it consisted of a "front house" and a "back house",
facing one another across a courtyard, the former occupied by the
parents and the latter by the children. The other two sides of the

square were filled in by domestic and estate offices. With the passing of the years Heiligenberg* blossomed into a full-grown *schloss*, with sixty rooms and two towers.[2] Here the Battenberg children spent their happy childhood. Soon the German Emperor was to describe them as the most handsome family in Europe. Soon, also, he was to cast anxious eyes towards them as, taking over the mantle of the Glücksburgs and the Coburgs, they planted their seed wide among the palaces of Europe.

Prince Alexander of Hesse and the Rhine began his adventurous and gay career at the age of sixteen. The herald was the Grand Duke Cesarevitch Alexander Nicholaievitch, eldest son of the Emperor Nicholas I of All the Russias.[3] Twenty-one-year-old Alexander was touring Europe with an eye open for a bride. He had already been to London. There he had danced with the young Queen Victoria and set her heart a-flutter. She made him sit near her, and she told Lord Melbourne: "I think we are great friends already and get on very well; I like him exceedingly."[4] This had urged the backers of Albert of Coburg to still greater efforts.

But the young Russian was looking for someone with more allure and less imperious enthusiasm than *la petite Reine*, and he found her, almost by accident, at the Grand Ducal Palace at Darmstadt. The young Princess Marie was allowed to join the grown-ups after dinner, and he fell in love with her ethereal beauty. To the Romanoff men, there was something irresistible about the ladies of Hesse. The couple were married at St. Petersburg on 28th April 1841.[5]

Prince Alexander of Hesse was one year older than his sister, Marie, and there was a strong bond between them. The Emperor therefore invited him to accompany Marie to St. Petersburg. The Prince already had his own tie with the country, for Alexander I had been his godfather and had commissioned him as a Second-Lieutenant in the Russian army on the day of his christening in 1823. On arrival with his sister he was promoted to First-Lieutenant in the Chevaliers Gardes, and two months later was a Colonel in the same regiment.[6]

* It is now a Teachers' Training College.

Marie did not find life easy at the Russian court. Her mother-in-law was Prussian by birth and made it no secret that she thought little of Hesse and the Rhine. Her father-in-law was awe-inspiring, and she was always shy in his presence. Court circles criticised her clothes and her lack of conversation. The cold winter winds from the swamps and the steppes played havoc with her weak chest, and she suffered from coughing and fever. The frequent arrival of children weakened her still further.[7]

On the other hand her brother revelled in the grandeur, the gaieties and the military life. He was a born soldier. In October 1843 he was promoted to Major-General and given command of the 2nd Guards Light Cavalry Brigade. In December he received the outstanding honour of being made Colonel-in-Chief of the Borissoglebosky 17th Lancers and having them named "Prince Alexander of Hesse's Lancers".* He had his amorous adventures. He made advances to the Grand Duchess Olga, sister of his brother-in-law, but here found his way barred. The Emperor had decided that his daughter should marry Charles, heir to King William of Würtemberg, and the wedding took place in July 1846. As an antidote to a bruised heart and a lost love, Prince Alexander volunteered for service in the Caucasus, where Shamyl, leader of the Caucasian tribes, was waging a holy war against Russia and, in his romantic fight for independence, earning for himself a legendary reputation throughout Europe. Alexander distinguished himself in the fighting, one of his achievements being to gain possession of Shamyl's Koran and some of his papers.†
The Emperor awarded him the Fourth Class of the Order of St. George for valour under fire.[8]

Prince Alexander's military career continued to prosper and in 1850 he became Commander of the Guards Cuirassier Division. But in affairs of the heart he was less fortunate in finding favour. The Emperor wished him to marry his niece, the Grand Duchess

---

* Earl Mountbatten of Burma has in his possession a letter written to his sister, Queen Louise of Sweden, by the Emperor Nicholas's second daughter, the Grand Duchess Tatiana, announcing with great pleasure that she had been made Colonel-in-Chief of this very Regiment, thus retaining the family connection.

† These are now at Broadlands, home of Earl Mountbatten of Burma, together with Prince Alexander's pistols.

Catherine Michailovna. This Alexander refused to do. It was his first crime. His second was committed in 1851, as a result of falling head-over-heels in love with one of his sister's ladies-in-waiting, twenty-six-year-old Countess Julie of Hauke.* Once again, the liaison was against the wishes of the Emperor. But this time Alexander took matters in his own hands, and he bolted with Julie. They were married in Breslau in October 1851. Nicholas I dismissed the Prince from the Russian army and stripped him of his General rank.

As a result of his love Alexander found himself an unemployed soldier of fortune and, as he had married morganatically, with a wife without a title. His brother Louis, now Grand Duke, came to his rescue in the latter direction. He created Julie, Countess of Battenberg, after a small town in the north of his territory.† Seven years later he elevated her to Princess, thus giving the rank of Prince and Princess to her children.

Although Prince Alexander was a Major-General in the Hessian army, there was no command for him in Hesse, so he applied to young Emperor Francis Joseph of Austria for service in the Imperial Austrian army. The two met at Geneva and Francis Joseph agreed. Then there came the question of rank. Here the Cesarevitch came to the rescue, successfully pleading with his father for the restoration of Alexander's Russian military status. So the Prince of Hesse became a General in the Austrian forces, and for ten years served Emperor Francis Joseph well and faithfully. He fought in two wars and covered himself with glory at Solferino. In 1862 he retired,‡ taking his family to live at the

* Daughter of Maurice, Count of Hauke. Of German origin but Polish nationality, he became General of Artillery in the Russian army, and Minister of War in the Kingdom of Poland. He was killed in the Polish revolution of 1830, while defending the Warsaw Palace against revolutionary cadets. He was instrumental in saving the life of the Governor-General, the Grand Duke Constantine, brother of Nicholas I. Hence the interest of the Emperor in his daughter, Julie.

† Battenberg was lost to the Grand Duchy as a result of the adjustment of boundaries after the Seven Weeks War.

‡ He was awarded the highest decorations of valour of four countries: Austria (Order of Maria Theresa), Prussia (Pour le Mérite), and Electoral Hesse (Order of Military Gallantry), as well as being advanced to the Third Class of the Russian Order of St. George for Gallantry. This was a most astonishing distinction for a General, as all were won for valour on the field of battle.

Castle of Heiligenberg, which had been bequeathed to him by his mother.[9]

The Battenberg children were all born during the period of their father's Austrian service, and each at a different place. The eldest, Marie, arrived at Geneva in 1852, where her parents had journeyed to meet the Emperor Francis Joseph. Thereafter the soldier's wife knew many homes. The following year Louis was born at Graz, where the Prince was stationed in command of a Cavalry Brigade. He was a Brigade Commander at Verona when Alexander ("Sandro") was born in 1857 and at Milan when Henry ("Liko") was born the following year. The youngest, Francis Joseph ("Franzjos") arrived in 1861 at Padua, where his father was a Lieutenant-General in command of the 7th Army Corps.[10]

Meantime Marie, by the death of Nicholas I in 1855, had become Empress of Russia. Between 1843 and 1860 she had six children—Nicholas, who died in 1865 while engaged to Princess Dagmar of Denmark, sister of the Princess of Wales; Alexander, later Emperor Alexander III, who married Princess Dagmar in 1866; Vladimir;* Marie, who was to marry Princess Alice's brother, Alfred, Duke of Edinburgh, in 1874; Sergius (Serge), who was to marry Princess Alice's daughter, Ella, in 1884; and Paul.†

The duties of Empress proved onerous to the delicate Princess from Hesse. The crown and the regalia were too heavy for her weak frame. In time she came to realise that she had lost her husband's love. The hand which stole him away was that of a girl thirty years younger than himself, Princess Catherine Dolgoruky. With the passing years, the secrecy was laid aside. Catherine was installed in rooms above those of the Empress, and bore the Emperor three illegitimate children.[11]

Now the Empress Marie only found peace amid the gardens and woods at Heiligenberg. As often as she could manage she would escape there with her younger children. Thus, on occasion, the assembly of young people at the castle was considerable. There

---

* Married, 1874, Marie, Duchess of Mecklenburg-Schwerin.
† Married, 1889, Alexandra of Greece.

were the five Battenbergs, three daughters of Prince and Princess Louis, three or four Russians, and possibly representatives from among the younger children of Queen Victoria, and William, Charlotte and Henry from Berlin.

Lord Milford Haven thus recalled those impressive days at Heiligenberg:

> Every summer the Imperial family travelled into Germany. The Emperor first went to Ems to take the waters, whilst my aunt and her younger children came to the Heiligenberg. Here the Emperor (he was never spoken of as Tsar in those days) later joined her, accompanied by one or another of his elder sons. The annual "Russian" invasion was a great event. We all—that is, my parents, we five children, tutor and governess—evacuated our own rooms and concentrated in the "Back House".
>
> The Imperial couple and their children, with their maids and valets, moved into our proper rooms. The only member of the suite lodged at the Heiligenberg was the Mistress of the Robes, for many years Countess Pratassoff. The remainder of the large suite occupied villas and hotels in Jugenheim, but always drove up to the Heiligenberg for dinner at one and supper at eight o'clock. For the former meal, served in the Garden Saloon, the gentlemen wore evening tail coats with stars of orders, evening waistcoats, black bow ties and pearl grey trousers. Frockcoats were worn for supper, served in the Terrace Saloon.
>
> After the meal the long table was removed and card tables set out, for "Yeralash", which is practically modern "Bridge" but for the dummy hand. After the midday dinner, for which we children were admitted for dessert, the gentlemen played bowls, a very heating amusement which the Emperor delighted in. After a short siesta the carriages came round (our stables were filled up with horses from Uncle Louis's stables) and the family started off on an expedition to some place such as the "Fürstenlager" at Auerbach, Seeheim, the Frankenstein, Felsberg, etc., where "Dick milch" (*sour cream*), tea or coffee was served.
>
> The Emperor had a black retriever who used to take up a good deal of room on the floor of the open "Korbwagen" (literally a "basket carriage"), in which the Imperial couple and my parents always drove. Whenever the carriage passed a brook or pond the dog used to jump out, plunge into it and return to the carriage. Neither my aunt nor my mother were allowed to say a word when the dripping, long-haired dog dried himself on their skirts, which in their amplitude were still reminiscent of the crinoline.

The question of careers for the Battenberg boys was a difficult one. There was little scope in Hesse. Austria had been robbed of her glory. Everything Prussian was anathema. Britain was too foreign. Prince Alexander's sojourn in Russia had ended in expulsion. Out of the blue, in 1868, came fourteen-year-old Louis's own, unchangeable decision. He wanted to be a sailor. His aquatic experience to date had been limited to the lagoon at Venice, but the fire was in him. It had been kindled by Prince Alfred, who wore his naval uniform whilst studying at Bonn and told sailors' yarns before the fire on his visits to Heiligenberg.[12]

Princess Alice heard of the boy's ambition, and had a long and earnest talk with him. As a result she took introductory steps and received a favourable reply from London. On 30th June Princess Marie of Battenberg wrote in her diary: "Our parents are frightfully against making an Englishman of him, but Louis's passion for the sea has won the day. It is a very grave decision."[13]

In September Louis travelled with his father to England. In October he took the Oath of Allegiance to Queen Victoria and became a British subject. He was entered as a Naval Cadet in the Navy, and placed on the books of *Victory*. On, of all days, the ever fateful 14th December, he took his examination. His eyes were none too strong, and he knew it. He had been primed that his examiners might ask him to read the time shown by the clock on the Dockyard tower. Before going in, he had synchronised his own watch with it. He managed to get in a furtive look just before the question was asked. He was through.[14]

Thus began the career of one of Britain's greatest sailors. That the British people did not reap the full harvest of his knowledge and experience was their loss, and his tragedy.

A Nurse Called Alice

IN 1870 TWO SPECIFIC MATTERS OCCUPIED THE ATTENTION OF Princess Alice, one domestic and the other international. The first was the marriage of her twenty-two-year-old sister, Louise, and the second, the storm clouds which were blowing up over France and Germany.

As to the first, the country of origin of the proposed bridegroom was of the utmost importance to the Princess, for so divided were the loyalties of the Royal Family already that the choice of any Continental Prince would be sure to lead to further schism. A husband from Denmark would lead to more bitterness in Berlin. One from Russia, where the sister of the Princess of Wales was waiting her turn to be Empress, might lead to countless complications. One from a country allied to France would be disastrous, and Princess Alice had had an ample sufficiency of differences between sisters and sisters-in-law.

In the event, a number of candidates had been put forward for the hand of pert and pretty Princess Louise—among them the Crown Prince of Denmark. On 7th May 1868 *Dagstelegraphen* had reported that the engagement had taken place, only to be followed by a semi-official denial in *The Times*. Then the awful spectre of "Citron", Prince of Orange, had again materialised, only to be exorcised once and for all by Queen Victoria. In the autumn of 1869 the Crown Princess weighed in with the suggestion of a Prussian Prince (she had a tame one standing by). This was too much for her mother, who decreed that "neither Louise nor I would ever hear of the Prussian marriage, which must be considered *at an end.* . . ."[1]

Princess Louise had decided that she would marry a man of her own country and make her home in Britain. He had already been selected. He was not royal. The Queen had agreed in principle. Not since Mary, daughter of Henry VII, married Charles Brandon, Duke of Suffolk, in 1515, had the Sovereign sanctioned the union of a Princess with a man who was not a member of a reigning house.*[2]

It was the lot of the Marquess of Lorne, heir to the Duke of Argyll, to make the break with tradition.

Strangely enough, it was Victoria who welcomed the new order, and the modern-thinking Prince of Wales who clung to the old. She explained to him her reasons and her way of thinking:

> The Prussian marriage, supposing even Louise wished it and liked the Prince (whereas she has not even seen him since she was a child), would be one which would cause nothing but trouble and annoyances and unhappiness, and which I *never* would *consent* to. Nothing is more unpopular here or more uncomfortable for *me* and everyone, than the long residence of our married daughters from abroad in my house, with the quantities of foreigners they bring with them, the foreign view they entertain on all subjects. . . .[3]

This extraordinary *volte-face* had been accomplished in less than a decade. In 1862 she had cried out that everything in her yearned for the Germany of her mother and her husband.[4] Then she had begged Alice to spend her early days of marriage in England. She had announced that the presence of a married daughter in her house was essential. Suddenly Germanic views had become "foreign" and the visits of Alice an embarrassment and an encumbrance.

Yet it was not without certain pressure that the Queen had

* Official recognition had not been given to the marriage of James II and Anne Hyde at the time of the union in 1660.

agreed to countenance the presence of a peer's son in a royal bedroom. Princess Louise had proved very determined on the matter. If thwarted, she had threatened to enter the Anglican Sisterhood at Clewer,[5] or take even more drastic action in another direction. She was to be one of the two daughters of Queen Victoria to marry for love, and, sadly, she was to live to regret it.[6]

On 3rd October 1870 Lorne, a guest at Balmoral, proposed to Louise on a walk from the Glassalt Shiel to the Dhu Loch.[7] The engagement was received with delight by the British public, and with rudeness in Berlin. Aristocratic circles were not enthusiastic, as royalties were only honorary members of the Establishment. Lady Amberley wrote:

> People don't consider the Royal family so much above as apart from others, made & kept so by established forms & etiquettes— & it will be a great pity if these forms & etiquettes ramify into families hitherto free from them—I think that for the comfort & well-being of society, it's better for Royalty to "keep itself to itself" as servants say of one another when they mean the highest praise— probably it's not best for the poor Royalty—but that seems to lead to the conclusion that Royalty's a bad thing! from wch awful con- clusion I shrink with horror . . . & so hasten to change the subject— only adding that I believe the young pair really to be attached—wch after all is the chief matter as regards right or wrong in their marrying —& that I shall be heartily glad if this or anything else tends to give a truer meaning to the words "marrying beneath one"—but such a thing there still will be—Bertha Hamilton* has married beneath her & so has the lady who ran off t'other day with her coachman— What if Frank were to marry a virtuous housemaid? . . .[8]

Princess Alice, with plenty of troubles of her own, kept her views on the marriage to herself, merely commenting that she was sure Louise would be happy with "such an amiable young man".[9]

Once again the hurricane of war had swept her on to the rocks of bitterness and horror. Through the early months of 1870 Bismarck had planned and engineered his duel with Napoleon. So well did he scheme that it was left to his adversary to fire the first shot, and bear the aggressor's blame. On 15th July the Franco-Prussian war began.

* She married the Marquess of Blandford.

Lord Milford Haven, serving at the time on the *Royal Alfred*, was on leave and thus able to witness the opening stages:

> In those days Alsace and Lorraine were still French, so that from the clock tower at the Heiligenberg we could see French Strassburg and the whole French frontier across the Rhine.
>
> It was said that the French army was short of Artillery horses, and as we fully expected them to invade Germany in a few days, my father arranged for his carriage horses to be turned adrift in our woods and preparations were made to bury the jewels and silver in the garden. Meanwhile the German mobilisation had begun and all railway trains were monopolised by the Government. No-one could travel by rail, no letter or parcel could be sent, no telegrams. For letters a horse post was organised a little later. Our almost daily amusement was, since the French invasion was apparently deferred, to drive to the station at Bickenbach and cheer on the trains full of soldiers going south to the frontier.

Throughout Germany, except in the heart of Bismarck, there was fear of an early defeat, and a greater fear of the aftermath. The Crown Princess wrote to her mother: "It is a dreadful trial for us—enough to strike terror into stronger hearts than mine. . . . The odds are fearfully against us in the awful struggle which is about to commence. . . ."[10] She sent an urgent message to Princess Alice to come at once with her children to Potsdam, where the King of Prussia had placed the *Neues Palais* at her disposal.[11] But Alice's roots, and her duties, were in Darmstadt, and there she intended to stay, invasion or no. As fate seemed to have decreed for her at times of crisis, she was expecting a child in the autumn.

Prince Louis was in command of the Hessian Division. Early on the morning of 26th July Alice wrote to her mother from Kranichstein:

> I parted with dear Louis late in the evening on the high road outside the village in which he was quartered for the night, and we looked back until nothing more was to be seen of each other. . . . I must be in town by nine o'clock: so much rests on me, and there are so many to help—the poor forsaken soldiers' families amongst others! I have seen all is ready to receive the wounded, and to send out help. I sent out fourteen nurses for the field-hospitals.[12]

The Princess was far more precariously placed than her sister in Berlin. The Rhine start-point for the Second Prussian Army was at Mainz to the north, and that of the Third Army, consisting of South German troops, commanded by the Crown Prince, at Speyer, to the south. She wrote: "I cannot leave this place until our troops should have—which God prevent!—to retreat, and the French come!"[13] In any event, Darmstadt would be a receiving centre for the wounded.

She turned her town house into a depot for the Red Cross, driving in from Kranichstein at nine in the morning, returning for lunch, and coming back to Darmstadt in the afternoon:

> Beside the large *Hülfsverein* for the wounded and sick, which is in our palace, I have daily to visit the four hospitals . . . we are so near the seat of war. This morning we got two large waggons ready and sent off for Pont-à-Mousson, where they telegraph from the battlefield they are in great want. . . .[14]

Yet, within a fortnight of the commencement of the fighting, it became obvious that the French hordes would not be allowed to sweep across Hessian soil. The Crown Prince twice defeated Marshal MacMahon on the Alsace frontier. On the 16th and 18th August the French were held at severe battles on the Chalons road. MacMahon headed north, but was penned by Moltke on the Belgian frontier. At Sedan, on the 1st September, MacMahon's army, of over 80,000 men, capitulated. Among those who surrendered was Napoleon III. He was taken into Germany. In Paris the crowds boiled with anger. A Republic was proclaimed. The Empress Eugenie fled, and was smuggled to the safety of England.

Lord Milford Haven recalled:

> The fallen Emperor was lodged a prisoner in the Castle of Wilhelmshöhe, a kind of small Versailles the Electors of Hesse had built for themselves near their capital, Cassel, and which was amongst the loot which the old King of Prussia (later German Emperor) got by annexing several German states after the civil war of 1866. Homburg, which had shortly before the war fallen to my Uncle Louis by inheritance, was another, also the little old town and district of Battenberg from which we derive our name and title and of which we were made honorary citizens when my parents came home from Italy. My sister and I were allowed to travel to Cassel with tutor and governess for a few days to see Napoleon, and on the

first day we had a good close view of him as he rode out of the gate of the Castle. He was accompanied by some Prussian officers in uniform, his jailors, and some French gentlemen. The Emperor, who looked very ill, and his people wore black plain clothes and tall hats.

While Alice grieved at the sad fate of the Emperor and Empress who had entertained her so well in Paris only three years before, "Vicky" was in transports of delight at the unexpected turn of events. Her fears faded away and she crowed in victory. "What will Bertie and Alix say to all these marvellous events?" she asked her mother. Having sermonised on the wickedness of the Parisian court, and its well deserved fate, she turned to the domestic and trivial. Fritz had diarrhoea. "Do not laugh at my long yarns as Affie would say, and pray excuse the blots on the paper."[15]

Yet in Berlin everything British was suspect. There it was being said that the Prince of Wales was openly backing the French, and munitions were crossing the Channel. The Crown Princess's loyalties were called in doubt, and even Princess Alice did not escape, eventually an accusation being made against her that she had passed military secrets to the French commanders.[16] Nothing that the Crown Princess did seemed to please the King and Queen of Prussia. She wished to help in the nursing field. At last she obtained permission to open, at her own expense, a hospital at Homburg. She ran it most efficiently, too efficiently for the Germans. Having referred to the doctors as "mischievous, stupid old things", the King recalled her to Berlin.[17]

Alice, on the other hand, built for herself, in Hesse and in England, a reputation bordering on that of Florence Nightingale. Here was the Princess who had nursed her father through his last illness and supported the Queen in her grief, who had revolutionised hospital services in the Seven Weeks War, now working all and every day, in her own hospital and others besides, regardless of the nationality of the wounded and the sick, and in permanent risk of catching a deadly disease.

Biographers of the period lavished encomiums upon her:

In the hospitals at Darmstadt, crowded with the soldiers, French as well as German, who had come from the battlefields maimed and racked with pain, she was foremost with her bright intelligence, her helpful sympathy, and her tender hand, in soothing pain and inspiring that sense of manly gratitude which is the best of human panaceas to a soldier's sick-bed. What she was, and what she did at that time, have embalmed her image in many a heart. . . . To her it was merely duty—duty to be done at every cost, but how much it had cost to that finely touched spirit, and to that delicate, womanly frame, might be read by all who could look before the surface, in the deep earnestness of her eyes, and the deeper earnestness of her thoughts.[18]

Newspapers carried stories which enhanced the legend. A wounded drummer boy was brought into the Princess's hospital. She wrapped a shawl around him, and told him that it had been knitted by the Queen of England. He clung to it, and was so doing when he died.[19]

Lady Bloomfield stopped at Darmstadt on her way back to England from Vienna, staying with the Moriers. Mr. Morier* was looking after the interests of the wounded in France, and his wife was nursing in the Hessian hospitals. The Princess sent for her and greeted her thus: "I hope, dear Lady Bloomfield, I have not got the small-pox." She went on to explain that she had just been helping to lift a wounded man when it was discovered that "the disease was full out upon him!"[20]

The Princess's way of life was anything but a salutary anteriority to child-birth. To add to her trials, her doctor came into touch with dangerous fever and dare not treat her for fear of passing on infection. Queen Victoria rushed a replacement out from London. On 6th October a son was born prematurely. He was named Frederick William, after the Crown Prince, and his mother called him "Frittie". She was very weak now. From outside the window came the constant beat of muffled drums as the funeral of some soldier passed on its way. Outside her door was a queue of women from her own hospital, now called the Alice Hospital, from other hospitals, and from the organisations in which she was interested. All queries came to her. There were 1,200 wounded French in a barracks at the end of her garden. The doctors demanded that she go away. She agreed to stay with her sister for three weeks in Berlin.

* Afterwards Sir Robert Morier.

At Army Headquarters, Versailles, on 23rd October, the Crown Prince included the following domestic item amid the military detail of his war diary: "My sister-in-law Alice has given birth to a second son, and my wife, the mother not being equal to the task, has several times already acted as wet nurse."[21] Alice told her mother that she had had to seek help in this direction, but did not reveal the identity of the wet nurse.

It was not until March that the troops came marching home. The Grand Duke met them at the Rhine and at the Ducal Palace in Frankfurt his family, headed by Princess Alice, was waiting to cheer them.[22] She had reason to be proud of her husband. Not only had he been decorated with the Iron Cross, but had also been awarded the highest Prussian award for valour, the "Pour le Mérite".

The Franco-Prussian war remained clear in the memory of Lady Milford Haven:

I have many recollections of 1870. At the beginning of the war we were living at Kranichstein. It was then really a peaceful summer resort—now it is almost a suburb of Darmstadt. Grandmama, Queen Victoria, had given us a small pony carriage and two Shetland ponies. A coachman drove them, walking alongside the carriage, while the nurse followed behind. But after the outbreak of the war we were escorted by a gendarme besides, as gypsies and the riff-raff of the big towns were flooding the region to follow in the wake of the armies and loot on the battlefields.

A bitterly cold winter set in very early and caught the swallows before they had left. "Orchie" used often to warm them up in our nursery till they were fit to fly away. We stayed at Kranichstein until November.

My mother was very busy with Red Cross work and regularly visited the wounded, both German and French, and I often accompanied her. Darmstadt being so near the frontier, an enormous lot of huts were built to house them. Some were in the Orangerie garden and numbers of huts were on the Exerzierplatz, which was the French prisoners' camp. I do not believe that there was any barbed wire round them, though sentries stood on guard. Towards the end of the war the prisoners were allowed to go into town for work and thereafter the little Darmstadt boys ran about wearing Képis, presented to them by the French prisoners. I fancy no French officers were detained at Darmstadt. Parole seems to have been given, but, I have heard, was frequently broken. In the New Palace my mother had two wounded officers, neither of them Hessian. One was very ill with typhoid and the younger had a shattered leg and liked to show us bits of bone he kept in a pill box.

My father brought back three pieces of loot from the war: a fine French cavalry horse, which lived to a great age and which I often rode, a little blue double-breasted jacket, which he picked up in a chateau where he was lodged, and the door knocker of a house in Orleans in the shape of a woman's hand holding an apple, which he brought back as a souvenir for my mother. My father said that the French troops lost their morale and their confidence in their leaders after the first battles. The cry of "nous sommes trahis", raised no one knew by whom or where, unnerved the soldiers. Some of the South German troops met with little animosity among the French population, and when in 1877 my father and mother passed through Paris, they officially called on the President, Maréchal MacMahon and his wife, whom they had known before the war. I cannot say that the same feelings prevailed in France towards the Prussians.

There were great illuminations when peace was signed. On the window ledges of the New Palace there were little saucers with wicks floating in grease. I can still remember how nervous we felt when our nursery-maid, Katrinchen, climbed on to the window ledges (third floor) to light them. The return of the troops, their helmets decorated with oak leaves, and the bands playing, thrilled us. The ranks were somewhat broken, the women and children clinging to the men as they marched past. Many captured cannon and mitrailleuses were brought to the town—the latter, the first quick firing guns in use in the armies, spoken of with awe and interest. Two guns with "N" and the Imperial crown over it stood for a long time on the terrace of the New Palace. Germany then, and for many years afterwards, was full of tales of the atrocities committed by Franc-Tireurs. According to the rules of war, as my father told us, any body of men registered as auxiliaries, and distinguished if but by an armlet, were considered combatants and taken prisoner. When the peasants took up arms independently and started a guerilla warfare, they could be shot off hand. It was a very natural movement on their part, but led to a great deal of private ambushing and sniping. I am convinced the old tales of the Franc-Tireurs led the Germans, during the Great War, to be extremely nervous when they heard unaccounted shots going off, believing them to be due to such snipers.

During the weary months of war Princess Alice had been dreaming of the peace and plenty of Balmoral. Keenly aware of her mother's recent attitude regarding disturbances to her routine, she broached the matter with care: "It seems too great a happiness to think of, that of our being allowed to come with our children to you, and to Scotland; and you know the smallest corner is enough for us, who are by no means particular—neither are our people."[23] Permission was granted. The invasion of Britain, with all five offspring, was arranged for August. Meantime there was a journey to be made to Berlin to watch the newly acclaimed Emperor of Germany, William I, welcome his victorious troops.

On medical advice, Prince Louis had arranged to take some sea air on the way to Balmoral. Accordingly, the hot August days found the family ensconced in an hotel on the beach at Blankenberghe. It was very bourgeois after the pomp of Berlin. The one small sitting-room was used for dining and also held the Prince's clothes. The children became lost among all the other children. The Princess wrote: "Everyone bathes together, and one has to take a little run before the waves cover one. We bathed with the three girls this morning, but I felt quite shy, for all the people sit round and look on. . . ."[24] They moved on to London and took over Buckingham Palace for a while.

Lady Milford Haven recalled:

> Every other year at least we went to some seaside resort with our parents, where we bathed and played on the sands to our heart's content. Blankenberghe, then a modest little place with a couple of big hotels on the "Dunes" with a town behind them, was one of the places we went to in the '70s. There was a fish market and a couple of shops, where one could buy little men made of lobster claws and boxes ornamented with shells. We went into the sea in a horse-drawn bathing machine which bumped and rocked as the driver, shouting "hue" to his horse, encouraged it to enter the water.

Princess Alice was in need of those few weeks of relaxation, for thereafter she had to steel herself to face the climax which had come to Balmoral, where her mother was lying ill and in low spirits.

The last year of the Queen's first decade of widowhood was the most critical of her reign. Politics, both at home and abroad, had proved an unceasing source of worry. The clamour against her seclusion had reached an uproar, and accusation about her suspected hoarding become increasingly bitter. There was mounting opposition to the generous financial provision for her married daughters and her sons when they came of age. The Prince of Wales, whose third son had lived for only a day,* had been subpoenaed in the Mordaunt divorce case, and it was being said that, despite his £100,000 a year, he was in debt. He was hissed at a race meeting.

The cataclysm had begun with the fall of Emperor Napoleon. On Sunday, 19th September 1870, noisy crowds gathered in Trafalgar Square. Caps of liberty were carried on poles and "The Republic of England" proclaimed. Republican clubs sprang up. From the platform Sir Charles Dilke fanned the flame. He made personal attacks on the Queen at Newcastle and Leeds, stressing the advantages of a republic. There was talk of abdication. Joseph Chamberlain and Charles Bradlaugh gave their support to Dilke, and writers, artists and poets joined in the clamour. And so did the less responsible section of the Press.

The Queen's family was referred to as a "litter", one scribe going so far as to call the Prince of Wales a "louse". There was sarcastic comment on the Court mourning ordered on the death of his baby son, this being described as "sickening mummery at Sandringham". "Common thief" was the label attached to Prince Alfred, and the accusation made that he had stolen from his ship's pay-chest:

> The Prince Consort's memory, dear to Her Germanic Majesty, was *dear* to her people also—had he not graciously left behind him a spawn of nine to be kept out of the taxpayers' pockets? And what— one need fall into no Brown study to guess the answer—what precisely were the functions of a certain stalwart Highland attendant upon Her Majesty's person?[25]

Premier Gladstone saw the danger clearly and did his utmost to stem the tide. But he was no Disraeli. He asked the Queen to delay her departure for Balmoral until the House rose. This request that she should alter her routine incensed her. She replied

---

* Alexander Charles Albert.

that, if there was a question of great importance to be decided, she would not hesitate to stay. "But where it is merely to gratify a fancy of the troublesome House of Commons, when it is their fault that Parliament has lasted so long—she must say she thinks it very unwise to yield beyond a certain point. She has been so much abused & attacked by the infamous newspapers that she cannot well be more. . . ." She agreed to three days' delay. She ended "What killed her beloved Husband? Overwork & worry—what killed Lord Clarendon? The same. . . . She must solemnly repeat that unless her ministers support her and state the whole truth she cannot go on & must give her heavy burden up to younger hands. . . ."[26]

The Queen had been overworking. The strain accompanying the recent wars on the Continent had taken its toll. Then, as since, few people realised how onerous is the burden of the Sovereign. Queen Victoria was known to have written as many as five thousand words in a day. With her relations, by blood or by marriage, scattered throughout Europe, there was so much that she could do, and never failed to do, to help to keep the balance and the peace. The postbag from Windsor was full of letters to Berlin and Brussels, Coburg and Copenhagen, Darmstadt and Vienna. She studied minutely every move of her Ministers and every Bill before the House. In the Budget of 1871 Mr. Lowe proposed placing a tax on matches. The Queen said that such a tax would make no difference to the rich, and would very much annoy the poor. Her opinion was generally agreed to be the correct one, and the tax was dropped.[27] Even when she disappeared with Brown and a few faithfuls to the Glassalt Shiel, and was cut off from the world, her Private Secretary never had complaint of lack of attention to the contents of the despatch boxes.

Somewhat to the disgust of many people in Britain, the Crown Prince and Princess had paid a summer visit to Osborne. One of the Queen's objects in extending the invitation was to bring them together with the Prince and Princess of Wales, and allow the bad feelings that had arisen as a result of the Franco-Prussian war to simmer down. A common ground was found in a general dislike of Bismarck, "Fritz" telling his mother-in-law that he would not be surprised if one day the Chancellor declared war on Britain. The two couples found another source of conversation of interest to both. This was the Queen, her behaviour, her seclusion, and the campaign being waged against her. Prince and Princess Louis were brought in, and it was decided that "Vicky", being the eldest, should write an explanatory letter, laced with advice, to her mother. It was to be signed by all the Queen's children. The letter was accordingly written. Then news came from Balmoral that the Queen was seriously ill. The Prince of Wales suggested that the delivery of the letter be postponed.[28] In the event, and most fortunately, it was never to reach her. If it had done, she would never have forgiven. No one was ever allowed to interfere with her arrangements and way of life with impunity. Gladstone had interfered with her departure date from Osborne. After, at long last, he was granted audience at Balmoral, he wrote: "The repellent power which she so well knows how to use has been put into action towards me on this occasion. . . . I have felt myself on a new and different footing with her."[29] She kept it that way until his death.

The Queen was suffering from rheumatic gout, neuralgia, and an abscess on her arm. She slept in a tent. The arrival of Princess Alice, her husband and children, followed by Prince Alfred, did not improve matters. She wanted to be alone with Princess Beatrice and Brown, the only people now who really understood her. There were rows over Brown. He had reached a stage of authority when he would throw open the billiard-room door, take a comprehensive view of the members of the Household, the Minister and guests there assembled, and gruffly announce: "All what's here, dines with the Queen."[30] Prince Alfred refused to shake hands with the Highlander on arrival. As a result he found that his orders were being countermanded. The Prince attempted to introduce naval discipline, only to find that the Queen was on the bridge at Balmoral.[31]

Yet it was fortunate that Alice, the experienced nurse, was with her mother at this time. By the beginning of September the Queen was so ill that, at one point, Sir William Jenner considered that she might die any day. It was decided to call in Professor

Lister.* He arrived on the 4th and decided that the swelling on her arm should be cut immediately. The Queen wrote:

> I felt dreadfully nervous, as I bear pain so badly. I shall be given chloroform, but not very much, as I am so far from well otherwise, so I begged the part might be frozen, which was agreed on. Everything was got ready and the three doctors came in. Sir William Jenner gave me some whiffs of chloroform, whilst Mr. Lister froze the place, Dr. Marshall holding my arm. The abscess, which was six inches in diameter, was very quickly cut and I hardly felt anything excepting the last touch. . . .[32]

She had kind words for her daughter: "Dear Alice was in and out constantly, and very affectionate and kind, helping my maids in moving me."

During the convalescent period, when the Princess's sole duty was to take her mother out for drives, she talked much with Henry Ponsonby, who had taken over as Private Secretary on the death of General Grey. She told him that only Disraeli could bring the best out in the Queen, and she urged him to show her mother the newspapers which attacked her most virulently—a suggestion with which the Private Secretary did not agree. The Princess also walked and talked with Mr. Gladstone. The Premier wrote to his wife:

> We breakfast six or eight. The Prince and Princess Louis of Hesse dine most days. To-day I walked with her and her party. She is quick, kind and well informed. I got her to-day on the subject of the religious movement in the Roman catholic church in Germany. She is imbued with her father's ideas, and I think, goes beyond them. She quoted Strauss to me, as giving his opinion that the movement would come to nothing. She said the infallibility was the legitimate development of the Roman system. I replied that the Roman system had grown up by a multitude of scarcely perceptible degrees out of the earliest form of Christianity, and if we adopted this notion of legitimate development, we ran a risk of making Saint Paul responsible for the Vatican council. . . .[33]

Princess Alice travelled south to Sandringham, to join the house-party which always assembled there for the great shoot held

* Afterwards Lord Lister.

157

on the Prince of Wales's birthday, 9th November. Sir Charles Dilke was still ranting and raving around the country about the iniquities of royalty. Prince Louis went back to his military duties in Germany. The children developed whooping cough. On 20th November the Prince of Wales became ill. Three days later it was announced that he had typhoid fever.

Meantime Princess Victoria of Hesse had been struck down with a lesser illness, which necessitated isolation:

The longest consecutive time we spent in Britain in my mother's lifetime was in 1871, from September until the end of January 1872. We were all at Balmoral at first, while Uncle Bertie and his family were at Abergeldie, and we children saw a great deal of each other. Unfortunately, all the children of both families contracted whooping cough there and I remember spending a dismal November at the top of Buckingham Palace, shut away, coughing my head off. We found in the former nurseries strange sorts of bicycles, with saddles and adorned with horses' heads and tails. These had belonged to our uncles and on them we careered down the corridor. The old royal nurseries were on the same floor and there we discovered a toy which fascinated us. It was a lion, and when you turned a crank it swallowed a figure—either a Russian soldier or an Indian Sepoy—I do not remember which.

It was during that November that the Prince of Wales was dangerously ill with typhoid, and my mother stayed at Sandringham to assist Aunt Alix in nursing him. When we were over the worst of our whooping cough, the Wales cousins and ourselves were moved to Windsor. We were not old enough to understand the anxiety Grandmama was going through when her son was at death's door, and were a very merry party of children. Our wild romps in the great corridor, in which Aunt Beatrice, a girl of 13, joined, were often interrupted by one of the pages bringing a message from the Queen that she would not have so much noise. In age, we formed a regular scale, Eddy (Duke of Clarence) coming between me and Ella, George (King George V) between Ella and Irene, while Louise Fife really belonged to the nursery party, Irene, Victoria, Maud and Ernie. Our greatest ambition, when we were with the Wales cousins, when no nursery dragon was in the room, was to steal lumps of sugar from the nursery store and melt them in the lighted candles. The result was burned fingers, an awful smell of burning wax—and no caramel.

There were lovely corners and curtains behind which one could hide and leap out in the dark. Outside the Queen's room there was always a table with lemonade and water, and a dish of biscuits which we used to pilfer.

It was generally assumed, and probably correctly, that the Prince of Wales had contracted typhoid at Londesborough Lodge, Scarborough, where he had stayed as the guest of the Earl and Countess of Londesborough on his way down from Scotland. Other guests there suffered ill effects, including the Earl of Chesterfield and Blegge, the Prince's groom, both of whom were to die from the same cause.[34] But there was another theory.

In July and August the Prince had made a continental journey, visiting Prince and Princess Louis at Darmstadt and the Russian Royal Family who were staying at Heiligenberg. Thereafter, travelling incognito as Baron Renfrew and accompanied only by General Teesdale, he had toured the French battlefields. After lunching in an hotel at Sedan, and successfully avoiding recognition, the time came to pay the bill. The General discovered that he had left his wallet behind. The pockets of the Prince were empty. They were in a predicament. If they sent a telegram for money, the French police and Press would be sure to uncover their identity. The Prince was very popular in France, and he did not want it to appear that he was glorying in the victories of the Germans. So he decided to pawn his watch. This unusual step for an Heir to the Throne was at length concluded, and the bill paid. But by this time the last train had left, and the two had to spend the night in Sedan, in the pestilential air of a town which had for many months been but one vast hospital for the sick and wounded. It was noted that the Prince had been in poor health from the date of this experience.[35]

It was indeed fortunate that Princess Alice was at Sandringham at this time. She knew well the terrors of typhoid. Her father had died of it. In 1870 she had nursed her husband through a mild attack. Her knowledge was backed by five years' experience in hospitals, and by now she was a competent matron. "Instantly she became the moral hope and stay of the house, taking charge of her sister-in-law, quiet and confident and responsible, and serving in the sick-room as a trained nurse."[36]

The fever raged through the Prince, proving a far more violent attack than that which had killed his father. On the 29th the Queen was sent for. Although Prince Albert had arranged the purchase of Sandringham and, with the Osborne agent, made the original planning of the estate, the Queen had never visited her son's home. Shadowed by Brown, she reached Wolferton station. She was not impressed. "The road lay between commons, and plantations of fir trees, rather wild-looking, flat, bleak country."[37] Alice and "Alix" met her at the door, and led her to a darkened room where one light burned low. She could see little, but it was the sound, the loud gasping for breath, which made the December nights at Windsor ten years before seem like only yesterday.

The Queen's journey to Norfolk set the interest of the country alight. Suddenly, no one wanted to hear what Sir Charles Dilke and Joseph Chamberlain had to say. It was not that the people were attached, to any large degree, to the person of the Prince of Wales, but here at last was a strong royal story, with all the elements of deep human interest. Would he, by strange coincidence, die on the same day as his father? The Princess, who, ten years before had, by her devotion, won the title of "Angel of Windsor", was again by the invalid's bed. Would she win the struggle for life this time? Tales of her wonderful work in the hospitals of two wars were recalled. The trust of the public rested on her.

The Press descended on Norfolk in a horde. There was a wild search for accommodation and transport. Outside the lodge gates there was a constant gathering of riders and carriages, awaiting the next bulletin. The sight of the day was to watch the Press dog-carts racing away to be first at the telegraph.[38]

To allay public anxiety, the Queen returned to Windsor on 1st December. There, the Wales and Hesse children joined her, under the care of Lady Churchill. Prince Louis hurried back from Germany. The royal yacht was kept in immediate readiness to fetch the Crown Princess.

On the 8th the Queen received a telegram telling her that her son's temperature was 104 and that she should come at once. It

Princess Victoria of Hesse and Prince Louis of Battenberg in 1883

Princess Elizabeth of Hesse and the Grand Duke Serge of Russia at
the time of their wedding in 1884

was eight o'clock by the time she reached Sandringham, through the deep snow hardened by the frost. This time there was only a lady-in-waiting to meet her. Alice and "Alix" were at either side of the patient's bed. They were still there when the Queen retired, and far into the night.

There now arose the problem of accommodation. Prince Leopold and Princess Beatrice were summoned. Princess Louise had come with the Queen. Sandringham was bulging at its seams. Demands were coming in all the time, from relations near and not so near, to be allowed to be present during the crisis. Among the most persistent was the Duke of Cambridge, always anxious to be to the fore at royal occasions, gay, sad, or ceremonial. He received permission on the 9th, and ordered a special train. He further increased the accommodation problem by probing the bedrooms for smells. Finding one in Princess Louise's room, he demanded that she be moved. Pinning down a workman whom he thought was a plumber, the Commander-in-Chief read him a fierce lecture on sanitary matters, only to find that the unfortunate man came from the gas works.[39]

Before dawn on the 11th the Prince had a severe spasm. Everyone was knocked up. The Duke was quartered at the home of General Sir William Knollys. He thus described the experience:

> The awfulness of this morning, I shall *never, never* forget as long as I live. Between six and seven the General knocked at my door to say we were sent for to the house. I rushed out of bed, dressed hurriedly, and ran to the house in tense agony. The morning was desperately cold, and the damp rose from the snow. . . .[40]

The spasm passed, but now matters were becoming dangerous in the sick-room. Objects were flying around as if a poltergeist had taken charge. Short, sharp words, unusual in royal homes, were echoing along the corridors. The Princess of Wales crept in on all fours, but when she rose, her husband dropped her with a pillow.

By the 13th the Prince was quieter, and much weaker. A fit of coughing seized him. White faced, Alice turned to her mother and whispered, "There can be no hope." He was grasping now, at objects which were not there. The Queen sat by the bedside, holding his hand. Alice and "Alix" rested for a while, and then took over the night vigil. Slowly the hours ticked by towards the 14th. Midnight passed, and still he lived. At four he fell asleep. He woke at breakfast-time, and asked for a glass of ale. He swallowed it, and asked for another. His mother came in. Her nightmare was over. He smiled up at her and said, "So kind of you to come."[41] Then he went to sleep again. Whether ale was a new cure for typhoid remained uncertain, but it was an idea that appealed to the men of Britain. On the 14th December 1871 it was the Prince of Wales who lived, and Republicanism which died.

Looking for the angel who had brought about this bedside miracle, the Press and the public settled for Princess Alice. Poet Joseph Gwyer wrote lines now cherished by collectors of such period pieces:

> The royal prince is sick and weak,
> His wife is watching by his bed,
> His mother looks so anxious there
> And sister Alice props his head.[42]

So widely were the virtues of Alice stressed that Queen Victoria became perturbed. To her way of thinking, it was a wife's job to keep watch by a sick husband, and hers the reward in the case of recovery. In the days when trained nurses were rare, she looked upon the main duty as one of spiritual support rather than medical expertness. There were certain things that women should not know, and the thought of men and women studying together in the dissecting room revolted her.

In truth, the Princess of Wales had kept ceaseless watch over her husband, often until sheer weariness overcame her. But this was her first experience of such emotional strain, and she had no medical training. Of natural course, she leaned on her sister-in-law, to whom death had become a commonplace and disease a daily risk.

But the Queen was not inclined to let the cap of Florence Nightingale rest on her daughter's head. Mrs. Gladstone visited Osborne, and the Queen had a little chat with her. She stressed that it was the Princess of Wales who had done the nursing, never leaving her husband day or night. She added that "apparently people imagined that it was his sister, Princess Alice of Hesse, who nursed him. She begged Mrs. Gladstone to take every opportunity of making this known."[43]

14

In Search of God

T HE LIKENESS BETWEEN PRINCESS ALICE AND HER FATHER
was strong. She had inherited his intelligence. Like him,
she liked to probe, and to originate a train of reasoning.
Like him, she lacked a sense of humour and seldom found light
relief with the little things of life. When troubles came, both faced
up to them with courage, but in the struggle they gave too much
of themselves, and both early paid the price.

Alice's happiest days were when she was in her teens, when
the horrors of the Crimean war were over and her parents enjoying
a period of comparative marital peace after the birth of Princess
Beatrice. Then Lord Clarendon had said of her: "Our *little friend*
is so full of larks that *she admits she doesn't know what to do with
herself. . . .*"[1]

Thereafter she had to endure the extraordinary emotional
display staged by her mother on the death of the Duchess of Kent;
her father's death and the impenetrable gloom which succeeded
it; the strain in her early married days, when attempts to overcome
hostility in Hesse were hampered by her mother's constant
demands for her presence; three wars and the consequent poverty;
and, most telling, the frequent arrival of children, often at the most
awkward of times. In 1871 she was twenty-eight, a tired woman

164

open to every ill, consumed with a desire to better the lot of the sick and to further the emancipation of women, her restless mind probing into the mysteries behind the painted picture of God.

The Princess's absorption with religion began in the period of nervous strain after the death of her father. She read Professor Jowett's *Essays and Reviews* and F. W. Robertson's *Sermons*, starting her along the path to spiritual freedom. She conversed with the leading churchmen, who were among the few visitors to the Queen in the initial mourning period, and before she was twenty had engaged Dean Stanley in an earnest discussion on the Apocalypse and the Psalms.[2] She posed problems to men of the calibre of Mr. Gladstone and Sir Charles Lyell. In the words of her sister, Princess Christian:

> The Princess at all times loved to gather around her people of distinction, of whatever denomination. To discuss abstruse subjects with them, and become acquainted with their opinions, was her great delight. She had a peculiar talent in drawing others out, and an inclination to enter, for the time at least, into their thoughts.[3]

The religious dilemma into which she drifted was thus summed up by E. F. Benson:

> She had been brought up to accept the creed of orthodox Christianity without question, and there presently came to her that inward necessity, known to many such, of determining for herself whether her belief was sincere, or whether, in accepting it emotionally, she was not stifling intellectual honesty. Christianity to her was not a profession to be made lightly. If she could not embrace its essential doctrines with her whole soul and without reservation it became a meaningless lip-service which it was a clear duty to abandon.[4]

Lost in the swirling mists between earth and Heaven, the Princess groped in vain for the ladder which linked the two. Her husband was little help in the matter. He was an amiable man, absorbed with his shooting and military affairs. A man who did not worry, and who liked his little joke. A not-too-German German.[5] Her parents-in-law accepted matters as they were, and had no leanings towards exploration. Princess Marie of Battenberg was a dedicated member of the Evangelical Church, disapproved of attractive hair styles and skated by herself to avoid the ordeal of being lifted to her feet by a strange man if she fell.[6]

There lived in Darmstadt from 1865 to 1872, David Friedrich Strauss, theologian, Biblical critic, man of letters. He was in his early sixties. A follower of Hegel, his *Life of Jesus* had been published in 1835. In this he had expounded his theory that, while the life of Christ had historical basis, the supernatural element in it was mythical. His destructive method caused a sensation, and brought forth wide and bitter criticism. His appointment to a chair of theology at Zürich university caused such a clamour of protest that he was pensioned off before he was installed. In orthodox circles in Berlin he was loathed. An exception was to be found in the Crown Princess, who admired the efforts of Strauss "to rid the purely historical and credible from all earlier and later embellishments".[7]

Princess Alice was drawn irresistibly towards Strauss and he became a frequent visitor at the New Palace. Among the subjects that the two discussed were Voltaire and his antipathy to priest-craft, the Princess suggesting that Strauss should make notes on the life of the French philosopher as a basis for a series of lectures. When these were finished in January 1870, she asked him to read them to her and a select circle of friends, including Robert Morier,* at her home. Then Prince Louis and the children developed scarlet fever, and, from fear of infection, the audience decided that it would be wiser not to attend. The Princess invited Strauss to read the lectures to her alone, if he did not fear the risk. So he was seen making his way to the Palace for his tête-à-tête sessions with her.

From the beginning Strauss had planned to dedicate the lectures, in their printed form, to the Princess. But when the moment for publication came he shrank from exposing her to the criticism that he knew would come in the train of such dedication. She settled the point for him. She asked him to dedicate the work to her. He hesitated, pointing out the mischief that might be made. "But," she later said, "I insisted, and he wrote a charming dedication."[8]

* Secretary of Legation at Darmstadt, 1866–71.

The result was as only to be expected. Berlin was furious. The Empress Augusta ranted that Alice was "a complete atheist", and never forgave her. When she died, the Empress commented that it was probably just as well for her children, owing to their mother's views on religion.[9] Although the Princess kept from her mother the full story of her activities in Darmstadt, the appearance of her name in print was concrete evidence of her leanings. A lady-in-waiting, writing of a "very terrible trial" that came to the Queen, said: "For some months a most interesting correspondence passed between the Princess and the Queen, the letters of the latter being most touching in their solicitude for her daughter's spiritual welfare."[10]

It was during Princess Alice's sojourn in the wilderness that her sixth child, and fourth daughter,* was born, on 6th June 1872. It has been suggested that the mysticism in the future Empress of Russia was due to her being conceived at a time when her mother was in a state of tension over her religious convictions.†[11] The Princess wrote to her mother: " 'Alix' we gave for 'Alice', as they murder my name here: 'Alicé' they pronounce it. . . ." The baby was also known as "Alicky", "Sunny", and "Princess Sunshine".[13]

It was tragedy that returned the Princess to the smoother, straighter path of her childhood beliefs. Her younger son, "Frittie", suffered from haemophilia. This dread disease, at this time still wrapped in mystery, entailed the constant surveillance of the child to see that he suffered no bruise or bodily damage which might initiate the escape of blood, possibly bringing death within a few hours.

Queen Victoria had transmitted the disease to three of her daughters, Victoria, Alice and Beatrice, and to her youngest son, Leopold. Haemophilia appears almost exclusively in males, but is transmitted by the females. In this event it was to be a subsidiary cause for the eventual toppling of the thrones of Spain and Russia.

The Queen, bewildered, pointed out that there was no trace of the illness on her paternal side, the Hanovers. It is therefore to

---

* Victoria Alix Helena Louise Beatrice.

† Frances, Countess of Warwick, was of the opinion that Princess Alice was both clairvoyant and psychic.[12]

be deduced that it was passed on to her by her mother, the Duchess of Kent, a Coburg.[14] The haemophylic strain was hereditary in that family, and Prince Albert's brother was tainted with it.[15] When Albert was wooing the young Victoria, a story ran round the London clubs that Lord Melbourne opposed the marriage because of this strain in the Coburgs, and that he had only been persuaded to change his mind when he was told that Albert was not Duke Ernest's son.[16] The value of this story lies in the knowledge that the danger was appreciated at this early date.

It was in February 1873 that the Princess finally learned that her son suffered from the bleeding disease. "Frittie" cut his ear. For three days the flow of blood continued, until the poor child's hair and neck were matted with it. An exuberant, playful boy, from now on his mother had to keep constant watch over him. On the morning of 29th May, while she was still in bed, her two sons came in to wish her good morning. They had a game. From the bow window of her room it was possible to see through that of the room next door. They would race to see who could be the first at the windows. On that morning they were half open. "Frittie" ran across the bedroom, as "hard as he could tear". To stop himself, he put his hands on the frame. It gave way. He fell through, landing on a stone balustrade twenty feet below. By the evening he was dead.[17]

Alice never recovered from the shock. Even the birth of another daughter, "May",* her last child, the following year did not alleviate the pain. The memories of her dead son seemed to grow fresher with the passing of time, and every anniversary of every little happening in his short life became an agony. Her letters to her mother were pathetic in their sadness, the wording so often reminiscent of that which the Queen had used when she was widowed. After a while, in her replies, the Queen began to temper advice with her sympathy. She pointed out the dangers of "baby-worship", and then turned to the question of the control of nerves. To which her daughter replied:

> People with strong feelings and of nervous temperament, for which one is no more responsible than for the colour of one's eyes, have

---

* Maria Victoria Feodore Leopoldine, born 24th May 1874.

things to fight against and put up with, unknown to those of quiet, equable dispositions, who are free from violent emotions, and have consequently no feeling of nerves. . . . One can overcome a great deal—but *alter* oneself one cannot. . . .[18]

Neither did the Queen allow her daughter's grief to infringe on maternal discipline. In the summer of 1873 Prince Alfred,* somewhat to the dismay of his mother, announced his engagement to the Grand Duchess Marie, only daughter of Emperor Alexander II of Russia. The Queen wished to inspect the bride on British soil. The Emperor thought otherwise and said that she was a "silly old fool". To smooth matters, the Empress, backed by Alice, suggested that the Queen should come to Germany. Whereat the Ruler of Great Britain exploded:

> You have *entirely* taken the Russian side, and I do *not* think, dear Child, that *you* should tell *me* who have been nearly 20 *years longer* on the throne than the Emperor of Russia & am the Doyenne of Sovereigns & who am a *Reigning* Sovereign which the Empress is *not,—what I ought to do*. I think I know *that*. The proposal received on *Wednesday* for me to be *at Cologne* . . . tomorrow, was one of the *coolest* things I ever heard. . . .[19]

Visits to Britain were less frequent now, and when the Hesses stayed at Osborne in 1875 it was the first time that they had seen the Island for six years. Holidays were strictly limited by finance. "We can get nothing at Scheveningen except at exorbitant prices, so we go to that dreadful Blankenberghe—without tree or bush, nothing but a beach and sand banks. . . ." "There is not a soul one knows."[20] An excitement there was that Prince Louis saved a visitor from Scotland, Mrs. Sligo, from drowning. Houlgate was better, but the house was "wee", and, oh, so dirty.[21]

The holiday which the Princess enjoyed most was to Italy, alone with her husband. Rome entranced her. "The sun was bright, the distance blue—the grand ruins dark and sharp against the sky. . . ."[22] Palm Sunday at St. Peter's, the museums of the Vatican and the Capitol, the frescoes of the Sistine Chapel, the pictures which her father had loved so dearly. Everywhere she walked and

---

* Created Duke of Edinburgh, 1866.

gazed, he was beside her. He had talked so much to her of Italy. Then south they went to Sorrento and Capri.

They were travelling incognito, but word of their presence leaked out. The Crown Prince and Princess of Italy bade them to the Quirinal, and they saw the Blue Grotto from the luxury of the Empress of Russia's yacht. Then back again to anonymity in a crowded railway carriage. One journey was very unpleasant, as they were cooped up for hours with "some very rude English".

This Jekyll and Hyde existence of the Princess, one week being treated as the daughter of "the Doyenne of Sovereigns" and pampered at the Courts of Emperors and Kings, the next shunning hotels because they were too expensive and squeezing into crowded railway carriages, was inclined to upset the equilibrium of the Princess, but certainly taught her the common touch.

An English lady, delightfully described as being "of high position", took a house in Darmstadt for a time. She received a message that the Princess would call upon her for tea. In the ensuing excitement a roll of best red carpet was ordered, a selection of the finest Hessian cakes obtained, the staff briefed. Before the appointed time of arrival a man was posted on the roof, so that he could give audible signal when the Princess's carriage came into sight at the end of the street. The hostess took her position in the hall, her staff around her. The clock chimed, but no signal came from the roof. A few minutes later the door bell rang. Alone on the pavement stood a woman wearing a mackintosh and goloshes. "I have made a point of not treading on your beautiful carpet," said Princess Alice. [23]

Her hostess saw that a change had come to the young lady who, at one time, only talked to the Clarendons and who had been the sole charted channel between the Ministers and the dark harbour of the Sovereign.

To royal travellers the informality of Darmstadt became an antidote to the sword clanking in Berlin. Sir Howard Elphinstone, Governor to Prince Arthur, was delighted when they reached the peace by the Rhine. He wrote to the Queen: "Your Majesty will find on the whole that Prince Arthur is improved by this visit to

Darmstadt. It has smoothed down some of the angularity acquired by the military spirit of Berlin. . . ." To which the Queen replied that she was glad, as "the Military Angularity of Berlin would never do HERE."[24]

Because it was the home of the daughter of Queen Victoria and because it was supposed that a better accent could be assimilated there, Darmstadt was a popular choice for up-and-coming young Britons who wished to polish up their German and learn more of the country's ways and history. Princess Alice would ask them round to tea, to play tennis at the Orangerie in the summer and to take sleigh rides to Kranichstein in the winter. Among these young men was George Arthur,* and for him there was a special attraction. "It is possible to say without hesitation or reservation that . . . Princess Ella was the most lovely child one has ever looked upon."[25]

Another British caller at the New Palace was the only person on record to have scored a direct hit on the Prince Consort with a catapult. This was Rowland Prothero,† son of the Rector of Whippingham, Isle of Wight, who had officiated at the wedding of Princess Alice.

The present church of St. Mildred was designed by the Prince Consort, the stone on the outside wall of the South Porch being all that remains of the original building, erected by FitzOsborn, kinsman and councillor of William the Conqueror.[26] The Prince took a great interest in the rebuilding and on occasion visited the site. One day young Rowland, armed with a catapult and a bag of marbles, was lurking among the tombstones on the wait for a target. On the platform erected round the tower he saw three figures. One was his father, one the builder, an exceeding fat man, and the third, a stranger, wearing a tall white hat and shepherd's plaid trousers. Rowland was having a feud with the builder. He aimed at his wide posterior, and away went the marble. Unfortunately, while he was correct for elevation, he was out of line. The marble bit deep in the plaid trousers. The Prince leaped into the air, grasping his smitten part. The rector and the builder gripped

* Afterwards Sir George Arthur, personal Private Secretary to Lord Kitchener.
† Afterwards Lord Ernle.

him before he fell. To the boy's great relief, the Prince did not tell the Queen.[27]

In the intervening years Prothero's interest had switched from catapults to religious matters. As a result, there were many conversations with the Princess.

> One evening, taking up a volume of F. W. Robertson's *Sermons* which was lying on her table, she asked me if I knew them. I replied "Yes"; that my father had them all; that, as undergraduates together at Brasenose College, Oxford, Robertson and he had been great friends; and that my father called him the "Crusader" . . . "What an excellent name!" she said; "it exactly expresses his fighting spirit and the fire of his faith." . . . She then asked if I knew Dean Stanley. . . . By a natural transition from Stanley, the Princess asked me whether I knew Professor Jowett . . . and what I understood his religious views to be. "Well, Madam," I replied, "I think that Professor Jowett holds Christianity to be not so much a doctrine as a life, of which charity and self-sacrifice for the good of others are the essential characteristics." The Princess then talked of the similarities between the attitude of Stanley and of Jowett towards doctrinal questions. I agreed that, in one sense, they approached theological discussion from the same angle, but suggested that the historical side of Christianity, which meant so much to Stanley, made no appeal to Jowett. "No one," I said, "imagines that the Dean would ever say, as Jowett is believed to have said—Voltaire has done more good than all the Fathers of the Church put together." "Did he really say that?" she asked. "How much that would have interested David Strauss."[28]

In their "digs", in conversation round the table after supper was over, these young visitors from Britain learned what the ordinary folk thought of the wife of their Prince Louis. There was general and genuine love and admiration for the Princess, for the work that she had done in the hospitals during the wars, for her care of sick children and the mentally deficient, and for her efforts to improve living accommodation for the poor. But on the point of higher education and more jobs being opened to women, opinion was divided. The older generation was dead set against such emancipation, fearing that it would lead to neglect of home duties. The younger was more open in its opinion, asking endless questions about the work of Octavia Hill and Mary Carpenter.

Underlying the objections was a marked resentment that a Princess from England should try to teach Germans how to order their lives, which lent the assumption that matters were better arranged in the land of her birth than in the land of her adoption, and thus savoured of patronisation.

At a meeting convened to discuss the building of a block of workers' flats, Princess Alice put forward the view that there should be a bathroom on each floor, for common use. This new-fangled notion on the necessity for personal cleanliness met with some surprise and opposition. An elderly and irate gentleman rose to his feet and roundly condemned the idea as modern nonsense and obviously English, and unwanted in Hesse. Before sitting down he announced that he himself had never had a bath in his life.[29]

There were also sniffs of disapproval over the *Frauen-Tag*, or Women's Conference, which had been held at Darmstadt under the leadership of the Princess and Miss Mary Carpenter. In this case the disapproval was shared by Queen Victoria, who viewed further emancipation of women with suspicion and mistrust. The Queen also feared the effect that Alice's modern ideas might have on the Grand Ducal family, and her letters were full of warning. But the Princess soothed her mother's doubts, telling her that there had been no word in the four-day discussions about "the emancipated political side", and that subjects had been restricted to those dealing with better education for girls, the employment of women in posts and telegraphs, improved instruction for nursery-maids, and matters concerning nursing generally.[30] There was a crispness in her letters, a concentration on fact rather than sentiment, which pointed to the success she might have had in organisation for some worthy aim, if aided by the sheltering wall of agenda and minutes and not always alone, on show, as the daughter of Queen Victoria.

Lady Milford Haven reviewed the work and aims of her mother:

> My mother was interested in every kind of movement in her time and knew many of their leaders. I have seen Professor David Strauss, author of the *Life of Jesus*, who dedicated his *Life of Voltaire* to her.

He was a very thin, dried-up looking man, whom I saw when he came to read his Voltaire in manuscript to her in 1870.

She was also greatly interested in the woman movement and there was a Women's Conference at Darmstadt in 1872. I remember a Mrs. Carpenter, who was one of the guests at our house for the occasion, one of the initiators of the movement for the education of women in India. I fancy it was also then that I saw Miss Octavia Hill, whose educational work among the poor is well known. Women's Welfare associations had already been started in Germany, but my mother founded the "Alicefrauenverein" for Hesse, the chief branch of which was the training of Red Cross nurses. She consulted Florence Nightingale about the work and the first matron of the Alice Hospital, their centre, was trained in London under Miss Nightingale.

Another branch took over the supervision of destitute orphans, provided for by the town rates, which, by my mother's advice, were given homes in respectable working men's families instead of being assembled in orphanages. When my mother married, there was no provision in the country for lunatics and it was she who persuaded the State to take over a lunatic asylum she had started with money collected by means of bazaars, which we children attended, having been supplied with money for our purchases.

She founded a shop called "Alice Bazaar", where poor ladies could be given work, which they sold. She further created a school where girls were given training as clerks and teachers of handicraft and needlework. This school was later taken over by the town and became a technical school for women workers.

When I was nineteen my father made me President of the "Alice Verein."*

Strange it was how the last years of Princess Alice followed the pattern of those of her father. In the summer of 1876 her devoted Lady-in-Waiting, the Hon. Emily Caroline Hardinge, died. Grief-stricken, she turned towards Balmoral to find the tonic to set her up, as Deeside had done for the Prince Consort after the worries caused by the death of the Duchess of Kent. But she warned her mother that she was so weak that, for the first few nights at least, she would be unable to come down to dinner.[31] This was a most

* In due course Princess Louis of Battenberg handed over her post to the Grand Duchess Eleonore, the Grand Duke Ernest Louis's second wife, and the family connection is continued today by Princess Margaret of Hesse and the Rhine. 1967 being the centenary year, a record of the work of the Alice hospital has been compiled by a German historian.

unusual happening at Balmoral where the rule was, if one was still alive, one was punctual for meals. But to Alice, as to Albert, Scotland was ever a strong wine, and soon she was once again in the carriage beside her mother, trotting as of old through the pages of the *Highland Journal*, with John Brown, of course, on the rumble.[32]

Now the gremlin, who operated the Curse on the Coburgs on behalf of the Kohary family, instituted a train of tragic happenings on a par with those which had hastened the end of the Prince Consort. In March 1877, Prince Louis lost his father, Prince Charles, and three months later the Grand Duke Louis followed his brother to the family mausoleum at the Rosenhöhe. At the lying-in-state the corpse was exposed. While this somewhat shocked young George Arthur, he found recompense in the passing of the Head of State. He was, somewhat against his will, in training at the time for some athletic sports, and the diet forbade the consumption of potatoes and vegetables. Now the sports were cancelled, and Arthur once again able to indulge in his beloved *Gemüse*.[33]

For Princess Alice the elevation to Grand Duchess and the new position of *Landesmutter* (Mother of the country) was a crown too heavy for her tired head. Yet worried as she was as to whether her strength would allow her to carry out her duties, she had some reward. When, after a seaside holiday, she drove into Darmstadt beside Grand Duke Louis IV for the official reception, it seemed as if all the population was in the streets—"flags out, bells ringing, people bombarding us with beautiful nosegays . . . Louis's old soldiers, singing. . . ."[34] The Princess from Britain had found her way into the hearts of the Hessians and they had taken her unto themselves as their own.

Remorselessly, the duties piled up upon her. It was, in part, her own doing. She had started so many organisations for the betterment of education, health services, living accommodation and the lot of women, and now those responsible for their administration turned to her with their every query. She had taken on too much, as her father had done. At the end of October she wrote to her mother: "Too much is demanded of one; and I have to do with so many things. It is more than my strength can stand. . . ."[35]

To the Queen might have come the echo of the words spoken by her husband sixteen years before: "It is too much. You must speak to the Ministers."

15

The Kiss of Death

ON THE 3RD SEPTEMBER 1878 THE PLEASURE STEAMER *Princess Alice* tooted her way down the Thames river, accordions playing, children cheering. She had seven hundred passengers aboard, Sunday school teachers and their classes, Cockney families who had saved up for a day out, young people in love. Very few of them could swim.

On the way back, off Woolwich, the *Princess Alice* was run down by the *Bywell Castle*. For a few minutes the dark, fast running waters were thick with struggling figures, their cries echoing from shore to shore. Then the waters were empty again. Over six hundred were drowned that tragic day.

One of the first messages of sympathy for the bereaved relatives came from Princess Alice, Grand Duchess of Hesse, and with it was a contribution for the fund set up for their relief.[1]

The Grand Duchess, with her husband and children, had spent part of the summer at Eastbourne. The holiday was a gift from her mother, who considered that she needed the rest. But Alice could not relax. She spent the days in visiting charity organisations, educational establishments and hospitals, and in studying the methods of Octavia Hill, planning to put what she had learned into practice when she returned home. She agreed to become

Patroness of the Albion Home at Brighton, despite the prejudice that she knew then existed against homes which cared "for those poor girls".[2]

Darmstadt—after tea on the 5th of November, 1878. Princess Victoria was sitting on the sofa, reading to her brother and sisters, who were on the floor around her. The Grand Duchess was resting on a settee, talking to Katie Macbean. The Macbeans lived in Darmstadt and were close friends of the Hesses—a Scottish family, "simple pious people to whom belief in a Personal Saviour was as the breath of their nostrils".[3] Miss Macbean* was standing in for the lady-in-waiting, who was on leave.

Victoria had complained of a stiff neck that day and her mother called her over to inspect, thinking that it might be mumps. She looked flushed, but there appeared nothing to worry about. Then "May" plagued "Mother dear" for more cake, and the others asked Katie to play the piano.[4] They danced for half an hour, and then went to bed. Any Victorian evening.

Next morning the family physician, Dr. Eigenbrodt, announced that Princess Victoria had diphtheria. No one was allowed to visit the Palace. By the 11th Victoria was out of danger, but the relief was short-lived, for the next day "Alicky" became ill. In quick succession "May", Irene, "Ernie" and the Grand Duke were victims. "Ella" was sent to her grandmother, Princess Charles, and in the event was the only one to escape. Telegrams to Balmoral followed one another with such frequency that there it was hard to follow the extent of the outbreak.[5]

On the night of the 16th a piece of membrane crossed the wind-pipe of little "May", and she was gone in a moment. The Grand Duchess steeled herself to break the news to her husband and her daughters. She knelt on the stairs, looking through the banisters, as her best loved child was driven away through the sunlight to the Rosenhöhe. Victoria was convalescent now, "Alicky" and the

---

* Miss Katharine Macbean married Brevet-Colonel Alexander Gordon Duff. Thomas Abercromby Duff (born 1802), having inherited the estate of Haddo in Scotland, fell into pecuniary difficulties and went bankrupt. He moved with his family to Hesse, and his descendants merged into the life of Darmstadt. His son, Robert William, married Marianne Georgina, daughter of Colonel Forbes Macbean, of Kirkleathen, Yorkshire. Their son, Alexander Gordon, married his first cousin, Katharine Macbean.

Grand Duke on the mend, Irene still on the danger list, and there were fears that "Ernie" might die any day. For a time he was not told that "May" was dead. He kept asking after her, sending her messages and, one day, a book. Then his mother told him, and in a sudden flood of emotion that was too much to bear, she bent down and kissed him.

On 7th December, her invalids all on the way to recovery, the Grand Duchess went to the station to see the Duchess of Edinburgh, who was passing through on her way to England.[6] That evening she felt unwell and next morning the doctors confirmed diphtheria. In her weakened state, and after her trials, she had no chance. The Queen sent out Sir William Jenner.* On Friday, 13th December, the doctors told the Grand Duke that she was dying. That evening he went into her room. She lay still, her eyes fixed on his, and whispered "Good night".

"Good night," he said, "I'll see you in the morning."

But for her there was no morning.

Windsor Castle, the 14th December 1878, the bedroom of Queen Victoria:

> This terrible day come round again! Slept tolerably well, but woke very often, constantly seeing darling Alice before me. . . . I asked for news, but none had come. Then got up and went, as I always do on this day, to the Blue Room, and prayed there. When dressed, I went into my sitting-room for breakfast, and met Brown coming in with two bad telegrams: I looked first at one from Louis, which I did not at first take in, saying: "Poor Mama, poor me, my happiness gone, dear, dear Alice. God's will be done." (I can hardly write it!) The other from Sir Wm. Jenner, saying: "Grand Duchess became suddenly worse soon after midnight, since then could no longer take any food." Directly after, came another with the dreadful tidings that darling Alice sank gradually and passed away at half past 7 this morning! . . . That this dear, talented, distinguished, tenderhearted, noble-minded, sweet child, who behaved so admirably during her dear father's illness, and afterwards, in supporting me, and helping in every possible way, should be called back to her father on this very anniversary, seems almost incredible, and most mysterious![8]

* Professor Oertel, of Munich, was also in attendance.[7]

179

The strange coincidence of the happenings on 14th December struck many people hard, and none more than the Prince of Wales. It was Alice who, of her own decision, had summoned him to his father's deathbed. It was Alice who had nursed him when he had all but died on the same date in 1871. Now he turned to his mother and said, "It is the good who are always taken."[9] He wrote to Lord Granville: "She was my favourite sister, so good, so kind, so clever. . . ."[10] She had understood him better than anyone else, and he owed her much. She had acted as an elder sister towards him. When in 1867, he had got himself into trouble for paying too much attention to the pretty ladies of St. Petersburg and Moscow, it was Alice who had read him a lecture, and to her whom he had listened.[11] He would take criticism on the point from no one else, not even his mother.

Princess Alice, Grand Duchess of Hesse, was deemed by many to be the outstanding child of Queen Victoria and Prince Albert. Certain it was that she made her mark on the nineteenth century by her own talents and her own energies. Handicapped in individuality by her formidable mother, she nevertheless brought a new approach to the care of the sick and the unfortunate in the land of her adoption, and her name lives there still.

Widely known among educational, nursing and charity services in Britain, there was a message of deep loss in the obituaries carried by the newspapers on 16th December. *The Times* devoted four columns to her passing and her life, repeating the tributes which had been paid to her the previous day in St. Paul's, Westminster Abbey, St. Margaret's and the Chapel Royal, Savoy.[12] A memorial service was held at Windsor on the 18th.

The Earl of Beaconsfield addressed the House of Lords:

My lords, there is something wonderfully piteous in the immediate cause of her death. The physicians who permitted her to watch over her suffering family enjoined her under no circumstances whatever to be tempted into an embrace. Her admirable self-restraint guarded her through the crisis of this terrible complaint in safety. She remembered and observed the injunctions of her physicians. But it became her lot to break to her little son the death of his youngest sister, to whom he was devotedly attached. The boy was so overcome with misery that the agitated mother clasped him in her arms, and thus she received the kiss of death.[13]

On the evening of the 17th the coffin of Princess Alice, Grand Duchess of Hesse, was taken by torchlight from the Grand Ducal Palace to the church in the old castle. Dense crowds made dark walls along the way. The next day the funeral took place at the mausoleum at the Rosenhöhe. The Prince of Wales, Prince Leopold and Prince Christian had come from England. The Emperor of Germany had forbidden the Crown Prince and Princess to attend for fear of infection.[14] A Union Jack was draped over her coffin. On the afternoon before she died she had expressed the wish that she should go "with the old English colours above her".[15]

The tomb was by Boehm, bearing a recumbent effigy representing the Princess holding in her arms the Princess Marie. A similar monument was placed in the mausoleum at Frogmore.*

On 29th December Princess Ella wrote to Queen Victoria:

We all wish you, dearest Grandmama, a happier New Year than this has been and that you may take comfort in the thought that dear Mama is happy at last. It has been said that death is a dark lattice that lets in a bright day. . . .[16]

Lady Milford Haven paid tribute to her mother:

My mother's death was an irreparable loss to us all and left a great gap in our lives. She had, indeed, been mistress of the house, a wise and loving wife and mother, whom we respected as much as we loved her. My childhood ended with her death, for I was the eldest and most responsible for her children.

*On 14th December Queen Victoria walked with the Prince of Wales to the Mausoleum in the gardens of Frogmore, and there placed a wreath on Prince Albert's tomb. Later she wrote in her diary: "I decided with Bertie as we left the Mausoleum . . . to have a reclining statue of our beloved Alice placed there, and he at once suggested Boehm in which I quite agree . . . Told Bertie I should like to add sweet little May to Alice's statue, which he equally thought would be very appropriate and beautiful . . ." The Queen's words appear below the statue: "To the memory of my much loved and lamented daughter, Alice, Grand Duchess of Hesse, who survived but a few days the fever-stricken child beside whom she had watched, 'not counting Her Life dear to Herself'."

Years later young Meriel Buchanan* was taken by her governess to the Rosenhöhe. "I can recall my feeling of awe, as I stood before that white recumbent figure so ineffably peaceful and serene." She walked, too, in the woods of Kranichstein. "The old grey castle itself seemed to me like the enchanted palace of the Sleeping Beauty, its walls and battlements reflected in the waters of the lake, deserted, silent. . . ."[17]

After his wife's death, the Grand Duke closed Kranichstein,† and it returned to the slumber from which Alice had awoken it fifteen years before. The ghost of her was alone in the rooms that she had loved. People who walked in the woods told how they had seen her face at the windows, and heard her happy voice calling her children in from play.[18]

* Daughter of Sir George Buchanan, Chargé d'Affaires, Darmstadt, 1892–1900.
† *Jagdschloss* Kranichstein is now a museum devoted to hunting and the chase.

16

Intermezzo

NOW THEY WERE SIX. GRAND DUKE LOUIS WAS FORTY-ONE years old. Victoria was fifteen, Elizabeth fourteen, Irene twelve, Ernest ten, and Alix six. Victoria, cultured, calm, accustomed to taking the lead, did her best to fill the gap left by the Grand Duchess. "Ella", beautiful, blessed with her father's sense of fun, outshone Irene. The two youngest were the hardest hit by their mother's death.

Little "Alicky" was completely lost. She had spent all of her days with her sister "May", and Princess Alice had always fussed the babies of the family. Now there was no mother to crawl into bed with in the mornings, no baby sister to play with and accompany on walks, not even any toys to play with, as they had all been burned for fear they might carry the infection. But there was still Mrs. Orchard, the English nurse who had been with the children since 1866,[1] to care for her.

The events in the first decade of "Ernie's" life had so deep an effect upon him that they influenced his outlook and character for the remainder of his years. At six he had taken the rebound of his mother's grief after "Frittie's" fatal fall from the window. His brother's end, the subsequent mourning and the visits to the Rosenhöhe, filled his mind with thoughts of death, and his nights

183

with dreams. Perhaps unwisely, his childish comments on the subject were treasured. One day he said to his mother: "When I die, you must die too, and all the others: why can't all die together? I don't like to die alone, like Frittie. . . ."[2] In 1879 he was a boy who needed very gentle handling.

Happily, there was another pillar of strength in the house. Miss Margaret Hardcastle Jackson, "Madgie" to the girls of whom she was the governess, was beloved by all the Hesse children, and had the confidence of the boy. Princess Alice had been much impressed by her modern ideas on education. Broad-minded, deeply interested in the social problems of the day, Miss Jackson concentrated on moulding the moral characters of her pupils, and trained them to talk on abstract subjects.[3] She was just the person to have around the Palace as the tidal wave of diphtheria spent itself, the dead were buried, and the sick nursed back to health.

Queen Victoria was quickly to the rescue. She wrote to Grand Duke Louis, urging him to come to Osborne with his children as soon as it was safe to travel. The Grand Duke agreed, and on 20th January the Prince of Wales sailed from Gravesend for Flushing in the royal yacht to collect the sad family and accompany them to Osborne.[4] There, and at Windsor, they stayed for two months.

The Queen ordered every detail of the children's lives. Progress reports on their education were to be submitted at regular intervals. Patterns for the girls' frocks were to be sent for approval prior to making. The elder girls were to be prepared for confirmation. Regular photographs were to be taken. They would make annual visits to Britain (the Grand Duke usually chose Balmoral in the autumn so that he could enjoy the shooting), and their British uncles, aunts and cousins would make regular calls at Darmstadt. As "Alicky" said when she married and became Empress of Russia: "Have you not been as a mother to me since beloved Mama died?"[5]

The stoicism of Queen Victoria on losing a child for the first time was in strange contrast with the extravaganzas of emotion in which she had indulged eighteen years before. It seemed that the Highland logic and calm of John Brown had been absorbed into her nature. She was in her sixtieth year, about to become a great-grandmother,* and admitted that Alice's death had taken "the elasticity"[6] out of her, but she kept her grief to herself† and did not allow the mourning to interfere with the happiness of others.

Prince Arthur‡ had become engaged the previous spring to Princess Louise of Prussia. The Queen had picked her out as a bride for him at her birth, saying that she "had a man in mind for the new little lady". But Prussian brides had become unpopular, and Prince Arthur had spent the 1870s travelling round Europe in search of a wife, his Governor clasping a well-thumbed *Almanach de Gotha*. At railway stations messages from the Queen were waiting, to spur them on. "Money *without* goodness or affection is useless." She heard of a perfect specimen—"*Quite* lovely . . . tall . . . élancée . . .'—but by the time the Prince reached her castle the fairy had bolted.[7] Then, in Berlin, he fell head over heels in love with Louise, as his mother had prophesied, despite the fact that her father, Prince Frederick Charles, disliked Britain, and Britain disliked him.

The Queen decided that the marriage of her favourite son should not be postponed any longer than absolutely necessary. He had become rather absent-minded of late, and had toppled out of a window at Buckingham Palace, landing on the head of a policeman below. She settled on 13th March, Arthur saying he did not care what date it was as long as he married Louise. On the eve of the wedding the Queen gave a dinner for twenty-six royalties at Windsor. Glancing at her son, she gave the order that he "must be looked after and *dosed*, for he is yellow and green".[8]

The loss of her daughter was felt keenly by the Queen when she reached Balmoral in May. Alice had known every hill and burn, track and cottage, and memories live long and clear on Deeside.

---

* The Crown Princess's eldest daughter, Charlotte, had married the Duke of Saxe-Meiningen in 1878, and the following year gave birth to a daughter, Feodora.

† Henceforward Queen Victoria always wore a locket on which was a miniature of Princess Alice. A miniature of Prince Leopold, Duke of Albany, was placed on the reverse side upon his death in 1884.

‡ Created Duke of Connaught and Strathearn and Earl of Sussex in 1874.

At a quarter to six walked with Beatrice to look at the Cross which I have now put up to my darling Alice. It is in *Aberdeenshire* granite, twelve feet three inches high. It is beautiful. . . . We then walked on to Donald Stewart's, where we went in; then down to Grant's. In both places they were quite overcome to see us . . . and poor Grant began sobbing and could not come into the room where we were. . . .[9]

Meantime the Prince of Wales was busy with a plan for solving the problems of the Hesse family, and in this he had the approval, outwardly at least, of his mother. The plan was that the Grand Duke Louis should marry Princess Beatrice,[10] and the news began to circulate in Darmstadt.[11] But there were two obstacles. Firstly, such a marriage was illegal, and, secondly, the Queen had no intention of losing the services of her youngest daughter. She would only tolerate a son-in-law who would spend all his time in her home, and obviously the Grand Duke's duties would not allow of this.

Princess Beatrice was twenty-two. In the words of her daughter, Queen Victoria Eugenia of Spain: "She had to be in perpetual attendance on her formidable mother. Her devotion and submission were complete. . . ."[12] As a result her many talents were apt to be overlooked. The fear of losing Beatrice obsessed the Queen. The word "engagement" was not allowed to be used at the dinner table, and when Ponsonby erred in this direction, he later received a note of reprimand.[13] Prince Louis of Battenberg was considered to be somewhat too familiar when on a visit to Osborne, and was despatched to a distant sea for a while. The Princess had been allowed some heart flutters over the Prince Imperial, only son of Napoleon III, who was serving with the British army, but such a union was, from the standpoints of religion and politics, obviously out of the question. The Queen had given the Prince permission to join the campaign in Africa, and that was that.*

The Prince of Wales threw himself heart and soul into the fight to end the prohibition of marriage with a deceased wife's sister, thus making it possible for Louis to wed Beatrice. On 6th May

* On 1st June 1879 the Prince Imperial was killed by *assegais*, in an ambush by the Ityatosi river.

1879, when the second reading of the Deceased Wife's Sister Bill came before the House of Lords, he rose from his place on the cross-benches and presented a petition signed by 3,258 Norfolk farmers, praying for the ending of the prohibition. He also made a speech.[14] But the Bishops were banded against him, and the Bill was thrown out.* "Incredible!"[15] commented the Queen, but the danger of losing Beatrice had, once again, faded away.

The Hesse children now had a new home during the summer months—Wolfsgarten, the summer palace of the Grand Dukes, cradled in deep wooded country between Darmstadt and Frankfurt. Originally a hunting lodge, when the forest around harboured wolves, wild boar and deer, two wolves were still kept in a cage by the gates. It was straight from a novel by Dornford Yates. Trees, in serried rows, stood sentinel beside the rides. Red, low-storied buildings flanked a wide courtyard. The smell of roses came from the pergolas, and new-mown hay from the stables.

At the head of the courtyard, approached by flights of stone steps, stood the *Schloss*, known as Big House. Here were the apartments of the Grand Ducal family, and the guest rooms for visiting royalty. Ladies and gentlemen-in-waiting, less elevated visitors and the staff lived in the sandstone houses to either side, and the stables completed the fourth side of the square.[16]

To Wolfsgarten every summer, for their holidays, journeyed Prince and Princess Christian, with their children, Christian Victor, Albert, Helena Victoria and Marie Louise.† Marie Louise and "Alicky" were of an age, and more like sisters than cousins. They would spend hours by the fountain in the courtyard's centre, trying to catch the goldfish with their hands.

"Alicky" was already showing some of the characteristics which were to become so pronounced after her marriage. One day her cousin said to her: "You always play at being sorrowful: one day the Almighty will send you some real crushing sorrows and then what are you going to do?"[17]

The flow of young men from Britain to Darmstadt, to learn

---

* The Bill was passed in 1896, being sponsored by the Prince of Wales.
† Born in 1867, 1869, 1870 and 1872.

German, continued, and they were accordingly asked round to play tennis. Among them was young Henry Wilson.* As was the case with all the other young men, he considered "Ella" to be the most beautiful creature that he had ever seen. "Alicky", with her golden hair, he thought somewhat indolent and apt not to pay attention. He teased her about it when they were partners.[18] Three young people laughing in the sun, each of them condemned to assassination.

Queen Victoria became a more frequent visitor to Darmstadt now, so arranging her Continental itineraries that she could keep an eye on her grandchildren. In 1880 she went over for the confirmation of Princesses Victoria and Elizabeth. She was glad to see that their mother's bedroom was kept the same as it was when she died, and she made her pilgrimage to the Rosenhöhe. Later she returned for the confirmation of Princess Irene.[19]

In her sixties, the Queen was more tolerant with her grandchildren than she had been with her own children. When one of them (not a Hesse) was told to kiss her hand, the imp spat on it instead. The Queen merely sent for a handkerchief to wipe it off.[20] As a young mother she would have clouted the miscreant smartly across the face, as she did when Prince Alfred was caught making an ugly face during a procession. In her old age the intolerancy returned. Entering a room at Windsor, she saw a movement behind the curtains. Tearing them open, she came upon a Page, whose distended cheeks showed that he was sucking some circular confectionery. Uttering, "You horrid small boy!" she smacked his cheek. Whereat a bull's-eye was propelled across the Castle floor.

Queen Victoria disapproved of her granddaughters smoking, but her keen scent for nicotine told her that certain of them indulged when the opportunity arose.

Lady Milford Haven recalled:

> I remember secretly smoking up chimneys and out of windows. Though my father did not object, Miss Jackson did, authorised thereto by Grandmama. A propos of my smoking, it was the

---

* General Sir Henry Wilson, shot on his own doorstep in Eaton Place, London, on 22nd June 1922, as he returned from unveiling a war memorial.

Emperor William who first trained me to the habit when, as a student from Bonn, he always offered me cigarettes.

Ella never cared about smoking, but even Queen Victoria could not break me of the habit. On one of my visits to Balmoral, before my marriage, guessing that I probably had cigarettes about me, and the midges being especially annoying, she bade me smoke to keep them away, and even took one of my cigarettes, giving a few puffs at it. She declared she thought the taste horrible! Of course we might not smoke openly in the house and one of the young maids of honour, Amy Lambart,* who, though a smoker herself, had come without any cigarettes and whose room was below ours, was supplied by me with a few at a time let down by a piece of string from window to window!

The Queen never for a minute relaxed her watch on the education of the Grand Duke's children, and the financial stringency, which had been evident during their mother's life, no longer applied. It was decided that Miss Jackson needed help in the schoolroom and an addition was found in Miss Pryde, daughter of a deceased army officer. There had been little money in the Pryde family home, and she was over-awed both by the majesty of Windsor and the Queen. While there with her charges, she had to submit daily progress reports, and, in addition, she was bombarded by queries in note form, some of which had obviously been written in the early hours. She was in some doubt about her adequacy for the post.

One evening Miss Pryde was in her bedroom, washing and changing for dinner. Her bosom and midriff were bare, and below a red flannel petticoat were bare legs, without shoes. There came an imperious tap upon the door. Looking around for her dressing-gown, Miss Pryde asked who was there. "It is I," said Queen Victoria, and marched in. She took one look at the blushing face and the expanse of nudity which two hands were vainly trying to cover, burst into laughter and collapsed on a chair. She had come to give the governess an inscribed locket as a token of appreciation for her work.[21]

While the children of Princess Alice continued with their studies, the girls under a governess and Ernest at the universities

---

* The Hon. Amy Gwendoline, Maid of Honour 1877–1884; married 1884 Major the Hon. Henry Charles Legge.

of Leipzig and Giessen, their cousins of Battenberg had been launched into the world.

Princess Marie had married Gustavus, Count of Erbach-Schönberg,* and had a family of three sons and a daughter.

Louis was carving out for himself a distinguished career in the British Navy:

> His first ship was the Frigate "Ariadne" in which the Prince and Princess of Wales toured the Mediterranean during the first half of 1869. In June 1869 he joined the "Royal Alfred", an old 74-gun Line-of-Battle ship; a fully rigged sailing ship but with an 800 h.p. auxiliary engine. He was rated Midshipman on 2nd October 1869 and altogether served four and a half years in the West Indies in her. On his return, with a beard, his parents hardly recognised him. As a Sub-Lieutenant he accompanied the Prince of Wales on his tour to India in the "Serapis" 1875–1876 and was promoted to Lieutenant on 18th May 1876. He next served for two years on board the "Sultan" at the request of the Captain, Alfred, Duke of Edinburgh. In 1880 he joined the "Inconstant", an iron frigate and a wonderful sailer. During this commission the Flying Squadron, to which the "Inconstant" belonged, did a cruise round the world. In June 1882 the Flying Squadron was ordered to the Mediterranean on account of the insurrection in Egypt. Prince Louis was landed in command of the Naval gatling gun battery and received the Khedive's Star.[22]

The three younger brothers all followed in the footsteps of their father and chose military careers. Alexander ("Sandro") fought in the Russo-Turkish war and subsequently transferred to the Royal Prussian Gardes du Corps. In 1879 he was elected Sovereign Prince of Bulgaria, the new state set up by the Treaty of Berlin of the previous year. While the Sultan of Turkey still claimed suzerainty over this autonomous principality, Russia regarded it as tied to her by creed and race. The Emperor of Russia, Bismarck and the Grand Duke of Hesse all backed "Sandro's" appointment, although he was only twenty-two.

Henry ("Liko") was serving with the Royal Saxon Hussars, and Francis Joseph joined "Sandro" in Sofia on the completion of his military training.[23]

Their aunt being Empress of Russia, the Battenbergs had con-

* He became a Prince (Fürst) in 1903.

siderable status in Europe. But on 3rd June 1880 the Empress Marie died at St. Petersburg. She was all alone. Her husband was at Tsarskoe-Selo and there was not even a nurse in the room.[24] Her struggle against the rigours of the Russian climate, her eternal fear of the assassin's bomb, her bitterness over the mistress who slept in the room above her, all were now mercifully over. Within a month the Emperor had married Catherine Dolgoruky, legitimatised her children, created her Princess Yourievsky, and set in train plans to make her Empress. Six attempts had already been made on his life, and, on 13th March 1881, the seventh succeeded. Bombs exploded around his sleigh as he returned to the Winter Palace from a military inspection, and within a few hours he was dead.[25]

Now the sympathies of the royal courts underwent a change, there were new ties of loyalty, and Bismarck was quick to note them. The wife of the new Emperor, Alexander III, was the sister of the Princess of Wales. Her name of Dagmar had been changed to that of Marie Feodorovna. In the family she was known as "Minnie". The marriage was a very happy one, and brown-eyed "Minnie" exercised considerable influence over her husband. Bismarck knew full well that the Royal House of Denmark would never forget, or forgive, the Schleswig-Holstein war. While Alexander II had harboured strong German sympathies and even spoke German in private, the feeling was not passed on to his son, who had made no secret during the Franco-Prussian war that his sympathies lay with France. Thus, for the first time, Sandringham became something more than a country home, in Norfolk, England. And a further development was that the new Emperor did not view with favour the appointment of "Sandro" of Battenberg as Ruler of Bulgaria.

17

Love and Marriage

S UDDENLY THE GARDENS OF WOLFSGARTEN AND HEILIGENBERG
were filled with lovers. The children of Queen Victoria's
children began pairing off among themselves, or finding
partners from among the offspring of Marie of Russia and of her
brother, Alexander. Victoria of Hesse was in love with Louis of
Battenberg, William of Prussia with "Ella" of Hesse, "Ella" of
Hesse with Serge of Russia, Victoria of Prussia* with "Sandro"
of Battenberg, and, in a less mature state, Marie Louise of
Schleswig-Holstein with Ernest Louis of Hesse, and Henry† of
Prussia with Irene of Hesse. To add to this welter of amourettes the
Grand Duke Louis, ever lonely after the loss of Princess Alice and
aware that his daughters would soon be leaving him, sought solace
in a lady's company. The news of this liaison was kept from the
ears of his mother-in-law.

The first love to be wrecked on the rocks of disillusionment was
that of William of Prussia for "Ella" of Hesse, whose heart, from
childhood, had been given to Russia. William was a very trying
young man, and already a considerable source of anxiety to his
parents. He was for ever attempting to prove that, despite his

* Second daughter of the Crown Princess, born 1866.
† Second son of the Crown Princess, born 1862.

Prince Henry of Prussia and Princess Irene of Hesse in 1887

Prince Alexander of Battenberg
Alexander I, Sovereign Prince of Bulgaria, 1879–1886

withered arm and weak leg, he could ride a horse, shoot a gun, row a boat, as well, if not better, than anyone else. His mother encouraged his visits to Darmstadt, hoping that the homely, informal life there would round off the angularity of Berlin. But instead he took advantage of Prussia's senior role in Germany, and automatically appointed himself leader among the young people. He would decree that they would ride in the woods, then change his mind and say that they would row on the lake. In the middle of a game of tennis he would throw down his racket and order the players to gather round him while he read from the Bible.[1] He was already earning for himself the nicknames that were soon to stick—"Gondola Billy", "William the Sudden", and "The Only".

He had a dimple on his chin. To physiognomists this points to a desire to attract the worship of the opposite sex. It was certainly true in William's case. The more beautiful, the greater the desire, and the photographs of the two most lovely women in Europe, Princess "Ella" of Hesse and the Princess of Wales, were ever on his desk. And he had a strange habit. His burning wish was to kiss well fashioned hands. In later years, he would have the lady of his choice brought to him, veiled. Then, impatiently, he would carry out his little strip-tease act. He would order her to take off her veil and coat. He himself would carefully withdraw the glove, then passionately kiss the hand and grip the little finger.[2]

On his visits to Darmstadt he shadowed "Ella", his eyes following her every movement. He was only silent when she was speaking, so that he could listen to her voice.[3] But soon he saw that he had no chance against his rival, and he did not like rivals. In 1881 he married plump Princess Augusta of Schleswig-Holstein-Augustenberg,* but addressed very few direct remarks to her when outside the bedroom. For many years he could not bring himself to meet "Ella" again, but he never ceased to love her. When the last wave of disaster swept over her, Kaiser William did his utmost to save her.

The first romance to come safe to harbour was that of Lieutenant

---

* Daughter of Prince Frederick, who, in 1864, had claimed the throne of Schleswig-Holstein.

Louis of Battenberg and Princess Victoria of Hesse. The sailor, home from his adventures in the Mediterranean, proceeded on leave to Heiligenberg, and on 1st July 1883 the engagement was announced. What joy this would have been to Princess Alice, who had arranged for the young Prince of Battenberg to join the British Navy fifteen years before. Louis had returned to Darmstadt on every occasion that his service would allow. There had been the thrill of expectation at his coming, the fun at listening to his tales of distant lands, the heart pangs at his going.

In their Reminiscences the engaged couple recalled those happy days. The Princess wrote:

> In spring grandmamma had as usual invited Ella and me to go with her to Balmoral, but I was not keen about it. The onlooker proverbially knowing more than the actor, Ella said to Papa: "If Victoria does not go with me to Scotland she will become engaged to Louis Battenberg." She was right, and we became engaged in June, when I was at Seeheim and Louis at Heiligenberg.

Prince Louis remembered:

> By this time I had set up my own stable—a pair of black Hungarian light horses, so-called "Juckers", which I drove Tandem in a big and high Dogcart built in England, dark green with brass fittings and brass mounted black harness. I drove nearly every day to Seeheim. Of course a high-wheel cart was bad for hilly work. However I had only one bad spill; the wheeler in the ditch, the cart on one horizontal wheel on the road above, the leader on the opposite bank, in a cat's cradle of reins and traces.
>
> We had many expeditions with the Seeheim party in a variety of pony carts and carriages, with tea baskets, and games to follow. At last one day on a bench in Seeheim grounds, I plucked up courage and asked Victoria of Hesse if she would marry me. My parents were delighted, my mother especially, who felt sure I would now say goodbye for ever to that unstable element, the sea.
>
> I was very kindly received by Queen Victoria, who was much relieved, as she had always been convinced that I meant to marry Aunt Beatrice! I was only allowed to see my fiancée by stealth, as the Queen did not approve of engaged couples "spooning".

Victoria was the "man" of the Hesse family, a role exaggerated by her mother's death. It was said that she was drawn to Louis because he was firstly a sailor, and only secondly a Prince.

Inheriting from her mother the interest in education, she would have liked to have been a schoolmistress. Cultured, but without particular talents, she was equally at home talking on Bach to musicians or Bulgaria to statesmen. With her golden hair brushed back, she was an impressive young lady, and a great favourite of Queen Victoria.[4] The first grandchild to be named after her, the Queen had wished to adopt her as a child.[5] She realised that Princess Victoria would make an ideal wife, friend and adviser to the young sailor for whom she had particular affection. In September she appointed Louis to the Royal Yacht *Victoria and Albert*.[6]

Grand Duke Louis had promised Princess Alice that he would allow their children to marry for love, and he readily gave his consent to the marriage. But elsewhere the news did not receive the same approval. In Berlin insulting remarks were made about the Battenberg antecedents, and in Russia Prince Louis received only the precedence of his naval rank. Queen Victoria wrote to her eldest daughter: "Of course, those who care only about great matches, will not like it, but great matches do not make happiness."[7]

On 26th February 1884 the Grand Duke gave his blessing to another engagement—that of his second daughter, "Ella", to his first cousin, the Grand Duke Serge of Russia.* The fruition of this romance had long been taken for granted. The two had been sweethearts since childhood and, when together, had been in a world apart. He was tall, fair, with light green eyes, and strikingly handsome in a saturnine way. A pious man, often misunderstood, fierce fires burned within him, and yet with "Ella" he had always been gentle and at ease. He had been in Italy when his father was murdered, and there was hate in his heart against the perpetrators. Having the instinct that he would one day share the same fate, he wished to marry "Ella" quickly to ensure their happiness together for as long as destiny would allow.

The next romance could be classified as political dynamite. The lady in the case was Princess Victoria, second daughter of the

---

* The Grand Duke Sergius was the fourth son of Emperor Alexander II and Empress Marie.

Crown Prince and Princess of Germany, born in 1866. She was the tallest of the daughters, and her father's favourite. She had blue eyes, fair hair and a pink and white complexion.[8] She was an incurable romantic and on one occasion had to be hastily removed from a naval base for the general security of both sexes. In the family she was known as "Vicky" and "Moretta". In 1883 Princess Victoria met "Sandro" of Battenberg, Sovereign Prince of Bulgaria, in Berlin, and fell violently in love. The attraction was mutual and the couple became engaged, with the initial approval of her parents.[9]

But there were thorns on the path of romance. In Bulgaria "Sandro" had been evincing a marked reluctance to playing the role of vassal to Russia. In 1881 he had issued a proclamation demanding absolute powers for himself. Two years later he dismissed Russian advisers.[10] Relations with Alexander III became strained. As it was Bismarck who had urged the young Prince of Battenberg to accept the position of Ruler of Bulgaria, developments there were being closely watched from Berlin. Friendly relations with Russia were vital to the aspirations of Germany, and the Chancellor was determined that Alexander III should not be antagonised. The marriage of "Sandro" to Princess Victoria would obviously arouse strong resentment in St. Petersburg.

Therefore, while the Crown Prince and Princess, backed by Queen Victoria, were anxious that the romance should develop, Emperor William, Empress Augusta and Prince William were equally determined that it should not. Bismarck avowed that, at this time, he was ignorant of the matter, but, considering the efficiency of his internal espionage service, this would appear to be in doubt. In the case of Prince William, his aversion to the union was not only political. He did not consider the family of Battenberg, with its morganatic element, of sufficient elevation to provide a husband for his sister.

Yet it was not the loves of the young in heart which were to steal the limelight when Prince Louis of Battenberg and Princess Victoria of Hesse were married on 30th April 1884, but a more mature affair. This was the liaison between the Grand Duke and

Alexandrine von Kolemine, or Madame Alexandra de Kalomine as she was known in Paris. She was thirty, the daughter of Count Adam of Hutten-Czapsky and Countess Marianne Rzewuska of Paris, and had been born in Warsaw.[11] She had married a Russian diplomat, from whom she had obtained a divorce. She had been introduced to the Grand Duke by Prince Isenburg and his wife, who were now encouraging the friendship.[12] She has been described in widely differing forms. Emily Crawford, Paris correspondent of the *Daily News* and *Truth*, described her as "one of the most beautiful and highly-accomplished women of her time".[13] Lady Ely, to whom fell the unenviable task of apprising the Queen of the situation, labelled her as "depraved" and "scheming".[14] Her name was to be placed in the locker at Windsor reserved for the incarceration of unspoken names, together with those of Julie de St. Laurent, Mrs. FitzGeorge, Nellie Clifden and others.

The two elder girls were fully acquainted with their father's friendship, and sometimes accompanied the couple on their walks. But when the rumour ran strong around Darmstadt that a wedding was in the air, Princess Victoria declared: "Dear Papa will never marry again."[15] Emily Crawford wrote: "This lady was liked by the Grand Ducal children, who were glad to think she would be with their father when they married off themselves."[16] The Grand Duke himself admitted that "he could hardly bear the thought of the further loneliness in his life when she (Princess Victoria) left him".[17]

Everybody seemed to know about the friendship between the Grand Duke and Alexandrine von Kolemine except the person who counted most—Queen Victoria.

Now, as the train which bore her made its way towards the Rhine, stopping for the engine driver to have his lunch and, by prior notification, to allow of the red carpet being unrolled, at station buffet and convenience, her spirits were far removed from those customary at nuptial festivities. Her eyes were brooding with sadness, for she had lost two men who were dear to her. The previous year John Brown had died of erysipelas, and the key turned in the door of his bedroom at Windsor. Only a month before, on 28th March 1884, her youngest son, Prince Leopold,

197

Duke of Albany, had died suddenly at Cannes, a victim of haemophilia. A fall downstairs had led to an infusion of blood in the brain and an epileptic convulsion.[18] His mother wrote: "I am a poor desolate old woman, and my cup of sorrow overflows!"[19]

Travelling with her was Princess Beatrice, still as yet showing no sign of wishing to change her role of secretary-companion. Other guests on the move towards Darmstadt were the Prince of Wales, the Crown Prince and Princess of Germany, with Princess Victoria, and the Princes "Sandro" and "Liko" of Battenberg. The Prince of Wales was a worried man. Well informed on the Kolemine affair, he feared the developments that the next few days might bring.

As the trains came in, the Grand Duke was on the platform to meet his guests. He was in high spirits, sparkling with compliments and jokes. And the crowds were out, to see the royalties, the uniforms, the suites, for there had not been a day like this in living memory. "The festivities and functions were elaborate and heavy. On one day there was a royal confirmation in the morning to be attended in full uniform, a banquet which lasted two hours, the christening of a royal baby in the afternoon, again in full uniform, later a 'Punch' and a heavy dinner in the evening, after which a Russian Colonel 'played beautifully on the pianoforte'."[20]

The wedding took place, and at a banquet in the Kaisersaal Crown Prince Frederick proposed the health of the bride and groom.[21] Then the Grand Duke left his guests for a while. Unnoticed, he made his way to a room in the Schloss.[22] There a woman and three men were waiting for him. Without delay Prime Minister Starck married Grand Duke Louis to Alexandrine von Kolemine, the witnesses being Prince Isenburg and the bride's brother.[23] Utmost secrecy was observed, the bride staying that night with friends. The marriage was not consummated.[24]

Lady Milford Haven clarified the situation:

> The evening of my wedding day, my father was privately married in a room in the Schloss to Countess Alexandrine Hutten Chapsky, divorced from M. de Kolemine who, as Russian Charge d'Affaires, had been two years at Darmstadt with her, the couple separating as soon as the ceremony was over. Influenced, I fancy, by Madame de

Kolemine's dread of opposition to the marriage, nobody had been told of it, except his children and prospective sons-in-law. Though Louis and Serge were in despair about it, they gave their promise to keep the secret. We others quite liked the lady, who was full of attentions towards us, and I hoped my father would feel less lonely when married to a woman he was much in love with.

Gradually the news leaked out. The Crown Princess told the Prince of Wales. Someone had to tell the Queen. Lady Ely undertook the task. There were tantrums behind closed doors, but outwardly the Queen retained her calm. She sent for her eldest son. She ordered him to interview Alexandrine von Kolemine and arrange that the marriage be declared null and void. She had spoken. A member of the Prussian suite informed Empress Augusta of developments by telegram. The old Empress, already angry over Princess "Ella's" engagement to the Grand Duke Serge and the romance between Prince "Sandro" of Battenberg and her granddaughter, Victoria, ordered the immediate return to Berlin of the Crown Prince and Princess, with their suite. After a hasty dinner, they caught a train on the evening of 2nd May.[25]

Poor Darmstadt! The bunting seemed tawdry now, and the gilt was off the gingerbread. Poor Grand Duke! He had not realised that his family ties with the Imperial Houses of Britain, Germany and Russia entailed so complete a surrender of his personal freedom. The Palace became deserted. Court officials developed colds and were confined to their rooms. Ministers found urgent business to attend to in nearby towns.

The story reached the Press and London boiled with rumours. Mr. Gladstone announced that the conduct of the Grand Duke in not informing Her Majesty before her departure was unjustifiable. The Duke of Cambridge, who, in his earlier days, had been guilty of a similar indiscretion, had strong views now, declaring that "when a man, through some unfortunate accident, makes a great mistake he must abide by it!"[26]

Queen Victoria was not above interpreting the sacredness of marriage to suit her own convenience, and in this case she saw nothing sacred about it. The unwinding process continued apace.

In June Hermann Sahl, formerly her German Secretary,* who had retired to Darmstadt, reported to Sir Henry Ponsonby:

> You will be glad to hear that *substantially* the untieing of the morganatic knot is now accomplished, and by degrees the *formal* severance will be pronounced by a Court of Law convened for this purpose. Diplomatists and Lawyers are never embarrassed about finding a suitable *form*—as soon as they have secured a convergence of views and aims in *substance*.[27]

That the Queen surmounted the difficulty of her son-in-law's remarriage with unexpected calm and lack of recrimination may be attributed to the fact that, while in Darmstadt, her attention had been focused on another example of romantic attraction. This effervescence more closely affected her own peace and comfort, and therefore took priority. Her eyes had shown her only too clearly that Princess Beatrice was falling in love.

The Princess had become well known in Court circles for her frigidity towards the opposite sex. One glance at the raised shoulders was sufficient to warn off would-be trespassers. But just as she made it abundantly clear when advances were not welcomed, so now nature decreed that she should make it equally obvious when her feelings were in reverse. To observers it appeared, and correctly so, that she was falling head over heels in love. To further enliven the interest, the man involved was yet another Battenberg, younger brother of Prince Louis, who was marrying her niece.

Prince Henry, known as "Liko", was twenty-five, eighteen months younger than Princess Beatrice. He was serving with the Prussian Household Cavalry, the Gardes du Corps, in Potsdam. Like his brothers, he was tall and good-looking. Even in Berlin, the Battenbergs were known as "the most handsome family in Europe". But as yet there had been no signs of a romance. Mme Lacroix, the most famous match-maker in Europe, had done her best, but given him up.[28] His intertwined family connections with Russia, Britain, Germany and Bulgaria appeared somewhat formidable to would-be brides. Mme Lacroix had not raised her sights high enough.

* Also librarian at Balmoral and Osborne.

When, on their return to Windsor, Princess Beatrice informed her mother that she was in love with "Liko" and intended to marry him, there began the most extraordinary vendetta mixed with tantrums ever staged by this formidable and emotional Queen. For seven months, from May to November, although the two lived side by side and ate together, she addressed no word to her youngest daughter. The only communication was through notes, pushed across the table,[29] her eyes averted. She had lost Albert, Brown, Beaconsfield, Leopold—no earthly power would now rob her of Beatrice. The "softening up" treatment continued—her aim being, should the romance mature, that she would be able to dictate her own terms. Beatrice stood firm by her love—it was her only stand in all her long years of devoted service. Yet when, in December, the armistice came, it was Queen Victoria who laid down the terms. "Liko" was to retire from his military service in Germany, and make his home with her. And so it was.

18

Strange Journeys

A T HALF PAST SIX ON AN EVENING IN EARLY JUNE 1884 THE
families of Hesse and Battenberg waited on the platform
of Darmstadt station for the train which was to carry them
to Berlin on the first stage of their journey to St. Petersburg.
There, on the 15th, Princess "Ella" was to be married to the
Grand Duke Serge.

"Ella" was a favourite with her father's people. Yet, on this
historic evening when she left to wed the Emperor's brother, there
were few to see her off. The affair of Alexandrine von Kolemine
was still too fresh in their minds.[1]

There was scant approval for the union in Britain, where the
Russian advance into Afghanistan was being watched with
anxiety. Queen Victoria would have liked her granddaughter to
marry a German and wished that she had accepted the early
advances of Prince William, knowing that "Ella" would have had
a steadying influence on him. In Berlin the opposition was violent.
Before Sir Howard Elphinstone visited Germany that summer he
received instructions from Balmoral:

> The Queen writes to Sir Howard to *warn* him *not* to enter with the
> Empress (Augusta) *on* the *subject* of the *Grand Duke* of Hesse and his
> daughter, against whom she is filled with spite and unchristian
> feelings. Please cut it short; say *you* know nothing. . . .[2]

The Princesses of Hesse had not been so far away from home before. Their journeys had been restricted to visits to their aunt in Berlin, their Grandmama in Britain, and holidays at French seaside resorts. Now, for endless hours, they were borne across the empty plains leading to St. Petersburg.

As their train drew into the station they were transported, in a matter of seconds, into a world of dreams. A gilt coach was waiting for the future Grand Duchess. It was drawn by white palfreys, and at their beplumed heads stood servants in liveries of gold. The magnificent procession wound its way through the streets to the Peterhof, where the members of the Court awaited.[3]

"Ella", Irene and "Alicky" were bewildered at the sights and way of life which surrounded them—"the golden domes and spires of the cathedrals, the baroque immensity of the Winter Palace, the all-pervading smell of sunflower-oil and leather and cigarettes, the fountains spraying scented water, the teeming rabbit-warrens of rooms and corridors on the upper floors of the palace, the inadequate sanitary arrangements. . . ."[4] The wedding itself proved as great an ordeal for "Ella" as a similar occasion had proved for her great-aunt Marie over forty years before. The Grand Duke had refused to allow his daughter to change her religion prior to marriage, so two services, Lutheran and Ortho-dox, were necessary.

"Alicky" was only twelve years old, yet, once the shyness had worn off, she sparkled at St. Petersburg. Too young to take part in the long ceremonies and be overawed by the strict discipline of the Court, she was spoilt by the giant Emperor and soon made friends with his eldest son, Nicholas. They played hide-and-seek about the Palace, and her shrieks of delight echoed along the corridors. It was this first journey to Russia which sealed her fate.

Lady Milford Haven thus described her sister's wedding:

The orthodox wedding took place in the Chapel of the Big Palace and was followed by the Protestant wedding in one of the drawing rooms. Ella's wedding dress was the Russian Court dress, all white and cloth of silver and, according to old custom, the Empress was supposed to "coiffe" her on the occasion. This consisted in handing some hairpins to the coiffeur and superintending the placing of the tiara and Grand-Ducal Crown on her head, as Ella sat in front of the vermeil looking-glass of the Empress Anne I. The diamond tiara, Crown, necklace and ear-rings to match, had all belonged to the Empress Catherine and were worn by every bride for her wedding. The ear-rings were so heavy, that they had to be suspended by a wire round the ears and this wire gradually cut into the flesh. A further discomfort to Ella was that the "garçon de noce" (bridesman), in order to bring luck to the Bride, had put a gold 10 rouble piece in her right shoe, which dug into her toes.

From old times, the Emperor's sons were presented with a cloth of silver dressing-gown with cap to match trimmed with sable—and a silver night pot! Serge presented his to Ernie as a souvenir.

Sadly, "Ella" watched her father and his sisters begin their journey back to Darmstadt. She was very much alone and had a great deal to learn. There were those who feared for her future with the young Grand Duke, with steel in his eyes and a streak of cruelty in his heart. Quick as he was to reprimand her if she transgressed the rules of etiquette, he was deeply in love with her, satisfied her every wish, and lavished jewels upon her. He cherished her beauty. Their tragedy was that they had no children, for Serge, like all the Romanoffs, adored them.

The Grand Duke commanded the Preobrajensky Guards and was Governor of Moscow.[5] He had two homes, the Sergueivskia Palace in St. Petersburg and Illinskoje, a country estate some forty miles from Moscow. Illinskoje was a square, wooden house, with a wide veranda. Here "Ella" was happiest. There were lovely gardens, and, in the park, cottages for guests, and a farm. As her mother had done when she built the New Palace in Darmstadt, the Grand Duchess imported chintzes and furniture from England and recaptured the atmosphere of her childhood days.[6]

Lady Milford Haven enjoyed holidays at her sister's country home:

> Illinskoje lay on the left bank of the Moskva, west of Moscow, at a distance of about an hour and a half's carriage drive from there, and it was connected by the only metalled highroad in the neighbourhood. All the other roads were merely broad sandy tracks. I speak of Illinskoje in the past, for after Serge's death, when it passed to Dimitry Pavlovitch, the main house was pulled down and most of the park sold.

The main building was a two-storied house, flanked on both sides by terraces and broad sloping approaches on arches, which were called "les pentes douces". The entrance faced away from the river and had a pillared portico. On the river side a broad balcony ran along the first floor, on which we used to have breakfast and sit after meals. The house stood on the high bank of the river which you reached by a small winding path in a minute. The opposite bank was flat meadowland. A number of boats were moored at the little landing stage just below the house, and were in the charge of two sailors of the "equipage de la garde". Boating and fishing were one of our chief amusements, as also bathing. The river was full of shallows and sand banks and many a time did I get stuck on one and had to step into the water to push off, especially when using a quaint water conveyance which consisted of two broad poles pointed at either end connected by a raised seat on a platform.

Meantime Princess Louis of Battenberg was settling down to a less exacting life as a sailor's wife at "Sennicotts", a country house near Chichester. As her husband was still serving on board the Royal Yacht, based at Portsmouth, the location was convenient, and also handy to Osborne.

Lord Milford Haven recalled an amusing incident about the Royal Yacht:

In those days the paddle yacht "Victoria and Albert" used to be laid up in the autumn until the following summer, up Porchester Creek, the ship's company joined the dockyard as "Riggers" (they were all Petty Officers), while the officers and a couple of boats' crews, removed into the "Royal George" at the next buoy. She was the old sailing yacht of George IV., wonderfully ornamented with gilt carvings inside and out. Of course all the married officers lived on shore, but generally came off in the forenoon, and after a heavy lunch, went back to the beach. The captain disappeared altogether (he lived at Hamble), so did the Commander and one of the two Lieutenants. The other had to sleep on board and so did the Navigator, Staff Commander Tracy, a charming little man, a bachelor, who went mad the next year; so did the other Lieutenant, who did not survive long after he had gone to the madhouse.

The smaller paddle yacht "Osborne" was set aside for Uncle Bertie [the Prince of Wales], and he took frequent trips to the continent in her. One day a telegram was received, through the C. in C. Portsmouth (Sir G. O. Willes) ordering the "Osborne" with all despatch to Flushing to embark some foreign Prince invited to Sandringham. As usual the only officer available was the Navigating Lieutenant, married and living at Gosport, near the ship's buoy. A Commander and two Lieutenants made up the complement. All three were away. Presently a telegram arrived from the captain (afterward Admiral Sir W. Fawkes) for the First Lieutenant—"Am delayed. Take the ship to Dover, where I will join." This was very soon followed by another from the First Lieutenant to the Second Lieutenant (whose turn for duty it was)—"Am delayed. Ask Captain kindly to pick me up at Dover." And yet a third telegram arrived from the Second Lieutenant to Navigator: "Am delayed. Ask Captain kindly to pick me up at Dover." The meeting of the captain and his two lieutenants at Charing Cross taking tickets for Dover must have been a sight. Admiral Willes was so furious that he wished to try everyone by Court Martial, and it required Uncle Bertie's personal intervention at the Admiralty to save Fawkes.

It was while they were at "Sennicotts" that Prince and Princess Louis became worried over the impasse which faced Princess Beatrice in her matrimonial intentions. In the hope of solving it they asked Prince Henry ("Liko") of Battenberg to stay with them for Christmas.

On 23rd December there was a dinner party at Osborne House. The beech logs burned in the open grate and the spirit of Christmas was strong and gay. The Queen chatted away to her youngest daughter as if the long silence had never been. On the 29th she wrote:

> Received a letter from Liko Battenberg saying that my kind reception of him encouraged him to ask my consent to speaking to Beatrice. . . . I let Liko know, to come up after tea, and I saw him in dear Albert's room. Then I called the dear child, and gave them my blessing.[7]

Yet this was but a short interlude before another storm. Berlin raved in anger and indignation over the engagement. In a letter to Queen Victoria, the Empress was distinctly "unamiable". "Fritz", the Crown Prince, considered Prince Henry to be an unsuitable brother-in-law for the future Emperor of Germany, as he was not of *Geblüt*.* Prince William and his wife, "Dona", were "insolent, impertinent and unkind".

The Queen, now as whole-heartedly on the side of "Liko" as

* Stock.

previously she had been against, was furious. Not only did she fix her verbal bayonet in his defence, but she moved into the attack. The Empress, she parried, had "no right to write me in that tone". She accused the Crown Prince of regarding the breeding of the Battenbergs as if they were animals. "Dona" she dismissed as "foolish" and a "poor little insignificant Princess". "As for Willie, that very foolish, undutiful and, I must add, unfeeling boy, I have no patience with and I wish he could get a good 'skelping' as the Scotch say and seriously a good setting down." She added that "morganatic marriages were unknown in England and if a King chose to marry a peasant girl she would be Queen just as much as any Princess".[8]

Having repulsed the attack, the Queen moved on to the offensive She shattered the opposition by pointing out that the Empress's son-in-law, and his brothers and sisters, "were the children of a Fräulein von Geyersberg, a very bad woman, and that they had been acknowledged by the whole of Europe as Princes of Baden".[9]*

Having shown that, single-handed, she was the master of Berlin, the Queen concerned herself with domestic planning, firstly for the birth of Princess Louis of Battenberg's child, and, secondly, the wedding of Princess Beatrice.

On 25th February 1885 Princess Louis had her baby in the same bed, in the same room overlooking the Long Walk at Windsor,[10] in which she had been born twenty-two years before. There was so much else that was the same. Queen Victoria sat beside her, stroking her arms, from seven in the morning until five in the afternoon,[11] just as she had done for Princess Alice at her first accouchement. The new baby† became another Princess Alice, and the Queen attended her christening at Darmstadt in the spring.

The wedding of Princess Beatrice and Prince Henry was arranged for 23rd July, in the Isle of Wight. Once again the families of Hesse and Battenberg gathered at Darmstadt station

---

* Empress Augusta's only daughter, Louise, married the Grand Duke of Baden.
† Victoria Alice Elizabeth Julie Marie, afterwards Princess Andrew of Greece and mother of Prince Philip, Duke of Edinburgh.

for a marital journey. This time they were so numerous that a special train was needed. With the Grand Duke Louis were his son, Ernest Louis, and his daughters, Irene and "Alicky", both of whom were to be bridesmaids. With Prince Alexander of Hesse were his wife, the Princess of Battenberg, their daughter, Marie, with her husband, Gustav, and their sons, "Sandro" and "Franzjos". For this august occasion the suites were considerable, including some "Bulgarian gentlemen". Prince Louis of Battenberg came over in the Royal Yacht *Victoria and Albert* to Flushing to meet them.

It was a never to be forgotten journey. A storm blew up and lashed the Channel for sixteen hours. In the early hours Princess Marie could stand her cabin no longer and decided to go on deck. Her maid was howling in the misery of *mal de mer* and beyond the stage of being able to assist. Somehow she managed to pull some clothes about her and make her slow way upwards. She came across the Grand Duke of Hesse, Ernest Louis, and Henry of Prussia crouching together for shelter. In a corner was "Sandro", beside him the disconsolate form of his Bulgarian secretary, holding a basin to his chin. She passed them by and stumbled on to the highest part of the deck, where she settled in a "sort of glass case".

> There I sat for hours, staring at the grey waves ceaselessly storming up at us; nothing could arouse me from my heavy apathy. Once the Grand Duke came and said, "Marie, you should go and see after Gustav; he has been lying deadly sick ever since a sailor found him at the foot of a stairway half-senseless with sea-sickness." "Oh! really?" I replied, quite indifferently, and continued to stare out at the waves. After a time came Louis: "You truly ought to go to mamma, her condition is really very bad; the doctor has been putting ice compresses on her head for hours!" "How dreadful!" said I, without moving from the spot. "The shield has been torn away from the bow in the storm," said "Sandro", who was feeling better again. "You don't say so!" I answered indifferently.[12]

Then guns were heard above the storm and there followed the blessed calm of the Cowes roadstead. But under the hides of the passengers the movement lingered on. Gaily, members of the Royal Family came out in launches to greet them, and a lunch was served. There were empty places, and plates were pushed away. On the shore crowds had gathered. As the shaken party came in to land, Princess Marie sat, mesmerised, watching her husband in the bows. He was wearing a top hat above a green face, and in his eyes was all the agony of a man who knew that, before all those staring, inquisitive spectators, he might be forced to pay yet another tribute to the sea.[13]

Princess Beatrice and Prince Henry were married at St. Mildred's, Whippingham, which had been designed by the Prince Consort. It was the first occasion that a daughter of the Sovereign had wed in a parish church. This break with tradition posed the problem of what the ladies invited to attend should wear. The Queen seemed vague, and Osborne was showered with queries. At last the Mistress of the Robes, the Duchess of Buccleuch, took matters in her own hands. She had her "body", suitably arrayed, displayed in Bond Street.[14]

But the Queen was determined on the garb for "Liko". She insisted on the white uniform of the Gardes du Corps. The result appeared out of character with the village setting, and the mischievous Princess of Wales dubbed him "Beatrice's Lohengrin".[15]

Already there were signs of rivalry between the Sandringham Set and the Osborne, or German, Set, a rivalry which was to reach its zenith when the yachts of the Kaiser and the Prince of Wales competed against each other at Cowes. Batting strongly for Norfolk were the three daughters* of the Squire of Sandringham, known as "the Whispering Wales's girls". In their own estimation they had been poured direct out of the salt-cellar of God.

For Queen Victoria there now began a decade of great, and unexpected, happiness. Once again there was a man about the house, and a handsome and gay one at that. Once again there was a man to laugh with over meals, for she seldom laughed with women. With him as a partner, she even danced again. Then there were babies,† crawling about her on the floor and leaving

---

* Louise, born 1867, afterwards Duchess of Fife, Princess Royal; Victoria, born 1868; Maud, born 1869, afterwards Queen of Norway.
† Alexander ("Drino"), born 1886, afterwards Marquess of Carisbrooke; Ena, born 1887, afterwards Queen Victoria Eugenia of Spain; Leopold, born 1889, afterwards Lord Leopold Mountbatten; and Maurice, born 1891.

their toys in her room, children who turned to her for advice and fun more often than they did to their busy mother.

Happy as he was in his life with his wife and his mother-in-law, moving with regular monotony around the royal homes of Britain, there was ever an element missing in the role of Prince "Liko". He had been denied the task of individual struggle which had been granted to his elder brothers. He had the tinsel. He was created Royal Highness and made a Knight of the Garter. He was a Privy Councillor, Governor and Captain of the Isle of Wight, Governor of Carisbrooke Castle, Honorary Colonel of the Isle of Wight Rifles.[16] The Queen gave him a yacht, in which he cruised from the Mediterranean to the Western Isles. He played tennis, and mastered the perils of the new-fangled bicycle. He took his part in amateur theatricals, in which his pretty sister-in-law, Louise, so delighted. He studied, with deep interest, the historic records of the Isle of Wight. But it took more than gilt and favour, a sinecure and a yacht, sport and babies, to fully occupy the mind and talents of a Battenberg. There were those who forecast that there would soon be dangers, perhaps pretty ones, along his way. Yet he had one absorbing problem to hold his attention—the progress of his brother "Sandro" in Bulgaria, and his ill-starred romance with Princess Victoria of Prussia.

"Sandro" was in a very difficult situation in Bulgaria. He believed that he was acting in Russia's interests in developing the country's resources, civilisation and military strength. "But that was a misconception. Alexander II was dead, and the new Russia wanted no developed Bulgaria. It wanted a weak one, in order to be able to control it more easily. It wanted no federation with the West, to which the Prince's efforts were directed. Bulgaria was to be isolated by a Chinese wall, and content itself with the crumbs of culture that fell from Holy Moscow's meagrely furnished table."[17]

In September Eastern Roumelia, that part of Southern Bulgaria which had been torn apart by the Berlin Treaty of 1879, demanded reunion with the North, under the leadership of Prince "Sandro". In fury, Alexander III struck his cousin's name off the list of the Russian army. Serbia, encouraged by Austria, declared war on

Bulgaria, but was defeated at the battle of Slivnitza. "Sandro" became a national hero. But in the heart of the Russian Emperor there grew a deadly, personal hatred against him, and plans were made to bring about his downfall.

Bismarck noted all this. He knew that the romance between "Sandro" and Princess Victoria must come to an end. He was forced into the open by the probability of a visit to Berlin of Queen Victoria, accompanied by Princess Beatrice and Prince Henry of Battenberg. He advised old Emperor William that he must refuse his consent to the marriage. He told Moritz Busch, his henchman:

> The old Queen is fond of matchmaking, like all old women, and she may have selected Prince Alexander for her granddaughter, because he is a brother of her son-in-law, the husband of her favourite daughter, Beatrice. But obviously her main objects are political—a permanent estrangement between ourselves and Russia —and if she were to come here for the Princess's birthday, there would be the greatest danger that she would get her way. In family matters she is not accustomed to contradiction, and would immediately bring the parson with her in her travelling bag and the bridegroom in her trunk and the marriage would come off at once.[18]

The Crown Princess, determined that her daughter should marry the man whom she loved and realising that she was being spied upon by Bismarck, went underground. Her letters to "Sandro" in Sofia were sent by devious secret routes, one of them being via "Liko" in England.[19]

The Russians now organised a small and discontented section of the Bulgarian army. Threat after threat reached "Sandro" that he was to be kidnapped or murdered. He ignored them, and nothing happened. But on 21st August 1886 a gang of one hundred and fifty broke into his palace in the early hours and dragged him away. They subjected him to every form of ignominy and made pretence that they were going to shoot him.[20] They spread the rumour that they had found him in bed with the sister of one of the conspirators. They put him on a train, under guard, for the Austrian frontier. On arrival there he wrote to his sister: "I am horribly tired—broken in body and spirit."[21]

Europe moved close to war, and Queen Victoria saw, behind

the Russian moves, a threat to Constantinople.[22] But the people of Bulgaria rose against the conspirators, silenced them, and demanded the return of their Sovereign Prince. Prince Louis was at Heiligenberg at the time, and he hurried to his brother's side. On the 29th they journeyed to Sofia, amid scenes of jubilation.[23]

In a last attempt to heal the bitterness, "Sandro" sent a placatory telegram to Alexander III. It was treated with vicious contempt, and as a sign of weakness.[24] The Emperor made it clear to the world that only the abdication of "Sandro" could bring friendly relations between Russia and Bulgaria. The threats continued, and he was warned that he would be killed in the Cathedral. On 7th September, weary and disillusioned, he abdicated, and his people wept as they saw him go.

In December Prince "Sandro" visited Windsor. At breakfast he told the Queen that he had slept well for the first time, "as he has been constantly in the habit of waking, still seeing those faces and hearing those words and cries of the dreadful 21st August".[25] But now doubts were born as to whether this embittered deposed ruler, old beyond his years, would make a suitable husband for the innocent and sheltered Princess Victoria of Prussia. Meanwhile Europe became absorbed with another man's tragedy.

19

Forbidden Love

IN JANUARY 1887 THE CROWN PRINCE OF GERMANY COMPLAINED of an irritation in the throat, and his voice became hoarse. On 6th March he saw a German specialist, who diagnosed a small growth on the left vocal cord. For the moment the infection aroused little speculation, as Berlin was preparing for great celebration on the 22nd, the ninetieth birthday of Emperor William, when it was rumoured that an announcement of interest would be made. Royalties poured in, including the Prince of Wales and Crown Prince Rudolf of Austria.

The Crown Prince led the procession of Generals up to his father, and delivered his speech of congratulation. Many noted the hoarseness in his voice.[1]

The announcement followed. Prince Henry, twenty-five-year-old son of the Crown Prince and Princess, and Prince William's only surviving brother, was engaged to twenty-one-year-old Princess Irene, daughter of the Grand Duke of Hesse and Princess Alice.[2]

This was an exaggerated example of "marrying in-and-in". On the maternal side, the couple shared the same grandparents in Queen Victoria and Prince Albert, who were double cousins. On the paternal side, Frederick William II of Prussia was a common ancestor to the Crown Prince and the Grand Duke Louis. He was the great-grandfather of the Crown Prince. King Frederick William's son, William, married, in 1804 Mary Anne, daughter of Landgrave Frederick V of Hesse-Homburg. Their daughter, Elizabeth, married Prince Charles of Hesse and the Rhine, and were the parents of Grand Duke Louis IV.[3] This proximity did not worry Queen Victoria, but she did foresee difficulties over divided loyalties in the years ahead. She wrote to Emperor William:

> It is strange that in the year in which you celebrate your 90th birthday I shall reach the 50th anniversary of my accession. And in this year, so important for us both, our grandchildren have become betrothed. I cannot think unmoved of the union of the children of my two dear daughters. Henry should consider himself fortunate to win such a wife as my beloved Irene. You were always so kind, dear brother, to my never to be forgotten Alice, that I cannot doubt that you will be glad to welcome her daughter as your future grand-daughter. She is a most charming girl.[4]

Prince Henry was a professional naval officer. Amiable enough at heart, he was bullied by his elder brother, whom he was inclined to ape. When filled with the propaganda of Berlin he was difficult to manage in the home. There was never the same bond of love and harmony between the three elder children, William, Charlotte and Henry, and their mother, that existed between her and her younger children, whom she had nursed herself. The Crown Princess confided in Queen Victoria: "The dream of my life was to have a son who should be something of what our beloved Papa was, a real grandson of his, in soul, and intellect, a grandson of yours. Waldie gave me hopes of this—his nature was full of promise from the first, and I saw it with such pride and pleasure, and thought I could one day be of use to him! He is gone, and I can be but of limited use to Henry, and of none to William in any way!"[5] She also complained that Henry was "as obstinate as a mule",[6] but added: "He is always nice when he has been with us for some time, but not when he has been set up by others, and his head stuffed full of rubbish at Berlin. . . ."[7]

But on the engagement day all was domestic bliss. Henry had

long set his heart on marrying Princess Irene, and two years before had braved the ire of Berlin by travelling with her to England for the wedding of Princess Beatrice. In the evening, in combination with his sister, Victoria, he staged a theatrical performance called *Kürmärker und Pikarde*, which delighted his father.[8] It was to be the last happy and trouble-free evening that the Crown Prince was to spend with his family.

The condition of his throat worsened and daily he was subjected to the agony of attempts to lassoo the swollen parts with a wire snare. Then six German doctors gave a unanimous diagnosis of cancer of the throat. They favoured an operation. Bismarck would not allow the operation to take place without the patient's consent. It was decided to seek another opinion, and an English specialist, Dr. Morell Mackenzie, was called in. Queen Victoria wrote to the Crown Princess:

> Not knowing him at all (and I had never heard of him) I thought it best to send Dr. Reid up to see him and send him off. Sir William (Jenner) said Dr. M. Mackenzie certainly is very clever in that particular line about throats! but that he is greedy and grasping about money and tries to make a profit out of his attendance. . . .[9]

Dr. Mackenzie said that he could not advise an operation until proof had come from under the microscope that cancer existed. He removed part of the growth and sent it to Professor Virchow for examination. The Professor replied that he could find in the sample no indication of a cancerous nature. The operation was postponed, and Dr. Mackenzie said he would like to treat his patient in England, holding out hopes of effecting a cure there.[10]

This exactly suited the book of the Crown Princess, for a number of reasons. Firstly, she liked and trusted Morell Mackenzie. It was he who refused to accept that cancer was present and she firmly believed that, once free of the experiments of the German doctors and at peace in England, her husband would regain his strength. Secondly, she wished to attend the Jubilee of Queen Victoria, and see her husband take his rightful place in the procession. Thirdly, she wished to have a free hand to further the romance of Princess Victoria with Prince "Sandro" of Battenberg, a freedom which was denied to her in Germany. She knew that the Empress

Augusta had turned pressure on the Emperor to stop the marriage at any cost, urging him to disinherit the Princess if she did not give him up.[11] She also knew that the Emperor had not more than six months to live, at the end of which she would be able to arrange matters her own way.

The Crown Prince's decision to travel to London for the Jubilee aroused a storm of protest in Berlin. Prince William, backed by German doctors, announced that he would take his father's place. Herbert Bismarck* declared that Mackenzie was a fraud. The Crown Princess was accused of shortening her husband's life to satisfy her own ambitions. But the Emperor gave the decision that his son was a grown man and must make up his own mind. On 12th June the Crown Prince and Princess set out for London, where they stayed at a house at Upper Norwood. It was considered that the air there would prove beneficial.[12]

On 21st July, in brilliant sunlight, a mighty procession moved from Buckingham Palace, up Constitution Hill, along Piccadilly and through Whitehall to Westminster Abbey, to celebrate the fiftieth year of Queen Victoria's reign. Thirty-two Princes rode in the cavalcade, towering among them Frederick, the Prince Imperial of Germany. The crowds were aware of his illness, and he was a centre of attention. He wore the wholly white uniform of the Cuirassiers, with silver breast-plate, and on his burnished steel helmet the great silver crest of an eagle with outspread wings. His brother-in-law, the Marquess of Lorne, who had himself been thrown from his horse soon after leaving the Palace, described him as looking like "one of the legendary heroes embodied in the creations of Wagner".[13] Yet the thoughts of the Crown Prince were far removed from war and conquest on that brilliant day. There were found in his clothes, after his death, pencilled notes that he had made about the ambulance arrangements, the cabmen's shelters, and the drinking troughs for horses.[14]

Throughout the celebrations the Queen showed particular favour to her two sons-in-law from Germany, the Crown Prince and the Grand Duke of Hesse. After the service in the Abbey, her relations passed by her, kissing her hand. She called back "Fritz"

* Son of the Chancellor.

and Louis, and embraced them, as she had done her own sons and daughters.

While in London the Crown Prince and Princess visited the Throat Hospital* in Golden Square, and were shown over by Dr. Wolfenden, who was acting in concert with Dr. Mackenzie. In one of the beds was a little girl who had undergone the operation of tracheotomy, a word that was to have such dramatic meaning to the visitors in the months ahead. The girl was nursing a doll and the Crown Prince asked her which of them had been operated upon. She replied: "Sure I don't know which it is, my dear."[15]

From Norwood the Crown Prince moved to the Isle of Wight, and from there to Scotland, staying at the Fife Arms, Braemar. By this time the Court at Berlin was beginning to wonder when their Prince Imperial would return home and bitter remarks were passed that his medical headquarters was obviously operating from Buckingham Palace, a supposition which was, to a large extent, correct.

The air of Deeside had a recuperative effect on the Crown Prince. He paid frequent visits to Balmoral, where his future daughter-in-law, Princess Irene of Hesse, was staying. He helped the Queen to entertain visitors from India, and she wrote of him: ". . . he is wonderfully better, still hoarse, but not without any voice, as when he arrived in England. He seems in excellent spirits."[16] He returned to Germany, and on 7th September, buoyed up by new hope, the Queen knighted Dr. Morell Mackenzie in the drawing-room at Balmoral.

The Crown Prince was now in the personal care of Dr. Mark Hovell, senior surgeon to the Throat Hospital. Dr. Hovell knew full well that his patient had cancer, thus being in disagreement with his superior, Sir Morell Mackenzie.[17]

As the climate of Potsdam was not considered favourable, the family moved around southern Europe in search of more kindly air, travelling from Toblach in the Tyrol to Venice, on to Baveno

---

* After the Emperor Frederick's death, the Empress asked Mr. Rennell Rodd (afterwards first Lord Rennell of Rodd) to write the story of her husband's life, the proceeds of the sale of this book going to the funds of the Throat Hospital.

near Lake Maggiore, and settling for the winter at the Villa Zirio in San Remo, which they reached early in November. There the Crown Prince took a turn for the worse, and Sir Morell Mackenzie was sent for. The Crown Prince asked him direct if he was suffering from cancer. The reply was: "I am sorry to say, sir, it looks very much like it, but it is impossible to be certain."[18] But the German doctors were certain, and hope lived alone in the heart and prayers of the Crown Princess.

Now all the venom of a nation's spite poured upon her tired head. She was accused of shortening her husband's life by entrusting him to the care of an incompetent British doctor, who had refused to believe the diagnosis of the German specialists. The Press, urged on by Herbert Bismarck, ranted that power in Germany would never pass into the hands of an Englishwoman. Her three elder children were unsympathetic and at times hostile, and Prince William already strutted around as if he was the Emperor.

On 9th March Emperor William I died. On the 11th Emperor Frederick and Empress Victoria* arrived at Berlin in a special train. The cold was intense and deep snow lay everywhere.[19] There were early signs that there would be opposition in the new reign. On walls and on placards were the words: "The Emperor of the Hebrews, Frederick II, alias Cohen"[20] and "Cohen I, King of the Jews".[21] The new Emperor's award of honours to brilliant men of Jewish extraction was not to be forgotten by the right wing extremists.

Empress Victoria now turned towards the fulfilment of her heart's desire, the marriage of her daughter with Prince "Sandro" of Battenberg. She persuaded her husband, against his better judgment, to agree. Princess Victoria wrote: "He gave me his consent personally at Potsdam, and how lovingly we embraced one another. I believe he planned to bring about the marriage there and then. . . ."[22] "Sandro" was invited to visit Potsdam.

Such a move had been foreseen by Bismarck, his son, Herbert, and Crown Prince William. William sent a message to "Sandro" that, if he married his sister, he would never speak to him again.

* Her rightful title while her husband was Emperor.

On 31st March Bismarck, in an interview with the Emperor, raised violent objection to any German military rank or honour being given to the Prince of Battenberg. The Emperor cancelled the invitation to the Prince and asked the Chancellor to submit a report on the question. Three days later the report arrived. In it Bismarck gave his opinion that, in view of the attitude in Russia, there should be no engagement, and if his opinion was not accepted, he would resign. He regarded the matter simply as an attempt by Queen Victoria to upset relations between Germany and Russia.[23] The romance now assumed the importance of an international crisis. The battle between the giants grew nearer.

Meanwhile Queen Victoria was behaving with the utmost circumspection. She told her daughter in Berlin: "Don't contemplate marriage without full consent of William. It would never do to contract a marriage he would not agree to. . . ."[24] She also pointed out to her Ministers that "Sandro's" engagement could not possibly interest or concern the Emperor of Russia, now that he was no longer concerned with Bulgaria, a point which Alexander III confirmed.[25] Then there came to her ears from Darmstadt the news that "Sandro" had fallen in love with one of the opera stars at the Court Theatre there, Johanna Loisinger,[26] and wished to marry her. The Queen confided this information in confidence to Herbert Bismarck through the Ambassador in Berlin. Herbert Bismarck received the news with "surprise and delight",[27] but there was no let up in the tirade of hate against Britain in the German Press. It was a trial of strength, and it seemed there was to be no peace until Emperor Frederick III was dead, and the possibility of a marriage between "Sandro" and the Princess ended for ever.

Colonel Swaine, British Military Attaché in Berlin, wrote to the Prince of Wales, confirming that "Sandro" had *"ein zärtliches Verhältniss* with a member of the histrionic art". He went on:

> It seems as if a curse had come over this country, leaving but one bright spot and that is where stands a solitary woman doing her duty faithfully and tenderly by her sick husband against all odds. It is one of the most, if not *the* most, tragic episodes in a country and a life ever recorded in history.[28]

On 22nd March Queen Victoria, with Princess Beatrice and her husband, left England at the start of a month's holiday in Florence. On 8th April she received a cypher telegram from Lord Salisbury, the Prime Minister:

> . . . The newspapers say that Your Majesty is going to Potsdam or Berlin. I would humbly submit that this visit at this time would expose You to great misconstruction and possibly to some disrespectful demonstration. German Chancellor is reported by his son to be in a state of intense exasperation. . . .[29]

Cold fury filled the Queen. No arranged demonstrations in the streets were to rob her of the chance of saying goodbye to her dying son-in-law, or of settling her differences face to face with Bismarck. She had been handling statesmen for over fifty years, and she had learned much of their ways.

On the 23rd she began her journey to Germany. At Innsbruck the Emperor Francis Joseph was waiting to greet her. The platform at Munich was peopled with royalties, headed by the Queen Mother of Bavaria. "The Queen, who is the mother of the unfortunate King Ludwig, drowned two years ago, and of the present mad King Otto, is the only and younger sister of Princess Charles of Hesse, and reminded me much of her, only much better-looking."[30] When she awoke next morning the train was nearing Berlin, and in the grey light she could see soldiers drilling in the fields.[31] She drove through silent crowds to the Charlottenburg Palace.

Throughout this and the two following days the Queen paid frequent visits to the bedside of the Emperor Frederick. Each time she kissed him. He gave her a nosegay and, bravely, she told him that he must come and stay with her as soon as he felt better. She had come to terms with death now, and down-graded its priority to below that of the business of ruling.

In the afternoon she drove through the streets of Berlin. Again the crowds stared, and were silent. She called upon the Empress Augusta. She found her old friend crumpled up in a chair, half paralysed, hidden beneath the long veil of mourning. The Queen commented: ". . . really rather a ghastly sight".[32]

A request came from Prince Bismarck that he might see the

Queen. A meeting was arranged for noon on the morrow. They had never met before. The diplomats held their breath, for at last the moment had come.

Bismarck was nervous when he arrived at Charlottenburg Palace. Major Bigge,* who received him, noted this as he answered various questions upon procedure.[33] There followed a short wait, during which the tension increased. Then Sir Henry Ponsonby arrived and led the Chancellor through a series of rooms. The conversation was confined to their decoration. Sir Henry Ponsonby took the caller to the Empress. She led him to the room in which the Queen was waiting. The door closed on a page of unwritten history.

When the door opened half an hour later, Bismarck came out smiling and with admiration writ clear on his face. He wiped the perspiration from his forehead and said: "What a woman. One could do business with her!"[34]

Then the sun came out, and the cheering began. In the afternoon the Queen drove out again through the streets. "Almost the whole way we passed through double lines of carriages, and when we got into the town there were great crowds, who were most enthusiastic, cheering and throwing flowers into the carriage. . . ."[35] So great was the acclamation that fears arose in St. Petersburg that a rapprochement was in preparation between Germany and Britain.[36]

That evening the Queen sat opposite to Bismarck at dinner. He was in gay mood and, seeing a bon-bon bearing on it the picture of Empress Victoria, he seized it and pressed it to his heart. An international crisis had faded clean away. But the turmoil and the sadness in a heart had not. Princess Victoria was told, gently but firmly, that her romance with Prince "Sandro" of Battenberg was at an end. It was with mixed feelings that she watched the preparations for her brother's wedding.

Prince Henry and Princess Irene of Hesse were married in the private chapel of Charlottenburg Palace on 24th May, Queen Victoria's birthday. The Prince of Wales came from England and the Grand Duke and Duchess Serge from Russia. From somewhere the Emperor found the strength to rise from his bed, and he was

* Afterwards Lord Stamfordham.

at the station to meet Princess Irene when she reached the capital.[37]

Wearing a general's uniform, he attended the wedding. While the rings were being exchanged and the couple blessed, he stood erect, by the wheel-chair which held the twisted form of his mother, garbed in black. Then, as the organ played Handel's *Largo*, he walked from the chapel. It was his last, unaided exit.[38] Eighty-seven-year-old Field Marshal Moltke turned to a friend and said: "I have seen many brave men, but none as brave as the Emperor has shown himself today."[39]

The sight made a divergent impression on Herbert Bismarck. He remarked to the Prince of Wales that a Sovereign who could not enter into debate should not be allowed to reign. The Prince, in retailing this to his mother, commented: "If I had not taken into consideration that good relations between Germany and England were essential, I should have thrown him out."[40]

Another guest there was Lady Milford Haven:

> I assisted at Irene's marriage to Henry of Prussia. It was a sad wedding. Uncle Fritz [the German Emperor] was in the last stage of his illness. He attended it in uniform, but with the collar open, as he had to breathe through a tube. He was quite unable to speak and would write anything he had to say on little slips of paper. The recently widowed Empress Augusta was also in a bad state of health. Shaking all over with palsy, she assisted at the wedding in a bath chair.

On 15th June Emperor Frederick died. His widow, Empress Victoria, became the Empress Frederick. Their eldest son became Emperor William II. His first act was to cordon off the house, in which his father's body lay, with a regiment of Hussars. Unmounted, and with rifles in their hands, they appeared from behind every tree and statue.[41]

The news that "Sandro" no longer wished to marry Princess Victoria had been kept from Emperor Frederick and in his will he charged his son with the duty of ensuring that the union took place. William's immediate action was to announce that, in accordance with his father's wish, the union would not take place.* [42]

* Princess Victoria married Prince Adolphus of Schaumburg-Lippe in 1890.

Lady Milford Haven recalled the upset that the affair caused in her family:

> Unfortunately, immediately after Uncle Fritz's death, in the high and mighty Hohenzollern fashion, William sent the Prussian diplomatic representative to my father-in-law to announce that all question of a marriage must be at an end, as the Emperor would never countenance it. My poor father-in-law was furious at the impertinence of such a message being delivered to him, as he had never asked for the hand of a Prussian princess for one of his sons. The letter Sandro received from William ignored the fact of the engagement and was, therefore, no help to break it off in the desired manner. Grandmama, with whom Sandro had become a great favourite and who was full of sympathy for Aunt Vicky, was, privately, equally indignant.
>
> How badly William treated his mother after his father's death is no secret to the world any longer. I can recollect how William had been her favourite son in his youth and how well they understood each other until he, the future heir to the throne, came under Prince Bismarck's influence. When Prince and Princess Bismarck called on Aunt Vicky to take leave of her after Bismarck's downfall, the Princess lamented to her how ungratefully this loyal servant of the throne had been treated. Aunt Vicky has told me that her reply was: "When one has trained a young man to have no respect or regard for his parents, how can one expect him to treat his ministers with more consideration?" The Prince remained silent during the whole of this conversation with his wife.

Prince "Sandro" of Battenberg now applied to the Grand Duke Louis for a non-royal title, and in January 1889 he became Count Hartenau.* In February he married Johanna Loisinger. Queen Victoria contented herself with one of the most human and understanding comments of her reign. She said: "Perhaps they love one another."[43]

---

* Count Hartenau joined the Austrian army. The former reigning Prince, Commander-in-Chief of his army, the victorious Commander at the battle of Slivnitza, he stepped down to the rank of Lieutenant-Colonel in command of an infantry battalion, a sacrifice which must have cost him dearly. A parallel came sixty years later when his nephew, Earl Mountbatten of Burma, went down from a full Admiral, Supreme Commander and Viceroy to Rear-Admiral commanding a cruiser squadron in the Mediterranean. Count Hartenau died at Graz in 1893. His widow survived him by fifty-eight years, dying at Vienna in July 1951. They had a son and a daughter.

20

Marriage Mart

SWIFTLY NOW, THE OLD ORDER CHANGED IN HESSE. IN December 1888 Prince Alexander, the father of the Batten-bergs, died at Darmstadt. The Castle of Heiligenberg passed to his eldest son, Prince Louis, at thirty-nine a Captain, Naval Adviser to the War Office and Chief Secretary to the joint Naval and Military Committee of Defence. In the following years he spent most of his leave here, with his wife and children, Alice, Louise* and George.† ¹

Next came anxiety over the health of the Grand Duke Louis, who, since the marriage of Princess Irene, had only his youngest daughter, "Alicky", to care for him. He had never recovered from the worry and strain through which he had passed during the disastrous Alexandrine von Kolemine affair, and, as a result of the strained relations which it had engendered, he was seldom to be seen at the Russian and Prussian courts. He still visited Britain for family occasions, such as the wedding of Princess Louise of Wales and the Duke of Fife in 1889, but the gaiety and the enthusiasm were gone from him. He was content now with

---

* Afterwards Lady Louise Mountbatten, and Crown Princess and Queen of Sweden. Born 1889.
† Afterwards Earl of Medina and 2nd Marquess of Milford Haven. Born 1892.

224

Princess Alix of Hesse (centre), assisted by her sister, Grand Duchess Serge of Russia, and the English nurse, Mrs. Orchard, prepares for her first ball in 1889

Above, the children of Emperor Nicholas II and Empress Alexandra Feodorovna of Russia. From left to right: Marie, Tatiana, Anastasia, Olga and Alexei. *Below*, from left to right: Grand Duke Serge of Russia, Princess Alix of Hesse, Grand Duke Louis of Hesse, Grand Duchess Serge of Russia and Prince Ernest Louis of Hesse, in 1886

his circle of friends, in Darmstadt for the winter, and Wolfsgarten in the summer. To assist in regaining his strength he had spent two winters by the Mediterranean. Paris became his favourite resort. There he maintained such a strict incognito that his presence was not recorded.[2]

In the autumn of 1891 the Grand Duke was treated for heart disease[3] and in the first week of the following March a paralytic stroke[4] caused his family to gather by his bedside. To the Queen came the superstitious fear that "that terrible number fourteen" would again be connected with a death. But it was on the 13th that the telegram, telling of his passing, was brought to her.[5]

Lady Milford Haven deeply missed her father:

> His body lay in state for some days and the Hessian mourning for him was universal and sincere. He was one of the kindest-hearted and most just men I have ever known. He was as liberal as he was fair-minded and did not approve of Bismarck's "socialist laws". My father understood his people well and they him. To give an instance of this, when he drove himself home from a long day's shoot through very socialistically minded villages, the peasants, on hearing the tramp of his Hungarian "jucker" team, would put their lamps on the window sills to lighten up the streets.

Four days later, as a memorial service was held at Windsor,* the funeral of Grand Duke Louis IV of Hesse and the Rhine took place at Darmstadt. The Duke of Edinburgh, representing the Queen, and the Empress Frederick were there. In recent years the Empress and the Grand Duke, each with their troubles, had drawn close to each other, and he had been the greatest support to her during her husband's illness. She wrote to her daughter:

> Poor Uncle Louis, so kind and affectionate, so much beloved by us all. Those poor children! Alicky, without Parents and home, Ernie much too young and inexperienced for his position, poor Victoria who doted on her father and was his pride and support. . . .[6]

Ernest Louis, the new Grand Duke, was twenty-three. In looks he took after his father. In taste and intelligence and outlook he followed in the footsteps of his mother, the memory of whom was very precious to him. It was while he was studying at the

---

* A bust of the Grand Duke is in the Mausoleum at Frogmore.

universities of Leipzig and Giessen that he became influenced by the Art and Social movement started in Britain by Ruskin, his mother's friend, and William Morris. In 1884 he was made a Second Lieutenant in the 1st Hessian Life Guard Infantry and two years later joined the 1st Prussian Footguards. He passed his military examinations in 1888, but gave up his active military career on his father's death.[7]

Grand Duke Louis IV was but fifty-four when he died, and his son had not anticipated taking over the rule of Hesse for many years to come. He was entirely inexperienced in governing, but he knew full well of the dangers of playing a subsidiary role to Emperor William and Bismarck. The example of "Sandro" of Battenberg was clear before his eyes. The assumption of power was an experience which he did not relish, and at his father's death-bed he had thrown himself into the arms of Princess Marie of Battenberg, begging for her support.[8] Yet he had the advantage of following parents who were beloved in Hesse. Also he was unassuming, quick witted and as full of fun as his father had been when he had courted Princess Alice a third of a century before.

Queen Victoria saw the problem, and was quick to act. In April she spent a week in Darmstadt, teaching her grandson the elements of governing. But for her it was now a town of ghosts. She could scarcely believe that the two young people whom she had seen married at Osborne in 1862 were now lying side by side at the Rosenhöhe. As the train drew into the station she half expected Louis to jump into the carriage and greet her with kisses, as he had always done. Instead there were three young women, and their brother, standing, in deep mourning, on the platform. "No Guard of Honour, all silent and sad."[9]

Yet in a few months the exuberance of youth came to the rescue of Grand Duke Ernest Louis, as he found himself free to follow his own desires away from the narrow confines of military life in Berlin. With Princess Alice, something had died in Darmstadt. Now her freshness returned, and the decorators moved again into the Palace, working under the Grand Duke's direction. He loved flowers and gardens, and his artistic touch restyled Wolfsgarten. He wrote and he painted. Often he was to be seen at rehearsals at the Court Theatre, helping to design the scenery and lending his encouragement to new talent. He was even known to walk into flower shops and offer his ideas on display. Everything that he did was fast, an eternal search for new ideas, new gaieties. Fresh faces were seen at his weekend parties at Wolfsgarten, those of artists, writers, poets. The old ones about his Court panted to keep pace, dreaming of the slow tread of his grandfather's days. He was like his mother had been at seventeen, even to the brightness in his clear blue eyes.[10]

Often the pace grew too fast for the youngest sister who kept house for him. "Alicky", at twenty-one, was serious-minded and so shy that her brother's guests sometimes wrongly assessed hostility in her greeting. On occasion she would leave their parties and, alone in her room, become absorbed in some book on religion or the occult. The mental turmoil through which her mother was passing at the time of her birth had left its indelible mark.

Her confirmation in 1888 had had a profound effect upon her. Religious instruction was given by Dr. Sell, a Hessian divine who had been the choice of Princess Alice. Like her, he believed in searching deep for the truth, and the search upset the daughter as previously it had upset the mother. She became introspective, self-critical, and set her ideals high. When the time came for her to desert the Lutheran doctrine, she did so with deep regret.[11]

Once "Alicky" was "out" and in a position to play hostess for her father, "Ella" proved of the greatest help in showing her the intricacies of etiquette and procedure. She came with the Grand Duke Serge for "Alicky's" first ball at the New Palace, and then persuaded her father to bring the youngest sister to St. Petersburg for a long stay in the early months of 1889. There opera and ballet, ball and carnival, filled the nights, skating, tobogganing and bear hunts, the days. Always beside her was "Nicky", the Cesarevitch. He called her *Tetinka*, which means "Little Aunt". When she came back to Darmstadt at the beginning of Lent, she left her heart behind at St. Petersburg, in the care of the Emperor's heir.[12]

A summons now came to Princess Alix of Hesse to attend at Balmoral Castle. On arrival she learned that there was an underlying reason for the summons. Queen Victoria was looking for a bride for Prince Albert Victor, eldest son of the Prince of Wales.

Albert Victor, known as "Eddy", could be likened to a cartoon of his father at a similar age. The faults were exaggerated. Shapeless was the picture of his life, and apathetic his approach to its problems. "He was also backward and utterly listless. He was self-indulgent and not punctual. He had been given no proper education, and as a result he was interested in nothing. He was as heedless and as aimless as a gleaming gold-fish in a crystal bowl."[13]

Prince "Eddy" was in the 10th Hussars. The military routine irked him, and, although he played polo, he did not take it seriously. He was liked by his fellow officers, his easy-going and unambitious attitude giving them no cause to do otherwise. With his wavy hair, receding forehead and little waxed moustache he was somewhat of a joke figure. Because he had to wear an extra high collar to hide his long neck, his father nicknamed him "Collars-and-Cuffs".[14] "Dear and kind" as he was often described, there were many who turned away in horror from the thought that one day he would sit on the Throne of Great Britain.

"Eddy" had one drawback more serious than his apathy. This was a desire for the company of young ladies. It was a strong and undeniable desire, and only in the throes of his *amours* did the sleeping energy within him spur him into action. His father, long versed in the intricacies of such aberrations, was quick to spot the danger signals. For the sake of his own peace, he despatched his eldest son on long tours to distant seas, and the longer these lasted, the better he was pleased. The Queen thought that this was strange treatment for a future King, and considered that "Eddy" should familiarise himself with the Courts of Europe. The Prince of Wales contented himself by saying that there was a very good reason why this course was not being followed. The Queen put her own espionage to work, and discovered the truth. She immediately came to the same conclusion that she and Albert had reached in the case of the Prince of Wales, thirty years before. That decision was that a steady and level-headed wife must be found for "Eddy" without delay, else one day the British ship of State might be lured towards the rocks by some siren's sensual song. So it was that Princess Alix of Hesse sat on the sofa under the tartan at Balmoral.

Among Albert Victor's few Continental journeys had been one to Darmstadt, and he had noted well the ethereal beauty of his cousin, "Alicky". He was therefore well satisfied when the suggestion was put to him that she should become his wife. She, on the other hand, had very different ideas. Apart from being secretly in love with Nicholas of Russia, "Eddy" did not measure up to her standards in any way. He strove after no high ideals. His faith was restricted to Sunday morning strolls across the park to Sandringham's peaceful church. She decided that it could not be, but a year passed before the planners finally gave up hope. In May 1890 Queen Victoria wrote to the Empress Frederick saying that the affair was over:

> It is a real sorrow to us . . . but . . . she says—that if she is *forced* she will do it—but that she would be unhappy & he—too. This shows gt strength of character as all her family & all of us wish it, & she refuses the gtest position there is.[15]

Princess Alix was spared the sadness of fearing that she had blighted Prince "Eddy's" life, for within a fortnight he was madly in love with Princess Hélène of Orleans. To this alliance the Pope gave a definite No. The Prince ricocheted off and found a new target in Lady Sybil St. Clair Erskine. She kept his letters, but gave her heart elsewhere. In December 1891 he became engaged to Princess May of Teck. On 14th January 1892 he died at Sandringham. "The terrible 14th" had claimed once again.

Many young men wanted to marry Princess Alix, among them a supposed descendant of Madame Julie de St. Laurent.[16] She had sailor admirers by the score, German when she visited her sister, Irene, at Kiel, and British when she went with her father to stay with Prince and Princess Louis of Battenberg at Malta. But although she danced all night, and the memory of her lingered on in the island for a long, long time, she remained unattainable.

Within herself she was struggling with the problem of whether she could face up to the change of religion that would be necessary if "Nicky" asked her to marry him. A step towards the solution came in the summer of 1890 when she stayed with the Grand Duke

Serge and "Ella" at their country home near Moscow. Firstly, it confirmed her love for Russia, for its endless pine forests, flat meadows, distance beyond belief. She was entranced with the village fairs and, in contrast, the marvels of Moscow. Secondly, it was while she was there that "Ella" told her that she was going to change to the Orthodox religion, which she did the following year.[17] The break with her established beliefs did not now appear so formidable to "Alicky".

The shock of her father's death, coupled with the strain of the many duties she was now called upon to perform, brought Princess Alix to the verge of a nervous breakdown. Queen Victoria sent for her and took her on a tour of Wales. Her brother took her to Florence and Venice. For the present plans for finding her a husband were shelved, but in another direction they were very much on the table. The old Queen, who loved match-making, was busy selecting a bride for the Grand Duke Ernest Louis. Her eyes turned towards the Edinburgh girls.

Alfred, Duke of Edinburgh, who had married Grand Duchess Marie Alexandrovna in 1874, had one son and four daughters. The boy, Alfred, born in the year of their marriage, was being educated in Germany, and was very wild. The girls were Marie ("Missy") born in 1875; Victoria Melita ("Ducky") in 1876; Alexandra ("Sandra")* in 1878; and Beatrice ("Baby B")† in 1884.

The Duchess was stout. She was devout, and wherever she moved a Russian priest and two chanters went with her. She was dowdy, and her boots were so made that they fitted either foot. She did not believe in illness or fads, and her children had to clean up every morsel on their plates. When she asked a question it was as if she had fired it from a pistol. She was haughty, and very conscious of being the daughter of the Emperor of All the Russias. She preferred "Imperial Grand Duchess" to plain "Royal Duchess". She resented having to give precedence to the Princess of Wales and the Queen's daughters.[18] Having better diamonds, she flaunted them. Sometimes, when she came from the presence

* Married 1896, Prince Ernest of Hohenlohe-Langenburg.
† Married 1909, the Infante Alfonso of Bourbon-Orleans. Died 1966.

of her mother-in-law, she would stamp her feet and wave her fists in rebellion against the aura of omnipotence.

The Edinburghs* and Prince and Princess Louis of Battenberg were together at Malta at the end of the 1880s.

Lady Milford Haven recalled:

> I often took the three Edinburgh cousins out riding on their lovely ponies that used to gallop along the hard roads while I followed at a sober trot, as my pony had so hard a mouth that I never dare let him go into a canter for fear of his bolting.
>
> Ducky, my future sister-in-law, the second of the girls, was then thirteen and somewhat farouche, as she was shy. Missy, a remarkably pretty girl, was a year older, Sandra, a chubby little thing, and Bee, just a year older than my Alice. These two infants used to play together in the private garden, where Aunt Marie and I generally had our tea, for it was a very fine autumn and winter, rain generally only falling at night. It was a painful moment for the two mothers when one day Bee set up an awful howl, crying out that Alice had bitten her—which, unfortunately was quite true. What they had quarrelled about could not be discovered. Bee was somewhat critical at that early age already, declaring that Alice ate butter and bread, not bread and butter.

It was at Malta that Prince George of Wales came to know well the Edinburghs' eldest girl, "Missy". The Queen thought that she would make an excellent match for him. So did Prince George, although he thought her too young. The Duchess had different ideas, as had the girl's German governess,[19] and in June 1892 "Missy's" engagement to Ferdinand, heir presumptive to King Carol of Roumania, was suddenly announced. The Prince of Wales, considering that his son had been snubbed, was most angry.[20] But Prince George found his happiness with Princess May of Teck.

When her husband's appointment to Malta ended, the Duchess of Edinburgh repaired with her daughters to Coburg and thereafter spent much of her time at the pretty castle of the Rosenau. Her reasons for so doing were twofold. The first was that she wished to be out of the orbit of Queen Victoria. The second was

---

* The Duke of Edinburgh held the greatest naval or military appointment then available, that of "Commander-in-Chief, Mediterranean". He had an official residence, Admiralty House, in Malta, but commanded the Fleet from his flagship.

that her husband was to succeed to the dukedom of Saxe-Coburg and Gotha on the death of childless Duke Ernest. Prince Albert's brother was now seventy-four, but still regarded as a major menace to young women. The Queen took good care that diplomats despatched to Coburg were not accompanied by pretty wives or daughters.[21] She herself had not met him for many years, and had never forgiven him for an incident which had occurred during her last visit. Ernest had then banished John Brown to a distant servants' wing, far from her beck and call.[22] But on 22nd August 1893 the long life of lechery of Duke Ernest came to a close, and Alfred of Edinburgh reigned in his stead. The Empress Frederick confided in her daughter, Sophie:* "Aunt Marie will love being No. 1, and reigning Duchess, I am sure."[23]

Having failed in her attempt to put Marie of Edinburgh into line to become Queen of England, Queen Victoria was determined to have her own way over the second daughter, Victoria Melita, whom she called "Ducky". She had decided that "Ducky" would make the perfect wife for the Grand Duke Ernest Louis. A wish that this should come to pass had been expressed by his father shortly before his death. It was necessary to bring the two together without delay, and fortunately a ready-made opportunity presented itself. On 6th July 1893 Prince George, Duke of York, was to marry Princess May of Teck in the Chapel of St. James's Palace, and the royalties of Europe would be on full parade. The bridesmaids included "Ducky" and her two younger sisters, and two little Battenberg girls, Alice and Ena.

Lady Milford Haven noted:

Nicky of Russia was over for the wedding. His and Georgie's likeness at that time was so great that, at Uncle Bertie's garden party at Marlborough House, several people congratulated Nicky instead of George on his marriage, and one of the old English gentlemen in attendance on Nicky came up to George to tell him the exact hour at which the guests were going to assemble at Buckingham Palace.

On the wedding day of the future King George V and Queen

---

* Married, 1889, Crown Prince Constantine of Greece. Afterwards Queen of the Hellenes.

Mary, Queen Victoria gave particular favour to young Grand Duke Ernest Louis of Hesse and the Rhine. She walked into the Chapel on his arm, and she had the same support on the way out. At the luncheon afterwards he sat at her table.[24] In the evening the Grand Duke and Princess Victoria Melita were at a party given by the Prince of Wales.

The plot thickened. Guests at Balmoral that autumn included the Grand Duke Serge and "Ella", his wife. They departed and Alfred, Duke of Coburg, arrived, without his Duchess. The Duke went on to Sandringham for talks with the Prince of Wales, and then rejoined the Queen at Windsor. On 9th January 1894 he sent a telegram to his mother at Osborne: "Your and my great wish has been fulfilled this evening. Ducky has accepted Ernie of Hesse's proposal. . . ."[25]

Once again the Queen had promoted a match where first cousins were doubly related. The Empress Frederick, for one, did not approve of such close unions,[26] but the Queen explained: ". . . the same blood only adds to the strength & if you try to avoid it you will marry some unhealthy little Pcess wh wld just cause what you wish to avoid."[27]

There was another person who viewed the forthcoming alliance with considerable misgivings. This was Princess Alix of Hesse. She had been playing the part of "stand in" Grand Duchess since the marriage of her sister, Irene, and had become deeply interested and involved in Darmstadt affairs. Now a tall, dark girl, with violet eyes, four years her junior, with the assuredness of an Empress and the high spirits of a tomboy, was to take precedence over her.[28] She did not like the idea, nor that of Aunt Marie Edinburgh playing the dictator around Darmstadt.

The wedding was fixed for 19th April 1894, at Coburg. Towards the quiet little town converged a confluence of royalties almost unrivalled even in the great days of Thrones. Old Sir Henry Ponsonby, whose experience of such matters was unique, commented: "I never saw so many."[29] Among them were Queen Victoria, Emperor William, the Empress Frederick, the Prince of Wales, Grand Duke Vladimir (representing Alexander III), the Cesarevitch (nobody knew as yet why he was there), the Ferdinands of Roumania, Prince and Princess Henry of Prussia, the Connaughts, Princess Marie Louise, a strong force of Battenbergs and a full local contingent of Coburgs.

As the train neared the town Queen Victoria's heart was full of memories of the first time that she had made the journey with Albert. Then he had been standing at the open window, excitedly pointing out the landmarks as they came into view. Now two of his grandchildren, whom he had never seen, were to be married there. On the platform a squadron of her Prussian regiment of Dragoons was drawn up, a gesture of Emperor William. She drove to the Schloss Ehrenburg through gaily decorated streets and, as she passed under a triumphal arch, two girls, dressed all in white, dropped flowers all about her.[30]

The wedding was gay and pretty. Empress Frederick told her daughter: "Ducky looked very charming and *distinguée*. She had a plain white silk gown with hardly any trimming, and Aunt Alice's wedding veil, a light slender diadem of emeralds with a sprig of orange blossom stuck in behind."[31] But, as had happened at other royal weddings, a sudden and unexpected event was to turn the spotlight from the bride. Next morning, as Queen Victoria was finishing breakfast, the Grand Duchess "Ella" hurried into the room, her lovely face lit with emotion and excitement. She announced: "Alicky and Nicky are engaged!"[32]

21

To Russia—With Love and Tears

THE FUTURE EMPRESS OF RUSSIA WAS GROOMED FOR HER ROLE under the personal supervision of Queen Victoria. Shortly after her brother's wedding "Alicky" presented herself at Windsor, and the necessary priorities—language, religion and health—were considered. Princess Alix was suffering from sciatica and her grandmother decided that this must be put to rights. So off she packed her to Harrogate to take the cure. With her went a crate of Russian manuals, a teacher, in the person of Mlle Schneider, reader to the Grand Duchess Serge, and, to keep her company, her niece, Alice of Battenberg, daughter of Prince and Princess Louis.

While at Harrogate the Princess used the name of Baroness Starckenburg, but the people of Yorkshire soon guessed her identity. She lived quietly in a boarding-house, worked hard at her lessons and fitted happily into her new surroundings. She became very fond of her landlady. When the latter had twins, the Princess stood sponsor for them in person. The boy was named Nicholas and the girl Alexandra.[1]

Princess Alix spent much of her time with her eldest sister. Lady Milford Haven wrote:

Alix returned to England with us and went to stop with Grandmama at Windsor. It was there I saw the great Duse and her company perform the "Locandiera" in the Waterloo Gallery. I have also seen her act in the "Masterbuilder" of Ibsen.

Sarah Bernhardt I have seen act in London "Adrienne Lecouvreur" and in a small one act play. To my mind Duse far surpassed her. One had not the impression that she was acting at all. She was absolutely the person she represented. She was, besides, much more attractive to look at.

Alix had been suffering for some time from attacks of sciatica and took a cure at Harrogate against it. I spent a couple of days with her there; we had great fun going about in tricycle bath chairs, worked by a man sitting behind us. We used to urge them to race each other. When her Harrogate cure was ended Alix came back to us at Walton and there Nicky joined us for the 20th to the 23rd of June. He came quite alone with his old valet and he and Alix were free to spend as much time as they liked together. Then this private intermezzo came to an end and we four were fetched by a Royal carriage with an outrider to go to Windsor, much to the surprise of the Waltonians, who never realised who the important people stopping with us had been.

Initial religious instruction for the Princess came from Dr. Boyd Carpenter, Bishop of Ripon, who pointed out the similarities between the Orthodox Church and the Church of England. He handed over to Father Yanisheff, the Emperor's confessor, who journeyed from Russia.

When the Cesarevitch arrived, he bore with him a casket of pearls and diamonds, sapphires and emeralds. The Queen, remembering the comparative poverty of her girlhood days, turned down the corners of her mouth and remarked: "Now, do not get too proud, Alicky."[2] "Nicky" found that a disadvantage of life at Windsor was that not for one moment was he allowed to be alone with his fiancée, the old Queen having a suspicious mind where such matters were concerned.

The great event of the Cesarevitch's visit was the christening of the first-born* of the Duke and Duchess of York, at which he was to be godfather. A special train took the Queen and her party from Windsor to Richmond and dense crowds greeted her as she drove with "Nicky" and "Alicky" across the park to the White

* Afterwards King Edward VIII and Duke of Windsor.

Lodge. "The dear fine baby, wearing the Honiton lace robe (made for Vicky's christening, worn by all our children and my English grandchildren), was brought in by Lady Eva Greville and handed to me. I then gave him to the Archbishop and received him back. He received the following names: Edward Albert Christian George Andrew Patrick David."[3] He was known as David.

The wedding of the Cesarevitch was planned for the spring, but in the autumn the unbelievable happened. The health of the giant Emperor began to fail. Alexander III was only forty-nine. He was so strong that he could bend a poker in his hands or a coin between his fingers. In 1888 he had held up the roof of a railway carriage to protect his family after the derailment of the royal train.[4] But now he grew tired when hunting, and lost his appetite. He complained that all his boots were too small for him. He had no patience with doctors, but at length allowed a German specialist to examine him. The verdict was an acute form of Bright's disease. Thereafter he was taken to the warm climate of Livadia in the Crimea. To those who watched him, it was as if a magnificent building was crumbling away.[5]

In the middle of October the Cesarevitch wired to Princess Alix to come to Livadia at once. There was no time to arrange a special train and the future Empress reached Russia as an ordinary traveller. On the way she was joined by the Grand Duchess "Ella". The last fifty miles of the journey were covered in an open carriage. Alexander insisted on getting from his bed and dressing to meet her. On the morning of 1st November he died, his head resting against the cheek of "Minnie", his wife. "Nicky" became Emperor Nicholas II. The body of Alexander was embalmed and carried by his relations to the Cathedral of Livadia.[6]

On the morning of the 2nd Princess Alix of Hesse was received into the Orthodox faith. For the occasion the ladies put off their mourning and appeared dressed all in white. The Princess now became the Grand Duchess Alexandra Feodorovna. The Dowager Empress wished her to marry "Nicky" at once, even before her husband was buried, as he had expressed the wish that there should be no delay. But the uncles of the new Emperor, consider-

ing that the public should be able to see the ceremony, decided
that the wedding should be held immediately after the funeral.[7]

Family mourners, including the Prince and Princess of Wales,
arrived at Livadia, and on the 8th began one of the strangest,
most spectacular journeys ever staged for a dead man, beginning
under the cloudless Crimean sky, with the air as mild as midsummer, and ending amid the domes of St. Petersburg, white
with snow.

Laurel leaves and branches of the cypress tree covered the road
as the Cossacks escorted the coffin to the jetty at Yalta, where lay
the cruiser *Pamiat Merkuria*. Six battleships of the Black Sea Fleet
escorted her over a dead calm sea to Sebastopol. It was the passing
of a Caesar.[8]

Be-plumed, black draped, decorated with the emblems of imperial power, the long train began its slow, thirteen-hundred-mile
journey, from one side of the Empire to the other. "Three times
it halted while the priests chanted their intercessions for the dead;
at every station, as it rumbled slowly through, crowds of peasants
fell upon their knees in prayer. At night it would draw up at some
wayside halt, and as it stood there, black and forbidding and surrounded by guards, people swarmed out of the countryside, and
knelt for hours in the frost."[9] The eerie nights and days had a
strong and lasting effect upon the travellers from Britain, upon the
young woman who had been plucked from the peace of Darmstadt
and Windsor, and upon the Prince of Wales, dreaming of the
pheasants at Sandringham. Throughout the land it was looked
upon as an ill omen that the future Empress should make her
baptismal journey in a saloon coupled up to a funeral car.

At Moscow the corpse lay in sepulchral state in the Archangel
Cathedral in the Kremlin. The crowds filed endlessly by and there
were lengthy services, all of which the Prince of Wales attended.
By this stage he was becoming somewhat worn. He had passed his
fifty-third birthday in the funeral train and had been robbed of
the gay house-party that was an annual event in Norfolk. As there
was still another full week of journeying and mourning services to
survive, he came to the conclusion that he needed some support.
And who better to give this than his only son, the Duke of York.

If there was one thing in the world that "Georgie" did not wish to do, it was to travel to St. Petersburg in November for a funeral. He always preferred the high seas to foreign railways, and he had a hearty respect for anarchists. In addition, he did not want to leave "May". After a shaky start, when he had learned that his new wife did not take kindly to the spartan furnishings of York Cottage which he had ordered from Maples, the couple had fallen deeply in love. It was the one occasion on which Queen Victoria's principle that, if a suitable young man and woman were put in a room with a double bed, eternal love was sure to be born, proved correct. The Duke even went so far as to say that he was sure he would become ill if long away from his "May".[10] But he was a dutiful son, so he drove with her to Wolferton station, and sadly set off eastwards.

Alexander III, his hand on the coffin's side, lay in the island-fortress Church of Saints Peter and Paul, the mausoleum of the Romanoffs. The procession which accompanied him there took two hours to pass any point.[11] There were daily services, to be attended in full uniform, and Prince George arrived in time to take part in seven.[12] He wrote to his wife:

> After the service was over, we all went up to [the] coffin which was open & kissed the Holy picture which he holds in his hand, it gave me a shock when I saw his dear face so close to mine when I stooped down, he looks so beautiful and peaceful, but of course the face has changed very much, it is a fortnight today.[13]

The Duke was a pall-bearer at the interment which took place on the 19th. The service lasted two and a half hours. At the opening chant the congregation knelt, unlit candles in their hands. Burning tapers were passed swiftly and noiselessly among them, and suddenly the whole cathedral was full of light. Then the old reign was over and the new one began. As the carriages rolled away the bands broke into lively music, cannon thundered, and the scene was set for the wedding of Emperor Nicholas II.[14]

A week later "Alicky" went to the altar of the chapel at the Winter Palace. She carried a candle and there was a crown on her head. Her dress was of silver tissue, the long train edged with ermine. The Imperial mantle of cloth of gold hung over her shoulders. The total weight was such that, when she was left alone for a moment after the ceremony, she found she could not move.[15]

There was no immediate honeymoon, the Emperor and Empress staying with their guests at the Anitchoff Palace. When they appeared next morning, the Prince of Wales was at breakfast. He afterwards remarked to Lord Carrington* that they behaved just as if nothing had happened.[16]

* Lord Chamberlain to the Queen, who had accompanied the Duke of York to St. Petersburg.

22

The Soldier's Return

IN THE AUTUMN OF 1895 PRINCE "LIKO" OF BATTENBERG WAS suffering from an attack of ten-year-itch. He was restless. He wished to be away from British shores. He boarded his boat and departed on a prolonged voyage.[1] His long absence was noted by those Press correspondents whose job it was to watch any untoward happenings in royal circles.

He was thirty-seven. For a decade he had circled Buckingham Palace, Balmoral, Windsor, and Osborne, varied by regal excursions to the Continent. His only relaxation had come with trips in his schooner, the *Sheilah*, but now even messing about with boats was not enough to satisfy him. The liveliest of the Battenberg brothers, he wanted a home of his own and an active military career.[2]

His brother, Louis, was Captain of the *Cambrian*, a cruiser of 5,000 tons,[3] and one of the most accomplished officers in the British Navy. "Sandro's" short career had been crammed with drama and excitement as Ruler of Bulgaria. "Franzjos", the youngest, still unmarried, had also had his adventures in Bulgaria and fought against the Serbs at the battle of Slivnitza. He was now in Paris and a central figure in a political intrigue. Prince Ferdinand of Saxe-Coburg and Gotha, who had succeeded

"Sandro" as Ruler of Bulgaria in 1887, had run foul of the Russians. A move was on foot to replace him with "Franzjos" of Battenberg, and his chances looked good if he could find the necessary financial backing. He therefore spent the Parisian evenings by the side of Miss Consuelo Vanderbilt, whose mother was in search of a son-in-law of high position. But the Prince's cool confidences about his ambitions proved startling to the American heiress, and even the dull routine of afternoon tea in an English stately home seemed preferable to bullets whining through the streets of Sofia and knives flashing in the cathedral. So she married the Duke of Marlborough.[4]

In contrast, "Liko's" days seemed tame indeed. And life in the royal homes was not always easy. He had won the confidence and the love of the Queen, but, by so doing he had aroused envy and opposition in certain directions.[5] There was some anti-German bias seeping from Sandringham, and true it was that the Prince of Wales often found that his young brother-in-law had more influence with the Sovereign than he had himself.

Boredom was his enemy, and this went so far as to include some of his relations. The chief offender was his brother-in-law, Alfred. In the smoking-room of an evening the Duke of Edinburgh and Coburg would either play the fiddle or take the chair and talk about himself for hour after hour. "Liko" gave up smoking.[6]

His main handicap was that he had to live his life according to the rules and memoranda laid down by Prince Albert over thirty years before. He went to endless pains to try to modernise his mother-in-law, and to a certain extent succeeded. He even made her dance again.[7] When he came on the scene, smoking was still a sin. At Balmoral the black sheep of the family, Prince Christian, had been allocated a dingy room furnished only with a table and chair where he could indulge in the vice in solitude. Access was through the servants' quarters and across the yard. "Liko" wheedled another room out of the Queen, and desks and easy chairs. He managed to get the rules relaxed at Osborne, but could do nothing about the Windsor custom that smoking was confined to the billiard-room after eleven.

It was to this restless Prince that young King Prempeh of Ashanti came to the rescue in October, 1895. King Prempeh was indulging in human sacrifice, slave trading and raids upon the peaceful people of the Gold Coast. He was also in league with French agents who were attempting to establish French influence in his territory. On 31st October the British Government sent an ultimatum demanding that a British Commissioner be allowed at Kumassi and that a British protectorate should be established over Ashanti. It was also decreed that all blood-letting and slave trading should end forthwith. No answer came to this ultimatum. It was therefore decided to send an expedition against King Prempeh, under the command of Colonel Sir Francis Scott, Inspector of the Gold Coast Constabulary. It was to be composed of a composite battalion of selected British troops, backed by a West African native contingent.[8]

On 11th November Lord Wolseley asked the Queen if it would be in order for Prince Christian Victor, son of Princess Helena and Prince Christian, to accompany the expedition. The Queen gave her permission, and thereby set a precedent. "Liko" saw his chance, and made his way to the War Office in search of similar permission. There he was discouraged. He was told that it was to be but a small and short affair, with little action and considerable danger from fever. If, it was suggested, he could wait a year or so, there was a much more interesting campaign coming up on the other side of the Continent. The Prince said he was sorry, but he could not wait that long. He did not reveal the reason. The reason was that he was being hotly pursued by a Lady.[9]

On 17th November he told the Queen of his plan. She answered, firmly, that "it would never do".[10] She summoned her physician, Sir James Reid, and asked him to convince the Prince of the inadvisability and the dangers. Next day she spoke with Princess Beatrice, who backed her husband. She told her mother that "Liko" "smarted under his enforced inactivity, and this was about the only occasion which presented no difficulties, as he would go as a volunteer without usurping anyone's place".[11] "Liko" prepared to sail.

When the news broke, rumour chased rumour through the

columns of the newspapers and round the chairs in the clubs. The one which annoyed the Prince most was that he would not accompany the battalion to which he was attached, but that a special saloon had been reserved for him in a passenger liner sailing from Liverpool for the Gold Coast.[12]

On 6th December he knelt before the Queen, kissed her hand, and said goodbye. Next morning he boarded the troop train at Aldershot. His wife waved to him from the platform and the bands played *Auld Lang Syne*.[13]

The Queen, considering that adequate arrangements had been made for the safe return of her son-in-law, which was expected at the latest in February, turned to another domestic event of immediate interest. The second child of the Duchess of York was due at any moment. On 14th December, "Mausoleum Day", a boy arrived at York Cottage, Sandringham. It was only fitting that he should be named Albert.* The family feared the result of this intrusion into her annual day of mourning, but fortunately she became possessed of "a feeling that it may be a blessing for the dear little boy".[14] In the event the blessings proved few, but included the best wife a man could ask for, two delightful daughters, some good shooting and the satisfaction of a job well done.

Surprisingly, the Queen had underestimated the portent of "the terrible fourteenth". Death was to cause the postponement of the baby's christening.

The British Expedition reached Cape Coast Castle on Christmas Day. On the 27th the march towards Kumassi began, in oppressive heat, through bush and swamp and forest. By the time the River Pra was reached a week later there were a number of casualties from fever among the British troops. At Prahsu "Liko" went for an evening walk with the camp commandant, Major Ferguson, who was looking unwell. Two days later Ferguson died. The Prince struggled on to Kwisa, forty miles short of Kumassi, and there malaria overcame him. The doctors ordered him back to the coast. On a rough stretcher, borne by natives, he began his journey. On the 12th the War Office received a telegram:

* Afterwards Duke of York and King George VI.

"Battenberg just arrived at Prahsee—state of health worse." Then the cable between Bathhurst and Accra broke down, and there was silence. The next news came five days later when the Prince reached Cape Coast Castle. There still seemed no grounds for anxiety. He was taken on board H.M.S. *Blonde*, England bound. A relapse followed, and he died on the morning of the 20th. On the same day the British expedition entered Kumassi.[15]

To preserve the body of the Prince it was placed in a tank contrived out of biscuit tins and filled with rum. This information reached the ears of his children, with the result that they suffered from nightmares for months afterwards.[16]

It was not until the 22nd that the news came to Osborne, and it resulted in a mental devastation as if a bomb had fallen from the winter sky. "God in His mercy help us!" wrote the Queen. "It seems as though the years '61 and '62 had returned. . . ."[17] Princess Beatrice had been preparing to go out to Madeira to meet her husband. Now her bags were put away. There began the long wait until 5th February when, at his wish, the Prince was to be buried at Whippingham Church.

To make the tragedy even more poignant there were family disagreements. It was questioned whether "Liko's" death was sufficient ground for the postponement of the christening of the Duke and Duchess of York's baby. Then the petulant and pretty Princess Louise began to behave in a most unfeeling way. Ever since she had been involved in a sleigh accident in Canada in 1880, when she had been dragged along the ice by the hair and lost an ear,[18] she had had an aversion to her husband and become so difficult that her mother seldom asked her to stay. Princess Victoria of Prussia, on a visit to Windsor, had commented to her mother: "Auntie Lou is not right at all—she complains of everything, but is charming as usual to look at."[19]

Now Princess Louise tried to take over the role of chief mourner. When the Duchess of Teck arrived at Osborne she found Princess Beatrice in tears. The Duchess wrote to her daughter:

Louise has alas! *froissed* her terribly by calmly announcing, that *she* (Louise) was Liko's *confidant* & Beatrice, nothing to him, indicated by a *shrug* of the shoulders!—This Beatrice told me herself. . . .[20]

On an afternoon of this dark February the Queen and Lady Erroll drove out from Osborne in a sociable to take the air. The Queen was swathed in black and silence. In an attempt to liven up the drive, Lady Erroll made the offering of how nice it was to think of when they would meet all their dear ones in Heaven. The Queen answered with a straight "Yes". "We will all meet in Abraham's bosom," went on Lady Erroll, encouraged. "I will *not* meet Abraham," retorted the Queen, with the "r" much pronounced. "*Nothing* will *induce* me to meet Abraham."[21]

In the deaths of the Prince Consort and Prince Henry of Battenberg there was a similarity. Few realised the worth of their work until after they had gone. Prince "Liko" had played a vital, though passive, part in the Victorian story. He had come into the life of the Queen at a time when she was battered down by the deaths of John Brown and Prince Leopold. By his fun and his liveliness he had arrested her slide into old age, and by his modern thinking had saved her Court from becoming antiquated. A man at her right hand was an essential to Queen Victoria, and he was a worthy successor to those who had gone before. He had her complete confidence and trust, and he never abused them. That he was not content only to be at her right hand was because he was a Battenberg, for Battenbergs like to climb high with their own, unaided strength.

From this moment on the Queen lavished even greater love and care upon Prince Henry's children. Golden-haired Ena sat often by her in her carriage. Alexander, the eldest boy, she sent to Wellington. It proved a shock for both sides. The boys there thought him a little Lord Fauntleroy. The Prince considered that they were a lot of bloodthirsty hooligans.[22] Unaccustomed to handling loose cash, he soon ran into financial difficulties. He applied to his grandmother for more money. She replied that he must learn to keep within his allowance. A few days later he informed her that all was now in order, as he had sold her last letter to a boy and was in funds again.* [23]

---

* The Marquess of Carisbrooke was the first member of the Royal Family to enter business life.

The Queen had referred to Prince "Liko" as "the bright sunshine in our home".[24] When the sun set, the twilight came in fast. But there was left to her what she termed "her swansong" yet to sing.

23

Russian Roulette

O N WEDNESDAY, 23RD SEPTEMBER 1896, LADY MONKSWELL wrote in her diary:

> This is a great day all over the world. Today the dear old Queen has reigned longer than any British Sovereign. What a day of emotions for her. The young Emperor of Russia, Nicholas II, & the Empress, our Princess Alix, came to her at Balmoral & she sat waiting to receive them in a room full of trophies from Sebastopol! It was the anniversary of the fall of Sebastopol.[1]

It had been the idea of Lord Salisbury that the visit should be paid at this historic moment, for British troops were active in the Sudan and good relations with Russia were of the utmost importance. The Queen wished the visit to be private and informal. The Prince of Wales thought otherwise. He saw this as a heaven-sent opportunity to impress Russia, and the world, and he insisted that full ceremonial was essential. All the way from Leith there was pomp and ceremony. On Ballater platform the Duke and Duchess of York and the Duke of Cambridge, with a Guard of Honour of the Black Watch, were waiting to greet the Emperor and Empress. As the light went down an escort of Scots Greys led the cavalcade of carriages along the Deeside road. There were bonfires on every hill, the church bells were ringing, and men of

the Crathie and Ballater Volunteers and the Balmoral Highlanders, bearing blazing torches, lined the procession to either
side. Then, as they approached the Castle, the Queen's pipers took
the lead and their music filled the valley.[2] It was the most splendid,
touching moment in all the Balmoral story. So it was that Alice's
little girl, who had been brought up at Darmstadt, with second-
hand toys and a preponderance of stewed apples and rice pudding
in her diet, came back to the home which her mother had known
so well and loved the best.

It was soon noted that the new "Alicky" and "Nicky", the
Emperor and Empress of All the Russias, were very different to
the young lovers who had frolicked at Windsor and Osborne but
two years before. "Alicky" was a haughty woman dressed in
white serge. She no longer smiled. "Nicky" vacillated and was
impossible to pin down. In fact he was not enjoying Balmoral at
all. He was cold, he told his mother. The weather was terrible.
There were so many of his wife's relations there all wanting to
talk with her, that he hardly saw her at all. The Prince of Wales
dragged him out shooting, but the stags disappeared and he had
to be content with a brace of grouse.[3] His jewelled ikon seemed out
of setting against the tartan wallpaper. To supplement the army
of detectives, who hid behind every bush and tree to guard him
against any attempts by Nihilists, he kept a piece of dried garlic
in his pocket. He apparently believed that this talisman would
ensure his safety.[4]

Politically, the visit had little significance. Queen Victoria
could deal with a strong man, a clever man, a vain and vauntful
man like the grandson who ruled in Germany, but she could make
little progress with a weak man, who wavered and told half-truths,
and turned away his eyes. She now admitted that politics meant
more than family.

Lady Milford Haven watched the Emperor closely:

> I remember Nicky once at luncheon saying to Ernie how he
> envied his being a constitutional Monarch on whom the blame for
> all the mistakes made by his ministers was not heaped. Under other
> circumstances, Nicky would have made a remarkably good constitu-
> tional Sovereign, for he was in no way narrow minded, nor obsessed

by his high position. If one could have boiled down Nicky and William in one pot you would have produced an ideal Emperor of Russia. His father's dominating personality had stunted any gifts for initiative in Nicky.

The visit was probably most enjoyed by young David of York, who represented the fourth generation. He revelled in the pettings from the royal galaxy, and treated his great-grandmother as if she was a recalcitrant sheepdog. "Get up, Gangan," he would say as he tried to get her out of her chair. Failing, he would turn to an Indian servant and order, "Man pull it."[5]

A welcome diversion was created by the arrival of Mr. Downey with his new camera which took moving pictures. He set it up on the terrace and self-consciously the royalties walked up and down. The children were told to jump.[6] Throughout these, and many other, photographs, the face of Alexandra Feodorovna remained unsmiling, stern, her eyes hard. On 3rd October she wrote to her old governess, Miss Jackson; "Next Saturday morning, God grant, we shall be at dear Darmstadt."[7] So, with relief in certain quarters, the Balmoral interlude came to an end.

What then had brought about the change in the young Romanoff and his innocent bride from Hesse, she who had been known as "Princess Sunshine", in two short years? In her the change was more clearly defined. It was noticed everywhere, even at "dear Darmstadt". Meriel Buchanan, daughter of Sir George Buchanan, saw her there:

> ... Watching the official reception, the mounted troops, the State carriages, I wondered what had brought that look of cold aloofness to the face of the woman I had known as Princess Alix of Hesse.[8]

The cause of the transformation was undoubtedly the sudden and unexpected death of Alexander III. On average expectation "Nicky" could have looked for another fifteen to twenty years of preparation and training before taking over his difficult role. The same handicap applied to "Alicky". While her mother-in-law, the Dowager Empress Marie, formerly Princess Dagmar of Denmark, had been allowed fourteen years to prepare to be Empress, she had been limited to a handful of days. From the start, the job proved too big for the young couple to handle.

The troubles for Princess Alix had begun immediately on her arrival at St. Petersburg. The big balls, to which as many as two thousand were invited, were a nightmare to her. She admitted herself that, during the *cercles*, she wished the floor would open and swallow her up. She blushed, and her French deserted her. She was by nature very shy, and she received little assistance from her ladies-in-waiting. They gave her no advance information as to who people were or what should be said to them, apparently considering that the mere honour of meeting the Empress was sufficient in itself. So "Alicky" either stood silent before those who were presented to her, or reddened and made unsuitable remarks. Her timidity was put down to haughtiness, and her reserve, to pride. The traditional etiquette of the Russian Court was unvarying, and any departure from it was unforgivable. Because she had had so little time to learn it, the new Empress did make mistakes, and accordingly was not forgiven.[9]

There were few young people with whom the new Empress could make friends, for the Court was composed of contemporaries of Alexander III, and they were not old enough to wish to hand over their world to a new generation. They still looked towards the Dowager Empress, who, by a decree of her dead husband, held precedence over "Alicky". Empress Marie could, and undoubtedly would, have helped her daughter-in-law to a far greater extent if "Alicky" could have brought herself to seek that aid. But the reserve in her forbade it. Also there was in the Empress Marie the same characteristic that showed clearly in her sister, the Princess of Wales, afterwards Queen Alexandra. Both sisters considered that their husbands reigned on after they were dead· Neither gave high rating to daughters-in-law. In competition with the Empress Marie, an accomplished woman with all the imperial tricks up her sleeve, "Alicky" had little chance.

Nicholas II also suffered from the handicap of youth. He had three large and outspoken uncles with whom to deal, and to control them was needed a stronger will than his. Crash would go their fists upon his table as they demanded the fulfilment of their wishes, until "Nicky" came to dread their visits. The father, on like occasions, had shouted, "Stop playing the Tsar, Serge," but the son could not do that. It was the same with rival rulers. Alexander III had cut the German Emperor down to size with the devastating remark: "Don't act like a dancing dervish, Willy. Look at yourself in the mirror."[10] Nicholas II could not do that.

The result was that "Nicky" and "Alicky" withdrew into a little world of their own, a world in which religion was prominent, a world in which the belief in the sanctity of their imperial role became all-devouring. The weekly family dinners ceased. When with her relations the Empress hardly spoke at all. The eternal silences were most embarrassing. At last the Grand Duke Vladimir stumbled on a trick to start the colloquial flow. He would deliberately make a mistake when quoting from the *Almanach de Gotha*. The Empress would then spend an hour putting him to rights. He found the strain of this better than struggling to find something to say.[11] Count Bernstorff, unaware of this trick, once spent an hour with her in the waiting-room of Tsarskoe-Selo station, when the train bringing Princess Irene and Prince Henry from Germany was delayed, and it proved an experience that he was to remember all his life.[12]

Ill luck dogged "Alicky", and the Curse of the Coburgs hung in the offing. As a bride, she had travelled behind a funeral car. It was hoped that her first child would be a boy, a strong and healthy heir. This would have delighted Russia. But, on 15th November 1895, instead of three hundred guns, only one hundred and one were fired, denoting a girl.* Mrs. Carnegie,† whose husband was in the British Embassy at St. Petersburg, described the christening:

> The baby was dipped three times into the water in the orthodox way and then was straight laid into a pink satin quilted bag, undried and undressed, & returned to the gamp, who was very important in corded silk. . . . The Empress had a very bad time, & I was told by one of her ladies that the Emperor was crying in the next room, & the Empress Marie on her knees praying. Now all has gone well, & they say the Empress is almost well & nursing her baby which has astonished all the Russians. It is so nice of her . . .[13]

* Grand Duchess Olga Nicolaevna.
† Afterwards the Hon. Lady Carnegie.

In May 1896 came their Coronation, and with it stark tragedy. Moscow, dawn, 30th May:

A great popular fête had been arranged to take place on the Khodinsky Plain, a large park outside the city. Thousands of people had been encamped upon this open ground throughout the night, and daybreak brought great numbers of fresh arrivals, until, by six o'clock in the morning, some 500,000 persons were assembled. Gifts of "Coronation" mugs, cake and sweetmeats were to be distributed to the populace from a number of booths, round which no sufficient barriers had been erected to facilitate orderly approach and departure. Soon after 6 a.m. the crush round the booths became so severe that the officials began to dispense the gifts. The result was appalling. The surging mass of human beings swayed forward, those behind scarcely realising what was happening, and with such terrible momentum did the great concourse advance that no power could stop its progress. Hundreds of victims were trampled underfoot by their fellows in the gangways round the booths, and many of the officials perished. Order was at length restored by the arrival of a military force, but not until more than three thousand persons had perished, and many hundreds besides had been fatally or seriously injured. The Emperor and Empress were terribly distressed by the news of the awful catastrophe, but subsequently took their places in the imperial pavilion, and the fête proceeded to its end, for the sake of the survivors and in the interests of public order, even while the work of removing the injured and the dead was still going on.[14]

So read the description of a correspondent on the spot. But behind the scenes fierce quarrels broke out among the Royal Family, one section demanding the resignation of the Grand Duke Serge, Governor of Moscow, who had been largely responsible for the arrangements. The scene of the tragedy had previously been used as a training ground for military engineers. The trenches which they had dug were now filled with corpses.[15] The Grand Duke had been warned of this danger, but had taken no action. The older generation still backed him, and the cold, cruel smile never left his lips.

For that night the French Ambassador had arranged a ball of fantastic extravagance, against a backdrop of treasures brought from Paris. Some of the Emperor's family wished the ball to be cancelled. Others said that arrangements had now gone too far.

The ball was held, the Emperor and Empress attended, but there were many who turned away from it, sick at heart, as the grim figures from the hospitals and mortuaries rose and rose.[16]

Lady Milford Haven wrote of the celebrations:

> The coronation itself was a magnificent sight. Alix looked beautiful in her robes, crown and the obligatory side-curls. Nicky said the great Imperial Prayer in a clear and moving voice. One little thing, which has since been pointed out as of ill-omen, was when part of the Regalia, carried by Count Heiden, slipped off the cushion he held and would have fallen to the ground had it not been caught up in time. Admiral Count Heiden was a remarkable old man. The son of the Commander of the Russian Fleet at Navarino, he himself as a young officer had taken part in the battle in 1827.
>
> Among the foreign guests there were some interesting figures—the Emir of Boukhara in his silk kaftan adorned with Russian General's epaulettes mounted in diamonds; the great Li-Hung-Chang in his yellow jacket; and the Bishop of Peterborough in full canonicals with his mitre and crook staff. Sitting among the guests was an Indian Maharajah, a little spectacled man who assisted the following year at Grandmama's Jubilee. He was so keen to see the Russian Coronation that he accepted the condition that he must uncover his head in church, the same as the Christian is obliged to take off his shoes in a Mosque. There I saw him bareheaded with his turban in his hand during the ceremony.
>
> The Papal Nuncio in his robes was an imposing figure with dignified manners. Being a true Italian, however, he could forget his dignity when impulse moved him. Prince Ferdinand of Bulgaria (later King) was at that moment very much in the black books of the Holy See. He, a Roman Catholic, without any warning to the Vatican, had had his son and heir, Boris, baptised into the Orthodox Church. On his way to the Coronation banquet, as he passed through the room in which the Cardinal was standing, the latter, to mark his contempt, made the gesture of spitting at him. Ferdinand, not to be beaten, spat back!

The accident to the Regalia, involving the Imperial Chain, deeply upset Nicholas II and seemed to bring to him a sense of mystic resignation. Into his character crept "the discrepant mingling of a pacific idealism with an obscurantist faith in autocracy and brute force".[17] Both he and his wife lost their bond of sympathy with ordinary folk. In the Empress it became more and more marked as the years passed. She became unfeeling for the wishes and hardships of the people. Once, when pregnant, she gave strict instructions to the police, before travelling to the Crimea, that no crowds were to be allowed to gather at the stations to watch the royal train go by. But at one halt a crowd did gather, a crowd of peasants in their Sunday clothes, who had driven in from the countryside. Furious, she refused to pull back the curtains which hid her, nor would she allow her children to be seen.[18]

Her behaviour was completely out of character with the Hessian family from which she sprung, and also with that of Victoria and Albert. Whilst her mother had been filled with a like ferment of religious obsession, that ferment had brought her ever nearer and nearer to the poor and to the sick. Her father had walked happily with the man in the street. To find a parallel one must return to the behaviour of her great-grandfather, Edward, Duke of Kent, when he was Governor of Gibraltar. His autocratic policy there led to his recall.

Some of the iron which entered her soul stemmed from the Russian attitude towards health. Ladies were not expected to reveal that they felt unwell, or even that they were pregnant. Although the carrying of the regalia of an Empress demanded the physique of an Amazon, no allowance was made for weaker frames. The winter of St. Petersburg brought her constant ills, as it had done to her sad Hessian great-aunt, who had trod the same path half a century before. Yet the winter was the time of the Russian "Season", with its constant round of festivities. It was not revealed that the Empress was absent from them because she was ill. Few knew that sciatica bound her to a wheel-chair. Child-bearing further sapped her strength, as did her insistence on feeding her babies herself. All her daughters, with the exception of Olga, the eldest, were born in the spring. Sometimes for months before her confinement she had to keep to her bed, and the "Seasons" passed without sight of she who should have held the stage—the Empress.

Impatiently Russia waited for the coming of an heir, but there came no thunder of three hundred guns. Grand Duchesses filled the nursery. Tatiana was born in 1897, just before Queen Victoria's Diamond Jubilee. Marie followed in 1899 and Anastasia in 1901. The next year the Empress had a miscarriage and was very ill.[19] Hope faded. But on 12th August 1904 the guns roared the full fusillade to mark the birth of the Cesarevitch Alexei Nicolaevitch. He was covered with gold and ermine and made Colonel of many regiments. The Prince of Wales* and the Emperor of Germany were godfathers at his christening, and splendours of the celebration helped to relieve the anxieties over the war which Russia was waging with Japan. On 27th May, the anniversary of the coronation of "Nicky" and "Alicky", the Russian fleet was crippled at the battle of Tsoushima. The guns of the anarchists cracked once more. Then the Empress noticed that her baby son suffered from bumps when he tumbled at play. A dread terror seized her, but she kept it to herself. He fell as he climbed into a boat, and internal haemorrhage set in. Then she knew, and the doctors knew. There was no escape for her from the curse of haemophilia, the curse which had broken the heart and spirit of her mother, had robbed her grandmother of a son, and even now was blighting the happiness of her sister Irene and her Aunt Beatrice. She turned towards the dark shadow of Rasputin, believing that in the satanic cave of him lay a pool of magic healing. His haunting voice called her on, blind, unheeding of the portents, along the path which led towards Ekaterinburg.

---

* Afterwards King George V.

The marriage of Prince Andrew of Greece and Princess Alice of Battenberg at Darmstadt in 1903

Eleonore, Princess of Solms-Hohensolms-Lich
Wife of Grand Duke Ernest Louis of Hesse and the Rhine

24

La Ronde

A S THE LAST SUMMERS OF THE OLD CENTURY TICKED AWAY
Wolfsgarten became the scene of the "with it" weekends
for young royals. The over-thirties were old and out, and
elderly members of the Court and the suites stayed behind at
Darmstadt, sipping tea and shaking their heads, and dreaming of
the days of Grand Duke Louis and his uncle before him.

The bells were ringing for the end of an era, and the beginning
of a new. Now there were electric light and telephones, bicycles
and motor-cars, and people were dreaming of wireless and
powered flight. The ghost of Albert was dim.

Etiquette went by the board at these parties organised by the
Grand Duke and Duchess of Hesse. Nicknames ousted titles.
Guests did as they liked. They sat on the floor and painted pictures,
not the classical sketches of Queen Victoria's youth, but fresh in
idea, in line, in colour—"cheeky, impertinent modernism, with
its usual contempt for established principles".[1]

They rode white horses through the woods and jousted on
bicycles. They went in a party to Frankfurt races. If someone
there was important enough to have a special train standing by,
they would use it to make an expedition to a place of interest.
They also became rough. By a reedy pond the Grand Duke had

built a chute, down which a flimsy boat descended at speed. On its impact with the water the occupants were showered with mud and weed. Lovely Georgina Buchanan, wife of the British Minister, was inveigled into riding in the machine. She was wearing a new and very best dress. By malice aforethought, the boat was overturned, and a limp, black creature struggled to the bank.[2]

In the evenings, in the lamplight, they would read aloud to one another from blood-curdling thrillers such as *Dracula* or *The Beetle*,[3] or play "Consequences", with scant respect for the feelings of others. Often they would dance all night. The Duke and Duchess of York—"Georgie" and "May"—very respectable and much married, visited their Hessian cousins, arriving at seven in the morning. The Grand Duke and Duchess met them on the platform and smilingly announced that they had been dancing until four.[4]

Among the guests at the house-parties were to be found Prince Nicholas of Greece,* Prince Henry of Prussia and Princess Irene, the Grand Duke and Duchess Serge, the Emperor and Empress of Russia (although the Empress played little part in the festivities), Russian relations of the Grand Duchess Victoria Melita and chosen members of the international set.

Princess Daisy of Pless arrived.

> One night we played *Consequences*—I think it is called. . . . The Grand Duchess asked: "Why does virtue take so many different forms?" To which someone replied: "Because, being a woman, she likes to change dresses." . . . I asked: "Do you believe in eternal joy after death?" To which Prince Nicholas replied: "I believe that joy is a sensation entirely moral and that, as such, it is inseparable from the soul." I also wanted to know: "Would you rather have a great love that might die, or an everlasting affection?" Prince Nicholas said: "Before having experienced either I am inclined to believe the second preferable; but usually a man's egotism is more flattered by the passion he inspires, however brief, than by winning a sincere and lasting affection."[5]

The Grand Duchess wanted to know why one so often hurt the person one loves best, which, in view of later events, was a most telling enquiry.[6]

* Father of Princess Marina, Duchess of Kent.

To Nicholas II, Wolfsgarten and Darmstadt were oases where he could relax for short intervals, oases in the desert of responsibilities and troubles through which he struggled at home. There was the relief of being able to call relations by their Christian names, an intimacy seldom allowed in Russia. At a dinner at the German Embassy his brother-in-law, Prince Henry, had made a remark to him, prefacing it with "Nicky". To which the Emperor had replied: "Don't call me Nicky in public."[7] At the family home of his wife he behaved like a schoolboy, was completely undignified in his pranks and took his fun while he could.

The wild parties were also a safety-valve for his host and hostess, the Grand Duke Ernest Louis, and Victoria Melita, his wife. People, gay people, were an essential additive to their lives. Without people their married life was unbearable, for, even after a year of conjugal living, they were drifting towards the rocks of divorce.

"Ernie" and "Ducky" had been allowed little real chance to get to know one another during their engagement period. Because they both were great fun at parties and both loved art and painting, they, and their families, thought that they were suited to one another. But they were quick to find that it needs more than a fiesta and a picture to make a marriage. Their channels flowed from a background of very different hills. Her father was a sailor. Prince Alfred had been the most mischievous and pugnacious of Queen Victoria's children, and later sown his wild oats, in particular with a young lady of Malta. Her haughty mother was the daughter of Alexander II, who had discarded Marie of Hesse for Catherine Dolgoruky. The amiability in the Grand Duke came from his father. The sensitive, idealistic strain came from Princess Alice, back to the Prince Consort and his mother, the tragic Louise of Gotha.

Victoria Melita soon lost patience with the constraints and traditions of the little German Court. She did not feel her way, as Princess Alice had done, through the thicket of hostility that met the stranger. She did not devote herself, as Princess Alice had done, to bringing progress gently by introducing the necessary organisation. Grand Duke Louis III had purposely kept progress in retard, two wars had impoverished the Grand Duchy, and there had been no Grand Duchess since the tragic death of Alice in 1878. Hesse now needed a very tactful *Landesmutter*.

Instead the Hessians received a highly volatile young woman, plunging from moods of jubilation to those of deep melancholy. She was contemptuous of local practice. She resented the inroads on her time resulting from the many duties which she was expected to perform, often a legacy from Princess Alice. "She forgot to answer letters; she postponed paying visits to boring old relations; at official receptions she often caused great offence by talking to somebody who amused her, and ignoring people whose high standing gave them importance."[8]

Such dereliction led to reproaches by the Grand Duke, and the reproaches led to temper. Not the temper born of subdued anger, but the overt variety, expressed by the dropping of a tray of tea things to the floor or the projection of any handy object. "Ernie" did not appreciate such treatment.

Horses were another bone of contention. While the Grand Duke regarded them as a means of transport, his wife adored them. She had horses from Vienna and horses from Russia, and ponies from England. She would ride out into the woods and forget all about appointments. She was equally happy with a high-stepper in a dog-cart or when flicking and calling over the backs of a six-in-hand. She had a great black stallion called Bogdan. He would obey no one but her. She would let him go in the courtyard and he would prance round helping himself to the decorations on the hats of any ladies unfortunate to be about at the time. One day he got the seat out of the Grand Duke's pants as he bolted up the steps to seek safety in the house.[9] Such antics did not lead to marital bliss.

Three Empresses found themselves involved in this emotional crisis. Victoria, Empress of India, had arranged the marriage, but now found that her daughter-in-law was loth to bend the knee. The Empress of Russia, who had hastened her own marriage to avoid having to play second fiddle to Victoria Melita in Hesse, was wholeheartedly behind her brother. "Dona", the Empress of Germany, was equally strong in backing the Grand Duchess, "the fighting Grand Duchess" as she was known at the Berlin Court. She was also known as "the little spitfire".

Victoria Melita liked the grandeur and the vastness of the Prussian mode of life, and it was said that her temper and discontent stemmed largely from the patronage she received from the Empress.[10] She was a foil for "Dona". They both loved horses, and liked to ride in the massive military parades organised with such delight by the Emperor. On the parade ground the ample bottom of the Kaiserin could be seen slowly rising and falling to a regular movement, while behind her pirouetted the slim and lovely figure of the Grand Duchess of Hesse.

For at least once in her life, the Empress Frederick kept free of an imbroglio, although she did express the opinion that "Ducky" was prettier than any of the Hesse girls, even "Ella".[11] She admired the way she dressed and did her hair, avoiding "the mops" to which her own daughters adhered:

> She is wonderfully handsome with the graceful fashion she wears her hair, in large waves back over the head showing the roots turned back in the middle of her forehead, which is so pretty because one sees that it is a person's own hair. The towsel and fringe like a thick sponge over the forehead suits Aunt Alix* but no one else. It spoils Maudie's† pretty face, and May‡ wears a wig front. . . .[12]

The only child of the Grand Duke and Duchess was born in March 1895. During the winter the Empress Frederick noted that "Ducky" was "looking very pulled, thin and drawn in the face, which usually denotes a little girl, as people say, but these sayings are mostly nonsense".[13] But the guess was correct, and the daughter was named Elizabeth. The Grand Duchess was to become pregnant on two subsequent occasions, but she was impatient and refused to take care of herself, and no babies arrived.

In 1896 came a journey to Moscow for the coronation of Nicholas II. Victoria Melita and Marie, her sister, in dresses of cloth of gold decorated with autumn leaves and violet irises,[14]

* The Princess of Wales, afterwards Queen Alexandra.
† Of Wales, afterwards Queen of Norway.
‡ Duchess of York, afterwards Queen Mary.

261

stole the ball scene. "Ducky" stole also the heart of the Grand Duke Cyril. He did not ask for it back, but took hers instead. Cyril was the handsome son of the Grand Duke Vladimir, one of the giant brothers of Alexander III. The birth of the love affair was clear to see. Like was calling to like.

Rumours began to buzz around Darmstadt as wasps buzz round a jam pot. Old ladies, over their tea, passed around photographs of the Grand Duke Cyril, remarking how good-looking he was. More and more malicious grew the buzzings. The Grand Duke, it was said, was visiting a lady in the town. Strange and wild were the tales told of the parties at Wolfsgarten. Echoes reached the ears of Queen Victoria. She summoned her Chargé d'Affaires. Mr. Buchanan was in a quandary. On the one side he was in a position of trust, on the other lay his duty. He said very little, but the Queen was wise. Tears washed her tired eyes and she said: "I arranged that marriage. I will never try and marry anyone again."[15]

Her long match-making career was over. The failures included not only Louise and Lorne, "Ernie" and "Ducky", but also another granddaughter, Marie Louise, Helena's daughter, whose marriage to Prince Aribert of Anhalt was proving a major disaster. In the Queen's young day duty and family had overridden the truth that, in life partnership, one loves and the other suffers to be loved. In the new, fast-moving world the amount of suffering to be endured was becoming less and less.

Queen Victoria would not tolerate divorce. When, in due season, the Grand Duke Ernest and his consort implored her to allow them to part, she not only would not hear of it but expressed herself very strongly about the proposition.[16] What troubled her most was the fate of little Princess Elizabeth, whom she adored. When she reached eighty in 1899 it was Elizabeth whom she asked to see first and wish her happy birthday.[17] "Granny Gran" the child called her, and the Queen called her "my precious".[18] Then death took the protecting arm from around the little girl.

The Grand Duke Ernest Louis was fortunate in being able to rely on the commonsense of his eldest sister. Lady Milford Haven commented on the estrangement:

In October 1901 I had a letter from Ernie, who had been spending a short time at Capri, saying that Ducky had informed him that she had decided to ask for a divorce. I was really less surprised and startled by her decision than he. Though both had done their best to make a success of their marriage, it had been a failure. Their characters and temperaments were quite unsuited to each other and I had noticed how they were gradually drifting apart. As I had known Ducky well from a child, since the time that she lived with her parents at San Antonio, she had often spoken freely to me on the subject of her married life. She had confidence, that I hope was not misplaced, in my fairness of judgement and, in spite of my being devoted to my brother, I can only say that I thought then, and still think, that it was best for both that they should part from each other.

On 21st December 1901 divorce ended the marriage of Grand Duke Ernest Louis and Grand Duchess Victoria Melita. She returned to Coburg to live with her mother, Princess Elizabeth, sharing her time between her parents. Once again there was no *Landesmutter* in Darmstadt. For some of the months there was a fair-haired, blue-eyed girl to watch tripping home from school. She was called Princess Sunshine, as her Aunt "Alicky" had been.

Europe seethed with the scandal of divorce. The Empress of Russia took a hard line against the sister-in-law whom she had never really liked. In unison for once, King Edward VII and the Emperor William clothed themselves in garb of outraged indignation, each emerging pure white from a speckled past. But "the fighting Grand Duchess" fired back, and she never forgave.

In the autumn of 1903 the Grand Duke Ernest Louis and Elizabeth stayed with the Emperor and Empress of Russia at their shooting box at Skierniewice in Poland. Elizabeth had the bacillus of typhoid in her before she left Darmstadt. She sickened quickly and died on 16th November, before her mother could reach her.[19] Heart-broken, the Grand Duke returned with her body and buried her at the Rosenhöhe. All kinds of rumours circulated as to the cause of her death, including one that the child had eaten a poisoned dish intended for the Emperor. But the post-mortem showed the truth.

Two years later the Grand Duke married Eleonore, Princess of Solms-Hohensolms-Lich, and with her found true happiness. They had two sons, George Donatus, born in November 1906, and Louis, in the same month of 1908.[20] November was proving the vital month in the lives of the Hesses, and was to prove more vital still.

In the same year that Ernest Louis remarried, Victoria Melita was wed to the Grand Duke Cyril. Alexandra Feodorovna poured all of her pent-up fury upon the head of her former sister-in-law, refusing to receive her at St. Petersburg. On her instigation the Grand Duke Cyril was deprived of all his decorations and privileges and banished from Russia. His father, Vladimir, ranted and raved, and threw his decorations down on the table before his nephew, the Emperor. But "Nicky" stood firm. It was not until 1909 that the Grand Duke and Duchess Cyril, with their two little girls, were allowed back to Russia.[21]

Theirs was a great love. The climax of it came in 1917. The Bolshevik patrols were after them. She was pregnant. He took her in his arms and carried her to safety across the frozen Gulf of Finland.[22]

25

Swan-Song and Wedding March

ON 22ND JUNE 1897 QUEEN VICTORIA SANG HER SWAN-SONG all the way from Buckingham Palace to St. Paul's and back again. It was her Diamond Jubilee.

A never-to-be-forgotten day. No one ever, I believe, has met with such an ovation as was given to me, passing through those six miles of streets. . . .[1]

I wore a dress of black silk, trimmed with panels of grey satin veiled with black net and steel embroideries, and some black lace, my lovely diamond chain, given me by my younger children, round my neck. My bonnet was trimmed with creamy white flowers, and white aigrette and some black lace.[2]

She was the flagship of Britain and the Empire. She meant more to a nation than anyone ever had before her. But now the guns of fate opened up upon her and the firing went on until, with the first year of a new century, she settled slowly into the waters of eternity. She was still the admiral and still upon the bridge.

Swiftly tragedy followed upon tragedy. Crisis and worry strained the weak eyes and stiffening legs. In the summer of 1898 the Empress Frederick was thrown from her horse, which had reared with terror at the approach of a traction engine.[3] She delayed consulting a specialist. When she did so it was to receive the verdict

I*

that she had cancer, and no longer than two years to live.[4] They were years of agonising pain and it was doubted whether she would outlast her mother.* The Duchess of Teck died. So did Annie Macdonald, the Queen's beloved wardrobe maid,[5] and Mrs. Simmonds, who kept the shop at Balmoral. She felt their loss more than she did the passing of Mr. Gladstone. King Humbert of Italy was assassinated. Elizabeth, Empress of Austria, was stabbed at Geneva. With the knife still in her back she walked on to a lake steamer, and died. The Empress's sister, the Duchesse d'Alençon, was burned to death, with two hundred others, in a fire which raged through a charity bazaar in Paris. In 1899 Prince Alfred of Coburg died of consumption, and his father of cancer the following year. The Queen had to settle the question of the Coburg succession. She took "young Charlie" of Albany, posthumous son of Prince Leopold, away from Eton and despatched him to Germany.

But the strain of battle was the primary reason for the shortening of her days. From the outbreak of the Boer War in October 1899 she gave every ounce of her energy, of her courage, of her humanity and of her wisdom into the effort for victory. She suffered personal loss. Her grandson, Prince Christian Victor of Schleswig-Holstein, who had been with Prince Henry of Battenberg in the Ashanti campaign, died of enteric fever contracted on the battlefields of South Africa. He was the third Prince of her time to die in the continent which she had never seen.

Rays of sunshine came to her at the births of great-grandchildren. A clutch of twenty arrived in her twilight years. The last to be born in her lifetime was Louis Francis Albert Victor Nicholas of Battenberg.† The scene was Frogmore House, Windsor, where Prince and Princess Louis were living at the time. He was very much "a tail-end Charlie", as the brother above him in age was already eight, and his elder sister, fifteen. Louis early distinguished himself by knocking Queen Victoria's spectacles off her nose at his christening.[6]

Lady Milford Haven wrote of this day:

* The Empress Frederick died in August 1901.
† Afterwards Lord Louis Mountbatten and Earl Mountbatten of Burma.

On June 25th 1900, at about 6 a.m., Dickie was born, a healthy child, weighing over 8 lbs. He was christened on the 17th of July at Frogmore House. The Christening took place in the Duchess of Kent's drawing room, to the left of the gallery, at 5.30 p.m. It was a very hot day and Grandmama, who always suffered terribly from the heat—she never perspired, her hands used to be like hot bricks—had given orders that the room was to be made as cool as possible. To do this, the servants had put buckets full of ice behind and underneath some of the chairs, whose loose covers hid the buckets. Dr. Elliott, Dean of Windsor, who performed the ceremony, walked to Frogmore from Windsor in good time and was shown into the Christening room, where he sat down to await the arrival of the Queen. Unfortunately, the chair he selected was over an ice cooler and he did not realise this until he felt his legs thoroughly chilled. As a result he got sciatic inflammation in his hip, of which he was never cured. He hobbled about with the help of a stick ever afterwards.

Dickie was a very lively baby. As soon as he was handed over to Grandmama, he waved one of his little arms about so violently that he knocked her spectacles off, and his hand became entangled in her cap-veil. This she took in very good part.

She was not always so lenient towards the behaviour of small children. I remember when Alice* was a little girl of about four, she, like many grandchildren and great grandchildren before her, refused to kiss Grandmama's hand, and when Grandmama, in a severe voice said "naughty child" and slapped her hand, Alice slapped back, saying "naughty Grandmama". I hurriedly removed the offender.

Prince and Princess Louis were now very close in the Queen's confidence. The Prince had conducted a delicate mission for her in Russia with considerable success, and she had appointed him her personal naval aide-de-camp. She would have liked to have him as Captain of her yacht, but to that he would not agree.[7] She valued his opinions on both naval and domestic matters highly and one of her last acts was to appoint him Trustee to her private money.[8] "Victoria B.", as she called Princess Louis, had a unique position in her affections.

On 18th December Queen Victoria left Windsor for Osborne. There was a sadness about the crumpled figure that rivalled the occasion, exactly thirty-nine years before, when she had made the

* Princess Andrew of Greece.

same journey, leaving Albert's body in the Blue Room. On 2nd January she received Lord Roberts and gave him the Garter.[9] On the 13th she went out for a short drive, and in the evening she wrote her Journal. She had done the same on every evening through three score years and ten. On the pages' ending:

13th Jan 1901 . . . at five-thirty went down to the drawing-room, where a short service was held by Mr. Clement Smith, who performed it so well, and it was a great comfort to me. . . .

And at their beginning:

Meridon, 1st August, 1832 . . . At $\frac{1}{2}$ past 5 we arrived at Meridon; and we are now going to dress for dinner. $\frac{1}{2}$ past 8. I am undressing to go to bed. Mamma is not very well and is lying on the sofa in the next room. I was asleep in a minute in my own little bed which travels always with me.[10]

Here lay twenty-five thousand stories of the days of her time, stories of the moments that made history, intermingled with the little things of life, the blue of the sky over Lochnagar, dogs barking by the burn, children playing on the Osborne shore. Half the brilliant statesman, half the simple child.

She was dying of tiredness. Shorter grew the lucid times between the patches of mist. Young Leopold of Battenberg, Princess Beatrice's son, played to her upon the violin, and soothed her. At eleven o'clock on the morning of 22nd January she talked quite normally to her grandchildren about the weather and their pets. For two and a half hours during the afternoon the Emperor of Germany and Sir James Reid cradled her in their arms and, as the clocks struck half-past six, she went down, and there was only the bright ring of her left upon the waters.

They had thought she was immortal, and there were no plans for her burial. As her coffin left the Isle of Wight the arrangements for its reception at Windsor were not yet complete. The yacht *Alberta* carried her through a mighty avenue of ships of war to Portsmouth, as the sun went down in a red sky.[11]

> We took her silent form to glide
> Where reached from shore to shore
> Her glorious Fleet. Each warship's side

Rang, mile on mile, above the tide,
The Queen's salute once more![12]

It was cold at Windsor, and the horses drawing the gun-carriage, which waited for the coffin, grew fretful. The wheelers set off before the leaders and, struggling against the heavy load, began to kick and plunge. A flying hoof narrowly missed the new King. Away went the traces. As the men of the Artillery strove to quieten the horses, the van of the procession moved on. Frederick Ponsonby,* in charge of the arrangements, sent an N.C.O. to stop it and had a hurried word with King Edward. Then it was that Prince Louis of Battenberg made a suggestion. He said: "If it is impossible to mend the traces you can always get the naval guard of honour to drag the gun-carriage." To this idea the Artillery took strong exception, but the King decided that there should be only one man in command, and that was Ponsonby.[13] He had had enough of horses for one day. "Having piled arms, with proud and quick step the Bluejackets of the *Excellent* came up and using the traces of the horses, supplemented by a few yards of railway communication cord, they hitched on to the gun-carriage, and at half-past two the sad procession went on its way."[14]

Thus did a Battenberg pay his last service to his Queen, and establish a precedent. Nine years later Bluejackets were to draw the funeral carriage of King Edward VII.

At this point in her Reminiscences Lady Milford Haven gave her personal impressions of Queen Victoria:

Grandmama's death was a great personal loss to me. On account of our having lost our mother when we were so young, Grandmama had taken a special interest in her beloved daughter's children. Her affection for us was very warm and sincere and she proved it on every occasion. As the one of us who was the most in England, I was the one who was in closest touch with her.

My understanding of Queen Victoria grew with the years. In childhood, I had known her as a middle aged woman, and as I was approaching middle age, she had become a very old lady. Both of us had developed different traits of character during this time. In my early youth, Grandmama was a very formidable person in my mind,

* Equerry and Assistant Private Secretary to Queen Victoria. Afterwards Lord Sysonby.

some one whom my mother regarded with respect and almost awe. She herself, though very gracious to her grandchildren, expected perfect manners and immediate obedience from them and would look and speak severely to any offender. These are the years of Angeli's portrait, with its stern and rather forbidding expression of face. My mother's death broke through many of these outward barriers and the constant signs of affectionate pity and interest, gave to our intercourse a more natural ease.

If with the older grandchildren Grandmama had been somewhat strict, with the youngest who were, in age, a generation younger, she showed the proverbial grandmother's leniency, and to the Connaughts and to Aunt Beatrice's children she was the "Gan-Gan" whom they could coax and wheedle. People picture Queen Victoria to themselves as completely "Victorian", but I do not know what Victorian means, when applied to a period extending over sixty years. Though in various details she adhered to the customs of her happy married life, yet, gradually, many little rules had been relaxed and had been adapted to the times she was living in. This was specially noticeable in her treatment of her grandchildren.

In her dress she always kept to the old-fashioned style she was accustomed to. Her day dresses had wide sleeves, showing the finest lawn under-sleeves. There were pocket slits in the ample skirts, the pockets themselves being in the under-skirt in which the keys of dispatch boxes were kept, attached to a chain and her spectacles. She had two writing tables side by side, one for her public, the other for her private correspondence and when she had on a smarter dress, she would put on a little black silk apron. Evidently, in her young days, ladies protected their light dresses from the chance of ink specking.

Once when Aunt Beatrice was a little girl of about four, Grandmama was writing with her apron on, and the child was playing about the room. Having nothing better to do, she managed to untie the apron strings and knot them to the back rail of the chair without her mother's noticing it. When the nurse had removed the child and the Queen wanted to get up from her table, she found herself so securely tied to her chair that she had to ring for the maid to release her.

Though it is well known from her portraits that the Queen always wore some form of widow's cap, yet in the privacy of her own room she would sit without it, with only a little bow arrangement pinned on to the back of her hair, which it covered, leaving the greater part of the head free.

In the grounds she wore a broad brimmed straw hat in summer.

She was extraordinarily neat and tidy in her toilette and used a faint perfume of orange blossom. She once gave me a bottle of this scent, which was made at Grasse, but I in vain after her death tried to get it there and elsewhere.

She never went out without a collection of capes of different thickness, and many a time have I helped her in the carriage to take a thinner one off and put a thicker one on and vice versa. When she went abroad, she always took her own bed and bedding with her, and her personal housemaid.

For breakfast and tea Grandmama used two special cups and would pour the tea from one into the other to cool it.

Having suffered very severely from gout between the age of 45 and 60—once at Balmoral she had gout in both hands—the doctors had forbidden her to take any wine and she only drank whisky and water at her meals. The whisky, probably, was finished off by her servants and thence the legend has arisen of her drinking lots of alcohol. It is true that she was not particularly shocked at any of her Scottish servants taking a drop too much, but one must not forget that in her youth gentlemen, as well as servants, were given to hard drinking.

I have met many distinguished people at her table. I remember an amusing episode when Mr. and Mrs. Gladstone had been invited to Windsor to dine and, as usual, spend the night there afterwards. Mrs. Gladstone appeared for dinner wrapped up in a shawl, which was somewhat against etiquette. Grandmama, who always suffered from the heat and kept her rooms very cold, never understood that people could feel chilly and generally made remarks when she saw signs of it. However, nothing was said to Mrs. Gladstone on this occasion. When we had risen from table and were leaving the room, one of the gentlemen noticed that something was trailing at the back of Mrs. Gladstone's dress. When he stooped to pick it up Mrs. Gladstone exclaimed, "Oh that is the bodice of my dress I could not find. My maid must have pinned it on there. That is why I have had to cover myself with the shawl." Her untidiness is well known; she was only amused at her maid's precautions when packing.

The Queen was a very shy person all her life and her apparent stiffness on meeting people for the first time was due to embarrassment. Another marked trait of Grandmama's character, as one of her favourite ladies-in-waiting, the old dowager Marchioness of Ely, pointed out to me, was "that the stupidest man's opinion carried more weight with the Queen than the cleverest woman's".

For quite half a dozen years before her death, Grandmama's sight began to trouble her. The nerves of the eye were affected, and the various oculists she consulted agreed that no operation could prevent a progress of the trouble. The thought that one day she would go quite blind like her grandfather, George III, oppressed her greatly. I remember when for some reason she had to write some official letter to the Emperor of Austria, she called me in to assist her in making a fair copy. She could not see where the words ended, after she had interrupted her writing to dip her pen. I had to put my finger on the last word written before she could continue.

Grandmama was always very proud of being a soldier's daughter and the interest she took in the Army was very sincere. In the Navy it was less pronounced, as the Admiralty had deeply offended her and hurt her feelings when it refused to give the Prince Consort an Honorary rank in the Service. I may say it was not until Louis became her grandson by marriage and she heard so much more about Naval life and Naval doings, that her personal interest became keener. Neither her naval step-nephew, Prince Ernest Leiningen, nor her naval son, the Duke of Edinburgh, had been able to do so.

Grandmama had essentially what was called a womanly nature, and her likes and dislikes were influenced by personal contacts. This was the secret of Lord Beaconsfield's charm for her; he never overlooked the woman in the Sovereign.

Prince Louis became personal naval aide-de-camp to King Edward,* and afterwards to King George V.[15] In November 1902 he was appointed Director of Naval Intelligence and two years later promoted to Rear-Admiral. "P.L's" career kept his family on the move and the Princess had experience of setting up house in many places, among them Osborne, Frogmore, Walton-on-Thames, St. Albans and Sheerness. She also joined her husband at Malta, where she was long remembered for her invention of a card game entitled "Happy Families of Malta". But the roots of the Battenbergs were in Hesse and whenever possible the summer months were spent at the Castle of Heiligenberg. They also had apartments in the Old Palace on the Luisenplatz in Darmstadt.[16] Here the girls, Alice and Louise, attended the finishing school of Fräulein Textor.[17]

It was in 1902, the year that her brother George began his studies at Cheam preparatory school,[18] that seventeen-year-old Princess Alice fell in love. Gold of hair and brown of eye, she had upheld the tradition of Hessian beauty. She was slightly deaf and,

* His younger son, Earl Mountbatten of Burma, carried on this tradition, for he was appointed Personal Naval aide-de-camp to King Edward VIII and King George VI and Personal aide-de-camp to Queen Elizabeth II.

like her mother, outspoken and clear-minded. She went to school with his crumpled love letters in her pocket.

The man in her heart was a nephew of Queen Alexandra and entwined by birth and marriage with the Royal Houses of Russia, Greece, Germany and Denmark. Later ties were made with France and America, and his mother complained that when she had all her children and their spouses at home it was like living in the Tower of Babel. He was Prince Andrew of Greece, son of King George.* He was thirty and a soldier. In the course of his duties he was attached to the Hessian 23rd Dragoon Guards for training at Darmstadt,[19] resulting in the soft breeze of romance once again blowing through the gardens of Heiligenberg. Queen Alexandra was delighted with the news. She asked Princess Alice to stay with her in London, and who should be there but Andrew.[20] In June 1903 they became engaged at Sopwell, St. Albans, where Prince and Princess Louis were living at the time.[21]

The wedding of Princess Alice of Battenberg and Prince Andrew of Greece that October was the last gay royal fiesta to sparkle in Europe. The sky was blue and clear. Thereafter clouds piled slowly up from all around until, in August eleven years later, the thunder came. Once again, as in 1884, trains loaded with royalties converged upon Darmstadt, and this time there was to be no Alexandrine von Kolemine to turn the milk and honey sour. Queen Alexandra represented King Edward, Princess Beatrice travelled with her lovely daughter, Ena, the Emperor and Empress and the Grand Duke and Duchess Serge came from Russia, Prince Henry and Princess Irene from Berlin, and the Greeks were in force. "The procession of their Greek Majesties with a military escort, three four-horsed carriages *à la Daumont*,

---

* Prince William Christian of Schleswig-Holstein, second son of King Christian IX of Denmark, was nominated for the Greek Throne by Britain in 1862 and was recognised as King George of the Hellenes by the Powers the following year. He married the Grand Duchess Olga of Russia, niece of Alexander II. They had seven children. Constantine married Princess Sophie of Prussia, daughter of the Empress Frederick; George married Princess Marie of Buonaparte; Alexandra married Grand Duke Paul of Russia; Nicholas married Grand Duchess Helen of Russia, and they became the parents of Princess Marina, Duchess of Kent; Andrew; Christopher married (1) Mrs. N. Leeds and (2) Princess Françoise of France; and Marie married (1) Grand Duke George Mihailovich of Russia and (2) Admiral Perikles Joanides (known in the family as "Perks").

with outriders, and many paired-horsed carriages, was splendid."[22]

The preliminaries included a reception by Prince and Princess Louis in the ballroom of the Old Palace, and a gala performance at the theatre. The latter produced considerable feminine rivalry. Queen Alexandra, below a magnificent tiara, was as lovely as she had ever been. But Lord Gosford, who was in attendance upon her, was discovered leaning against a pillar, staring up at the box which contained "Alicky", Empress of Russia, and "Ella", her sister. Upon being asked what he was doing he replied that he was looking at the two most beautiful creatures in the world— a remark which, under the circumstances of his attendance, appeared to border on the unfaithful.[23]

The wedding day, the 7th, proved to be a religious marathon for the bride and groom. Princess Alice belonged to the Protestant Church, Prince Andrew to the Greek, thus entailing two services. Then, according to the law of Germany, there had to be a civil ceremony. In addition, King Edward wanted them to be married at the British Legation, as the Princess was a British subject. But the couple declared that being "spliced" three times was sufficient strain on their endurance, and they struck.[24]

The Protestant service took place in the castle chapel, from where the procession made its way to the Assembly Rooms and from there to the Russian Church on the Mathildenhöhe. In the words of Princess Marie:

> The arrival at the Russian chapel was wonderful. A fragment of Hellas in the North; deep blue sky, brilliant sunshine, flashing golden cupolas, a scarlet carpet on the steps. We were received by Russians and Greeks, blazing with gold, and led into the rich, beautiful chapel, where we were greeted by three priests in golden vestments. The bridal couple, who, of course, came last, stood on a carpet of rose-coloured silk—a symbol of the path of life.[25]

Now came the difficult part of the day for the Princess. She had been coached beforehand, but, becoming confused by the complicated procedure, she said "No" when asked if she was marrying of her own free will, and "Yes" when asked if she had plighted her troth elsewhere.[26]

The service lasted an hour, throughout which the congregation had to stand. The wedding-crowns, brought from St. Petersburg, were so heavy that four crown-bearers, all Princes, were necessary, and they took turn and turn about at holding them. Raising these crowns over the heads of the bridal couple, as they circled the altar three times, proved an operation of difficulty and some danger.[27]

The wedding breakfast afterwards was described by Mark Kerr,* naval friend of Prince Louis, as being more like a Bank Holiday on Hampstead Heath than a Royal ceremonial.[28] The tempo really heated up as the guests waited for Prince and Princess Andrew to change before leaving for their honeymoon at Heiligenberg. Servants and suites were dismissed, and little mercy was expected, or given. Mark Kerr had the job of holding Prince Andrew's coat and hat in anticipation of his coming. Prince George of Greece seized the hat and planted it upon the head of his aunt, Duchess Vera of Württemberg. As he did so he knocked her spectacles to the ground and upset her hair-do, which was the latest thing in bobs. She could see nothing without her spectacles, but, intent on revenge, she seized the hard hat and began to belabour Mark Kerr over the head with it. Queen Alexandra, always intent on mischief, ran over to Mark Kerr's sister, who was lady-in-waiting to Princess Louis, and whispered to her that her brother had put his hat on Duchess Vera and knocked her spectacles off. The sister, thinking that Mark Kerr had imbibed too well and too long, rushed to the rescue of the Duchess. It was then that she heard, behind her, the tinkling and unseemly laughter of the Queen of England.[29]

With Grand Duke Ernest Louis acting as butler, the wedded couple entered the car and drove away on to the Luisenplatz. Emperor Nicholas saw that there was a chance to catch up with them at the corner of the Wilhelminenstrasse, where spectators were standing six deep. "Come on," he shouted, and raced off, with children of the party hanging on his coat tails and a queue of tiaras and uniforms behind him. Horrified, the German detectives, who were thick on the ground, pounded in pursuit.

The Emperor charged the spectators head down, shedding children as he did so. He emerged through the front rank as their

* Afterwards Admiral, and Major-General, R.A.F.

Wolseley car was about to pass. Princess Alice was bowing and acknowledging the cheers. She received the contents of a rice bag in the face. A satin shoe followed. Adroitly, she caught it and, leaning over the back of the open car, proceeded to hit the Emperor on the head. At the same time, in the concise way Battenbergs have, she told him exactly what she thought of him.[30]

In the middle of the street, doubled up with laughter, stood Emperor Nicholas II of Russia, as the Wolseley bowled into the night on its way to the peace of Heiligenberg.

26

The Smell of Powder

JANUARY 22ND 1905 WAS "RED SUNDAY" IN ST. PETERSBURG.[1]
Columns of workers streamed in from Kolpino, Schlusselburg
and the Putiloff foundry, joining others from the city. They
headed for the square before the Winter Palace, intent upon seeing
Nicholas II and demanding better working conditions. But the
Emperor and Empress were at Tsarskoe-Selo.

The authorities, instead of halting the individual columns,
allowed the vast concourse to reach the square. The Governor-
General gave them three warnings to disperse, and then ordered
the troops to open fire.[2] The bodies lay thick as upon a battlefield,
and the fate of the Romanoffs was written in their flowing blood.

The Emperor decided that a more Liberal policy must be introduced, and he informed the Grand Duke Serge, Governor of
Moscow, of the new rulings. The Grand Duke did not agree with
them, and resigned.[3]

In London, on 8th February, *The Tatler* carried full-page photographs of the Grand Duke and Duchess. He was described as being
"feared throughout Russia". Grand Duchess "Ella", it was pointed
out, was the niece of King Edward and the daughter of "our
beloved Princess Alice". She was in full dress, and the pearls
were thick about her neck. It was the last time she was to be

photographed in all her beauty, and the pictures were a strange prescience of coming events.

The Russo-Japanese war was at its height and the Grand Duchess, as head of the Red Cross, had converted part of the Kremlin Palace into a store for comforts for the troops and sewing-rooms where clothes could be made. Daily she worked with her helpers, sorting and despatching the bales of bandages and clothing and the boxes of food. In the pressure of work no one noticed the young student, Kaliaev, who hung around the gates. There was a bomb in his pocket. He was waiting his chance to kill the Grand Duke. Several times that chance came, but on each occasion the Grand Duchess was also in the carriage, and Kaliaev turned away.

On the 17th the Grand Duke had arranged to go to the new Governor's house to clear out his private possessions. He said goodbye to his wife in their private apartments, and went to his carriage. She was preparing to visit a sick friend, and her carriage drew up. Minutes later an ear-shattering blast shook the windows. "Ella" needed no telling as to what it was—she had feared it too long. She ran, hatless, down the stairs and out into the cold. The carriage took her the short ride to the Spassky gate, where a crowd had gathered. Smoke drifted and there was the smell of powder. Alighting, she saw fragments of wood and wheels, mangled, twisted horses, the coachman lying on the ground.[4] She saw men holding Kaliaev, blood-stained and defiant. She saw soldiers covering with their cloaks the little bits of flesh which were all that remained of the body of the husband whom she had loved since her childhood days.[5]

Only the head of the Grand Duke was not completely disfigured. Such of his other remains as could be gathered up filled but a small box.[6] His widow placed them in a marble sarcophagus, which was taken to a special room, afterwards converted into a chapel.[7]

In those few terrible seconds out before the Kremlin, a woman changed completely, as if she too had been killed, and then reborn. The "Ella" of Darmstadt was gone for ever. No hate twisted her heart and mind, for it was hate which had caused the stream of blood to flow upon the stones. A reaction against all hate possessed

her. Into the empty rooms of her swept clear of feeling by
the shock and tragedy, came angels of forgiveness and sympathy.
The desire for the pleasures and the grandeurs of this world died
right away.

In secret she went to the Taganka prison, intent on reconciling
the assassin to his god.[8] The door of Kaliaev's cell opened and
before him stood the tragic widow in her weeds. She talked with
him alone, but found him unrepentant, though he expressed regret
that he had brought sadness to such a woman. The Grand Duchess
promised that she would care for his mother, and so she did until
the mother died.[9]

The funeral of the Grand Duke was quiet and private, the police
having warned the Emperor and Empress that their lives might be
endangered if they travelled from St. Petersburg for the ceremony.
But the Grand Duchess Elizabeth had the support of her eldest
sister, Princess Louis of Battenberg, and her brother, the Grand
Duke Ernest Louis.[10]

Lady Milford Haven recalled:

> I left England for Russia on the evening of the day that I received
> the news of Serge's death. Irene and Henry of Prussia were unable
> to go to Moscow, but travelled for a couple of hours with me in
> Germany. William [the German Emperor] met me at the Berlin
> station and gave me supper. He was very kind and thoughtful and
> much worried about Ella, for whom since his student days he had
> felt a strong devotion.
>
> I found Ella very brave and collected, trying to distract her mind
> by looking after everybody and everything in the house. The shock
> had, however, been a very great one to her nervous system. She could
> not sleep, neither could she touch a morsel of food. Contrary to the
> general belief, she and Serge had led a happy married life, though
> it was he who was completely the head and master of the house.
> Ella was very willing that he should be, and he was full of affectionate
> attentions to her. Both were fond of children and it was sad that they
> never had any of their own.
>
> Ella told me in confidence—she hoped it would not be spread
> about—that she had visited Kaliaev, the young assassin, in prison.
> She knew that Serge had a great feeling of distress for people dying
> unconfessed and unshriven and felt herself that, if she could awaken
> a feeling of repentance in him for the murder that he had com-
> mitted, she would be helping his soul. When she entered Kaliaev's

279

cell, he said, "Who are you?" She answered: "I am the wife of the man whom you have killed." He seemed moved by her visit, but considered that he had only acted up to his convictions. She did not remain with him long, nor discuss opinions with him. He did not resent her promise that she would pray for him. He had shown a certain regard for her before, as he had refrained from throwing a bomb at Serge a few days before when Ella was driving with him.

Ella was much distressed when the news of her visit leaked out. Later tales were spread that she even went so far as to beg for Kaliaev's life to be spared. That is not true. She said to me herself: "I have nothing to do with earthly justice. It was his soul, and not his body, I was thinking of." We never spoke to each other of that visit again.

The childless Grand Duchess now had no responsibilities in Russia except for the guardianship of her young nephew and niece, Dimitri and Marie. They were the children of Grand Duke Paul, youngest son of Alexander II and brother of Serge. Their mother, Princess Alexandra, daughter of King George and Queen Olga of Greece, had died when they were babies, since when the Grand Duchess Elizabeth had cared for them. She took them to her country home outside Moscow and retired from public life. Never again did she eat meat, and increasingly she devoted herself to good works. The Grand Duke's Palace in St. Petersburg she bequeathed to her nephew, and to him and to his sister went much of her priceless collection of jewellery. When Dimitri joined the army and Marie married Prince William of Sweden, the Grand Duchess sold the remainder of her possessions, even down to her wedding ring.[11]

With the proceeds she bought land on the southern bank of the Moskva and there began the erection of buildings which were to be the first step in the fulfilment of her new life's aim—the bringing of religious and bodily comfort to the old and the sick, the lonely and the needy. Moscow watched in wonderment as the Foundation took shape. "There was a big church dedicated to the Lord's Mother, the hospital proper with a large dispensary and an out-patients' department, a home for the aged, a house for the clergy, an orphanage, the community quarters, a guest house and a little church of SS Martha and Mary. Between the guest house and that church were to be three small rooms for the Grand Duchess, her office, a sitting-room and a tiny bedroom."[12]

After long and difficult negotiation with the religious hierarchy, the role of the women who were to staff the Foundation was at last settled, and in 1910 the Grand Duchess founded the Order of Martha and Mary, the only sisterhood of nursing nuns in Russia. In April she became their Abbess.[13] When she took the veil Bishop Triphonius said to her: "This veil will hide you from the world, and the world will be hidden from you; but it will be a witness of your good works which will shine before God and glorify the Lord."[14]

Yet the darker side of the world was not hidden from the Grand Duchess. From the seclusion of her Foundation she ventured forth into the slums, into filthy corners where no nursing sister had tended before. She went unaccompanied except for her faithful maid of bygone days, Varia, now known as Sister Barbara. One such corner was the Khitrovka market, where twenty thousand lost souls dwelt in squalor. Miss Almedingen, who ten years later was to work there with a Famine Relief Mission, thus described it:

> . . . filthy, narrow alleys, fringed by tumbledown hovels, converged on to a great irregular square, girdled by huge barrack-like buildings. . . . The middle of the square was occupied by the market proper where ramshackle stalls offered little more than secondhand clothing and food of the kind the poorest among the poor could afford. The barracky buildings were shelters. . . . Each such shelter had a big *"traktyr"* on the ground floor where boiling water might be purchased for a copper and where better-moneyed denizens might buy cabbage soup and meat-pies and—chiefly—vodka—made at the illicit stills of Khitrovka. In those doss-houses, *"Lebensraum"* was measured by careful inches.[15]

This was the haunt of burglars and fences, pimps and pickpockets, and those on the run from the police. Infant mortality was high, yet an emaciated baby was looked upon as an asset, as it produced more alms when displayed for begging purposes in the richer areas. Male children who survived the ordeal were quickly instructed in the art of picking pockets and scaling drain pipes, whilst few of their sisters remained virgins beyond the age of ten.

Through this nightmare walked the woman who, for a quarter

of a century, had been known as the most beautiful in Europe. In the stench of the drains lay the ever-present danger of contracting the disease which had killed her mother and her sister. Yet she was beyond fear now, mindful only of the example which had been set for her by Princess Alice. In the social world which she had left, opinion upon her new life was sharply divided. Some looked upon her as a saint, while others considered that the murder of her husband had upset her reason. The police, fearing that one day they would be called upon to retrieve the body of Grand Duchess "Ella" from the maze of alleys, were insistent that the errands of mercy should cease. The Grand Duke Ernest Louis wrote in his Reminiscences:

> Accompanied by a single sister, she often went into the slummiest streets and alleys of Moscow until, driven to despair, the police let her know that they could do no more for her safety. She sent them a message to thank them for their kindly solicitude but added that she was in God's hands and not in theirs.[16]

*   *   *   *

Anarchists were also busy in Spain. Their particular target was Alfonso XIII, the young man who had been born a King. He showed no sign of being perturbed about it. He had been warned, anonymously, that ten bombs were waiting for him. The first, of the "pineapple" variety,[17] had been thrown under his carriage as he drove through the streets of Paris on 31st May 1905, but he had escaped unhurt. Nine to go . . .

Alfonso was looking for a bride, and from Paris he proceeded to London. He had in mind one of the daughters of the Duke of Connaught, but Princess Margaret announced her engagement to Prince Gustavus of Sweden. It was therefore the photograph of the younger Princess, "Patsy",* which he carried in his baggage. Somewhat to the handsome Spaniard's surprise, he discovered that this Princess's affections lay, irrevocably, in another direction. It came also as a surprise to many others, including King Edward. At a supper party the chair to the right of Alfonso was left empty while the Princess chatted with a guardsman on the balcony. Next

---

* Afterwards Lady Patricia Ramsay.

day, at a lunch given by the Duke of Connaught, she was again placed beside him. During the meal the Spanish King turned to the Duchess of Westminster, on his left, and asked, "Am I very ugly? Because I do not please . . . I do not please the lady on my right!"[18]

Princess Victoria, King Edward's daughter, a keen matchmaker, stepped in and asked Alfonso which, among the collected bevy of Princesses, he thought the most beautiful. Without hesitation, he answered: "The fair one." He looked towards the pink and gold loveliness of eighteen-year-old Princess Ena of Battenberg. He had fallen in love with her without even knowing her name. Having met her, he vowed that he would eschew the company of women until such time as he married her,[19] which, for such a gay young man, was a considerable promise.

The troth was plighted, King Edward gave his blessing, and the necessary transference of the Princess to the Church of Rome was arranged, despite considerable clatter from the Church of England. There was also a change in her name—she became Victoria Eugenia. The wedding was arranged for 31st May 1906, the first anniversary of the bomb attempt on Alfonso in Paris.

It proved to be the most sensational and spectacular royal wedding in Europe's history, medieval in its splendour. Another superlative was that no Sovereign's marriage has ever been worse policed. The nuptial programme was so long that guests from Germany and Russia, Scandinavia and Britain, were away from home for a fortnight. They gathered in Paris and joined the *Sud Express*, which, despite its romantic name, proved to be noisy, unstable and indescribably dirty. If a bomb had been placed on the track, half of the royalties of Europe would have gone, including the future King and Queen of Great Britain.* [20]

King Alfonso had advance information that a bomb might be thrown on his wedding day, and his first anxiety came when his bride was late in reaching the Church of San Jeronimo. But she arrived safely and the service began. In the pews there were hearts which beat fast with anxiety, for the previous evening the King had entertained his guests with a lurid description of his narrow

* King George V and Queen Mary.

escape in Paris the previous year. The bride's aunt, Princess Marie of Battenberg, wrote:

> During the ceremony the thought suddenly occurred to me how easy it would be in the narrow, one-aisled church for an attempt to be made from above on all this princely assemblage. I little knew, then, by what a hair's breadth we had escaped this danger. . . .[21]

The fortunate chance which prevented Princess Marie and the rest from being blown to pieces in the church was the sudden recovery to health of an American journalist. At the last moment he felt well enough to attend. If he had not, his ticket would have gone to the assassin chosen for the job, syphilitic Matteo Morral, who had posed as a member of the Press. Thwarted here, Morral made his way to a balcony at No. 88, Calle Mayor, a narrow street through which the procession would pass on its way back to the Palace. In his hands was a bouquet of flowers. In the flowers was a bomb.

He watched the long procession passing, four storeys below. He took the bomb in his hands as the carriage of the Prince and Princess of Wales lumbered by. The next contained Queen Christina and Princess Beatrice, mothers of the groom and bride. The next was the bridal coach of Alfonso and Ena. The bomb began its long drop. Looking up, people saw only flowers in the sky. The coachman checked his horses, so that the King might acknowledge a particular outburst of cheering.[22] The bomb fell between the wheel horses. Twenty people were killed and sixty wounded.[23] A party of officers from the 16th Lancers* were watching the procession from a nearby house. They raced for the carriage and helped Alfonso and Ena, unhurt, on to the road.[24] Also racing in the same direction was Morral, who, seeing that his attempt had failed, now had a gun in his hand. But he could not get through the crowd, and made good his escape. Someone suggested to the King that he and his bride should shelter in the Italian Embassy, but the reply was so forthright and rude that the idea was abandoned. Saying, "Come on, Ena," he handed his

---

* Official delegates from the Regiment, of which King Alfonso was the Colonel-in-Chief.

Queen into the Coach of Respect,* which was travelling behind, and on they went to the Palace.[25]

There the guests already assembled knew nothing of the tragedy, thinking that the blast was ceremonial gunfire. As they dismounted Princess Marie noticed that the chain of King Alfonso's Order hung broken on his breast, and that his wife's wedding dress was splashed with blood:

> In indescribable excitement we rushed upstairs behind them, and accompanied them to their rooms. Ena was incredibly self-controlled, in spite of the deadly shock, and the terrible things she had seen, but she kept on repeating: "I saw a man without any legs."[26]

As they went out on to the balcony to show themselves to the wildly excited crowds, Marie, Duchess of Edinburgh and Coburg, remarked: *"Je suis tellement accoutumée à ces choses."*[27] Bombs had taken the lives of her father, Alexander II, and her brother, the Grand Duke Serge.

Although Morral was at large, and known to be desperate, King Alfonso completely ignored the danger, drove through the streets and continued with the arranged programme. Some of the guests considered that this bordered on the suicidal, and suggested that civilian clothes might make them less obvious targets. The King would not consider it, and was backed by the Princess of Wales. Her serenity, unruffled calm and complete lack of fear were the subject of universal comment and admiration,[28] but then the light of Queen Mary always shone its brightest in the critical days of her life. Her husband contented himself with the emphatic and Georgian remark: "Damn those police."[29]

After three days Morral was found in a village near Escorial. He shot his captor and then himself. There remained but the climax of the bullfight, which, by request of Parliament, the British Royal representatives were not to attend.

In the blazing heat, under her white mantilla and with red

---

* The reason for the inclusion of the Coach of Respect in the procession was that, if anyone in a carriage passed a priest on foot carrying the Host to a dying person, it was the ancient custom in Spain for the owner of the coach to stop and offer it to the priest, proceeding on foot himself. To avoid the King or Queen having to walk in such circumstances, an additional coach always accompanied them. This, in theory, could be offered to the priest.

carnations in her hair, the new Spanish Queen drove to the great arena where a crowd of fifteen thousand roared and cheered in competition with the music of the bands. She dropped her handkerchief, and the show was on. Behind her sat her aunt Marie of Battenberg, in the unusual garb of an Infanta.

> I tried to look as little as possible, as one horse after another was wounded and killed by the bull. . . . Only when all the horses lay dead about the arena did the fight between the wounded bull and the *banderillos* begin, and finally with the *torero*. . . . We saw nine bulls, one after another, done to death in this way, and from twenty to thirty horses. . . . I felt horrified but stood it out, for Ena had not only to control herself, but to smile. . . . "Once in my life, and never again," I thought. Poor Ena will have to go through it over and over again.[30]

Fortunately a thoughtful brother had previously apprised her that, if she altered the focus of her field glasses, only a blur would appear before her eyes.[31]

27

The Henrys of Prussia

PRINCESS IRENE, THE MIDDLE DAUGHTER OF PRINCESS ALICE, Grand Duchess of Hesse and the Rhine, took a middle path through life. She was small and delicate of figure, but she lacked the ethereal beauty of "Ella" and "Alicky", and the strong character of Victoria. At the Berlin Court she was described as being "an amiable woman, of domestic habits", but lacking in *esprit*.[1] She passed through life without scandal or intrigue touching her name, and her dual tragedy was that she was a carrier of haemophilia and, in World War I, found herself on the opposing side to her three sisters and a contributory cause to the resignation of her brother-in-law from high office. The four Hessian sisters were as close as the quarters in an orange, and the divided loyalties of war were hard to bear.

Before his marriage to her Prince Henry of Prussia had been a careless and little-read young man, indulging in as much riotous living as his allowance would permit.[2] His mother came to the conclusion, as had Queen Victoria in the case of "Bertie", that a nice, sensible girl must be found for him before there was an upset in the Imperial Household. She settled on his first cousin, Irene, and in so doing founded a marriage of love.

The cross in the lives of Henry and Irene was represented by

287

"big brother" William, William "The Only". William was for ever starting quarrels, just to make sure that his younger brother remembered who was Emperor. He was for ever pumping him full of the propaganda of grandiosity and setting him against his mother. Another cause of trouble was that Princess Irene did not get on with the Empress, who championed the Grand Duchess Victoria Melita in her marital squabbles with Grand Duke Ernest Louis.

The Empress Frederick had arranged that, on their marriage, Henry and Irene should live at the Villa Carlotta in Sans Souci Park at Potsdam. Before they could move in William became Emperor. He decreed that the Villa was Crown property and at his disposal, and he gave possession to a favoured Baron.[3] It was an act of spite and defiance aimed at his mother, and she never forgave him for it.

The Prince and Princess set up their first home at the Schloss at Kiel, and it was there that the Empress fled when her eldest son made life impossible for her in Berlin. She was much attached to her daughter-in-law, called her "dear little Irene", and found peace in her house. Henry, she noted, was much more tractable now. The Empress wrote to her daughter, Sophie, in Greece: "Henry and Irene were so nice, and the Schloss looks so clean and well-kept and comfortable. They are so happy and their home so peaceful and harmonious because they are away from Berlin, and mischief-making. . . ."[4]

In 1896 Prince Henry purchased the estate of Hemmelmark by Eckernförde, near Kiel, and this became their home for life. He died there on 20th April 1929, and his wife, whose name meant "Peace", on 11th November, Armistice Day, 1953.[5] The Empress Frederick visited them as they were moving in. "It is a fine property, with barns and cow houses, some woods and a good sheet of water, but very damp and low. . . . Henry and Irene are quite devoted to the place, and the thought of it being their own makes them love it, they enjoy perfect liberty there, and live à la Robinson Crusoe."[6]

"The Henrys of Prussia" had three sons. The first, born in 1889, and the second, in 1896, had the very German names of

Emperor Nicholas II and King George V, with their heirs

Prince Louis of Battenberg
First Marquess of Milford Haven

Waldemar* and Sigismund,† but were given the sobriquets of "Toddie" and "Bobbie". The third, Henry, born in 1900, had the bleeding disease and died at the age of four. It was his illness and death which bound Princess Irene so closely to her younger sister in Russia, fighting to preserve her only son from a like fate.

The Prince and Princess, known as "the very amiables", were popular everywhere, and were to be seen at weddings, anniversaries and christenings from Madrid to St. Petersburg. The last sound that Prince and Princess Andrew of Greece heard as they set off on their honeymoon was the loud "Hoch-ing" of Henry.[7] Queen Victoria liked them, but complained about their casual attitude. When they declined her third invitation to stay at Windsor, she became angry and told the Empress Frederick that she would not ask them again.[8] But she did, and Princess Irene proved a great support to her in her last days. She and Princess "May", Duchess of York, were with the old Queen during her last stay at Balmoral,[9] when her strength was failing fast.

With the contentment of marriage Henry did all in his power to avoid squabbles with the Emperor. One cause of rancour had been the contents of his speeches. Henry did not welcome the mental effort of such composition, and he therefore hit upon a bright idea. The Emperor should write his speeches for him, thus saving him not only the effort but also from the danger of recrimination. He would say to his older brother: "Do not forget about that speech of mine for the Marine Club dinner", or "If you cannot come on Thursday, be sure to telephone me the speech". This was just the kind of flattery that the Emperor liked, and on one occasion he was heard to say: "Now I shall have to telephone the speech Prince Henry is expected to deliver tomorrow. To be the intellectual giant of one's family has its drawbacks."[10]

It was this ruse of Prince Henry which landed him in hot water.

In 1897 the Emperor and the newly appointed Foreign Minister, Count von Bülow, decided to boost the strength and significance of the German Navy. On the excuse of the murder of two German

* Married, 1914, Princess Calixta of Lippe.
† Married, 1919, Princess Charlotte Agnes of Saxe-Altenburg.

missionaries, a spectacular expedition was mounted and des-
patched to China. In command was Prince Henry. Before the ships
departed, in the wild scenes of excitement which gripped Kiel,
Henry spoke his farewell words. At the beginning: "Exalted
Emperor, Puissant King and Master, Illustrious Brother . . ."
At the end: "Our sublime, mighty, beloved Kaiser, King and
Lord for all times, for ever and ever—hurrah, hurrah, hurrah!"
In between he defined his mission: "I will carry forth the evangel
of your Majesty's person; I will preach it to those who want to
hear it and also those who do not want to hear it."[11] Poor Henry
was reciting the words concocted for him by his brother, and he
did not know that he was being reported. His sister, Charlotte,
who knew all, commented that William would be inviting Luna
to sleep with him next.

Prince Henry's words rang around the world. Early on Sunday,
19th December, the *Deutschland* arrived off Spithead, and a royal
salute was fired. But the frigidity around Portsmouth was very
noticeable, and not due to the wintry weather. The Prince went
to Osborne to see his grandmother.[12] When he returned to the
Deutschland he was a very chastened sailor. He proceeded on his
way to Port Said.

There he entertained Sir J. Rennell Rodd* and the German
representative in Cairo. Rodd thus described the meeting: "We
dined on board with the Prince, who was very cordial and discussed old times in Berlin. He spoke to me rather apologetically
about a speech of his delivered on the eve of his departure, which
had been a good deal criticised, especially for the words addressed
to his brother, whose menaces to China had been unpleasantly
reminiscent of Attila, in which he accepted 'the gospel of Your
Sacred Majesty'. He had, he said, been very hard worked up to
the day fixed for sailing, and final preparations, together with the
leave-taking from his family, had imposed a considerable strain
upon him. At the very last minute the Emperor had announced
his intention of coming on board to dine. 'You know,' Prince
Henry observed, 'how my brother warms you up when he speaks.'
The Emperor had there charged his younger brother to carry

* Afterwards Lord Rennell of Rodd.

overseas the 'mailed fist' which became thereafter historically notorious. Prince Henry responded with what he described as a rousing quarter-deck speech, not in the least, he maintained, realising that it was a public occasion, and that reporters were present who would telegraph his words all over the world. It was only when he touched at Portsmouth on his outward journey that he became aware of the publicity which had been given to the speeches, and he was, he said, not at all surprised that 'people were annoyed in England'."[13]

The Empress Frederick commented: "I wish with all my heart Germany would let alone all these adventurous plans and puerile ambitions...."[14]

During his prolonged absence Princess Irene learned, as her sister Victoria knew so well, the hardships of a sailor's wife. In 1902 her husband went away again, this time to America and Canada. Ostensibly he went to see the launching of the Emperor's new racing yacht, *Meteor*, but it was suspected that there was an underlying reason. He visited Washington, St. Louis and Niagara, and everywhere was received with enthusiasm.[15] The enthusiasm extended to the Vanderbilts.

The Emperor, like all those of the Coburg strain, had a great respect for wealth, and he was particularly tactful and pleasant with the Vanderbilts, whose finances were, he believed, so great that they could undermine a nation. He was therefore very upset on the occasion when Mr. William K. Vanderbilt was marched away from the gates of the *Neues Palais* at gun point. The sentry, who understood but the one word "American", was taking no chances with a civilian from a republic which boasted no King or Princes.[16] Suitable apologies arrived before the German Empire was brought to financial ruin.

Kiel Yachting Week of July 1903 was, for the Germans, a brilliant affair. The Emperor and Empress were on board the *Hohenzollern*. The Ormondes* arrived on *The Mirage*, Mrs. Goelet† on *Nahma*, and the Cornelius Vanderbilts on their beautiful boat,

---

* 3rd Marquess of Ormonde and Lady Elizabeth Harriet, daughter of the 1st Duke of Westminster.
† Miss May Goelet married the 8th Duke of Roxburghe in November 1903.

North Star. Most of the racing yachts were owned by business gentlemen, and as they were barely accepted by the élite, the latter took little part in the sport for which they had assembled.

The female visitors from abroad quickly discovered that the rating of women was low in Germany, the local ladies seeming content to sit around the Empress hoping for a kindly word to be dropped from the imperial height. Even when they were invited on board a yacht they found that they were classified as "hands", and their numbers limited. Princess Daisy of Pless came to the conclusion that this was the only occasion on which women counted for anything. In the evening the men all departed to *bierabends* at the Club, leaving their wives to the doubtful amusement of "hen parties". Princess Daisy was invited to one given by Princess Henry. The game of "Up Jenkins" was played. Acidly, Princess Daisy described this as "thrilling".[17]

She was invited by the Vanderbilts to dinner on the *North Star*, Prince Henry also being a guest. As usual, when the meal was over, the men departed for their *bierabend*. "We women were left all alone on board with two Frenchmen, but in about an hour, to my astonishment, the launch reappeared with several men *and* Prince Henry, who disappeared down below with Mrs. Cornelius Vanderbilt, our hostess, a fascinating (though snobbish) little American, but with much charm; I always imagined the Prince stiff and shy, certainly without a soupçon of flirtation but—still waters run deep. . . ."[18]

King Edward liked Prince and Princess Henry, finding their amiability and easy-going ways a pleasant contrast with the touchiness of the Emperor and his wife. The two came over for his Coronation in June 1902, staying at Wimborne House. Field Marshal Count von Waldersee was representing the German Army, and a private battle began between Prussian officers regarding the precedence of the two parties. Prince Henry settled it by quietly stating that he did not mind in which carriage he and his wife travelled. Then the news broke that the King was ill and to have an operation, and everyone went home.[19]

The King made Prince Henry a Vice-Admiral of the British Fleet[20] and conferred the Royal Victorian Chain on him.[21] When he visited Kiel in the summer of 1904 he took the opportunity of dining with the Henrys at Hemmelmark, but, to his annoyance, the Emperor, who insisted upon being present, stood up and made a pompous speech of welcome.[22] In fact William suspected his brother of suffering from Anglomania.

King Edward, with Queen Alexandra, was at Kiel again in 1908, this time *en route* to see Emperor Nicholas II at Reval. The journey across the North Sea was a nightmare. The R.Y. *Victoria and Albert* bucked and twisted its way through a violent storm, and the state-rooms were empty except for Queen Alexandra, who sat sipping her tea and nibbling at the cakes just as if she was on the lawn at Sandringham. Then a mountain of a wave smote the yacht. Away went "the Sea King's daughter", chair and all, on to the floor and into a corner, teapot and plates all around her. She picked herself out of the mess of butter and jam, and roared with laughter. The Danish Royal Family had that kind of sense of humour.[23] Prince and Princess Henry were waiting at Kiel to comfort them, but the warmth of the family reunion was dimmed by the grim silhouette of the German High Seas Fleet, lying in the port.

The threat of Germany's naval strength had by this time become a source of considerable worry and anxiety in Britain, and was clearly shown in Britain's attitude, which was distinctly cool. Apparently worried about this, Prince Henry, who had been appointed to the chief command of the German battle fleet, had a heart-to-heart talk on the subject with Frederick Ponsonby, Assistant Private Secretary to the King, early in 1910. On being told that it was considered that Germany was building up her fleet with the object of attacking Britain, Prince Henry became very excited and said that nothing was further from German thoughts. All Germany wanted to do was to defend her commerce. Invasion was impossible. Any attempt to do so would cripple their finances and ruin their trade. He added that there were people in his country who thought that Britain was only waiting for an excuse to smash the German Navy. His general attitude appeared to be that, as Britain had a fleet, why should not Germany? He appeared to regard battleships as prestige symbols. Ponsonby pointed out that they cost much in taxation, their ultimate purpose must be for war, and Britain kept her fleet where it was most likely to be wanted. Prince Henry replied: "You are the first that has dared to tell me that."

Next day Prince Henry saw Mr. Asquith. Years later the question arose as to whether the Prince was a knave or a fool. Mr. Asquith thought the former. Ponsonby came to the conclusion that, being a friend of Britain, the Prince was trying to smooth matters out. "He was a perfectly straightforward man and never gave the impression of having any Machiavellian cunning."[24]

When George V became King, the ties between "the Henrys" and the British Royal Family became closer still. George of Wales, Henry of Prussia and Victoria and Irene of Hesse had been born within four years of one another and had played together as children. Both boys had become sailors, and both girls married sailors. Yet the divided loyalties which had split their parents' generation now threatened to split theirs. Visits between them were frequent, but saddened by the shadows of war. There was the visit to Sandringham of December 1912. Prince Henry then asked the King direct if, in the event of Germany and Austria declaring war on France and Russia, Britain would come to the aid of the latter. The King replied: "Undoubtedly Yes—under certain circumstances." When Prince Henry reported the conversation to his brother, William read into it what he wanted to read, and decided that Britain would remain neutral. He went ahead with his plans to attack France.[25]

A few months later the Prince of Wales,* on a tour round his German relations, was invited by Prince and Princess Henry to stay at Hemmelmark. Of the many relations whom he met Uncle "Harry"† impressed him most. "He preferred working about his property or in his garage to the more pompous pastimes of those days. Uncle Henry sponsored modern ideas and inventions with vigour and enthusiasm. In fact his great interest in the still comparatively primitive motor-car brought him often to Great Britain, where he competed in automobile endurance tests."[26]

* Afterwards Edward VIII and Duke of Windsor.
† As he was always called in the family.

Lady Milford Haven was a victim of his enthusiasm:

In the early days of cars there were a certain number of people, Henry among them, who believed in steam as a better propelling force than petrol. There were great drawbacks about Henry's motor car, however. First of all, between Kiel and Hemmelmark, you had to replenish the boiler, stopping at some farmhouse on the way to get water in a bucket. Then, in accordance with the force of the draught created by the car, flames and steam would envelop the passengers in the back seat, and the temperature would become uncomfortably high. Coming back from Hemmelmark I was frozen up to the waist by the icy wind we faced, while the lower part of my body was being roasted like St. Laurence on the gridiron!*

Prince Henry paid a visit of considerable length to England during the summer of 1914. On 8th May he had breakfast with King George, and subsequently paid his cousin a number of visits. They were men of the same stamp, frank and simple.[27] They discussed the international situation. The Prime Minister regarded these conversations as "a diplomatic channel". Such channels had worked before, and might be of assistance now.[28] Prince Henry was an admirer of Britain, but his ties went deeper than that. His wife's sister was married to a British subject. He could not bring himself to believe that Britain and Germany would come to war. His feelings were shared by his sister, Sophie, by this time Queen of Greece, who, in July, brought her children and their English nurse to spend their holidays at Eastbourne.

During that month Prince Henry was yachting at Cowes. On the morning of the 26th he called in at Buckingham Palace and asked the King if there was any news. The King told him that the news was very bad, and that he had better get back to Germany. Prince Henry asked what Britain would do if war broke out. The King answered: "I don't know what we shall do, we have no quarrel with anyone and I hope we shall remain neutral. But if Germany declared war on Russia, and France joins Russia, then I am afraid we shall be dragged into it. But you can be sure that I and my Government will do all we can to prevent a European war!"[29] The Prince replied that, if hostilities broke out, he hoped

---

* In the midst of his torments the Saint is reputed to have said to his judge: "I am roasted enough on this side. Turn me round, and eat."

that their personal friendship would not be affected. He said that he would first call in on his sister Sophie[30] at her Eastbourne hotel, and then proceed to Germany. This he did, reaching Kiel two days later. The Queen of Greece returned home, but left her children to continue their holiday in the care of their English nurse. It is apparent that, if Prince Henry and his sister had anticipated war, the children would have immediately returned to Greece.

From Kiel Prince Henry wrote to the Emperor. He quoted King George as having said: "We shall try all we can to keep out of this and shall remain neutral."[31] Again the Emperor read the words as he wished to read them, although Prince Henry later admitted that, in the tense moments of excitement, he had interpreted an "anxious hope" as a "definite assurance".[32]

The armies were marching, but Emperor William (now referred to simply as "The Kaiser") told Admiral von Tirpitz, doubtful on the point of neutrality, that he had the word of a King.[33] War was declared on the 4th August, and six days later the Kaiser telegraphed President Wilson that he had been assured by King George V that Britain would remain neutral.[34] *

An urgent message reached King George from Queen Sophie of Greece, begging him to arrange a safe passage home for her children and their nurse. The dangers from submarines and mines in the English Channel were considerable, but a boat was chartered and, accompanied by a destroyer, took the stranded party to Holland.[35] The children were the nephews and nieces of the Kaiser.

In those first few anxious weeks of war discussion began on the strange situation that Princess Henry of Prussia was the sister of Princess Louis of Battenberg, whose husband was First Sea Lord.

---

* It was not until 1938 that final proof came of the actual words used by King George in his last talk with Prince Henry.

28

Dropping the Pilot

T HROUGH THE REIGN OF EDWARD VII AND INTO THAT OF
George V the career of Prince Louis of Battenberg gathered
brilliant achievement and fitting reward. In 1905 he was
in command of the 2nd Cruiser Squadron, the manœuvring and
smartness of which created a sensation when on a visit to the
United States and Canada. In 1908, the fortieth year of his service,
he was confirmed as Vice-Admiral and appointed as Commander-
in-Chief of the Atlantic Fleet. He was still a very fit sailor, troubled
only by occasional attacks of gout, as had been his cousin, the
Grand Duke Louis. In 1911 he commanded the 3rd and 4th
Divisions of the Home Fleet, the fine old Admiralty House at
Sheerness becoming the family home for a while. It was at East-
church Aerodrome, under his command, that the first Naval
officers were trained as pilots. "P.L." gave them personal and
enthusiastic support, and Battenbergs, of both sexes and all ages,
became airborne. Among those pioneer airmen were some, like
Samson and Longmore,[1] whose names were soon to be writ in
stars across the sky.

Lady Milford Haven now achieved a personal record by becoming the first Princess to fly:

> That summer we had our first experience in aeroplane flying.

The planes were not made to carry passengers and for our short flight—for Louis would not allow me to be taken on a long one—we perched, securely attached, on a little stool hung on to the flyer's back. Commander Sampson took Louis and me and Lieutenant Longmore* took Louise and Dickie.

On 9th December 1912 Prince Louis was appointed First Sea Lord, which meant that he was virtually operational Commander-in-Chief of all the Fleets and the professional head of the Royal Navy.[2] Objective achieved. "He was never defeated in manoeuvres until 1912—and was, in the opinion of many, the greatest naval officer of his day."[3] The Battenbergs moved into Mall House, with its marble staircase and the splendour of its rooms.

The younger generation grew up apace. Prince George of Battenberg left Cheam in 1905 and went to the Royal Naval Colleges of Osborne and Dartmouth. Lady Milford Haven recalled an early voyage of her elder son:

> On the 26th April 1909, Georgie passed out fourth from Dartmouth. In June he started in the cadet training ship, the *Cornwall*, for a tour of the Baltic. He found relations in each of the countries that line it, and after asking permission to visit his cousin, Queen Maud, in Norway and his cousin Daisy† at Stockholm, the commander grew somewhat suspicious when he wished to visit an aunt‡ in Kiel, an aunt§ in Moscow, and another‖ in St. Petersburg, and was not convinced of the genuineness of these Russian relations until he showed a telegram from Ella inviting him to visit her.

Prince George went to sea as a midshipman in 1910 and the following year, whilst in the *Cochrane*, accompanied King George and Queen Mary to the Delhi Durbar. Promoted Sub-Lieutenant in 1913, he did the round the world cruise in the *New Zealand*, the battle cruiser given to the Royal Navy by New Zealand.[4]

"Little Prince Louis",¶ the youngest in the family, had a very full childhood. He was known as "Dickie". He followed the Flag

* Air Chief Marshal Sir Arthur Longmore.
† The first wife of Crown Prince Gustavus Adolphus, whom he had married in 1905, was Princess Margaret (Daisy) of Connaught.
‡ Princess Henry of Prussia.
§ Grand Duchess Elizabeth.
‖ Empress Alexandra Feodorovna.
¶ Thus called to avoid confusion with his father.

to Gibraltar and Malta, spent his summer holidays at Heiligenberg, and travelled with his mother to stay with his Imperial uncle
and aunt in Russia.[5] In his early days his achievements in the air
were more spectacular than those on the sea. Although he flew in
a biplane at ten, this was not his first experience of leaving the
ground. Four years before he had been at Wolfsgarten when a
Parsifal airship was sent over for the inspection of the Grand Duke
Ernest Louis. It was a very hot day. The passengers were in the
basket, waiting for the moment of lift, when the captain decided
that he needed a sandbag to counteract the effect of the expansion
of the gas. On the ground a little boy was looking up in wonderment. "This will do," said the Grand Duke. Leaning down, he
took "Dickie" by the collar of his coat and lifted him in.[6]

"Dickie" went to Locker's Park preparatory school in 1910 and
three years later arrived at Osborne as a cadet. He had achieved
the status of uncle in 1905 when a daughter, Margarita, was born
to Princess Andrew of Greece. Theodora followed the next year,
and Cecile in 1911.

In 1913 Prince Louis spent a short holiday with his sister,
Marie,* at her lovely home of Schönberg, only a few miles from
Heiligenberg when one rode through the woods. Alone, they made
the days an experiment in time and went back to the chapters of
Alice. Princess Marie had bought herself a small motor-car and
together they drove to scenes and towns which they had not seen
since before the Franco-Prussian war. One baking hot afternoon
they drove across the flat lands, past the little farms, to the great
river which flows by the hills to the west. She wrote in her diary:

> Under the trees of a little inn, down on the Rhine, we drank coffee.
> The river glittered golden behind the poplar avenue. On the oppo-
> site shore one saw like a faint pastel drawing the blue peaks of the
> Bergstrasse.
> On the water gay tugs and barges steamed along, and little naked
> boys were turning somersault on the horizontal bars at the swimming
> pool, their bodies flashing in the clear air. A dog was swimming in
> the river, shook himself on the opposite bank, and jumped once more
> into the water.

* Princess Marie's husband, Gustavus, Prince of Erbach-Schönberg, had died in
1908.

For long we sat enjoying the peaceful, beautiful water picture. When Louis had to leave again he said to me, drawing a deep breath: "Oh! I shall come now every year to you, to rest. This is at last possible, now I don't go to sea any more, but live in London." *Auf Wiedersehen.*[7]

On 28th June 1914 the Archduke Francis Ferdinand of Austria was murdered at Sarajevo. In July Prince Louis organised the first test mobilisation of the British Fleet.* The officially advertised dates were from Wednesday 15th to Monday 27th, and the combined Home Fleets were to concentrate at Spithead for the review by King George V from the 17th to 18th.

Excitement and activity swept through every branch of the Navy—except for one. Over the Royal Naval College, Osborne, where Cadets spent their first two years before going on to Dartmouth, there hung a cloud of gloom and disappointment. The Cadets had been told that they would not be required to man the Reserve Fleet. Strong was the protest at being left out, and no voice more indignant than that of young Prince Louis of Battenberg, by now in his fourth term.

Then came reprieve. The news flashed round Osborne that the Cadets were to be divided among the capital ships and cruisers, and to witness the mobilisation and the visit of the King. Young Prince Louis was "mobilised" on board his brother's ship, the battle cruiser *New Zealand*. His father and the First Lord, Mr. Winston Churchill, shared the Admiralty yacht, *Enchantress*.

After the "Steam Past" and "PZ", and the Cadets had been disembarked, the vast Fleet sailed for exercises based on Portland. The manœuvres which took place ensured that virtually the whole of the Royal Navy was at a strength and pitch of training never before achieved in history.

One by one the lights went out in Europe. On the 23rd Austria delivered to Serbia an ultimatum, the terms of which were almost impossible of acceptance. The Belgrade Government was given

* Prince Louis first put up the idea of a test mobilisation in 1912, when he was Second Sea Lord and Chief of Naval personnel. With the approval of the First Lord (Mr. Winston Churchill) he arranged for this mobilisation to be carried out when he was First Sea Lord. Such a test required months of preparation and notice to foreign countries.

only forty-eight hours to agree. The time of expiry was six o'clock on the evening of the 25th.

It was a Saturday, and Prince Louis settled down to a weekend at his desk at the Admiralty. Mr. Winston Churchill had travelled to Cromer to see his wife, Clementine, who was unwell. The Prime Minister, Mr. Asquith,* and the Foreign Secretary, Sir Edward Grey,† were also out of London. Prince Louis commented: "Ministers with their week-end holidays are incorrigible."[8]

The Serbian reply to the ultimatum was very conciliatory, but Austria refused to accept it, and the Austro-Hungarian Minister left Belgrade. The Austrians mobilised eight Army Corps,[9] and the Serbs appealed for help to their ally, Russia.

Through Saturday evening and Sunday morning Foreign Office telegrams and special editions of the newspapers reached Prince Louis in rapid succession. As the hours passed the news became more and more alarming. By midday on Sunday Prince Louis knew that he had to make a decision.

On Monday the big Fleet at Portland had orders to disperse, demobilise and give leave.[10] The Powers had been informed of the date when the mobilisation test would end. To keep the Fleet in being, on a war footing, if war did not break out, might be considered a provocation and prove the spark which would ignite such a war. To allow the crews to disperse, if war did break out, would leave their ships impotent pending the recall of the reserves. Prince Louis took it upon himself to countermand the demobilisation orders. He spoke with Mr. Churchill on the telephone. The First Lord, and the other Ministers, returned that evening to find all arrangements made for keeping the Fleet intact.[11] By 1st August a state of war existed between Germany and Russia, and next day German troops marched on to French territory. On the 4th they violated the sanctity of Belgium, and at midnight Britain entered the war.

Prince Louis had, by his initiative, enabled the British Fleet to be ready for any eventuality when the dread moment came. But, if he had been proved wrong, he might well have had to

---

* Afterwards Earl of Oxford and Asquith.
† Afterwards Viscount Grey of Fallodon.

resign. He had done a great service to the country of his adoption, but he was to receive few thanks.

Meantime Prince Louis had another worry, for his wife and daughter, Louise, were in Russia. They had travelled there in mid-July in order to take part in an interesting trip through the country with the Grand Duchess "Ella". Lady Milford Haven described in detail her adventurous journey to the Urals:

In 1813 the tricentenary of the reign of the Romanoff dynasty had been celebrated in Russia, and Nicky and Alix visited the home towns of the family, Jaroslaw and Kostroma on the Volga. One of the river inspector's ships had been fitted out as a yacht for them. It had not been returned to its usual service, and Nicky had suggested that it might be used by us for our trip. We embarked at Nijni Novgorod (renamed Gorky) and after visiting that town, then in its somnolent period before the great autumn fair, we steamed down the Volga to Kazan. We spent a couple of days there, Ella attending church services and we doing sight seeing and all lunching at the Governor's house in the Kremlin. All the old fortified centres of Russian cities went by that name. It was interesting to see the Tartar population still in their distinctive Oriental clothes. There seemed to be a lot of eye disease amongst them, for there were many blind or half-blind people walking about.

From Kazan we steamed up the Kama,, which falls into the Volga a little lower than that town, and went as far as Perm. The immense breadth of the Volga was most imposing, but the shores were not very picturesque and, owing to the great width of the river, often far off, while the banks of the Kama offered much variety. There were little towns with their churches showing among the woods and meadows topping the banks.

We landed at various spots, where Ella had to visit convents. At one place I remember a large wood of lime trees in full bloom, and the scent was delicious. The population of the villages all turned out in their best clothes to receive Ella. There we saw a man of the Tcheremiss tribe, strikingly different from the Russians.

We often ate small sterlet, freshly caught, which I consider much better than the great fat sterlet people make such a fuss about. The ship, though not luxurious, was very comfortably furnished and a good big bathroom had been built in it. Our river voyage ended at Perm, where Ella and we separated, she going to visit various convents, one of which was at Alapaievsk, the place in which she was interned in the schoolhouse during the revolution and from where she was taken out to be murdered.

Meanwhile Louise and I made a tour in the Urals by special train. One of the first places we visited was the town of Kishtym, where no member of the Imperial Family had been since Alexander I. Though not the rose, I was near enough to it, being the Empress's sister, and we were officially received there during two or three days. At all the other places we stopped we were very hospitably welcomed too, both officially and privately, and were presented with gifts and souvenirs. At Kishtym there was an exhibition of Home Industries and we were given complete peasant costumes.

There we visited an interesting cave on the banks of the small river, which had only been discovered a year or two before. The weather being exceedingly hot and the cave being very cold, elaborate preparations were made for us to put on thick stockings, overcoats and wraps in a tent specially erected for this. We were not allowed to stay very long in the cave for fear of getting inflammation of the lungs from the extreme and sudden change of temperature. We had to crawl through the entrance, sheepskins having been laid down on the ground in the passage on the rocky soil. The limestone ridge was not high, nor was the cave very deep, faint daylight penetrating into it, yet the temperature was permanently below freezing point. In one corner there was a great mass of smooth ice of a lovely blue colour, and the roof of the cave was encrusted with large and perfect ice-crystals of fascinating shape, for the air was absolutely still. They were so brittle that our walking about would cause them to fall down. When we left the cave, we felt exactly as if we were entering an oven. The official and opulent banquet that evening was a very trying performance!

From Kishtym the train took us into the Ural Mountains, where we visited various mines. The furthest point we went to was a little beyond the sign post on the old road, one arm of which was marked "Europe" and the other "Asia". The scenery of the Urals reminds one of Scotland. There are no great mountain peaks and the hills are often covered to their summits with firs, while rivers and lakes can be seen in the valleys.

The biggest town we visited was Ekaterinburg. I did not think the town attractive and the population did not seem particularly pleased at the official visit. I noticed it especially at an evening entertainment of fireworks, where the crowd was quite unenthusiastic. We also attended a sort of afternoon party on the banks of a lake, driving through woods and forests not far from the spot where the remains of the destroyed bodies of Nicky, Alix and their children were found.

The Ipatiev house at Ekaterinburg, where Nicky, my sister and family were interned, lies on a big square, and I have several times driven past it and remember that it was pointed out to me as belonging to a rich merchant.

Meanwhile the political outlook was so threatening that any hopes of Louis and Dickie being able to join us on this holiday were given up, and Alix warned Ella that we had better return to St. Petersburg as soon as possible as war might break out any day. We went straight back to Perm, and our journey from there to St. Petersburg was a slow one, as mobilisation was in full swing and our train had several times to be shunted off the line to make way for the troop trains to pass. War between Russia and Germany was declared while we were under way.

We reached St. Petersburg on the evening of August 4th, on the very day England also declared war. Sir George Buchanan and Isa Buxhoeveden, one of Alix's ladies-in-waiting, received us at the station and the latter took us to the Winter Palace. Alix, with the two eldest girls, came to see us next morning, and I spent the next day with her and her family at Peterhof. She came again to see us before we left and, with loving forethought, equipped us with thick coats and other serviceable clothing for the sea journey, we only having the lightest of summer clothing with us.

We had to provide ourselves with a largish sum of money in golden sovereigns, which was rendered possible through special Imperial permission. I believe it was £200, which we divided up, each one of the party having a share of the money in small bags worn round our waists under our dresses. We left St. Petersburg on the afternoon of August 7th. I little dreamt that it was the last time I should ever see my sisters.

We were taken by special train to the Russian frontier, at Torneo, at the head of the Gulf of Bothnia. Lying at a wayside station, I caught sight of another saloon carriage on the line opposite to us, in which I recognised Aunt Minnie,* her daughter Olga and party at tea. We dashed across to speak to her and get the latest news. Aunt Minnie had come from England and Olga from France, and they had been sent out through Berlin and Sweden and were now nearing home.

We boarded the last steamer leaving Bergen. They had managed to secure cabins for us from Oslo. The ship was crowded with the last tourists and anglers coming from distant parts of Norway, and people slept on the floor of the dining saloon. We crossed the North Sea going as high up as Petershead and coasting down from there to Newcastle. We had good weather and an undisturbed voyage, but we found all the warm clothes Alix had provided us with most useful in the fresh sea air.

* Dowager Empress of Russia.

We arrived in London on the 17th of August, ten days after we left St. Petersburg. We found Louis absorbed in his work, which went on at night as well as by day. As to Dickie, whose leave from college had begun several days before, he had been quite solitary at the Mall House till we arrived, and tried to find occupation in the care of some white mice he had bought for that purpose.

In the first wild, frenzied, uncomprehending weeks of war there welled up in Britain a hatred of Germany, and all things German, such as has never exploded between one nation and another. People cursed the day when George I took over from Queen Anne. Dachshunds were stoned and shops with German names had their windows smashed. Abuse flowed through the mail to anyone who could, to any degree, be associated with the hated Hun. Even the youngest daughter of Queen Victoria, Princess Beatrice, did not escape, for her title was Princess Henry of Battenberg. She received a rude letter asking what part she was playing in the war. As she was already engaged in war work, and planning for the hospital that she later ran so efficiently in Hill Street, this riled even this most docile of ladies. She tartly replied that she had already lost her husband on active service and that her three sons had left for the front on 12th August. She did not see what more she could do.[12] Of those sons, Prince Alexander was serving with the Grenadier Guards, Prince Leopold, despite being a sufferer from haemophilia, had joined the Isle of Wight Rifles, and Prince Maurice had been commissioned into the 60th Rifles in 1910.

The tirade against Prince Louis was not long in starting. Why, it was asked, did Britain need a man of German origin, and a Hessian General to boot, at the Admiralty? Could not Britain produce a sailor of her own? Three old cruisers were torpedoed in the North Sea, and some of the allegations in certain sections of the Press bordered on treachery on the part of the First Sea Lord.[13] In his post came anonymous letters crammed with vilification, and the clubs buzzed with rumours. It was said that letters had been received from Germany containing the definite information that Prince Louis was a spy. If such letters were received, it was clear that they were part of a German ruse to spread confusion. But the newspapers, headed by the *Globe*, which were on the hunt

305

and intent on a kill, would hear no reason. A sense of mortification and a great, deep sadness swept through the old sailor. On 28th October he picked up his pen and wrote to Mr. Churchill a letter that seemed to sweep away all the usefulness, all the message, of his life. He resigned his appointment as First Sea Lord.

> I have lately been driven to the painful conclusion that at this juncture, my birth and parentage have the effect of impairing in some respects my usefulness on the Board of Admiralty. . . .[14]

The forces ranged against Prince Louis could, briefly, be divided into four sections. The first was small, and composed of senior officers, mostly on the retired list, who had for many years been jealous of "P.L.'s" ability, his promotion, and of the great respect which his subordinates felt for him.[15] This section was responsible for the rumours in the clubs. The second was made up of the mass of readers who devoured the pages of the accusing Press, ever anxious to see a head fall from a high place.

In the third section were upper-class die-hards, whose families had never accepted the invasion of German royalty and still drank the King's health with their glass over the finger-bowl. They were Stuart-minded, and looked down on German Grand Dukery. In their travels abroad they had made their attitude abundantly clear. Although the main objective for Germany in declaring war was expansion in land and trade, a side issue was a chance to have a duel with the stately homes of England and Scotland. The common man and the Royal Family were little involved.

The fourth, and last section, comprised those who suddenly woke up with a start to realise that German spies were in their midst, and had been for some years. They were not previously anti-German, but suddenly became so, and began looking for spies in every churchyard. That spies had been carefully planted around Britain since the early days of King Edward's reign was soon discovered and accepted. The swift realisation, coupled with the bitter feeling of having been fooled, meant that everyone remotely connected with Germany was considered guilty. When the zeppelins came in, and lights from below guided them to their main targets in the Midlands, the fears of these people were, in the main, justified. Those so sociable Germans, who had travelled round the countryside with their sketch-books, and then disappeared overnight, were vividly recalled.

Mr. Churchill deeply regretted the loss of Prince Louis. So did King George. "At 4.0 I saw poor Louis, very painful interview, he quite broke down. I told him I would make him a Privy Councillor to show the confidence I had in him, which pleased him."[16] So did the Prince of Wales, who called upon him and noticed that "the hurt showed in his tired, lined face".[17] So did Labour statesman, Mr. J. H. Thomas, who wrote to *The Times** about it and paid his tribute. So did a multitude of those fortunate enough to know the truth. A valued message came from the Commander-in-Chief, Grand Fleet:

> . . . The whole Fleet will learn the news . . . with the deepest possible regret. We look to you with the greatest loyalty, respect, and gratitude for the work you have accomplished for the Navy.[18]

But Prince Louis did not allow his personal tragedy to drown his sense of humour. Walking along Pall Mall, he met General Sir Henry Wilson. The two men had known one another since the days when young Wilson had visited Darmstadt to learn German. "Hello, Admiral," called out Sir Henry. "I'm uncommonly glad to see you. Heard you were in the Tower."

"P.L." answered: "Behind the times as usual, Henry. I was shot last Thursday."[19]

The shock for the Battenberg boys was severe. For George the load was lightened. When the news reached the *New Zealand*, his turret's crew asked to see him. They wished to tell him that they considered the treatment meted out to his father was terrible, and to give him their deepest sympathy.[20] But for fourteen-year-old "Dickie" the cross was harder to bear, for youth feels more deeply, yet proffers less sympathy. If tears welled on that October day at Osborne,[21] they can be readily excused and understood. Idols, such as that boy's father, can never be replaced undamaged upon their plinths.

Much of the responsible Press commented little on the resigna-

* 4th November 1914.

tion, but a page of *The Sphere* of 7th November summed up the sudden poignant sadness of the events which had overtaken the Battenbergs. Three pictures filled the page's top. On the left was that of Prince Louis, with the caption that his resignation "caused a very lively regret in naval circles". In the centre was that of his successor, Lord Fisher of Kilverstone. To the right was a photograph of twenty-three-year-old Prince Maurice. He was dead. He had fallen while fighting a gallant rearguard action at Ypres during the retreat from Mons on 28th October.[22] He had already been mentioned in despatches. He was the first lad from the Isle of Wight to lay down his life. Field Marshal Sir John French[*] wrote in his diary:

> On this day Prince Maurice of Battenberg died of his wounds. He was a young officer of great promise, and much beloved of his regiment, the 60th Rifles.[23]

The Commander-in-Chief informed Lord Kitchener that on this occasion he was prepared to make an exception and allow the Prince's body to be returned to England. But Princess Beatrice would accept no preference, saying that her son should be buried, with the others, somewhere between the Somme and the sea.[24] As Queen Ena despatched her wreath to Ypres, she received a telegram. It was from Kaiser Wilhelm, offering his condolences. He received the stiffest of stiff replies.[25]

The King and Queen, Queen Alexandra, Empress Eugenie of France and two Field Marshals, Kitchener and Grenfell, attended the memorial service at the Chapel Royal, St. James's. It was only the second time in her life that the aged Empress had attended an Anglican service,[26] but she was intent on showing her loyalty to a family which had befriended her.

It was to the Isle of Wight that Prince and Princess Louis now retired, living at Kent House, Osborne, which Princess Louise, Duchess of Argyll, made over to her niece, Victoria. The Prince busied himself with Red Cross activities and began work on a history of naval medals.[†] He also helped his wife in the garden

---

[*] 1st Earl of Ypres.
[†] Later completed by his younger son and to become a basic study.

and was often to be seen striding out on his walks, a lonely figure staring out to sea.

In 1917 King George swept away the princely German titles, and into history went Coburg and Teck, Schleswig-Holstein and Battenberg.* Prince and Princess Louis became the Marquess and Marchioness of Milford Haven. Prince George,† using his father's second title, became Earl of Medina. Prince Louis ("Dickie") received the courtesy title of Lord Louis Mountbatten, and his unmarried sister, that of Lady Louise Mountbatten. Princess Henry of Battenberg became plain Princess Beatrice again, as, in fact, she had long been known. Her eldest son became the Marquess of Carisbrooke‡ and her younger, Lord Leopold Mountbatten.

The name of Battenberg, resurrected from obscurity two-thirds of a century before to give title to the family of a gay Hessian Prince who had bolted from Russia with a lady-in-waiting of the Empress, died once more. Those who had first borne it had written their names in large and glittering letters across the pages of their time. They all had tried to climb the peak, risking the fall. Louis, "Sandro", and "Liko" were all colourful men. They passed the colour on.

---

* Prince Francis Joseph of Battenberg, who had married Princess Anna Petrovitch-Neigosh of Montenegro in 1897, died in 1924. There were no children.

† Married, 15th November 1916, Countess Nadejda (Nada) Torby, daughter of Grand Duke Michael Michailovitch of Russia. They had two children, Lady Tatiana Mountbatten, born in 1917, and David, Viscount Alderney, afterwards 3rd Marquess of Milford Haven, born 1919.

‡ Married Lady Irene Denison, 19th July 1917. They had one daughter, Lady Iris Mountbatten, born 1920.

29

The Cellar and the Shaft

O N A DAY AT THE END OF JULY 1918 PRINCESS MARIE LOUISE
travelled from Windsor to the Isle of Wight. They were
the most terrible hours of her life. In her handbag was
a letter from King George V, addressed to his cousin Victoria,
Marchioness of Milford Haven. The letter contained the news
that Victoria's sister, Alix, her brother-in-law, Nicholas, and their
five children, had been murdered in a cellar at Ekaterinburg, a
town on the eastern foothills of the Ural mountains.

Lord Milford Haven took that letter and told of its contents to
his wife. Shortly afterwards she went to the Princess's room to
thank her for bringing it in person. Thereafter, through the three
weeks during which Princess Marie Louise was a guest at Kent
House, the tragedy was not mentioned. Through the meaningless
summer days the three worked in the garden. In the evenings
they read aloud to one another. There were comforts to be knitted
for the troops.[1]

At the peak of happenings there come moments that are too
strong for words. There were echoes always in the three minds,
the blast echoes of the bombs which had killed Alexander II and
the Grand Duke Serge, and filled a narrow Madrid street with the
dead and the screaming as Queen Ena looked down at the blood

upon her bridal dress. To those moments time had given focus. But there could only be harm now in probing into the present possibilities and the probabilities—the bodies hacked to pieces in the dust, the searing acid, hands of assassins groping through underwear in the search for jewels, the fearful stench of the slow fire in the empty forest.

There were other worries and fears for those working in the island garden. What could be the fate of their many friends and relations caught in the Russian maelstrom? Louis's aunt had been the ill-fated Empress Marie, and there were many ties. For Victoria there was a great unanswered question. What would the Bolsheviks do to her sister "Ella", the Grand Duchess Elizabeth, working in her Convent in Moscow?

Victoria, Marchioness of Milford Haven, was a woman of superb courage. She faced the tragedy of Ekaterinburg with the same calmness and strength that she had shown in Moscow after the death of the Grand Duke Serge, and at the time of the resignation of her husband. Through these, and the sorrows to come, she never allowed her sadness to intrude into the lives of those around her.[2]

Empress Alexandra Feodorovna began her walk to Ekaterinburg on an autumn evening in 1912 when her only son, the Cesarevitch Alexei, lay near to death at the Imperial shooting lodge at Spala. The doctors had given up hope and Princess Henry of Prussia, who was staying with her sister, asked the Household to disperse early, as the news was so bad. Then it was that the Empress, in her desperation, turned for help to a so-called faith healer whom she had first met in 1906. His name was Gregory Novikh, but he was called Rasputin, which means "debauchee". She asked Rasputin to pray for her dying son. He agreed, and in the morning the Cesarevitch was out of danger.[3] Thereafter she put her trust in him, regarded him as Holy man, a man of God, moved under his influence and venerated him even after the bullets had cut through his already poisoned body. His prayers had saved her boy's life! The same powers of healing had been bestowed upon two glasses of beer swallowed by the Prince of

Wales on 14th December 1871 when he was miraculously snatched from the jaws of death.

Rasputin was a peasant. He was born in the province of Tobolsk, Siberia, in 1871. He received little education and his youth was associated with many dubious activities, including horse-stealing. He married, and was the father of three children. In 1904 he came under the influence of a priest and became imbued with the idea that he must repent. Bearing chains, he travelled from monastery to monastery, picking up prayers and fragments of the Gospels as he did so. His magnetic eyes, his great strength, his apposite quotations, combined to build up his reputation as a "Holy man". His appetite for wine and women was prodigious, but, after each indulgence, he made extravagant repentance. He encouraged others to sin so that they might obtain forgiveness, and this suited well some of those who listened to him. He made several long pilgrimages, including one to Jerusalem. Then he set his eyes upon St. Petersburg and the Court of Nicholas II. Through priests, who thought that he spoke with the mouth of the people, and ladies-in-waiting, who were either mischievous or had not enough to occupy their minds, Rasputin made his preordained way to the Empress Alexandra Feodorovna. He held her firm through his power, supposed or real, of being able to alleviate the sufferings of her son, and she succumbed to his magnetic mantle of the super-natural. Patronage from the Palace went to his head and he began to interfere in church affairs. Through his influence the strangest of people rose to high position. Then rumours of debaucheries at Court began to circulate. It was said that Rasputin was sexually involved, not only with the Ladies there, but also with the Empress. Any fabrication began to find a hearing. Russia and Germany went to war—and the Empress was a German. In 1914 an attempt was made on his life, but failed. Two years later a group of men of high position decided that the menace of Gregory Rasputin must end, and that he must die.[4]

The reasons why Alexandra Feodorovna fell so easily, even willingly, for the wiles of Rasputin, stemmed from the day of her birth, and thereafter built up through the years.

Two of Queen Victoria's grandchildren were born at moments

when their mothers were passing through times of great emotional stress. The first was William, first child of the Princess Frederick William, Princess Royal of England. On the one hand the eternal chivvyings and exhortations and recriminations received daily in the post from her mother, on the other the bullying and spite with which she had to contend at the Berlin court, had reduced her to a state of nervous prostration. She was fortunate indeed to survive her labours and the child was only brought to life through the spanking of its body with a wet towel by the midwife.[5] The second was Alix, daughter of Princess Alice of Hesse, who at the time of her confinement was in a state of mental turmoil over her religious beliefs and the preachings of David Strauss. In each case an outstanding characteristic showed in the unlucky child. It amounted to the importance of "I", egotism in varying degrees, amounting in the case of Emperor William to megalomania.

Death hung closely around the childhood days of Princess Alix. She had lost a brother, a sister and her mother by the time she was six. The girl was a ripe subject for religious indoctrination and Dr. Sell, the Hessian divine who gave her this teaching, soon had a strong influence over her. When she changed her religion, she became more Orthodox than the Orthodox, as often happens with converts. She longed for the religious fervour of the past, complaining that her generation was denied the comfort and support of the saints.[6] That way of thinking suited Rasputin, as did the egotism—and yet another experience of her past.

On the death of Princess Alice, Queen Victoria had taken over the role of mother to Princess Alix. When "Alicky" visited her grandmother, as she often did, she saw, through the eyes of a child, that a peasant was the most important person in the Household. If one wanted anything, one asked John Brown. Brown was with her grandmother all the day through, and never took days off. Brown was the strength. As she grew older she heard strange stories, that Brown was fey, that he was a medium and in touch with grandfather Albert in Heaven. The stories were everywhere. Then, when Brown died, and Princess Alix came to Windsor as a grown woman, there was another man ever around the Queen, this time an Indian, "the Munshi", again with those apparent powers over the Sovereign. The Empress Alexandra Feodorovna was not breaking new family ground when she gave her trust and confidence to the peasant Rasputin. The men were very different, but the latent power in them was the same, and they each held the ear of the woman at the top.

There was no question of any sexual association between the Empress and Rasputin. Apart from the fact that rigid procedure of the Imperial Court would have made it impossible, "Alicky" and "Nicky" were in love, and remained so to the end. To one another they used the language of lovers, and immature lovers at that. But she was the wrong woman for him. He was not strong enough for her. Edward VII described him as weak[7] and George V as "the kindest of men".[8] He could not stand up to her insistent demands, and so there came into her hands a power which she did not understand how to wield.

She used her influence over her husband to make men, and to break them. In 1916 she wanted to be rid of Polivanov, the Minister for War, who detested Rasputin. She sent her husband a note—"Get rid of Polivanov". The Emperor stalled, and nothing happened. Two months later he received another note—"Remember about Polivanov". Two days later she followed this up with another—"Lovey, don't dawdle." Polivanov went.[9]

Russia was suffering severely from the ravages and shortages of war. Disaffection spread throughout the country, yet the Emperor would not allow changes to be made in the Constitution, changes which were clearly essential. He clung to the wording of his Coronation Oath, determined, as was his wife, that his mantle should pass unaltered to his son. Hatred for Rasputin became an obsession, and Prince Youssoupoff, the Grand Duke Dimitri Pavlovitch and others decided that his death was the only answer. On 29th December 1916 Rasputin was invited to the Prince's house. He ate poisoned cakes and drank poisoned wine, but with little apparent effect, the alcohol proving an antidote. He was shot, but still refused to die, clambering, clawing after his killers until further bullets stilled him for ever. His body was put through a hole in the ice on the Neva River.[10]

Rasputin had told the Empress that, if he was to go, the

Romanoffs would not long endure.[11] His prophecy was soon fulfilled. On 11th March the Emperor, who was at his Army Headquarters at Moghilev, was handed a telegram from Rodzianko, President of the Duma. It read: ". . . There is anarchy in the capital. The Government is paralysed. Transportation of food and fuel is completely disorganised. General dissatisfaction grows. Disorderly firing takes place in the streets. . . ."[12] It was a Sunday and the crowds were out in the streets of St. Petersburg, carrying red banners and shouting, "Down with the German woman".[13] At Tsarskoe-Selo the Empress's garrison mutinied.

The Emperor tried to get back to Tsarskoe-Selo, but the railway workers heard of the move and blocked the line. On the 14th the Emperor telephoned Rodzianko, saying that he was prepared to make concessions to the people. But Rodzianko could hear the sound of gun-fire in the streets, and he replied that it was too late. Next day Nicholas II abdicated in favour of his brother, the Grand Duke Michael. But Michael would only assume power if it were offered to him by a Constituent Assembly. He, too, abdicated, and the long innings of the Romanoffs was over.[14]

In Britain few tears were shed over the abdication. It was generally regarded as the end of an autocratic system, the corruption and incompetence of which had prevented Russia from using her vast potential in the war effort. But King George had received a request to allow the Emperor and his family to live in England. Fond as he was of his cousins, the King did not welcome the idea, preferring that they should go to Denmark, Switzerland or France. But in the circumstances he could scarcely refuse, and as a result received much abuse from the Left Wing.[15]

When the idea of leaving was put to the Emperor and Empress, they both stolidly refused. It was, in any case, they said, impossible at the moment as the children had measles. Secretly, they both hoped that they would be allowed to live quietly in Russia.[16] The red light was hidden from them by the mists of tradition. In the event it is doubtful if the new leaders, who were appearing through the chaos, would have let them go. These men were not content with abdication. They were intent on destroying for ever the image of the Romanoffs, of reducing those who bore the name to piteous

315

characters without garb or character, of pulling down the Palace structure brick by brick, of leaving no belief, no loyalty, no respect, no fairy tale on which the dynasty could be rebuilt. The quality of mercy did not enter into it.

The ex-Emperor and Empress were under arrest, and prisoners with their family at Tsarskoe-Selo. They were allowed to speak only Russian, and every word was listened to. Exercise was restricted to an hour in the garden in the afternoon. "Citizen Romanoff", as Nicholas was now known, decided to bicycle round the paths for relaxation. A soldier put his bayonet through the spokes of a wheel.[17]

After the Bolshevik rising of July the Provisional Government decided that the Romanoffs should be moved. Tsarskoe-Selo was too near to the capital and there was a danger that it might be attacked by extremists. On 13th August they were told to prepare to leave, but they were not told their destination. It proved to be Tobolsk, a quiet town in Siberia. The curtain of world disinterest began to fall upon the exiled Imperial family. Britain's offer of asylum was withdrawn.[18] They were alone now, "Nicky" and "Alicky", with their daughters, Olga, aged twenty-two, Tatiana, twenty, Marie, eighteen, Anastasia, sixteen, and Alexei, thirteen.

At Tobolsk, far removed from the centres of political activity, life became easier for them before it became worse. They had their suite and servants about them. They were allowed to go to church. There was little hostility among the population. But with the winter came intense cold. Money began to run out, and food became scarce. Clothes were threadbare. More and more they had to rely on gifts from nuns and sympathisers. The Empress was by this time an invalid, racked by sciatica and troubled with her heart. The Emperor was suffering from his kidneys. Alexei had to be nursed through from day to day, and became so thin as to be almost transparent.[19]

By the spring the new order reached Tobolsk, in the form of bands of soldiers from Omsk and Ekaterinburg. Properties and valuables were requisitioned. Fear ran through the countryside, and the interlude of comparative peace for the Romanoffs was over. Orders came that Nicholas was to be moved. At the time

Alexei was suffering from an internal haemorrhage, and his life hung in the balance. Alexandra Feodorovna was faced with the terrible decision—should she go with her husband or stay with her son? She decided on the former course.[20]

In the early hours of 26th April 1918 four springless carts drew up outside their house. Nicholas, his wife and daughter, Marie, their physician, Dr. Botkin, Prince Dolgorouki, a former Marshal of the Court, and three servants were ordered to climb into them. There were no seats, but some straw was fetched from a pigsty and scattered on the boards. All day they drove over icebound tracks. Sometimes they dismounted to cross frozen rivers on narrow planks, Nicholas carrying his wife in his arms across one running stream. They came to a station and a train. After four days they reached Ekaterinburg. They were lodged in the home of an engineer, Ipatiev. It was fenced in with wooden palings. They could see only the cross on a church steeple in an empty sky.[21]

A month later the children and remainder of the suite and servants arrived at Ekaterinburg station. Among the passengers were Baroness Buxhoeveden, Maid of Honour to the ex-Empress, and M. Pierre Gilliard, Swiss tutor to Alexei. They had been parted from the children, who were in a separate carriage. M. Gilliard thus described the moments:

> I tried to get out, but was brutally pushed back by the sentinel. I stood at the window. I saw Tatiana Nicolaievna carrying her little dog and dragging along painfully a heavy valise. It was raining, and I saw her sinking in the mud with every step she took. . . . A few minutes later the cab drove off with the children in the direction of the town. How little did I guess that I was never to see again those with whom I had spent so many years.[22]

M. Gilliard and the Baroness were told that they were free. For eleven days they sheltered in a fourth class railway carriage, but then were ordered to leave the area. Of the others on the train, only two, a footman and a kitchen boy, survived.[23]

May to July in Ekaterinburg. The wooden palisade around the prison was made higher. The window panes were painted over. Bars went up outside. Nagorny, the sailor who had cared for Alexei, was taken away and shot. Anastasia's shoes wore out, and she asked permission to get another pair from the luggage, which was in the loft. She was told that the pair she had would "see her out".[24] The parents and Alexei slept in one room, the girls in an adjoining one from which the door had been removed. Some of the guards slept on the same floor, others in the basement. There was free access to the prisoners throughout the day and night. Meals were shared, the table manners being in violent contrast with those which had been followed at the Winter Palace. Newspapers were not allowed, and there was no contact with the outside.[25] They did not know that Czecho-Slovak troops of the White Russian army were approaching Ekaterinburg. This advance was later to be given as a reason for the murders.

The death warrant of the Romanoffs was signed in Room 10 of the Hotel Amerika, Ekaterinburg, on the evening of 15th July. It had been premeditated, and the condemned had been allowed to attend a religious service the previous day, a Sunday.[26] On the 16th the fifteen-year-old kitchen boy, Sednew, was told that he could go and visit his uncle. Alexandra Feodorovna retired, and wrote her diary:

> . . . would like to know if this is true and if we shall ever see the boy again? Played bezique with N. 10½ to bed—15° of heat.[27]

It was after midnight when the family and those few left with them were awakened. They were told that the town was in a state of insurrection and that they were to be moved to a safer place. They dressed and packed a few oddments. They were led downstairs and told to wait in a ground floor room until the carriages arrived. With the Romanoffs were Dr. Botkin, Anna Demidova, maid, Haritonov, cook, and Trupp, valet. On request, three chairs were brought in. Alexei sat on the floor.

The guards came in, a dozen strong, grouped close around the door. There was only the sound of their heavy boots on the boards. Then their leader spoke: "Nicholas Alexandrovitch, your friends have tried to save you, but they have not succeeded. We are obliged to shoot you." The ex-Emperor replied: "Aren't we going to be taken somewhere else then?" Revolvers roared a salvo. Only Anastasia and the maid lived, screaming, running from wall to wall. Other shots rang out, and then bayonets were used.

Ekaterinburg still slept as a lorry, surrounded by men on horseback, made its way through the streets towards the forest. There were but three witnesses of its passing. An old woman and her son and daughter-in-law from a nearby village had risen early and set off in their cart with a load of fish to sell in the town. They met the riders and the lorry on a track. They were ordered back to their village, and told not to look behind them on pain of death. But the old woman had seen the grim load on the lorry. She spoke of her fears and peasants went out to inspect. They came against a ring of sentries.[28]

By a disused mineshaft, in a clearing in the forest, the bodies were hacked into pieces. It was while this was going on that the executioners discovered that the Grand Duchesses had, with great ingenuity, sewn jewels round the seams of their underclothes. Most were found, but some fell to the ground and were trodden underfoot. For three days the acid and the fire befouled the trees with smoke and stench. On the 20th the ashes were thrown down the mineshaft and it appeared to the executioners as if the traces of the killings had been brushed clear away. Yet, in the burnt grass and the hot soil there hid many little things—the false teeth of Dr. Botkin, a glass from the spectacles of Alexandra Feodorovna, the buckle of the ex-Emperor's belt, a button from Alexei's coat.[29]

Ekaterinburg fell to the White Russian forces on 25th July, and an enquiry as to what had happened in the clearing in the Ganina forest was instituted. Patient research uncovered, among many smaller items, the metal framework of six corsets.[30] There were six women to be accounted for—the Empress, her four daughters and the maid.

30

The Passing of Saint Elizabeth

IN THE AUTUMN OF 1916 THE GRAND DUCHESS ELIZABETH, Abbess of the Order of Martha and Mary, took leave of her patients in the Convent wards, of the home which she had started for the care of consumptives, from the war work which filled every spare moment of the day, and travelled to St. Petersburg.[1] She was a worried woman, for her mission was delicate. She was intent on persuading the Emperor to order Rasputin back to the village in Siberia whence he had come.

Eleven years had passed since the sight of her dead husband had driven her to forsake the pleasures and comforts of the world. For the last six, with shaven head, she had slept the short nights in a little whitewashed room, on a hard wooden bed. If there was a risk of a patient dying, in her Convent or in her home, she kept constant vigil by the bedside. She, who had tasted of the glories and wonders of Russia while "Alicky" was still at her lessons, knew things about the people that the younger sister could never know.

In St. Petersburg she sensed the deep, frightening, fanatical hatred that was building up against the Empress. She came to Tsarskoe-Selo. She had lost familiarity now with the pomp and tradition that once she had known so well, taken as part of life. Strange seemed the gold and the glittering glass, the hot-house

Prince Andrew of Greece and Denmark

Alice, Princess of Battenberg
Wife of Prince Andrew of Greece and Denmark

flowers and the scent of roses, the groups of chamberlains and ladies-in-waiting with time idle on their hands, the Cossacks riding round and the liveried servants, the mighty rooms, the paintings, the photographs of those with whom she had played in another world.[2] She was told that she could not see the Emperor, as he was engaged in the conduct of war. So she spoke with Alexandra Feodorovna. But she did not speak as an Abbess to an Empress, but as "Ella", the elder sister, to "Alicky", the younger.

The journey of the Grand Duchess Elizabeth proved to be in vain. Her sister would listen to no warning about Rasputin, brushing aside the rumours that he was influencing her, the Cabinet and even the politics of Russia. She was convinced that he was a saint, the saviour of her son, and no one, not even a beloved sister, was going to send him away from her. She believed that the peasant population had faith in their Empress, and would understand that the presence of the man who was protecting the life of their future ruler, was essential.[3] Sadly the Grand Duchess returned to Moscow. She never saw her sister again.

In the first flush of anticipated victory in 1914, and with the early success of the Russian forces, the popularity of the Romanoffs had run high. But the reverses of the following year brought a sharp change, and soon every catastrophe was being attributed to the machinations of the secret agents of the Kaiser. Even the inefficiency of the railway system was attributed to espionage and treachery. As in the case of the Empress, the Grand Duchess did not escape the vilification of everything German, and in the summer of 1915 her car was stoned as she drove from the station to her convent. The opposition against her was confined to extremists, and she ignored it, continuing to visit the Fronts and continually struggling to ensure that the trains carrying relief supplies did not get lost in the railway sidings.

As the food in the shops grew scarce, rumours began to circulate that sumptuous meals were still being served in the Convent of SS. Martha and Mary, that behind its walls German prisoners were being sheltered and cared for, even that from there a telephone line ran direct to the Kaiser. It was said that the Grand Duke Ernest Louis of Hesse had been seen in Russia and that he had come to negotiate a separate peace at the invitation of his German sisters, now dubbed "the Hessian witches".* But to the poor and the sick and the wounded, for whom "Ella" slaved, she remained "Mátuskha".[4]

When the Emperor abdicated and the slow hounding down of the Romanoffs began, accusations against the Grand Duchess increased, with the intent of destroying her image as a saint. An armed gang battered on the Convent door, demanding to be allowed to search for German officers who were believed to be sheltering there. The Abbess sent her nuns into the Chapel and was alone when she opened the door. She told the leader that she would allow five men in to search. She asked them to leave their rifles in the hallway and, with quiet dignity, she led them around the building. The tour ended in the Chapel. There the Grand Duchess held a short service and the searchers stood, bare-headed and silent, before her. Then they picked up their rifles and went away.[5]

But that was in the early days of the new movement, and there was still magic in the Cross. Some outside observers saw clearly along the path of things to come, and among them was Kaiser Wilhelm in Germany. He had had a horror of assassination ever since the boy Cohen had shot at his grandfather. It became a fixation with him and news of attempts, whether on friend or foe, would send him into paroxysms of rage. It was this fear which had stopped him from visiting Spain before the war, although it would have been politic for him to have done so. King Alfonso despised him for it. Wilhelm sensed the threat of assassination now—the victim none other but the beautiful "Ella" whom he had loved as a girl in Darmstadt, and never ceased to love. He sent an urgent message to her through the Swedish Minister, begging her to leave before it was too late, guaranteeing her safe passage to Germany and refuge there. But "Ella" was a very different person now to the beauty who had played in the Hessian gardens of so

* Yet there was little of the German to be seen in either the Empress or the Grand Duchess Elizabeth. They invariably spoke English or Russian. In *Russia and History's Turning Point* Alexander Kerensky recalls the Empress saying to him: "Why do people think I am siding with Germany and our enemies? There is nothing German about me. I am English by education and English is my language."

long ago. She lived only for her faith and her work. Maybe she thought that the Bolsheviks would have little interest in a nun of foreign birth whose sole role was attending to the sick. She knew that the people loved her.

The Red Guards came to fetch her on an April night in 1918. Again alone, she opened the door. She was handed a note, purporting to be from the Emperor, telling her to come to him at once. The ruse worked. She packed a bag and went with them. Sister Barbara insisted on going with her. They were taken to the railway station and there put on a train.[6] For some seven hundred miles they travelled east towards the Urals and Siberia. At Perm, a town on the Kama river, they were ordered out by their guards and thrown into prison. They joined other victims of the Romanoff round-up—the Grand Duke Sergei Michailovich, three young sons of the Grand Duke Constantine, and Prince Paley, morganatic son of the Grand Duke Paul and half-brother of the Grand Duchess Marie.[7]

On 1st May the prisoners were taken to Ekaterinburg, though it is doubtful if the Grand Duchess knew that her sister and family were held behind the palisade round the Ipatiev House. A few days later they were driven by night to Alapaevsk, a small town in the copper and iron mining area, close to the Siberian boundary. There they were incarcerated in a schoolhouse, the garden of which was surrounded by a high wall. No preparation had been made for their comfort, and they slept on the classroom benches.

The summer of foreboding reached its height. The sun beat down on the schoolhouse, and endless seemed the airless nights behind the barred and padlocked windows. No visitors were allowed, nor priest to administer to them. Services were conducted by the Grand Duchess. Each day brought the indignity of a search by the guards, and once-daily rations were issued, these consisting of horseflesh and dried fish. But seeds were provided, and soon the garden was producing vegetables, allowing the Grand Duchess to revert to her normal diet. She and Sister Barbara mended the men's clothes, cared for their ills and worked with them in the garden.

The quiet and polite behaviour of the prisoners was rewarded by the uncovering of a chink of humanity in the armour of the guards. Prince Constantine and Prince Paley were able to persuade them to smuggle out a few letters. These told of the daily routine, of the kindness and strength of "Aunt Ella", and that it was she who knew the most about growing vegetables. No trace was found of letters written by the Grand Duchess herself.[8]

On the late evening of 18th July a lorry drew up outside the schoolhouse. Armed guards hustled the prisoners on to it. They were taken to a lonely spot at nearby Sinjatschicha.[9] There gaped the mouth of a disused mineshaft. They were told, this grand-daughter of Queen Victoria, her devoted companion in nun's apparel, the man and the boys, that they were to be thrown alive into the shaft before them.

The Grand Duchess Elizabeth asked but one favour of her executioners—that she should be allowed to cover her head with her cape. This was granted. Then she folded her hands before her and began singing a favourite hymn.[10] Those who were to die sang with her. Slowly, steadily, she began her walk, as the hymn tune filled the night. . . .

"Hail, gentle Light . . ."

On she walked, this grandchild of the Sovereign who had reigned longer, more gloriously, than any in British history, who in sixty years had feared no man and been beaten by no man. They had been such good friends, Victoria and "Ella"—they had shared the same strength. Echoes from the Osborne shore and children laughing on the battlements at Windsor . . . picnics with her mother at Kranichstein . . . tennis parties at Wolfsgarten . . . her first ball and Serge's kiss. . . .

Slowly she sank to her knees by the mineshaft's lip. Then, as hands closed in around her shoulders, the voice of her came clear from the white tent of her veil. "Thou, dear God, forgive them, for they know not what they do."

She went over, and the singing ceased.

Praying, fighting, crying, the others also went. One by one the screams of the falling faded. Two hand grenades followed where they had gone and in the wake of their blast came utter silence.

Then there were only wheel marks on the turf, footprints in the dust and sentinels under the trees.

But the tragedy had not passed unobserved. From a distance a priest, Father Seraphim, a devotee of the Grand Duchess Elizabeth, had kept in touch with the doings of that night. When Admiral Kolchak's White Army took over the area shortly afterwards, the priest, with the help of White soldiers, climbed down the mineshaft. At the bottom, by a lantern's light, he found a scene of utter sadness. Several of the victims, including the Grand Duchess, must have survived the fall. Their wounds and fractures had been bandaged with strips of cloth torn from clothing.[11] It was "Ella's" last act before she lay down and died.

Her body, and that of Sister Barbara, were hoisted to the surface, and the priest provided coffins. Father Seraphim was a strong and handsome man, with long hair and a beard. He was also a man of means,[12] his father being a merchant in Moscow who had long admired the work of the Grand Duchess. His experience down the shaft had fired him with the determination that he would not rest until the bodies of the two saintly women lay at peace in a Chapel of God. To take them west was out of the question, so he turned towards the east, towards the endless plains of Siberia, Mongolia, China, and the sea.

When the body of the Grand Duchess was recovered it was noted with wonder by the peasants who helped the priest in his task, that there was no change or damage to her face, nor was there any sign of decomposition. This added to the belief that she was a saint, and the word spread through the countryside. As the coffins began their long journey across Siberia, people gathered in groups by the wayside to pray at her bier. "They evoked her in their prayers, and marvellous cures took place."[13] Then all traces of the little caravan were lost, swallowed by the wide steppes.

In the autumn of 1920 Princess Beatrice saw, in a newspaper, a picture of a little shrine in an Orthodox chapel in Peking. Here lay, the story ran, two coffins which were said to contain the bodies of Grand Duchess Elizabeth and her companion, Sister Barbara. The Princess immediately sent the newspaper to Lady

Milford Haven. Enquiries were instituted, and the truth confirmed.[14]

The coffins were shipped to Port Said, the faithful priest who
had cared for them for two and a half years still beside them.
They rested for the night in the Greek Church. There it was that
Lord and Lady Milford Haven knelt in prayer beside them.
Victoria and "Ella" were together again. The living stared at the
likeness of the dead, let in to the coffin lid.

Afterwards Louis and Victoria listened to the tale of the holy
man whose superhuman love for a saint had brought this miracle
about. It began on the night when the sound of singing ended by
the shaft. It ended, a thousand days and many thousands of miles
later, on a P. and O. liner, homeward bound. This rugged man
qualified as a saint himself, and his journey was a saga.

The mourning party travelled by train to Jerusalem, the priest
keeping watch by the coffins in the luggage van. Their destination
was the Russian Orthodox Church of Mary Magdalene, on the
Mount of Olives, near Gethsemane.[15] How fitting was this resting-
place, for the Church had been erected by the Grand Duke Serge
and his family in memory of their mother, the Empress Marie,*
another Hessian Princess who had suffered sadness in Russia. In
1888 "Ella" and Serge had travelled together to Jerusalem for
the inauguration service. The lady-in-waiting, who had accompanied them then, followed the coffins now.[16]

In a letter to Princess Beatrice, her brother-in-law described
the arrival scene:

> At the station we were met by all the Orthodox clergy, and as
> soon as the coffins had been lifted on to the platform, a service was
> held. After this, each coffin was placed on a motor lorry, decorated
> with green bows, two priests in black and silver funeral vestments
> sitting on each side of "Ella's" coffin. We followed in two cars sent
> by Sir H. Samuel, and many more, full of Russians, followed. We
> drove towards the town, then skirted the West and North Walls
> and down into the valley. At two places we stopped for short services.
> At the foot of the Mount the coffins were lifted out and carried up
> the steep, stony, zig-zag road to the church. Most of the carriers
> were Russian peasant women, stranded pilgrims, who staggered

* Aunt of Lord Milford Haven.

under the tremendous load, sobbing and moaning all the time, and almost fighting to get at some part of the coffin. I clung to one of the handles, and once had to climb over the body of one of the women who had tripped over a stone and fallen full length. One huge lay priest, with hair like a lion's mane, was happily at the head end, but it was a relief when we reached the church safely. A service was held at once, the congregation overflowing through the open doors. . . .[17]

So ended the story of the woman who was outstanding among the grandchildren of Queen Victoria and Prince Albert, a woman of such beauty that many declared that they had never seen the like, a woman who conquered fear and to whom Faith meant all, a woman who subjected herself to stern discipline and expected the same of others, a woman who was loved and respected, not because of her birth and marriage, but despite them.

31

Grecian Bends

THE GREEK IDYLL INTO WHICH PRINCESS ALICE OF BATTENBERG walked with Prince Andrew of Greece after their Darmstadt wedding, lasted until King George V ascended the British Throne. In 1903, George I, Queen Alexandra's brother, had reigned over Greece for forty years and, although he had kept a portmanteau packed in case the people should ask him to go,[1] no such request had come. He had proved a very successful Monarch.

He was a most democratic man. He walked about the streets without escort, talking in his bluff way to all and sundry. No "Royal Highness" enriched the nomenclature of his sons, and on the Athens pavements they were greeted with "Good morning, George, Christopher or Andrew". A distinguished visitor to Greece was invited to the Court ball and hired a carriage for the occasion. The driver asked him if he would mind arriving a little early, as he himself was going to the ball and had to change.[2]

King George occupied in Greece a position similar to that of his sister, Alexandra, in her "kingdom", the parishes around Sandringham. Both were welcome at any door, both were regarded as Solomons for the settling of disputes, and both were consumed with a love for people and for animals. Neither could tolerate the shooting of birds. While this democratic way of life

suited well brown-eyed and fair-haired Princess Alice of Battenberg, brought up among the movements and uncertainties of a
sailor's home, with interludes at peaceful Heiligenberg, it came
as a strong contrast to sisters-in-law arriving from more rigid
Courts, and on occasion they lost patience.

Prince and Princess Andrew spent the winters at the Royal
Palace in Athens and the summers at Tatoi. The Palace was vast.
It had an impressive bath, but unfortunately it was seldom that
hot water came through the taps. In the cold months the Royal
Palace posed many problems of light and heat. The vast entrance
hall heralded a grand staircase. Long, dim galleries led to endless
rooms, many of which were never used, and enormous ballrooms
ran the Palace's length. The china stoves and the oil lamps did
not have a chance against the draughts and the cubic feet.[3] When
the temperature became intolerable, the hearty King would take
remedial measure by summoning his children and his grandchildren to engage in tournaments of battledore and shuttlecock,
organise bicycle races round the ballrooms[4] or, on roller skates,
lead them along the corridors, the serpent-like line behind him
swaying wildly. Both the last occupations usually ended in a heap
of relations piled upon one another, which appealed vastly to the
Danish sense of humour.

Tatoi was the real home of the Greek Royal Family. Built by
King George, in English cottage style, in 1886, the house stood in
an estate covering forty thousand acres, some twenty-four kilo-
metres from Athens across the plain of Attica. A pine forest
covered much of the area, and no less than fifty miles of roads
ran between its trees. The house and gardens were surrounded
by evergreens, and these played a vital role when war-time
tragedy came to Tatoi. Here privacy was precious, and, although
there was an inn in the village, visitors were not allowed to stay
there longer than two days to prevent them becoming too curious.

It was a paradise for children, with its farm, nursery gardens
and orchards. Among the pines roamed red deer, wild boar, foxes,
badgers and peacocks. When the estate was first taken over wolves
had been numerous, and were a nightmare for the shepherds. But
when one trailed the King and a visiting Italian diplomat back

to the house, it was decided that something must be done, and shoots were organised.[5]

At Tatoi the Greek way of life of centuries past continued unchanged. There were the weddings, when a procession wound its way to a distant village and returned with a bride, demure, eyes downcast, as she sat with her mother on a cart. There were the festival days, when sheep were roasted whole and the men danced through the day and far into the night. At the height of the dance the King would arrive with a bag of sovereigns. According to custom he would press one firmly upon the forehead of each dancer. They were perspiring so freely by this time that the coins adhered to the skin.[6]

Holidays for the Greek Royal Family meant Corfu, the King's Palace there being the former Residence of the British High Commissioner of the Ionian Islands, which were under British protection from 1815 to 1864. High above the Adriatic, the house was built by the Adam brothers, and stood then as it had left their hands. Portraits of British Kings and Prime Ministers hung round its walls, and the furniture had been fashioned in the age of the great English masters.[7]

Two miles away, on a promontory, stood the villa of *Mon Repos*, a favourite spot of Queen Alexandra. All round the house gardens, full of olives, magnolias, cypresses, eucalyptus, oranges and lemons, swept down to the sea,[8] and the fragrance of those gardens gave undying memories to those who had sat in them. On the King's death *Mon Repos* was to pass into the ownership of Prince Andrew, who loved every inch of it. He and his wife were very proud of the lovely lilies which they grew there.[9]

The constant playmates of Princess Andrew's elder girls, Margarita and Theodora, were their three cousins, the daughters of Prince Nicholas of Greece. Prince Nicholas had married the Grand Duchess Helen of Russia, granddaughter of Alexander II and Marie of Hesse, in 1902. They had three daughters, Olga,* Elizabeth† and Marina.‡ Theodora and Marina were of an age,

* Afterwards Princess Paul of Yugoslavia.
† Afterwards Countess Toerring-Yettenbach.
‡ Afterwards Duchess of Kent.

being born in 1906. The Andrews's third daughter, Cecile, took junior station, as she did not arrive until five years later. They were all very English, had English governesses and, when remiss, were spanked with rolled up copies of *The Times*. Marina even prayed in English. When asked by Queen Olga why she did not do so in Greek, she replied:

> I have arranged it with God. I told Him I liked to talk to Him in English best, and he said: "Please yourself, Marina."[10]

The idyll ended in 1912. In Thrace and Macedonia the Turks were oppressing the Christian section of the population, which was mostly Greek, and the Balkan States decided that joint action must be taken to put an end to it. In October Bulgaria, Serbia, Montenegro and Greece declared war on Turkey. Three weeks later, after a brilliant campaign, Crown Prince Constantine entered Salonika at the head of his victorious troops. He was received with scenes of wild enthusiasm. The next day King George arrived. Throughout his long reign he had dreamed of this moment. He regarded it as the completion of his life's work. In order to "prove ownership", he decided to stay in the Macedonian capital for a while.[11]

On 18th March 1913 he went for a walk with his A.D.C. Despite the pleas of his family, he had no armed escort. They came upon a man sitting, apparently idly, on a low wall. His name was Schinas. As the King turned about to go home, Schinas shot him in the back. The bullet went through his heart. One more name was added to the list of Europe's murdered Sovereigns.

The new King, Constantine, known in the family as "Tino", was forty-five. He was married to Sophie, daughter of the Empress Frederick and sister of the Kaiser. They had six children, the youngest being born in the year of accession, when Queen Sophie was forty-three.

Constantine began his reign as a very popular King. He had led the Greek army to victory in the First Balkan War. He was a man with a deep sense of duty and he spoke plainly to people of all ranks, sometimes too plainly, as he possessed a unique vocabulary of Greek oaths.[12] But the Balkans were "a witches' cauldron in which wars and rumours of wars simmered perpetually over a fire assiduously fed by the great protecting powers".[13] In June the Bulgarians took aggressive action in Salonika. Greece and Serbia united against them, and the Second Balkan War began. The King retained his position as Commander-in-Chief, Prince Andrew serving on his staff. The Bulgarians were routed and peace came with the Treaty of Bucharest, signed in August.

On 26th June 1914, a fourth daughter was born to Princess Andrew at her Corfu home. She was called Sophie, after the Queen, but nicknamed "Tiny". On the 27th the Archduke Francis Ferdinand and his wife were murdered at Sarajevo. The whirlpool of war began to spin, and the ripples washed against the Hellenic shore.

King Constantine found himself in a most unenviable position as the Powers prepared to turn Europe into a battleground, a position difficult from both political and personal standpoints. The resources of his army had been strained by the two Balkan wars, and it was in no state to enter a major conflict. If Greece joined with Germany, the Allied fleets would pound her coasts. If she joined the Allies, German land forces would sweep down upon her. Neutrality seemed to be the obvious course.

This belief was strengthened by family ties. Queen Alexandra, the Dowager Empress of Russia and the Duchess of Cumberland were his aunts. His wife was the sister of the Kaiser and daughter of the Princess Royal of England—a woman of British ways and sympathies. His brother Nicholas and two of his sisters had made Russian marriages. His brother George was married to Princess Marie Bonaparte, descendant of Lucien, brother of Napoleon.[14] To add to the confusion, his brother Andrew's wife was the daughter of Britain's First Sea Lord. Never were loyalties so sharply divided.

When August came the antagonists made it crystal clear that neutrality was not acceptable. Those who were not for them were against them. The Kaiser announced that, if Greece did not join the German side, he would consider her an enemy state. The Allies were intent that Greece should become a cog in their machine, and in this they were aided by the enthusiastic support for their cause of the Prime Minister, M. Venizelos. France and Britain seized upon the overtures of Venizelos to condemn Constantine as being pro-German, and the stumbling block which prevented Greek aid. The campaign against the King and Queen Sophie, both in London and Paris, became one of bitterness and vilification. It became worse when, in September 1915, Bulgaria attacked Serbia, Venizelos mobilised the Greek army, and was at once dismissed by the King. Constantine clung to neutrality, but, with the Venizelists actively supported by the Allies, his time was running out.

He sent Prince Andrew to London, charged with the mission of assuring the British Government that Greece had no secret alliance with Germany and had no intention of attacking Allied forces in Salonika. Prince Andrew was horrified at the hate and hostility against his brother and sister-in-law and at the newspaper placards in the streets—"TINO'S NEW TREACHERY"—"ALLIED PLANS BETRAYED TO GERMANY BY TINO".[15] He talked with George V, who begged him to induce his brother to "see reason". But at the same time the British King was of the opinion that Greece was being treated somewhat roughly, and so he informed his Prime Minister.[16]

Yet wilder and wilder grew the stories and the rumours about King Constantine and Queen Sophie. The King fell ill with pleurisy, and two of his ribs had to be removed. It was widely circulated, and believed, that he had been stabbed with a knife by his wife.[17] Then it was whispered that the Queen had a private telephone line from Tatoi to her brother in Germany.

In July 1916 a strange car, containing four men, was seen about the Tatoi estate. It was loaded with petrol cans. On a morning of breathless heat a spiral of smoke, straight as the pine trees from which it sprang, rose into the summer sky. "A hush hung over the forest, even the birds were silent." Then away to the left and to the right, other spirals formed tall pillars in the sunshine.

Fires were an expected hazard in such weather, and King Constantine, Queen Sophie and their children set off to fight the nearest outbreak, not realising that there were others. Intent on their task, they did not notice the danger to their flanks. The

Queen, standing back from the men, realised their predicament first. Seizing her three-year-old daughter in her arms, she ran back a mile and a half to safety, collapsing on the grass amid the evergreens round the house. The King and his helpers worked on until the holocaust all but ringed them. The King, who knew every inch of the forest, raced for a goat path, his son Paul behind him. Through the smoke, above the screech and roar of the fire, he called to the others to follow. But they wandered, lost, amid the acrid fumes. As the King reached the forest's edge he stumbled over a tree root, fell, and sprained his ankle. Two soldiers reached him as the flames closed above his head. They took him to the blackened shell of Tatoi. But sixteen men never came back from the forest.[18]

More trouble loomed ahead. At the end of November a Franco-British squadron appeared at the Piraeus, carrying demands for King Constantine to comply with certain conditions. On 1st December a detachment of French and British marines marched on Athens.[19] In the heat of the moment, strengthened by the suspicions of certain Greek elements, they were fired upon. In a few minutes wild confusion reigned.

Princess Andrew was working, as was her custom, in the School for Greek Embroidery, when the guns of the squadron opened up and shells fell round the Palace. Wounded were being carried through the streets. She hurried home, to find that one of the nursery windows had been shattered by a bullet. She sought shelter with Queen Sophie and the children in the cellars. A shell landed by the King's study, and several others in the Palace gardens.[20]

When the Allies recognised the Revolutionary Committee of Venizelos in Salonika as the *de facto* Government of Greece, it was time for King Constantine to go. Crown Prince George could not take his place, as the French considered him pro-German, so on 11th June 1917 Constantine appointed his second son, Alexander, as his successor. Broken-hearted, he went into exile in Switzerland, leaving behind a son who was King only in name, a son condemned to be cut off from his parents for the rest of his days.

Constantine's brothers were also ordered to quit Greece. Prince and Princess Andrew were close friends of the new King and, seeing his need for support in his initial days, they purposely delayed their departure for as long as possible. A month passed before they followed the rest of the Royal Family to Switzerland.[21]

They spent the winters of their exile at St. Moritz, the summers at Zürich or Lucerne. Money was short for all of them, and they were assisted by the generosity of friends. These were troubled days, for the accusations that King Constantine and Queen Sophie were pro-German continued. An English nurse and a governess caring for the royal children were called to the British consulate and told that, if they did not cease to serve "traitors to their country", they would be deprived of their passports.[22] No communication with King Alexander, by letter or telephone, was allowed. Owing to her birth, the treatment of Princess Andrew was less severe, and in September 1917 she was able to pay a visit to England and to be reunited, after so long and dramatic an interval, with her parents.[23]

After the Armistice, other reunions became possible, Lord Louis Mountbatten making first contact in January 1919. In the summer the Marquess of Milford Haven, with his sister, Marie, travelled to Lucerne, where the Greek colony occupied the Hotel National on the lake. Princess Marie wrote:

> Their longing both for Greece and their lost German home was evident—one saw it in them all, even in the children, who sometimes sang the pathetic songs of their native land, and would ask again and again: "When may we go home?"[24]

Their time was near at hand. In October 1920 King Alexander was walking with his Alsatian in the grounds of Tatoi when the dog was attacked by a monkey belonging to one of the estate workers. In separating them, the King was bitten in the leg by the monkey. Blood-poisoning set in, and proved fatal. King Constantine was invited to return to Greece, but, before agreeing to do so, he demanded a plebiscite on the point. Out of 1,010,788 electors only 10,883 voted against his return.[25] So the King, whose heart had once been broken, went back, in the cruiser which had taken him away. The train which took him on the last stage to Athens was routed on to a side-line which ran through the streets. "When they saw it coming about a mile off, the people could not contain their emotion. The cry, '*Erchetai! Erchetai!*' ('He is coming! He is coming!') . . . rose like a roar of an ocean wave. The engine, all beflagged, was painfully ploughing its way through a seething mass of people yelling, crying, gesticulating, sobbing hysterically. Men were hanging on to the engine and the steps of the carriage like flies. . . ."[26] It was a true Grecian welcome.

Prince and Princess Andrew had preceded the King to Greece. The Princess wrote home: "The children are beside themselves with joy. Everything abroad seemed to them grey and desolate; their young hearts sighed for the ever-blue sky and the hot sunshine of Hellas."[27] The Princess had a reason beyond the exile's end and the blue skies to bring her happiness. She was expecting another child, after an interval of seven years, years which had seemed an age. She was thirty-six. It was on 10th June 1921 that Philip, Prince of Greece and Denmark, was born at his parents' home of *Mon Repos* on the island of Corfu.* He was sixth in succession to the Throne. For a short, short while it seemed that the Princess had left the storms behind her and that the voyage ahead led across a windless sea. Her husband and her brother-in-law were back in their rightful positions in the land of their birth. At home Britain had made amends to her father. On 4th August, the seventh anniversary of the outbreak of the war, Prince Louis, Marquess of Milford Haven, was specially promoted to Admiral of the Fleet on the retired list, an honour which had only once before been granted to anyone in the British Navy, and given the Grand Cross of the Military Division of the Order of the Bath.[28]

Yet the peace for the Princess lasted only long enough for her to taste its sweetness. Despite the rapturous reception given to him by the Greek people, Constantine had inherited many problems from the departed Venizelos, and also a legacy of war with Turkey. Prince Christopher summed up the position:

---

* The entire town of Corfu stood sponsor at Prince Philip's christening.

The King had come back to a country in the throes of still another war. . . . The Asia Minor campaign could only have had one end and King Constantine, practised soldier and far-sighted general, said so from the beginning, but he took over the reins too late to prevent it. The Greek force was already walking straight into the wasps' nest prepared by that military genius, Mustapha Kemal.[29]

Immediately on returning to his homeland Prince Andrew applied for reinstatement in the Greek army and in June 1921 was given command of the 12th Division. An experienced military leader, he noticed at once the deficiencies in equipment and the lack of training of the men. The Division was weak in artillery, its signals equipment consisted of only two heliographs, and one of its three infantry regiments had been recruited largely from punishment companies. Another danger for a force engaged in active operations was the divided political loyalties among the officers, kept alive by the propaganda of political exiles in Constantinople, concerned more with the downfall of King Constantine and his family than the outcome of the war.[30] These exiles picked Prince Andrew as their particular target, going so far as to put out the story that he had died of wounds, in an attempt to destroy confidence in Athens.

For a time the tide ran for the Greeks, and in July came victory at Eski-Shehr. In recognition of the part that Prince Andrew had played, he was promoted to Lieutenant-General and given command of the Second Army Corps, consisting of the 5th, 13th and 9th Divisions.[31] If victories had continued and the Turks had been conquered, Prince Andrew would have been ensured a place in the Hellenic hall of valour, but in the event a very different picture presented itself. Promotion brought increased worries to the Prince, and the chief of these lay in the person of the Commander-in-Chief, General Papoulas.

Later Prince Andrew was to be charged with "acting on his own initiative" and departing from battle orders.[32] That in fact he did, on occasion, act on his own initiative was because he considered that the only alternative to his not doing so would have meant disaster.

Meantime back in Athens the victory at Eski-Shehr had conjured

337

up dreams of the resurrection of the Byzantine Empire. "If any Greek had counselled self-restraint and moderation, both the rival parties, Royalist and Venizelist, . . . would have considered him a traitor to his country."[33] So General Papoulas ordered the advance on Ankara. Prince Andrew opposed this move unless the army was reinforced,[34] but speed was essential, as the advance and battle had to take place before the rains began early in September.

The Greek forces began to move across the hard 150 miles of country which lay between them and the Sakaria river, flowing fast through the hills which were the last bastion before the Nationalist capital. In Ankara the inhabitants began gathering their possessions together, in readiness for flight northward. The Assembly appointed Mustafa Kemal generalissimo of the Turkish army.

Mustafa Kemal hurried to the fighting line and personally supervised the retreat. He realised that every mile that he withdrew he further weakened the Greek line of supply. His own men knew every inch of the country, and left it empty behind them. Kemal had every advantage except that of numbers. Reaching the Sakaria line, he dug in and feverishly began to prepare for the counter-attack.

The battle of Sakaria began at dawn on 24th August. Kemal had injected new spirit into his men, and they fought continuously for twenty-two days. At last the Greeks, without water or rations and having suffered appalling losses, began their withdrawal to Eski-Shehr. The Turks were too spent to pursue them.

When the news of the defeat reached Athens, there was a complete reversal of feelings. Those who but a few weeks before had been shouting, "On to Ankara", were now the first to criticise the Greek command. There had to be a scapegoat. A story was put out that it had been on the insistence of Prince Andrew to the King, and against the advice of the Commander-in-Chief, that forty thousand men had been sent on a fifteen-day death march across a waterless desert. Such tales well suited those whose ultimate aim was the end of the Greek monarchy, but in truth was calumny against King Constantine, who had entered the war against his better judgment, fearing that such a disaster might

overtake his forces, and particularly against Prince Andrew.*
There were two main reasons for the defeat of the Greeks. The first
was that the men were insufficiently trained and ill equipped. The
second was the brilliant leadership of the Turks by Mustafa Kemal.
Relations between Prince Andrew and General Papoulas came
to such a state that the Prince asked to be relieved of his command.
His request was refused. Determined that he could not carry on

* The role played by Prince Andrew in the advance towards Ankara and the retreat
to Eski-Shehr was clarified in a documentary statement by Mr. John Terraine,
published in part in the *Sunday Times* of the 27th November 1966:

"Plans for a Greek advance from Eski-Shehr were outlined in a G.H.Q. Memorandum of July 28th (a week before Prince Andrew's promotion) signed by General
Papoulas. Prince Andrew wrote of this: 'In describing in the Memorandum the difficulties that might be expected, the most important was omitted—that is, the crossing
of the salt desert, the Axylos desert of the ancients, where there is not a drop of water.
This desert was crossed by the Second Army Corps with incredible suffering.'

"The Greek advance was resumed on August 14th and continued until September
4th against stiffening Turkish resistance. Fearing a battle of attrition, Prince Andrew
suggested carrying his Corps from right to left of the army, to produce a 'decisive force'
at that point. On September 5th General Papoulas wrote to Prince Andrew's Chief
of Staff: 'The plan which you wrote to me is being studied and we will carry it out
in five days . . .' But on the 9th G.H.Q. became seriously alarmed at the prospect of a
Turkish attack, and ordered the Second (and First) Corps 'to attack violently and
desperately'. Prince Andrew judged this impossible and set in hand the manœuvre
which he believed G.H.Q. to have approved in principle. He then received this
message from General Papoulas:

" 'Astonished at plan of abandoning your positions, I order corps to remain in its
position. Only person competent to judge and decide is myself as Commander-in-
Chief. Cancel all orders of transfer movements.'

"The following day G.H.Q. removed Prince Andrew's Chief of Staff, but refused
to accept his own resignation. Then, at 4 o'clock, he received peremptory orders to
carry out the very movement which he had initiated the day before, and for which
he had been rebuked. He remarked: 'The preceding day G.H.Q. had decided that
there was not sufficient time to make the transfer when there were no signs of an attack,
and now they ordered this same transfer after the attack had declared itself in the
middle of the battle. I think that comment is superfluous.'

"On September 12/13th the Greeks began a retreat which was not seriously
molested by the enemy. Colonel Hoare-Nairne, British Military Attaché in Athens,
reported: 'The Greek army of Asia Minor had suffered 30,000 battle casualties since
the middle of July, and its numbers had been further reduced by sickness.'

"During the retreat Prince Andrew learned that it was being said 'that it was on
account of my hesitation and indecision that the advance to Ankara had failed.' He
took this up with the C.-in-C., and General Papoulas replied: '. . . The suspension
of the advance to Ankara, and the return to the position before Eski-Shehr were not
in the slightest degree the consequence of any action or of any fault, but an action
which G.H.Q. had foreseen before the commencement of operations, and the execution
of which had been accepted as the only suitable one. The Second Army Corps has so
many heroic exploits to its credit, that its officers need not be disturbed at the propaga-
tion of senseless criticism of the corps' action.' "

under such conditions, he applied again. Again his request was refused—clear proof that General Papoulas did not wish to lose his services and experience. The Prince next asked for leave of absence, and this time his request was granted. He left for Athens on 30th September 1921.[35]

It was a sad home-coming, for that month a telegram to his wife from London had announced the death of the Marquess of Milford Haven, only a few weeks after Britain had repaid her debt to him. During August Lord Milford Haven had travelled to Scotland for a cruise northward with his second son, Louis, on board *Repulse*. He returned to London on 10th September, staying at the Naval and Military Club. Next day he was found dead in bed by the housekeeper.[36]

His body was taken to the Private Chapel at Buckingham Palace and thereafter to the Chapel Royal, St. James's. On the 19th the coffin was carried in procession to Westminster Abbey and then taken to the Isle of Wight, for burial at the Church of St. Mildred's,[37] the Church which had figured so prominently in his family story since its rector had assisted at the marriage of Princess Alice in 1862.

Meantime, Princess Andrew, with her son, was racing across Europe, but did not reach "Fishponds", Netley Abbey, the home of her parents at this time, until after the funeral. Thus did Prince Philip see England for the first time.

During October and November Prince Andrew worked on the Supreme Army Council, and then returned to Smyrna as a member of that Council.[38] During the next four months he did everything within his power to persuade the Commander-in-Chief to put an end to the disloyal plotting rife among the forces under his command, but with little, or no, success. Prince Andrew made clear that the continuance of the existing command could only end with disastrous results, and applied for, and was given, command of the Fifth Army Corps of Epirus and the Ionian Islands, with headquarters at Janina in Greece.[39] He thus severed all connection with Second Army Corps and the command of General Papoulas. Accusations that he was in part responsible for the forthcoming débâcle were therefore without foundation.

That débâcle was not long in coming. On 26th August Turkish forces, under the brilliant leadership of Mustafa Kemal, attacked the Greeks on the Eski-Shehr–Afion line, and drove them back in disorder to Smyrna. On 9th September Kemal entered Smyrna. Thereafter followed, swiftly and relentlessly, more cruelty, more suffering, more wanton damage than it has ever been the lot of a city to endure. The Greeks had previously been accused of savagery in captured villages, and now came the Turkish revenge. Many thousands of Christian civilians and Greek troops were burned alive, massacred with gun and bayonet, drowned, tortured. It was impossible to compute the loss of life. Smyrna was sacked, and then the flames went up, devouring all but the Turkish section of the town. The banks, consulates and business houses in the European quarter on the quay became a heap of smouldering ruins. Three years afterwards it appeared as if the damage had been done but three weeks before.[40]

The disaster rocked Greece, insurrection broke out, and was followed by revolution, fanned by the very officers whose disloyalty had been a primary cause of the defeat. These men demanded the abdication of the King. Constantine, weak in health as a result of a long visit to his army, could have resisted, as he still had a strong following, but the thought of civil war appalled him, and he considered that the time had come for him to go. He abdicated on 26th September,* in favour of his eldest son, George, who became but a king in name as his brother Alexander had been before him.[41] Prince Andrew was informed that he could stay with his family at his property of *Mon Repos*, provided that he agreed to resign from the army.[42] But this was but cover for the real intent of the revolutionaries.

A few weeks later there reached *Mon Repos* a peremptory demand for Prince Andrew to go to Athens to give evidence at the trial of former Ministers who were accused of instigating the Asia Minor campaign. He had no alternative but to comply. Princess Andrew noted that the house was under police surveillance.

There then arrived at Corfu her brother-in-law, Prince Christopher, who had hurried from Paris to see what aid he could give

* King Constantine died at Palermo in January 1923.

341

to his family and at the same time gain possession of funds and jewellery before they fell into the hands of the revolutionaries. As an insurance of his own safety he carried, and openly displayed, a substantial cheque which his wealthy American wife, formerly Mrs. N. Leeds, had made out in favour of the Greek Red Cross. He also had instructions to rescue, and return with, one spoiled and petulant white cat.

To his horror Prince Christopher saw the police shadowing *Mon Repos*, and hurried to Athens, having promised Princess Andrew that he would do all in his power to keep her in touch with developments. There he discovered that the summons had been but a ruse, that his brother Andrew had been arrested and was in solitary confinement awaiting trial.

Christopher went to see the King, but found that he was a prisoner in the Palace and could be of little help. He applied for permission to see Prince Andrew, and was refused. He looked about for a means of communication.[43]

Prince Andrew was being held in the house of a former A.D.C. and was closely guarded. The accusation against him was of military incompetence and part responsibility for the miscarriage of the campaign against Ankara. Each day he was taken, under escort, for examination by General Pangalos,[44] chairman of the commission of enquiry into the responsibilities for the Asiatic disaster. Pangalos had been at school with Prince Andrew, but now held peculiar animosity against this monocled, six-foot-four royal soldier. One day he asked the Prince how many children he had and, on being told five, replied: "Poor things, what a pity they will soon be orphans."[45]

Only his valet had access to Prince Andrew. Even the services of a dentist were refused when the prisoner broke a tooth. All letters and parcels were confiscated, and gifts of food were sliced through and through with a knife before the Prince was allowed to eat them.

At length Prince Christopher thought of a way to get round the guards. He wrote a message to him on a cigarette paper, carefully folded the tobacco inside it, and persuaded the valet to put it in his case. Prince Andrew took the proffered cigarette, appreciated the given signal, and put it away unlit. Back, through the same channel, came a message to Prince Christopher. The note was full of courage, but, reading between the lines, Christopher knew that his brother held little hope of being freed.[46]

Prince Christopher's visa to remain in Greece lasted only for a week and in that time he had much to do. Even so, before the seven days were through, a friend came to him and begged him to leave by train immediately. If he did not he might well find himself in the same predicament as his brother Andrew, and if he tried to leave by boat, he would be stopped at the gangway. But the Prince had planned to board an Italian steamer on the day that his visa ran out, and he had so much to do that he decided to take the risk and adhere to this arrangement.

With the aid of a former tutor and his lawyer, he collected securities and valuables belonging to himself and his brother Nicholas, and packed them in two suitcases. Then he rescued the jewellery of his sister-in-law, Princess Nicholas. This had been packed in a wooden box, the bottom of which was faulty, and the Prince had visions of tiaras sparkling along his trail. The baggage was completed by a wicker basket which contained the petulant white cat.

On the day of sailing the Prince hired a plain car and drove by a devious route to the quay. Instead of stopping by the tender which was to take passengers out to the Italian steamer, he and his companions continued for a while along the quay. There a rowing-boat was waiting, a man at the oars. Into it went the two suitcases, the jewellery box and the wicker basket, the passengers after them.

But the speed of the transference and the movement of the water proved too much for the nerves of the white cat. Dismal yowls echoed along the quayside. The Prince turned to the tutor, to tell him to stop the row, only to find that a suitcase had burst open under the strain and the unfortunate man was vainly trying to stuff back into it wads of notes and securities. A crowd was gathering as the oars dipped and took the boat out to deep water.

The fugitives mopped their brows, content now that they were out of trouble. But worse was to come. As they came alongside the gangway they saw a Greek sentry standing at its head. By

343

this time Prince Christopher was wishing that his father had never left the peace of Copenhagen to struggle with the sovereignty of Greece. He acted on impulse. He was a tall man. He jumped from the boat, raced up the gangway and punched the sentry hard in the stomach. He ran on until he reached the safety of his cabin. There he was under Italian authority. Doubled up, the sentry was too far gone to worry about his companions or their baggage.[47]

On its way to Italy the steamer called in at Corfu, and there Princess Andrew went aboard to hear the latest news about her husband. By this time she had become extremely anxious, and the report that she received from Prince Christopher made her even more so. He tried as best he could to soften the blow, but she saw the truth in his eyes, realizing that he feared that his brother's life might end before a firing squad. Regardless of her own safety she went straight to Athens, leaving her children in the charge of their English nurse, Miss Roose.[48]

Strive as hard as she could, the Princess could make little progress in the capital. The King was a prisoner at Tatoi. Old friends seemed powerless to help, but she was at last allowed to visit her husband for a short time daily.[49] Meantime she was sending out appeals to those with power in Europe. In this she was aided by other members of her family, including Queen Sophie, who appealed to King George V, M. Poincaré and King Alfonso of Spain. Princess Nicholas aroused the interest of the Pope.

First, six men were arraigned before the extraordinary court-martial of eleven officers. They consisted of three ex-Premiers, two ex-Ministers and the Commander-in-Chief. Venizelos saw the pressure building up to bring about their release. He sent a message to those conducting the trial: "Whatever you have to do, do it quickly. Tomorrow may be too late."[50] The death sentence was brought in in each case. Without being given time to make religious preparation or settle their affairs, the five ex-Ministers were shot against the prison wall. The Commander-in-Chief made a last-minute bid to gain the sanctuary of the British Legation, but was dragged back, and suffered the same fate.[51] Britain immediately severed diplomatic relations with Greece, and the Minister left Athens that night.

After seven weeks of imprisonment, on 2nd December Prince Andrew was tried in the Chamber of Deputies by a jury of officers, who had previously decided that he must be shot. Representatives of King Alfonso and the Pope left Madrid and Rome for Athens. King George V ordered H.M.S. *Calypso* to Phaleron and also took necessary steps which resulted in Lord Curzon* despatching Captain Gerald Talbot† in secret from London, bound for Athens. Captain Talbot, who in the past had rendered service to Colonel Pastiras, the Greek revolutionary leader, travelled fast.[52]

The finding of the court was due to be announced at midnight. All through Europe Prince Andrew's relations waited by the telephone. No news came. The crowd outside the gates of the Old Palace in Athens drifted away, as reporters were told that the court had decided to postpone judgment until the morning. Gerald Talbot had arrived.‡

In the morning came the news that H.M.S. *Calypso* rode on Phaleron Bay. The court reconvened and the sentence was given. Prince Andrew was to be banished for life.

The departure was swift and dramatic, for with the Prince and Princess on their way to Phaleron Bay drove General Pangalos, the accuser who but a few days before had forecast that their children would shortly be without a father. *Calypso* turned towards the sea and the second, and last, exile for a very good soldier began.

There was one more contact yet to be made with Greece. On the 4th *Calypso* called at Corfu and there the Prince and Princess picked up their four daughters, baby son[54] and the English nurse, Miss Roose. So much, in memories and possessions, was left behind in the rooms and in the gardens of the villa of *Mon Repos*.[55]

The crew of the cruiser made much of Philip, Prince of Greece and Denmark. They obtained an orange-box from the galley and fashioned it into a cot so that he would lie safely on the bunk.[56] The rescued family travelled to Rome, then Paris, and the Christmas lights were gay in the streets when at last they reached London.

* Foreign Secretary.
† Gerald Francis (Sir) Talbot, K.C.V.O., C.M.G., O.B.E., Commander R.N.V.R., one-time Naval Attaché at Athens.
‡ On his return to London Captain Talbot was received by King George, and given the K.C.V.O.[53]

32

The Altar and the Sky

IN THE FIVE YEARS AFTER THE ENDING OF THE FIRST WORLD WAR there was a flush of royal weddings to cheer the London scene. Princess Patricia of Connaught married Commander the Hon. Alexander Ramsay, Princess Mary married Viscount Lascelles, Princess Maud of Fife married Lord Carnegie and Prince Albert, Duke of York, married Lady Elizabeth Bowes-Lyon. There were two weddings in the Battenberg line, those of Lord Louis Mountbatten to the Hon. Edwina Ashley and of Lady Louise Mountbatten to Gustavus Adolphus, Crown Prince of Sweden.

Lord Louis had become engaged in February 1922 at Delhi, where he was on tour as A.D.C. to the Prince of Wales.[1] From then on the newspapers and the magazines were full of the pictures of the lovely goddaughter of King Edward VII, daughter of Colonel Wilfrid Ashley, M.P.,* and granddaughter of Sir Ernest Cassel. "The richest girl in England,"[2] they called her. Edwina Ashley was twenty.

They were married at St. Margaret's, Westminster, on 18th July 1922, and never before in the history of London had a wedding attracted a bigger gathering, with the exception of that of Princess Mary. Certainly never had so many naval uniforms

* Subsequently Minister of Transport; created Lord Mount Temple, 1932.

been seen at such an occasion. The King and Queen were there, and Queen Alexandra. The Prince of Wales was best man, fulfilling, an observer said, "his duties with a characteristic touch of delightful diffidence".[3] Among the seven bridesmaids were the four daughters of Prince and Princess Andrew of Greece, and after the ceremony Queen Mary and Queen Alexandra bent down to kiss the younger ones. That moment was recalled when, but a few months later, those four girls came back to London as exiles.

The following year Lady Louise Mountbatten became engaged to Crown Prince Gustavus of Sweden, whose first wife, Princess Margaret of Connaught, had died in 1920.* The Swedish Government asked for assurance that this granddaughter of Princess Alice was of Royal blood, as she had the title of "Lady" instead of "Princess", Swedish law forbidding a Sovereign heir-apparent marrying a commoner. The assurance was readily given and the wedding took place in London on 3rd November 1923,[4] in the Chapel Royal of St. James's Palace. Strangely enough, when talking of his younger daughter shortly before his death, Lord Milford Haven had said: "There is only one person in the world who would suit Louise, and that is Gustav of Sweden; and the only person who would suit Gustav is Louise." They met by chance at a London party two years later, and her father's prophecy was to prove so very right.[5]†

Yet the descendants of Princess Alice of England and Prince Louis of Hesse, who had fallen in love at Ascot races sixty years before, were thin upon the ground. Of their seven children four were dead, two in childhood, two by massacre, and there was left no generation after them. Irene had two sons, but they had been swallowed by the German mists. Victoria's eldest son, the 2nd Marquess of Milford Haven, had a daughter, Lady Tatiana Mountbatten, born in 1917, and a son, David, Viscount Alderney, two years later. It was therefore apparent that the strengthening of the Hessian ranks would first come from the marriages of the daughters of Prince and Princess Andrew of Greece, or of the two

* They had four sons and a daughter, Ingrid, who married King Frederick IX of Denmark.
† Gustavus Adolphus succeeded as King Gustavus VI Adolphus of Sweden on 29th October 1950. Queen Louise died in 1965.

sons, by his second marriage, of the Grand Duke Ernest Louis of Hesse and the Rhine. In 1923 George Donatus was seventeen and Louis fifteen.

The Grand Duke's happiest years lay between his second marriage, in 1905, and 1914. Then he was able to concentrate on the things that he wanted to do, which were mostly in the field of the arts. The Artists' Colony in Darmstadt, which he subsidised, staged exhibition after exhibition of contemporary European work, culminating in the Great Century Exhibition of German Art in the year when war broke out. Their success was due to his initiative, drive and support. He also built up the reputation of the Court theatre and orchestra,[6] and in 1911 organised a festival of music at Darmstadt.[7] A progressive ruler, he was a patron of science and encouraged the building of factories for the production of glass and painted china.[8] He was a man who loved a garden, and he left his mark on the landscape at Wolfsgarten and the Rosenhöhe. Hesse lost the gaiety it had known in the 'nineties, when royalties and the international set came for Frankfurt races, when Victoria Melita raced her black stallion through the woods and danced the whole night through. But the peace and the routine were back, and the new Grand Duchess cared for the schools and orphanages, hospitals and institutions which had been founded by the second daughter of Queen Victoria, her husband's mother. And she never forgot appointments or was rude to people whom she considered boring.[9]

Earl Mountbatten of Burma has described the Grand Duke Ernest Louis as "a man of peace". Certain it is that he was almost alone in Germany in opposing Kaiser Wilhelm's war plans in 1914.[10] Because of his principles, and also his relations both in Britain and Russia, no pressure was put upon him to engage in active service in the theatres of operation, and as a result accusations were made that his sympathies lay with the enemy, and even that he was passing information. But the same groundless accusation had been made against his mother during the Franco-Prussian war. Like her, he now devoted his energies, just as unsparingly, to the care of the wounded, and was generous with financial support. He was a frequent visitor to the hospitals and travelled on the ambulance trains with his wife. Then, as Germany tumbled towards the chaos of defeat, there came the news that "Alicky" and her children had been shot in the cellar at Ekaterinburg, that "Ella" had been thrown down the mineshaft. Since babyhood he had been haunted by the tragedy of death. When his brother, "Frittie", had fallen from the window and lay still on the terrace below, he had cried to his mother, "Why cannot we all die together?" The Princess had treasured his little philosophies about dying, retailing them in her letters to Queen Victoria,[11] like autumn leaves falling into the Albert gloom. Then Marie had gone, and his mother also, and from that date until his second marriage Ernest had been a lonely man. The bombshell from Russia was almost more than he could bear.

In the second week of November 1918 revolution swept through Germany. Hesse declared for the "Free German Socialist Republic" and the Grand Duke lost his throne.[12] A deputation of the new order invaded his Palace, making demands, but he went out to meet them, talked to them as he had always talked to his people, and they went away.[13] It was only a ripple on the waters. He steadfastly refused to abdicate, but could not avoid being deposed. By 1919 he had reached an amicable arrangement with the Republican Government and the Grand Duke, shorn of his power, remained a popular and well loved figure on the Hessian scene, he and his family always being treated with respect.

One of Ernest Louis's main preoccupations now centred round the rehabilitation of men whose minds and bodies had been shattered by the war. He gave them accommodation in his Palace and, by tact and occupation, nursed them back to normality. Sadly, some of those young men were to live to take part in another war. Happily, there are some who remember him still.[14] *

His sons grew to a marrying age. So did the daughters of Prince and Princess Andrew of Greece. This family was living quietly in Paris, Philip attending a day school at St. Cloud. The Princesses paid visits to their relations in Germany, and in the years 1930–1931, all four were married, within a space of nine months.

* A monument to Grand Duke Ernest Louis has recently been unveiled in Darmstadt.

The first to go was the youngest, Sophie. She was only sixteen. She remained fast in the tentacles of Victoria and Albert by marrying, in December 1930, a grandson of the Empress Frederick. He was a son of Margaret, the Empress's youngest daughter, who had married Landgrave Frederick Charles of Hesse in 1893. He was a twin, Princess Margaret being unique in royal history by having two pairs of boys. This was a great comfort to King Edward VII on an occasion when thirteen were present for dinner, the pregnant Princess among them. He was only persuaded to sit down when he was assured that two unseen persons were also at the table.

The name of Princess Sophie's husband was Christopher. He was known as "Cri Hesse". When he joined the Nazi Air Force, some wit renamed him "Cry Havoc". He was killed when flying over Italy in 1943.*

The eldest, Princess Margarita, also strengthened her ties with the House of Coburg. In April 1961 she married Godfrey, Hereditary Prince of Hohenlohe-Langenburg. His mother was Alexandra, third daughter of Prince Alfred, Duke of Edinburgh and of Saxe-Coburg and Gotha, her sisters being Queen Marie of Roumania, Victoria Melita, first wife of Grand Duke Ernest Louis of Hesse and afterwards Grand Duchess Cyril, and the Infanta Beatrice of Spain.

Princess Theodora married Berthold, Margrave of Baden, in August 1931. His father, Prince Maximilian of Baden, had the distinction of being the last Chancellor of the German Empire.[15]

There remains to be accounted for Princess Cecile, born at Tatoi in 1911. She moved the finger of time right back to Princess Alice. In February 1931 she married, at Darmstadt, George Donatus, the elder son of the Grand Duke Ernest Louis. He was a grandson of Princess Alice, and she was a great-granddaughter. They had three children, Louis born in 1931, Alexander in 1933, and Johanna in 1936.

The Grand Duke Ernest Louis's health began to fade. In the spring of 1937 he visited the family mausoleum at the Rosenhöhe.

---

* In 1946 Princess Sophie married Prince George William of Hanover, Duke of Brunswick-Luneburg, and Prince of Great Britain and Ireland.

The blossom was out and an apple tree, planted there when he was a boy, had pushed a bough across the path leading to the building. The pink and white and the green of it were bathed in sunshine. The sight gave him so much pleasure that he gave orders that, when his coffin passed that way, the bough was to be pushed aside and not cut down.[16]

His last months were cheered by the news of the engagement of his younger son Louis, who was at this time working at the German Embassy in London. His fiancée was the Hon. Margaret Geddes, daughter of Sir Auckland* and Lady Geddes.[17] The Grand Duke stipulated that, should he die before the wedding, the arrangements should proceed. So it happened, the long illness of Ernest Louis ending at Wolfsgarten on 9th October. The impressive funeral procession which followed his coffin through the Darmstadt streets to the Rosenhöhe, the dense crowds which lined the route all the way,[18] proved that, though he had lost his power in the land, he had not lost one iota of the respect and affection which his people felt for him. Through a mountain of flowers steel-helmeted soldiers carried him to join his mother, his father and his daughter.[19] With him, the old order passed away.

The wedding of Prince Louis was postponed from 23rd October to Saturday, 20th November.

At 1.53 on the afternoon of 16th November a three-engined Junkers J–52 airliner of Belgian Sabena Airways left Frankfurt, bound for Croydon. The pilot was Tony Lambotte, one of the most senior in Sabena service, with over six hundred thousand flying miles to his credit. In his crew were an engineer, a wireless operator and a mechanic. The passengers, bound for the wedding, were the Hereditary Grand Duke George Donatus; his wife; his two young sons, Louis and Alexander, who were to be pages; the Dowager Grand Duchess Eleonore; Baron Joachim von Riedesel, who was to be best man; and Mlle Lina Henar, the children's nurse. Only Johanna, the baby daughter, had been left behind in Hesse.

The Junkers was due to land at Croydon at around five o'clock. Lord Louis Mountbatten's chauffeur headed there to meet the

* Afterwards 1st Baron Geddes.

351

party. The Dowager Grand Duchess was to stay with the Marchioness of Milford Haven at Kensington Palace, the remainder with the Mountbattens in Park Lane. Prince Louis and Miss Geddes, after visiting the house in Chelsea which was to be their future home, also made for Croydon, preoccupied with their marriage plans. Miss Geddes was to have a retinue of eight grown-up bridesmaids and four children. She had chosen to wear a Bavarian peasant's gala frock, as she had met Prince Louis on a skiing holiday in Bavaria two years before.

The Junkers was scheduled to call at Ostend on its way. There, at half-past two, there was brilliant sunshine. But dense fog came suddenly in from the sea and, fifteen minutes later, visibility was down to twenty feet. People in the streets heard an aircraft circling low over the town.

At Steene, two and a half miles away, a chimney, one hundred and fifty feet high, towered over a brickworks. Pilot Lambotte brought his aeroplane in over Steene to land. The tip of a wing touched the chimney's top. The wing and an engine were ripped away and, a mass of flames, the Junkers crashed into the works below.

There was nothing that the workers there, the ambulance men, the doctors, could do. No one could approach that holocaust. When it was over, little recognisable was left.* There came from it a charred book on engineering, some photographs on porcelain such as are placed on Continental gravestones, and the body of an eight-months child, born in the crash.

At Croydon Prince Louis and Miss Geddes walked the tarmac. After a while they went to the offices to ask the reason for the delay and, reassured, continued their stroll. It was as they were watching an airliner take off that the manager of Imperial Airways walked up to Prince Louis and whispered in his ear. In the privacy of his office he told what he knew of the tragedy. Then it seemed as if the life drained from Prince Louis. Ekaterinburg . . . Alapaevsk . . . Ostend. . . . Father, mother, brother, sister-in-law, nephews,

---

* The famous Hessian pearls and the wedding veil worn by Princess Alice at her wedding in 1862, and used at every family occasion since that date, were lost in the crash.

Right. Bridesmaids at the wedding of Lord Louis Mountbatten and the Hon. Edwina Ashley at St. Margaret's, Westminster, on 18th July 1922. The daughters of Prince and Princess Andrew of Greece; from left to right, the Princesses Margarita, Cecile, Sophie and Theodora

Below. Hereditary Grand Duke George Donatus of Hesse and the Rhine, and his wife, Princess Cecile of Greece and Denmark

Princess Victoria of Hesse and the Rhine
Wife of Prince Louis of Battenberg, Marquess of Milford Haven

close friend, all dead within a few weeks. Relentlessly indeed had the curse on the Coburgs followed through Prince Albert to Princess Alice, her children, and their children after them.[20]

That evening a family conference was held at the Kent home of Sir Auckland Geddes. Then the strange, but wise, decision was taken to advance the date of the wedding from the 20th to the morrow, the 17th. Sir Auckland explained the reasons to the Press and asked that no members of the public attend.

Her wedding garb was a black coat and skirt, and her bridal veil was black, as Miss Geddes went to the Church of St. Peter, Eaton Square, at eight o'clock in the morning. The only decorations were chrysanthemums, lilies and palms on the High Altar. Lord Louis Mountbatten took the place of the best man who had died.[21]

Two hours later the Prince and Princess left for the scene of the crash, and then proceeded to Darmstadt. On arrival the Prince called a conference of those of his family who were left and announced that he and his wife had decided to adopt their fourteen-month-old niece, Princess Johanna.

That same day the coffins came to Darmstadt. Draped with the Hessian flag, they were borne on gun carriages to the Rosenhöhe, the Hill of Roses.[22] Strange now was the echo of Ernest Louis's prayer—"Why cannot we all die together?" But he had been spared the agony of this.

The tragedy was not over yet. In June 1939 Princess Johanna died and was buried at the Rosenhöhe. As Prince and Princess Louis were childless, there was no sunshine to take her place.

33

Alice in the Looking-Glass

THE COMINGS AND GOINGS OF THE HELLENIC KINGS CONTINUED. In October 1923 General Metaxas, the Royalist leader, originated a movement to overthrow the Revolutionary Committee. The revolt failed, but King George II was accused of being concerned in the plot.[1] He saw that his time for departure was drawing near, and took certain steps. He and his wife, Queen Elizabeth, were collectors of beautiful furniture and now, often moving at dead of night, they began moving it for safe-keeping to the houses of various friends.[2] The King refused to abdicate, but agreed to leave the country under duress. On 19th December he, his wife and Crown Prince Paul were escorted to the coast, and yet once more a warship took the Greek Royal Family into exile.

This time the absence was long. The King moved from Bucharest to Paris to London. He spent much of his time in hotels. He was reported eating fish suppers in Whitechapel, porridge in Scotland and drinking beer in remote countryside pubs. In 1935 his wife divorced him for desertion. He had married a brilliant woman, but one of high-spirited and temperamental stock. Queen Elizabeth was the eldest daughter of Queen Marie of Roumania, and granddaughter of Prince Alfred, Duke of Edinburgh and Saxe-Coburg and Gotha, and the Grand Duchess Marie Alexandrovna, she who had rebelled against the omnipotence of Queen Victoria. Now came a parallel with the case of Victoria Melita, her aunt, and the Grand Duke Ernest Louis. Queen Elizabeth painted to the standard of a professional artist, sang charmingly, contrived exquisite embroidery, was a brilliant cook[3] and knew all that there was to be known about flowers. She complained that she was mentally starved in Greece, and hungered for the music and art of Roumania.[4] The life of an itinerant exile was not for her.

King George was tiger-shooting with the Viceroy of India in the autumn of 1935 when he received an invitation to return to the Greek Throne. As his father had done, he asked for a plebiscite to be held on the point. The result proved an overwhelming demand for his restoration. On his arrival on 25th November he was accorded the now customary scenes of enthusiastic acclamation.[5] But it had all been done before. Prince Andrew, who had been too close to the prison wall ever to forget the experience, was not unduly impressed. He feared, and in the event correctly, that his nephew might be forced into yet another exile.[6]

Prince Philip was by now in his second year at Gordonstoun. After three years at Cheam preparatory school, where his uncle George, 2nd Marquess of Milford Haven, and his cousin David, had been, he spent three terms at the school of Salem Castle, Germany, owned by his brother-in-law, Berthold, Margrave of Baden.[7] It was during his time there that the Salem headmaster, Doctor Kurt Hahn, fell foul of the Nazi authorities. It was clear that there was no room for a liberal thinker such as he in the new Germany, and he was arrested as a Communist. Considerable pressure had to be put to bear to secure his release, and thereafter he left for Scotland to establish a similar school at Gordonstoun in Morayshire, in a house once owned by Sir Alexander Gordon-Cumming. There Prince Philip joined him.[8]

After the marriages of their four daughters in 1930–1931, Prince and Princess Andrew sold their home at St. Cloud. The Princess was tired. The trials and the hardships, the sadnesses and the dangers which had continually assailed her since the assassination of King George I twenty years before, had sapped her strength

355

and her resistance. The past decade had been a perpetual struggle to bring up a growing family on a restricted income. She became ill. She was treated for intermittent heart trouble in a Swiss clinic, and moved from sanatorium after sanatorium in an effort to regain her strength. Prince Andrew stayed on in Paris, remembering with bitterness his banishment and the events which had preceded it. He was determined that his son should be brought up free of the machinations and uncertainties of the Greek political scene.[9] Although he kept in close touch with Philip, getting endless pleasure from the letters from school, he was well content to let him remain in the care of his Uncle George and Aunt Nada Milford Haven, staying with them at Lynden Manor, their home near Maidenhead, with his grandmother at Kensington Palace, or with Lord and Lady Louis Mountbatten and their daughters, Patricia* and Pamela,† in Park Lane or at Broadlands.

Up to the age of fifteen Greece was to Prince Philip just a country about which his parents and relations talked, sometimes with longing, sometimes with bitterness. He had no recollection of the gardens at *Mon Repos*, the forest of Tatoi, the ballrooms of the Athens Palace. But the reality of his link came when newspapers referred to him by his title of Prince of Greece. Then his school friends would bestow upon him, from the wells of their imagination, extravagant and Ruritanian titles, sometimes of a questionable nature, and bow in mock respect before him.[10] But with the restoration of King George II the time had come for his introduction. His mother had returned to the sun and the blue sky, taking a little house in Athens, picking up again the threads of the charitable works in which she had always been deeply interested.[11] His father went back, but only for visits to see his nephew and old haunts again. For he and his brother Christopher the streets of Athens were full of flags, and the bells were ringing. They planned a tour of the Peloponnesus incognito, but instead found themselves involved in five days of speech-making, hand-shaking, triumphal arches and cheering crowds.[12] It was some consolation, but not enough.

* Born 1924. Married 7th Baron Brabourne, 1946.
† Born 1929. Married Mr. David Hicks, 1960.

Prince Philip took his place on the Greek royal tapestry when, in November 1936, he went to Athens for what the family termed "The Funeral". During the period of exile Queen Olga, King Constantine and Queen Sophie had died and been buried at Florence. It was now decided that their bodies should be taken to Greece and, after lying in state for six days in Athens Cathedral, be re-buried at Tatoi. To the sons of King George I, Princes Andrew, Christopher and Nicholas, standing on guard beside the coffins, the ceremony was a part of their own lives, every moment of the past fresh in their minds. To the younger generation, brought up in exile, it was more in the nature of an historical pageant, the actors in it all elderly relations.

On the last day of the lying in state there was a family dinner party. The lobster was not all that it might have been, and in the morning faces showed up ashen white under the tall black hats. None was whiter than that of Prince Philip.

There was considerable doubt as to whether the stomach would endure the strain of the funeral service. The whispered fear having been confided to his cousin Alexandra,* she began to shake with laughter below her veil, but made the practical suggestion of using the top hat as a receptacle.

The climax came afterwards, in the processional car. The top hat was put to its unaccustomed use. This posed the problem of its disposal. No solution showed itself. On arrival at the Palace, the Prince emerged from the car, the hat before him. Then it was that he caught the eye of an A.D.C. and thrust the hat towards the unsuspecting man. The A.D.C., trained to serve, took it.[13] If, in the future, he was suspicious of accepting proffered hats, he cannot be blamed.

In 1938 Prince Philip went again to Greece for a family occasion, the marriage of Crown Prince Paul, brother and heir of the King, and Princess Frederika of Hanover. The bride, who had completed her education at a finishing school at Bexhill, was the daughter of the Duke and Duchess of Brunswick and Luneburg. Her father was a great-great-grandson of George III. Her mother, Victoria Louise, was the only daughter of the ex-Kaiser. It was for the

* Daughter of King Alexander of Greece; afterwards Queen of Yugoslavia.

occasion of their wedding, in 1913, that King George V and Queen Mary had made their last visit to Berlin.

Fifty-five royalties attended the dual ceremony, among them the Duke and Duchess of Kent, the crowds roaring with delight at the sight of their lovely Princess Marina, in sky blue. Prince Philip was a best man, sharing his duties with Crown Prince Michael of Roumania and his cousin, Prince Peter, son of Prince George.[14] It was no sinecure, as forty bishops officiated at the Greek ceremony. There was then a German Protestant ceremony at the Palace, and every foot along the route of the procession stood the white-kilted Evzones.[15]

It was at an evening party that Prince Philip gave evidence that he had inherited the sense of mischief of the Danish royal family, most pronounced in the case of his great-aunt, Queen Alexandra. The magic of the old days had been reborn. Backs were very bare, and tiaras resplendent. The guests were grouped round the buffet, sipping champagne. The best man had emptied his glass. His eyes then fell upon a most tempting bare back. It belonged to a former Grand Duchess of Russia, his aunt Helen, mother of the Duchess of Kent. In her young days, ladies' bare backs had been severely left alone at evening entertainments at Tsarskoe-Selo. It was therefore with considerable alarm, indignation and shrinkage that she felt the ice-cold rim of a champagne glass pressed across her backbone. She spun round for the counter-attack, but her agile nephew had weaved his way like a shadow through the guests, and was lost to sight. Innocents, vainly declaring that innocence, had to withstand the onslaught of that outraged Grand Duchess.[16]

It was during this wedding season that the idea was born in certain Grecian minds that Prince Philip would make an excellent recruit for the Royal Hellenic Navy. Little hints were dropped as to how nice it would be if *Mon Repos* once again became his family home. Prince Andrew resisted the pressure. As for his son, the roots were deep in Scotland, at Lynden Manor, in Park Lane. The British Navy had called to his grandfather, two uncles and his cousin, and now it just as surely called to him. Greece was an interlude, and not a life. He returned to Gordonstoun, and his friends with the little boats.

On 8th April 1938 Prince Philip was called to Dr. Hahn's study and, for the second time in six months, told of a family loss. In November the news had been that Cecile, the loveliest of his sisters, had died in the Ostend air crash. Now he was informed that his Uncle George was dead. The 2nd Marquess of Milford Haven was only forty-six, a victim of cancer. Retiring from the Navy in 1932 to devote himself to a business career, he had been promoted to Captain on the retired list in 1937.[17] He had inherited the brilliant mind of his father, and only his illness robbed him of the chance of reaping the rewards. He had been a second father to Prince Philip, guiding his every step. On his death Prince Andrew asked Lord Louis Mountbatten to take on the role which had been so sincerely filled by his elder brother.[18]

A year later Prince Philip joined the Royal Naval College, Dartmouth, as a naval cadet. On 22nd July he was Captain's messenger for the day. In the afternoon the Royal Yacht, *Victoria and Albert*, dropped anchor in the river Dart. King George VI, Queen Elizabeth, Princess Elizabeth, Princess Margaret and Lord Louis Mountbatten came ashore. The King could well have chosen a more favourable date to visit the seat of his erstwhile nautical training. Not only was the rain pouring in from the Atlantic in sheets, but the College was partly immobilised by a joint epidemic of chicken-pox and mumps.[19] To ensure that the Princesses were kept free of infection, they were despatched to gardens and buildings outside the danger zone, under the care and general direction of the Captain's messenger. It was a new role for him, his own sisters being so far his senior. The elder girl was silent, the younger loquacious. He solved his problem with a compound of lemonade and croquet. Having dined on the Royal Yacht, he overslept, greeting the new day abruptly when his hammock was cut down by a petty officer.[20]

It has been the habit of Royal Families to co-operate with Heaven in the making of marriages. Queen Victoria, although she would never admit it, was not good at co-operation in any direction, having the tendency to take the chair. As a result there was often too much Victoria and not enough Heaven in the unions of her descendants. In late years, having noticed most forcefully that some whom she had brought together were unsuited, she retired from the co-operative field.

King George VI had learned much, from watching the experiences of his own family, of the dangers and pitfalls of matrimony. He had seen marriages in which Heaven was held to be one hundred per cent responsible, and he had watched the course of marriages which had received a helpful push from the Palace. His own union with the Lady Elizabeth Bowes-Lyon had proved a resounding success for the co-operative system. Yet, when the engagement received the blessing of his father, it had not been considered likely that the bride would undertake the role of Queen Consort.

The King was faced with a peculiar, and particularly difficult, problem, for it was clear that the man who married his elder daughter would one day be husband of the Queen. Continental Princes were out of fashion. German and Italian were ruled out automatically. Spanish, Grecian and Balkan were suspect. The regal past of France and Russia was history. There remained the homely states of Belgium, Holland and Scandinavia, should they be able to provide a candidate. The alternative lay in the historic families of Britain. But here there had been a marked reluctance among the sons to accept sinecures such as those which had been enjoyed by Prince Christian and the Duke of Teck, and a husband with an independent line of activity would be an obvious handicap to a young Queen.

That King George and Queen Elizabeth considered the problem at an early stage was an obvious and wise precaution. Their one thought was for the happiness of their daughter. They had to be certain. With so much at stake it was necessary that there be reins in their hands, but the guidance was given with reins of unseen, silken thread. Fortunate indeed was it that so little guidance was necessary.

When Princess Elizabeth and Prince Philip first came to know one another, they seemed, to outward appearances, to be far apart, in background, land of birth, religion. Yet for the old there was a differing picture. To Princess Louise, born in 1848, and Princess Beatrice, in 1857, living in Kensington Palace, Elizabeth was the offshoot of their eldest brother "Bertie" and Philip the offshoot of their gentle sister Alice. Among the children of Victoria and Albert it had been "Bertie" and Alice who had been the closest knit. There had been a bond of sympathy and understanding between them, and it was only in Alice that "Bertie" would confide. Now, only one long lifetime away, their great-grandchildren were drawn together by a similar bond. In the Alice line, time had proved tragic and cruel, through many changing homes and tumbling fortunes. In the "Bertie" line, the way through the years had followed a more equable course, and Windsor, Buckingham Palace and Balmoral remained much as they had been when Victoria and Albert moved about them with their children.

Yet there was little, either in looks or character, to be seen of "Bertie" in Elizabeth, or Alice in Philip. The waywardness, the tantrums, the love of gaiety, the panache of Queen Victoria's heir had been submerged in the more solid, down to earth approach to life of the Cambridges and the royal House of Denmark, while Philip was a true son of Prince Alexander of Hesse who had bolted from Russia with Julie of Hauke, his sister's lady-in-waiting. But the hands of "Bertie" and Alice stretched out towards one another through all the years. The first indication was the exchange of casual correspondence.

Prince Philip was rated Midshipman on 1st January 1940, joined the battleship *Ramillies*,[21] and was firmly in the footsteps of his grandfather and his uncles. But in his private life he faced certain difficulties. Firstly, he was a national of a country not yet at war with Germany and, although Prince Andrew had wished him to adopt British nationality in 1939, the outbreak of war had made such a step impossible. Secondly, his family was widely separated. His mother was in Athens, and there she remained throughout the German occupation, working every day in the crowded hospitals under the aegis of the Swedish and Swiss Red Cross.[22] His father was living in Monte Carlo, where he was to die of a heart attack in 1944, at the age of sixty-two. His three sisters were all in Germany. Communication was rare, and very difficult.

M*

When on leave Prince Philip had the use of a room in the Mountbatten's house in Chester Street. Meetings with Princess Elizabeth became more frequent. In 1943 they were together at a dance given by the Duchess of Kent at "Coppins", and that Christmas he was a guest at Windsor. In September 1945 a Greek newspaper published a report that an engagement would shortly be announced. This was denied. In September 1946 Prince Philip was a guest at Balmoral. The British Press forecast an engagement, and this was denied. He renounced his rights to the Greek Throne and in March 1947 became a British citizen, plain Lieutenant Mountbatten, R.N. On 10th July the engagement was formally announced. On 20th November Lieutenant Mountbatten became His Royal Highness, Philip, Duke of Edinburgh, Earl of Merioneth, Baron Greenwich, Knight of the Garter, and he drove from his grandmother's apartment in Kensington Palace to Westminster Abbey to marry Princess Elizabeth, Heir Presumptive to King George VI.[23]

There were twenty signatures on the marriage certificate of Philip Mountbatten and Elizabeth Alexandra Mary Windsor. Fittingly, the name of Alice appeared three times.* But standing out, bold and clear, was "Victoria".

The Dowager Marchioness of Milford Haven was eighty-four years old. She was the link between the years of then and now, this first of Queen Victoria's grandchildren to be born in Britain and the first to be named after her.

The marriage of the Prince of Wales and Princess Alexandra of Denmark had been hurried forward so that the scene could be set for her arrival. At Windsor the fineries of the wedding were stowed away and the nursery prepared. Alice was wearing the shift that her mother had worn at all her lyings-in, but the Queen was in tears because it was not she who was in the bed, preparing to give another child to Albert. All through the day she waited by her daughter. Then came the Irish peasant girl, who had to be bathed before doing service as a wet-nurse.

So soon did the trials start for Victoria of Hesse, and it seemed

---

* Princess Andrew of Greece; Princess Alice, Countess of Athlone; and the Duchess of Gloucester.

as if they would never end. "Frittie" falling from the window and lying still on the stones below. . . . Three wars, and poverty, and rice pudding for lunch. . . . Diphtheria raging through the family and claiming her mother and baby Marie, leaving her the keystone at fifteen. . . . Her wedding day shattered by the news of her father's secret wedding. . . . "Sandro's" expulsion from Bulgaria and "Liko's" death in the Ashanti campaign. . . . The murder of Serge and the bomb at Ena's wedding. . . . The scourge of haemophilia. . . . The retirement of Prince Louis as First Sea Lord and the shattering of his life. . . . Maurice killed in action. . . . Ekaterinburg. . . . Alapaevsk. . . . Her husband's sudden death but a few weeks after his belated recognition. . . . Prince Andrew's trial and rescue. . . . The air crash at Ostend. . . . Cancer claiming her elder son. . . . War again, and the worry of a daughter working in German-occupied Greece. . . .

So many homes had she known, but now all were memories. Kranichstein, deserted after her mother's death and haunted by the voice of her calling to her children. . . . The New Palace at Darmstadt, which funds from Queen Victoria had helped to build, now flattened by bombs of the Royal Air Force. . . . All the temporary resting-places of a sailor's wife. . . . The fine house in the Mall which they had left so sadly in October 1914. . . . Heiligenberg and Kent House, sold after the First World War. . . .

Victoria, Princess of Hesse and the Rhine, Princess of Battenberg, Marchioness of Milford Haven, was a woman of indomitable courage. The self-discipline which she imposed upon herself was of iron. She had her set of rules, and she adhered to them, and in so doing set an example the results of which are clear to see.

In the last of the evening, when the storms had blown away, the sun shone clear for the Dowager Marchioness of Milford Haven. With the birth of Prince Charles she saw the Line of Succession assured in the descendants of her mother and her uncle, King Edward VII, who had been so good and true a friend of herself and her husband. She died on 24th September 1950, a few weeks after Princess Anne was born, and was buried beside her husband in the churchyard of St. Mildred's, Whippingham. Her sister Irene, Princess Henry of Prussia, survived her by three years. Then the stitching ceased on this eventful roll of the long tapestry of Hesse and the Rhine.

THE END

BIBLIOGRAPHY

LETTERS AND DIARIES

Alice, Grand Duchess of Hesse: Letters to H.M. the Queen. (John Murray, 1885.)

Letters of Queen Victoria, 1837–1901. 1st Series edited by A. C. Benson and Viscount Esher; 2nd and 3rd Series by G. E. Buckle. (John Murray, 1907–1932.)

Further Letters of Queen Victoria. Edited by Hector Bolitho. (Thornton Butterworth, 1938.)

Letters of the Prince Consort, 1831–1861. Edited by Dr. Kurt Jagow. (John Murray, 1938.)

Leaves from the Journal of Our Life in the Highlands (1848–1861), Edited by Arthur Helps. (Smith, Elder, 1870.)

More Leaves from the Journal of a Life in the Highlands (1862–1882). (Smith, Elder, 1885.)

The Girlhood of Queen Victoria (2 vols.). Edited by Viscount Esher. (John Murray, 1912.)

George, Duke of Cambridge. Edited by Edgar Sheppard. (Longmans, Green, 1907.)

Letters of the Empress Frederick. Edited by Sir Frederick Ponsonby. (Macmillan, 1928.)

Dearest Child: Letters between Queen Victoria and the Princess Royal, 1858–1861. Edited by Roger Fulford. (Evans, 1964.)

The War Diary of the Emperor Frederick III, 1870–1871. Edited by A. R. Allinson. (Stanley Paul, 1927.)

"My Dear Duchess"–Social odd Political Letters to the Duchess of Manchester, 1858–1861. Edited by A. L. Kennedy. (John Murray, 1956.)

Queen Victoria at Windsor and Balmoral: Letters from Princess Victoria of Prussia, 1889. Edited by James Pope-Hennessy. (George Allen and Unwin, 1959.)

The Empress Frederick Writes to Sophie. Edited by Arthur Gould Lee. (Faber and Faber, 1955.)

Memoirs of Prince Hohenlohe (2 vols.). (Heinemann, 1906.)

Correspondence of Sarah Spencer, Lady Lyttleton, 1787–1870. Edited by Mrs. Hugh Wyndham. (John Murray, 1912.)

Henry Ponsonby: His Life from His Letters. By Arthur Ponsonby. (Macmillan, 1942.)

A Great Lady's Friendships: Letters to Mary, Marchioness of Salisbury, Countess of Derby. With introductions by Lady Burghclere. (Macmillan, 1933.)

Gladstone to His Wife. Edited by A. Tilney Bassett. (Methuen, 1936.)

A Victorian Diarist: Later Extracts from the Journals of Mary, Lady Monkswell, 1895–1909. Edited by the Hon. E. C. F. Collier. (John Murray, 1946.)

Letters of Lady Augusta Stanley, 1849–1863. Edited by the Dean of Windsor and Hector Bolitho. (Gerald Howe, 1927.)

In My Tower (2 vols.). By Walburga, Lady Paget. (Hutchinson, 1924.)

Reminiscences of Court and Diplomatic Life (2 vols.). By Lady Bloomfield. (Kegan Paul, 1883.)

Daisy Princess of Pless and *From My Private Diary.* Edited by D. Chapman-Huston. (John Murray, 1928 and 1931.)

A Royal Correspondence: Letters of King Edward VII and King George V to Admiral Sir Henry F. Stephenson. Edited by John Stephenson. (Macmillan, 1938.)

REMINISCENCES AND MEMOIRS

Reminiscences, by Princess Marie of Battenberg (Princess Marie zu Erbach-Schonberg). (Allen and Unwin, 1925.)

Social and Diplomatic Memories, by Sir James Rennell Rodd. (Edward Arnold, 1923.)

Things I Have Seen, by Sir Charles Oman. (Methuen, 1933.)

My Memoirs, by Princess Victoria of Prussia. (Eveleigh Nash and Grayson, 1929.)

My Memories of Six Reigns, by H.H. Princess Marie Louise. (Evans, 1956.)

The Queen Thanks Sir Howard, by Mary Howard McClintock. (John Murray, 1946.)

Recollections of Three Reigns, by Sir Frederick Ponsonby (Lord Sysonby). (Eyre and Spottiswoode, 1951.)

The Reminiscences of Lady Dorothy Nevill, by Ralph Nevill. (Edward Arnold, 1906.)

Uncensored Recollections. Anon. (J. B. Lippincott, 1924.)

Whippingham to Westminster, by Lord Ernle. (John Murray, 1938.)

Collections and Recollections, by George W. E. Russell. (Nelson, 1903.)

"Auld Acquaintance", by the Marquis of Huntly. (Hutchinson.)

George Douglas, Eighth Duke of Argyll: Autobiography and Memoirs (2 vols.) (John Murray, 1906.)

Memoirs of Sarah Bernhardt. (Heinemann, 1907.)

Not Worth Reading, by Sir George Arthur. (Longmans, Green, 1938.)

My Fifty Years, by H.R.H. Prince Nicholas of Greece. (Hutchinson, 1926.)

Once a Grand Duke, by Grand Duke Alexander of Russia. (Cassell, 1932.)

The Memoirs of Count Bernstorff. (Heinemann, 1936.)

Thatched with Gold: The Memoirs of Mabell, Countess of Airlie. Edited by Jennifer Ellis. (Hutchinson, 1962.)

Memoirs of H.R.H. Prince Christopher of Greece. (The Right Book Club, 1938.)

The Glitter and the Gold, by Consuelo Vanderbilt Balsan. (Heinemann, 1953.)

Afterthoughts, by Frances, Countess of Warwick. (Cassell, 1931.)

Recollections, by Louisa, Countess of Antrim. ("King's Stone" Press, 1937.)

Reminiscences, by "J.P.J." (Printed privately, 1929.)

A King's Story: The Memoirs of H.R.H. the Duke of Windsor, K.G. (Cassell, 1951.)

In Black and White, by Sydney Holland, Viscount Knutsford. (Edward Arnold, 1926.)

Reminiscences, by Louis, Prince of Battenberg, Marquess of Milford Haven. (Unpublished.)

Reminiscences, by Victoria, Princess of Hesse and the Rhine, Princess Louis of Battenberg, Marchioness of Milford Haven. (Unpublished.)

BIOGRAPHIES AND BIOGRAPHICAL STUDIES

The Life of William Ewart Gladstone (2 vols.), by John Morley. (Edward Lloyd, 1908.)

H.R.H. the Duke of Connaught and Strathearn, by Major-General Sir George Aston. (Harrap, 1929.)

The Royal George, by Giles St. Aubyn. (Constable, 1963.)

King Edward the Seventh, by Sir Philip Magnus. (John Murray, 1964.)

King Edward and His Times, by André Maurois. (Cassell, 1933.)

King Edward VII, by E. F. Benson. (Longmans, Green, 1933.)

King Edward VII (5 vols.), by Edgar Sanderson and Lewis Melville. (Gresham Publishing Co., 1910.)

King Edward VII (2 vols.), by Sir Sidney Lee. (Macmillan, 1927.)

Edward VII and His Circle, by Virginia Cowles. (Hamish Hamilton, 1956.)

Edward VII (2 vols.), by Sir Richard Holmes. (Amalgamated Press, 1911.)

Victoria's Heir, by George Dangerfield. (Constable, 1942.)

King Edward VII and His Court, by Sir Lionel Cust. (John Murray, 1930.)

The Private Life of Queen Alexandra, by Hans Roger Madol. (Hutchinson, 1940.)

Christian IX, by Hans Roger Madol. (Collins, 1939.)

Prince Consort, by Frank B. Chancellor. (Philip Allan, 1931.)

The Coburgs, by Edmund B. D'Auvergne. (Stanley Paul, 1911.)

The Prince Consort, by Roger Fulford. (Macmillan, 1949.)

Speeches of the Prince Consort. (John Murray, 1862.)

The Life of the Prince Consort, by Theodore Martin. (Smith, Elder, 1877.)

The Early Years of the Prince Consort, by Lieut.-General C. Grey. (Smith, Elder, 1867.)

Queen Victoria, by Richard R. Holmes. (Boussod, Valadon, 1897.)

Queen Victoria, by Sidney Lee. (Smith, Elder, 1902.)

Sidelights on Queen Victoria, by Sir Frederick Ponsonby. (Macmillan, 1930.)

Victoria the Widow and Her Son, by Hector Bolitho. (D. Appleton-Century Co., 1934.)

Queen Victoria's Relations, by Meriel Buchanan. (Cassell, 1954.)

V.R.I.: Her Life and Empire, by the Duke of Argyll. (Eyre and Spottiswoode, 1902.)

Queen Victoria, by Lytton Strachey. (Chatto and Windus, 1921.)

The Reign of Queen Victoria, by Hector Bolitho. (Collins, 1949.)

Queen Victoria, by E. F. Benson. (Longmans, Green, 1935.)

Victoria R.I., by Elizabeth Longford. (Weidenfeld and Nicolson, 1964.)

Queen Victoria As I Knew Her, by Sir Theodore Martin. (Blackwood, 1908.)

Victoria: Her Life and Reign, by Alfred E. Knight. (Partridge, 1897.)

The Mother of Queen Victoria, by D. R. Stuart. (Macmillan, 1942.)

Victoria, Queen and Ruler, by Emily Crawford. (Simpkin, Marshall, 1903.)

Life of Her Majesty Queen Victoria, by G. Barnett Smith. (Routledge, 1897.)

The Life of Queen Victoria, by W. W. Tulloch. (James Nisbet, 1901.)

Daughters of Queen Victoria, by E. F. Benson. (Cassell, 1939.)

Queen Victoria: The Story of a Noble Life. (Standard Library, 1901.)

The Queen's Resolve, by Charles Bullock. (Home Words, 1887.)

Concerning Queen Victoria and Her Son, by Sir George Arthur. (Robert Hale, 1943.)

The Private Life of the Queen, by One of Her Majesty's Servants. (C. Arthur Pearson, 1897.)

The Queen and Mr. Gladstone, by Philip Guedalla (2 vols., 1933). (Hodder and Stoughton, 1958.)

Queen Victoria and Her People, by C. S. Dawe. (Educational Supply, 1897.)

Queen Victoria, by Mrs. Oliphant. (Cassell, 1900.)

Our Queen: The Life and Times of Victoria. (Religious Book Society of Scotland, 1884.)

Queen Victoria's John Brown, by E. E. P. Tisdall. (Stanley Paul, 1938.)

Sixty Years a Queen, by Sir Herbert Maxwell. (Harmsworth, 1897.)

The Life of the Queen, by Sarah Tytler (3 vols.). (J. S. Virtue and Co.)

The English Empress, by Egon Conte Corti. (Cassell, 1957.)

The Empress Frederick, by Princess Catherine Radziwill. (Cassell, 1934.)

Prince Bismarck, by Charles Lowe. (Cassell, 1885.)

The Public and Private Life of Kaiser William II, by Edward Legge. (Eveleigh Nash, 1915.)

Kaiser Wilhelm II, by Emil Ludwig. (Putnam, 1926.)

The Private Lives of William II and His Consort, by Henry W. Fischer. (Heinemann, 1904.)

Frederick: Crown Prince and Emperor, by Rennell Rodd. (David Stott, 1888.)

"Fritz" of Prussia, by Lucy Taylor. (Nelson, 1891.)

The Emperor Francis Joseph and His Times, by Baron von Margutti. (Hutchinson, 1921.)

Alexander III of Russia, by Charles Lowe. (Heinemann, 1895.)

The Life and Tragedy of Alexandra Feodorovna, by Baroness Sophie Buxhoeveden. (Longmans, Green, 1928.)

The Minister of Evil, by William Le Queux. (Cassell, 1918.)

Rasputin: A New Judgement, by Heinz Liepman. (Frederick Muller, 1959.)

The Empress Eugenie and Her Son, by Edward Legge. (Grant Richards, 1916.)

Catherine Gladstone, by Mary Drew. (Nisbet, 1919.)

King Alfonso, by Robert Sencourt. (Faber and Faber, 1942.)

Victorian Gallery, by Meriel Buchanan. (Cassell, 1956.)

King George the Fifth, by Harold Nicolson. (Constable, 1952.)

King George V, by John Gore. (John Murray, 1941.)

Queen Mary, by James Pope-Hennessy. (George Allen and Unwin, 1959.)

Queen Mary, by Kathleen Woodward. (Hutchinson.)

Prince Louis of Battenberg, by Admiral Mark Kerr. (Longmans, Green, 1934.)

Grossherzog Ernst Ludwig, by Dr. Max Wauer. (Berlag, Darmstadt, 1938.)

Manifest Destiny, by Brian Connell. (Cassell, 1953.)

Last Viceroy, by Ray Murphy. (Jarrolds, 1948.)

Edwina: The Biography of the Countess Mountbatten of Burma, by Madeleine Masson. (Robert Hale, 1958.)

H.R.H. Princess Marina Duchess of Kent, by J. Wentworth Day. (Robert Hale, 1962.)

The Pearl from Plymouth. (British Technical and General Press, 1950.)

Prince Philip, by H.M. Queen Alexandra of Yugoslavia. (Hodder and Stoughton, 1959.)

An Unbroken Unity: A Memoir of Grand Duchess Serge of Russia, by E. M. Almedingen. (Bodley Head, 1964.)

HISTORY, POLITICS, AND MISCELLANEOUS WORKS

Monarchy in the Twentieth Century, by Sir Charles Petrie (Andrews Dakers, 1952.)

The Court at Windsor, by Christopher Hibbert. (Longmans, 1964.)

1914, by Field-Marshal Viscount French of Ypres. (Constable, 1919.)

Behind the Throne, by Paul H. Emden. (Hodder and Stoughton, 1934.)

A Century of British Monarchy, by Hector Bolitho. (Longmans, Green, 1951.)

The Story of Buckingham Palace, by Bruce Graeme. (Hutchinson, 1928.)

A Queen at Home, by Vera Watson. (W. H. Allen, 1952.)

Balmoral, by Ivor Brown. (Collins, 1955.)

Milestones to the Silver Jubilee. Edited by H. C. Dent. (Halcyon Book Co., 1935.)

The Royal House of Greece, by Arthur S. Gould Lee. (Ward Lock, 1948.)

Roumania and Her Rulers, by Mrs. Philip Martineau. (Stanley Paul, 1927.)

The Mountbatten Lineage. Prepared for private circulation by Admiral of the Fleet, The Earl Mountbatten of Burma. (1958.)

The Royal Family in Africa, by Dermot Morrah. (Hutchinson, 1947.)

Church of St. Mildred, Whippingham, by R. W. Trelease. (1958.)

Blair Castle. Compiled under the supervision of the 9th Duke of Atholl.

Coronation Commentary, by Geoffrey Dennis. (Dodd, Mead, 1937.)

Close of a Dynasty, by Vice-Admiral Sir Francis Pridham. (Allan Wingate, 1956.)

The Royal Marriage Mart of Europe, by Princess Catherine Radziwill. (Cassell, 1915.)

Le Tragique Destin de Nicholas II, by P. Gilliard. (Payot, Paris, 1921.)

Confessions of an Anarchist, by W.C.H. (Grant Richards, 1911.)

The Crown and the People, by Allan A. Michie. (Secker and Warburg, 1952.)

The Fall of the Romanoffs. Anon. (Herbert Jenkins, 1918.)

The House of Teck, by Louis Felberman. (John Long, 1911.)

Europe Since Napoleon, by Elizabeth Levett. (Blackie, 1913.)

The Windsor Tapestry, by Compton Mackenzie. (Rich and Cowan, 1938.)

Towards Disaster—The Greek Army in Asia Minor in 1921, by Prince Andrew of Greece. (Translated from the Greek by H.R.H. Princess Andrew of Greece.) (John Murray, 1930.)

Russia and History's Turning Point, by Alexander Kerensky. (Duell, Sloan and Pearce, New York, 1966.)

PERIODICALS AND MAGAZINES

The Illustrated London News
The Graphic
London Society (1863)
The Sphere
The Tatler

The Observer
The Times
The Sunday Times
The Daily Telegraph
The Morning Post

The Sketch
Punch
The Queen

The Sunday Express
The Daily Express
The Daily Mail
The Daily Mirror
The Daily Sketch

SOURCES

CHAPTER I

1. Barnett Smith: *Life of Queen Victoria*, p. 202.
2. Fulford: *Dearest Child*, p. 151; Kronberg Archives.
3. *Victoria, Letters*, 16th May 1843.
4. Longford: *Victoria R.I.*, p. 234.
5. Fulford: *Dearest Child*, p. 267; Kronberg Archives.
6. Crawford: *Victoria*, p. 269.
7. Barnett Smith: *Life of Queen Victoria*, p. 167.
8. Bolitho: *Further Letters of Queen Victoria*, 6th Oct. 1856.
9. *War Diary of Emperor Frederick*, p. 167.
10. Kennedy: *My Dear Duchess*, p. 232.
11. Crawford: *Victoria*, p. 344.
12. Lorne: *V.R.I.*, p. 150.
13. Crawford: *Victoria*, p. 244.
14. Wyndham: *Lady Lyttleton*, p. 338.
15. *Victoria, Letters*, 16th May 1843.
16. Ibid., 6th June 1843.
17. Wyndham: *Lady Lyttleton*, p. 339.
18. *Political Hits*, No. 11.
19. Graeme: *Buckingham Palace*, p. 250.
20. *Punch*, 1846.
21. Benson: *Daughters of Queen Victoria*, p. 25.
22. Bloomfield: *Reminiscences of Court and Diplomatic Life*.
23. Wyndham: *Lady Lyttleton*, p. 340.
24. J.P.J.: *Reminiscences*, p. 49.
25. Jagow: *Letters of the Prince Consort*, p. 233.
26. *Princess Alice*: Memorial Volume; Knight, *Victoria*, p. 134.
27. *Victoria, Letters*, 22nd May 1849.
28. Ibid., 2nd July 1850.
29. *Our Queen*, p. 150.

CHAPTER II

1. Information from the late Marquess of Carisbrooke.
2. *Victoria, Leaves*, 10th Sept. 1855.

375

3. Sheppard: *George, Duke of Cambridge* (I), p. 197.
4. *Punch*, Sept. 1855.
5. *Victoria, Leaves*, 29th Sept. 1855.
6. *Victoria, Letters*.
7. *The Times*.
8. Barnett Smith: *Life of Queen Victoria*, p. 332.
9. Corti: *The English Empress*.
10. Fulford: *Dearest Child*, p. 78.
11. *Greville Diary*.
12. Fulford: *Dearest Child*, p. 184.
13. Martin: *Life of the Prince Consort* (IV), p. 427.
14. *Uncensored Recollections*, p. 146.
15. Corti: *The English Empress*, p. 55.
16. Kennedy: *My Dear Duchess*, p. 72.
17. Ibid., p. 79.
18. Fulford: *Dearest Child*, p. 212.
19. *Victoria, Leaves*, 7th Oct. 1859.
20. Fulford: *Dearest Child*, p. 231.
21. Kennedy: *My Dear Duchess*, p. 91.
22. Ibid.
23. Ibid., p. 93.
24. *Uncensored Recollections*, pp. 142–4.
25. Kennedy: *My Dear Duchess*, p. 171.
26. Holden: *The Pearl from Plymouth*, p. 51.
27. Arthur: *Not Worth Reading*, p. 8.
28. Legge: *Empress Eugenie and Her Son*, p. 254; *Memoirs of Sarah Bernhardt*, p. 138.
29. Arthur: *Not Worth Reading*, p. 8.

CHAPTER III

1. *Victoria, Letters*, 25th April 1860.
2. Kennedy: *My Dear Duchess*, p. 102.
3. Ibid., p. 103.
4. *Victoria, Letters*, 25th April 1860.
5. Corti: *The English Empress*, p. 61.
6. Kennedy: *My Dear Duchess*, p. 96.
7. Fulford: *Dearest Child*, p. 257.
8. Jagow: *Letters of the Prince Consort*, p. 233.
9. Fulford: *Dearest Child*, p. 260.
10. Kennedy: *My Dear Duchess*, p. 106.
11. *Victoria, Letters*, 31st July 1860.
12. *Letters of Lady Augusta Stanley*.
13. Fulford: *Dearest Child*, p. 267.

14. Tilney Bassett: *Gladstone to his Wife*, p. 151.

15. Chancellor: *Prince Consort*, p. 260.

16. *Duke Ernest Memoirs*, IV, p. 55.

17. Chancellor: *Prince Consort*, p. 261.

CHAPTER IV

1. Corti: *The English Empress*, p. 64.

2. *Victoria, Letters*, 1st Dec. 1860.

3. Bolitho: *Further Letters*, 30th Nov. 1860.

4. *Victoria, Letters*, 1st Dec. 1860; *Princess Alice* Memorial Vol., pp. 16, 17.

5. Tytler: *Life of the Queen*, p. 182.

6. Corti: *The English Empress*, p. 64.

7. *Victoria, Letters*, 4th Dec. 1860.

8. Bolitho: *Reign of Queen Victoria*, p. 176.

9. Jagow: *Letters of the Prince Consort*, p. 356.

10. Arthur: *Concerning Queen Victoria and her Son*, p. 102.

11. Kennedy: *My Dear Duchess*, p. 136.

12. Creston: *Mother of Queen Victoria*, p. 286; Martin: *Life of the Prince Consort* (V), p. 54.

13. Kennedy: *My Dear Duchess*, p. 144.

14. Barnett Smith: *Life of Queen Victoria*, p. 345.

15. Cowles: *Edward VII and his Circle*, p. 49.

16. Lee: *King Edward VII* (I), p. 118.

17. *Victoria, Letters*, 26th Aug. 1861.

18. Lee: *King Edward VII* (1), p. 119.

19. Barnett Smith: *Life of Queen Victoria*, p. 346.

20. *Victoria, Leaves*, 27th Aug. 1861.

21. Kennedy: *My Dear Duchess*, p. 174.

22. Magnus: *King Edward the Seventh*.

23. Le Moine: *Quebec, Past and Present*.

24. Fulford: *Dearest Child*, p. 353.

25. Ibid., p. 355.

26. *Victoria, Leaves*, 20th Sept. 1861.

27. *Blair Castle*.

28. *Victoria, Leaves*, 8th and 9th Oct. 1861.

29. Ibid., 16th Oct. 1861.

30. Fulford: *Dearest Child*, p. 365.

CHAPTER V

1. Jagow: *Letters of the Prince Consort*, p. 369.

2. Corti: *The English Empress*, p. 69.

3. Jagow: *Letters of the Prince Consort*, p. 370.
4. Fulford: *Dearest Child*, p. 367.
   Magnus: *King Edward the Seventh.*
   Longford: *Victoria R.I.*, p. 293.
   Fulford: *The Prince Consort*, p. 264.
5. *Victoria, Letters*, 12th Nov. 1861.
6. Fulford: *The Prince Consort*, p. 51.
7. Longford: *Victoria R.I.*, p. 293.
8. Corti: *The English Empress*, p. 72.
9. Fulford: *Dearest Child*, p. 352.
10. *Prince Consort, Speeches*, p. 53.
11. Ibid., p. 52.
12. Jagow: *Letters of the Prince Consort*, p. 371.
13. Fulford: *The Prince Consort*, p. 265.
14. Barnett Smith: *Life of Queen Victoria*, p. 348.
15. Corti: *The English Empress*, p. 81.
16. Martin: *Life of the Prince Consort* (V), p. 421.
17. *Victoria, Letters*, 9th Dec. 1861.
18. Knight: *Victoria*, p. 242.
19. Longford: *Victoria R.I.*, p. 298.
20. Sheppard: *George, Duke of Cambridge* (I), p. 223.
21. Wyndham: *Lady Lyttleton*, p. 422.
22. Barnett Smith: *Life of Queen Victoria*, p. 351.
23. Bolitho: *A Century of British Monarchy*, p. 73; *Letters of Lady Augusta Bruce.*
24. Journal; Lorne: *V.R.I.*, p. 227.
25. Bolitho: *A Century of British Monarchy*, p. 75.
26. Ibid.

CHAPTER VI

1. Corti: *The English Empress*, p. 77.
2. Longford: *Victoria R.I.*, p. 307.
3. *Alice, Letters*, p. 307.
4. Tytler: *Life of the Queen*, p. 199.
5. *Memoirs of Prince Hohenlohe* (I), p. 88.
6. *Alice, Letters*, p. 307.
7. Sheppard: *George, Duke of Cambridge* (I), p. 224.
8. *Daily Telegraph*, 24th Dec. 1861.
9. Ibid.
10. *Victoria, Letters*, 24th Dec. 1861.
11. Kennedy: *My Dear Duchess*, p. 189.
12. Lee: *King Edward VII* (I), p. 126.
13. Kennedy: *My Dear Duchess*, p. 180.

14. Ibid.
15. Memo by Grand Duchess of Baden; *Princess Alice* Memorial Volume, pp. 18, 19.
16. *Private Life of the Queen*, p. 166.
17. Benson: *Daughters of Queen Victoria*, p. 68.
18. Kennedy: *My Dear Duchess*, p. 196.
19. Bolitho: *Further Letters of Queen Victoria*, 26th May 1862.
20. Kennedy: *My Dear Duchess*, p. 193.
21. *Illustrated London News*, 12th July 1862.
22. Kennedy: *My Dear Duchess*, p. 193.
23. *Duke of Argyll, Memoirs* (II), pp. 185–7.
24. Bolitho: *Further Letters of Queen Victoria*, 26th May 1862.
25. Watson: *A Queen at Home*, p. 157.
26. *Illustrated London News*, 5th July 1862.
27. Ibid., 28th June 1862.

CHAPTER VII

1. Journal, 1st July 1862.
2. Sheppard: *George, Duke of Cambridge* (I), p. 231.
3. *Illustrated London News*, 5th July 1862.
4. Journal, 1st July 1862.
5. Benson: *Daughters of Queen Victoria*, p. 76.
6. Aston: *H.R.H. Duke of Connaught*, p. 50.
7. *Illustrated London News*, 12th July 1862.
8. *Alice, Letters*, p. 13.
9. Jagow: *Letters of the Prince Consort*.
10. 7th Feb. 1862. Kronberg Archives; Corti: *The English Empress*, p. 80.
11. *Illustrated London News*, 12th July 1862.
12. *Punch*, 12th July 1862, p. 15.
13. Ibid., p. 14.
14. *Illustrated London News*, 19th July 1862.
15. Ibid.

CHAPTER VIII

1. Rodd: *Social and Diplomatic Memories*, p. 298.
2. Arthur: *Not Worth Reading*, p. 11.
3. Marie of Battenberg: *Reminiscences*, p. 25.
4. Longford: *Victoria R.I.*, p. 313.
5. *Alice, Letters*, p. 63.
6. Paget: *Embassies of Other Days*.
7. Corti: *The English Empress*, p. 93.

8. *H.R.H. Princess Louise*, p. 89.
9. Kennedy: *My Dear Duchess*, p. 201.
10. Cowles: *Edward VII and his Circle*.
11. Madol: *Christian IXth*.
12. Corti: *The English Empress*, p. 97.
13. Paget: *Embassies of Other Days*.
14. Corti: *The English Empress*, p. 97.
15. Lee: *Edward VII* (I), p. 154.
16. *London Society*, April 1863.
17. Ibid., March 1863.
18. Malmesbury: *Memories of an Ex-Minister*.
19. Kennedy: *My Dear Duchess*, p. 214.
20. Journal, 10th March 1863.
21. Kronberg Archives.
22. Buchanan: *Queen Victoria's Relations*, p. 51; Grand Ducal Archives.
23. Sheppard: *George, Duke of Cambridge* (I), p. 239.
24. *Our Queen*, pp. 217–220.
25. *Victoria, Letters*, 12th May 1863.
26. Barnett Smith: *Life of Queen Victoria*, p. 368.
27. *Victoria, Letters*, 18th May 1863.
28. *Alice, Letters*, p. 70.

CHAPTER IX

1. *The Mountbatten Lineage*, p. 305.
2. Sheppard: *George, Duke of Cambridge* (I), p. 244.
3. Bolitho: *Further Letters*, p. 137.
4. Morley: *Life of Gladstone* (I), p. 549.
5. Ibid., p. 547.
6. Tilney Bassett: *Gladstone to his Wife*, p. 151.
7. Marie of Battenberg: *Reminiscences*, p. 24.
8. Crawford: *Victoria, Queen and Ruler*, p. 346.
9. Corti: *The English Empress*, p. 97.
10. Tilney Bassett: *Gladstone to his Wife*, p. 153.
11. *More Leaves*, 7th Oct. 1863.
12. Morley: *The Life of Gladstone* (I), p. 551.
13. *More Leaves*, 13th Oct. 1863.
14. Benson: *Daughters of Queen Victoria*, p. 102.
15. Huntly: *Auld Acquaintance*, pp. 23, 24.
16. Crawford: *Victoria, Queen and Ruler*, p. 326.
17. *The Mountbatten Lineage*.
18. *Alice, Letters*.
19. Longford: *Victoria R.I.*, p. 325.
20. *Alice, Letters*; Crawford: *Queen and Ruler*, p. 324.

CHAPTER X

1. Kennedy: *My Dear Duchess*, p. 232.
2. *H.R.H. Princess Louise*, p. 121.
3. *Daily Telegraph*.
4. Kennedy: *My Dear Duchess*, p. 232.
5. Nicolson: *King George V*, p. 4.
6. Ponsonby: *Letters of the Empress Frederick*, p. 57.
7. Longford: *Victoria R.I.*, p. 369.
8. Kronberg Archives.
9. Lee: *Queen Victoria*, p. 360.
10. *Victoria, Letters*, 6th Sept. 1865.
11. *Alice, Letters*, p. 122.
12. Ibid., p. 112.
13. *The Mountbatten Lineage*.
14. Marie of Battenberg: *Reminiscences*, p. 69.
15. Tytler: *Life of the Queen*, p. 235.
16. Sheppard: *George, Duke of Cambridge* (I), p. 262.
17. Buchanan: *Queen Victoria's Relations*, p. 56.
18. Private information.
19. *Victoria, Letters*, 21st July 1866.
20. Marie of Battenberg: *Reminiscences*, p. 79.
21. *The Mountbatten Lineage*.
22. Tytler: *Life of the Queen*, p. 235.
23. *The Mountbatten Lineage*, pp. 261–2.
24. Benson: *Daughters of Queen Victoria*, p. 112.
25. Ibid.
26. *Alice, Letters*, p. 141.
27. Crawford: *Victoria, Queen and Ruler*, p. 390.
28. Ponsonby: *Letters of the Empress Frederick*, p. 66.
29. Radziwill: *The Empress Frederick*, p. 95.
30. Buchanan: *Queen Victoria's Relations*, p. 57.
31. McClintock: *The Queen Thanks Sir Howard*, p. 86.

CHAPTER XI

1. Hardinge: *An Account of a Night spent with the Duke of Kent at Ealing*. 1811.
2. Pope-Hennessy: *Queen Mary*.
3. Private information.
4. *Daily Telegraph*.
5. Dawe: *Queen Victoria and Her People*, p. 180; *Alice, Letters*, p. 89.
6. *The Private Life of the Queen*, p. 69.
7. Crawford: *Victoria, Queen and Ruler*, p. 332.

8. Longford: *Victoria R.I.*, p. 370.
9. *Alice, Letters.*
10. Ponsonby: *Henry Ponsonby*, p. 91.
11. Ibid., p. 71.
12. Ibid., p. 300.
13. *Alice, Letters*, p. 127.
14. Lee: *Queen Victoria*, p. 356.
15. Longford: *Victoria R.I.*, p. 370.
16. *Alice, Letters*, p. 179.
17. Marie of Battenberg: *Reminiscences*, p. 98.
18. Buchanan: *Queen Victoria's Relations*, p. 58.
19. Lee: *Queen Victoria*, p. 382.
20. Sheppard: *George, Duke of Cambridge* (I), p. 271; Tytler: *Life of the Queen*, p. 238.
21. Buxhoeveden: *Life of Alexandra Feodorovna*, p. 5.
22. *Alice, Letters*, p. 186.
23. Buchanan: *Queen Victoria's Relations*, p. 91; Grand Ducal Archives.
24. Hohenlohe: *Memoirs* (I), p. 346.
25. *Alice, Letters*, p. 205.
26. Ibid., p. 208.

CHAPTER XII

1. Mark Kerr: *Prince Louis of Battenberg*, p. 5.
2. Marie of Battenberg: *Reminiscences*, p. 33.
3. *The Mountbatten Lineage*, p. 267.
4. *Victoria, Letters*, 11th May 1839.
5. Buchanan: *Queen Victoria's Relations*, p. 89.
6. *The Mountbatten Lineage*, p. 280.
7. Buchanan: *Queen Victoria's Relations*, p. 89.
8. Information from Earl Mountbatten.
9. Ibid.
10. Ibid.
11. *The Mountbatten Lineage*, p. 270; *Queen Victoria's Relations*, p. 91.
12. Mark Kerr: *Prince Louis of Battenberg*, p. 7.
13. Marie of Battenberg: *Reminiscences*, p. 185.
14. Mark Kerr: *Prince Louis of Battenberg*, p. 9.

CHAPTER XIII

1. *Victoria, Letters*, 24th Nov. 1869.
2. Lee: *Queen Victoria*, p. 411.
3. *Victoria, Letters*, 29th Nov. 1869.

4. Corti: *The English Empress.*
5. *Western Morning News,* Oct. 1870.
6. Pope-Hennessy: *Queen Mary,* p. 211.
7. *More Leaves,* 3rd Oct. 1870.
8. Russell: *The Amberley Papers* (II).
9. *Alice, Letters,* p. 236.
10. Ponsonby: *Letters of the Empress Frederick,* p. 76.
11. Ibid.
12. *Alice, Letters,* p. 216.
13. Ibid., p. 217.
14. Ibid., 219.
15. *Victoria, Letters,* 6th Sept. 1870.
16. Ponsonby: *Letters of the Empress Frederick,* p. 395; *Empress Frederick: A Memoir,* p. 328.
17. Benson: *Daughters of Queen Victoria,* p. 138; Radziwill: *The Empress Frederick,* p. 105.
18. Martin: *Social Notes; Alice, Letters,* p. 330.
19. Queen Victoria: *A Noble Life,* p. 101.
20. Bloomfield: *Reminiscences of Court and Diplomatic Life,* p. 343.
21. *War Diary of Emperor Frederick III,* p. 167.
22. Ibid., p. 334.
23. *Alice, Letters,* p. 229.
24. Ibid., p. 243.
25. Dennis: *Coronation Commentary,* p. 17.
26. Guedalla: *The Queen and Mr. Gladstone,* p. 85.
27. Ibid., p. 82.
28. Longford: *Victoria R.I.,* pp. 383–5.
29. Guedalla: *The Queen and Mr. Gladstone,* p. 88.
30. Countess of Antrim: *Recollections,* p. 83.
31. Longford: *Victoria R.I.,* p. 386.
32. Journal, 4th Sept. 1871.
33. Morley: *Life of Gladstone* (I), p. 761.
34. Lee: *King Edward VII* (I), p. 321.
35. Holmes: *Edward VII* (I), 243.
36. Benson: *Daughters of Queen Victoria,* p. 164.
37. Journal, 29th Nov. 1871.
38. *The Graphic,* Dec. 1871.
39. Ponsonby: *Henry Ponsonby,* p. 99.
40. Sheppard: *George, Duke of Cambridge* (I), 303.
41. Journal, 13th Dec. 1871.
42. Gwyer: *Poems and Prose.*
43. Drew: *Catherine Gladstone,* p. 99.

CHAPTER XIV

1. Kennedy: *My Dear Duchess*, p. 102.
2. Lorne: *V.R.I.*, p. 282.
3. *Alice, Letters*, p. 28.
4. Benson: *Daughters of Queen Victoria*, p. 123.
5. Arthur: *Not Worth Reading*, p. 11.
6. Marie of Battenberg: *Reminiscences*.
7. Corti: *The English Empress*, p. 166.
8. Ernle: *From Whippingham to Westminster*, p. 63.
9. Radziwill: *The Empress Frederick*, p. 153.
10. *Private Life of the Queen*, p. 161.
11. Arthur: *Not Worth Reading*, p. 12.
12. Countess of Warwick: *Afterthoughts*, p. 272.
13. *Alice, Letters*, p. 248.
14. Longford, *Victoria R.I.*, p. 235.
15. Creston: *The Mother of Victoria*, p. 191.
16. Ibid.
17. *Alice, Letters*, p. 36.
18. Ibid., p. 282.
19. Longford, *Victoria R.I.*, p. 394.
20. *Alice, Letters*, p. 279.
21. Ibid., p. 303.
22. Ibid., p. 260.
23. *Our Queen*, p. 277.
24. McClintock: *The Queen Thanks Sir Howard*, p. 154.
25. Arthur: *Not Worth Reading*, p. 13.
26. Trelease: *Church of St. Mildred*.
27. Ernle: *From Whippingham to Westminster*, p. 6.
28. Ibid., pp. 61–3.
29. Information from Prince Louis of Hesse.
30. *Alice, Letters*, p. 252.
31. Ibid., p. 295.
32. *More Leaves*, 26th Sept. 1876.
33. Arthur: *Not Worth Reading*, p. 14.
34. *Alice, Letters*, p. 305.
35. Ibid.

CHAPTER XV

1. *Our Queen*, p. 276.
2. *Alice, Letters*, p. 39.
3. Arthur: *Not Worth Reading*, p. 12.
4. *Alice, Letters*, p. 42.

5. Journal, 13th–16th Nov. 1878.
6. *Alice, Letters*, p. 51.
7. Scott Stevenson: *Morrell Mackenzie*, p. 90.
8. Journal, 14th Dec. 1878.
9. Ibid.
10. Lee: *King Edward VII* (I), p. 592.
11. Magnus: *King Edward the Seventh*, p. 95.
12. *The Times*, 16th Dec. 1878.
13. Dawe: *Queen Victoria and Her People*, p. 183.
14. Taylor: *Fritz of Prussia*, p. 405.
15. *Our Queen*, p. 284.
16. Almedingen: *An Unbroken Unity*, p. 16.
17. Buchanan: *Queen Victoria's Relations*, p. 66.
18. Ibid.

CHAPTER XVI

1. *Alice, Letters*, p. 48.
2. Ibid., p. 277.
3. Buxhoeveden: *The Life and Tragedy of Alexandra Feodorovna*, p. 13.
4. Stephenson: *A Royal Correspondence*, p. 40.
5. Magnus: *King Edward the Seventh*, p. 248.
6. Longford: *Victoria R.I.*, p. 426.
7. McClintock: *The Queen Thanks Sir Howard*.
8. Ibid., p. 202.
9. *More Leaves*, 27th May 1879.
10. Magnus: *King Edward the Seventh*, p. 80.
11. Crawford: *Victoria, Queen and Ruler*, p. 384.
12. In a letter to the author.
13. Ponsonby: *Henry Ponsonby*, p. 119.
14. Lee: *King Edward VII* (I), p. 544.
15. Journal, 7th May 1879.
16. Princess Marie Louise: *My Memories of Six Reigns*, p. 61; Buchanan: *Queen Victoria's Relations*, p. 29.
17. Princess Marie Louise: *My Memories of Six Reigns*, p. 61.
18. Buchanan: *Victorian Gallery*, p. 33.
19. Barnett Smith: *Life of Queen Victoria*, p. 410.
20. Martineau: *Roumania and Her Rulers*, p. 119.
21. Stirling: *Victorian Sidelights*.
22. *The Mountbatten Lineage*.
23. Ibid.
24. *The Graphic*, 12th June 1880.
25. Ibid., 19th March 1881.

CHAPTER XVII

1. Buchanan: *Queen Victoria's Relations*, p. 94.
2. Fischer: *The Private Lives of William II and his Consort;* Legge: *The Public and Private Life of Kaiser William.*
3. Buchanan: *Queen Victoria's Relations*, p. 94.
4. Murphy: *Last Viceroy*, pp. 22–23; Mark Kerr: *Prince Louis of Battenberg*, p. 107.
5. Benson: *Daughters of Queen Victoria*, p. 122.
6. *The Mountbatten Lineage*, p. 323.
7. Longford: *Victoria, R.I.*, p. 479.
8. Pope-Hennessy: *Queen Victoria at Windsor and Balmoral*, p. 17.
9. Princess Victoria of Prussia: *My Memoirs*, p. 67.
10. Ponsonby: *Letters of the Empress Frederick*, p. 202.
11. *The Mountbatten Lineage*, p. 320.
12. Ponsonby: *Henry Ponsonby*, p. 301.
13. Crawford: *Victoria, Queen and Ruler*, p. 383.
14. Longford: *Victoria R.I.*, p. 477.
15. Ponsonby: *Henry Ponsonby*, p. 301.
16. Crawford: *Victoria, Queen and Ruler*, p. 383.
17. *The Mountbatten Lineage*, p. 320.
18. Holmes: *Edward VII* (I), p. 332.
19. Journal, 28th March 1884.
20. Ponsonby: *Henry Ponsonby*, p. 300.
21. Princess Marie of Battenberg: *Reminiscences*, p. 183.
22. *The Mountbatten Lineage*, p. 320.
23. Ponsonby: *Henry Ponsonby*, p. 303.
24. Information from Earl Mountbatten.
25. Ponsonby: *Henry Ponsonby*, p. 302.
26. St. Aubyn: *The Royal George*, p. 276.
27. Ponsonby: *Henry Ponsonby*, p. 303.
28. *Uncensored Recollections*, p. 127.
29. Information from the Marquess of Carisbrooke.

CHAPTER XVIII

1. Ponsonby: *Henry Ponsonby*, p. 303.
2. McClintock: *The Queen Thanks Sir Howard*, p. 229.
3. Buxhoeveden: *The Life and Tragedy of Alexandra Feodorovna*, p. 18.
4. Buchanan: *Queen Victoria's Relations*, p. 95.
5. *The Mountbatten Lineage*, p. 306.
6. Buchanan: *Victorian Gallery*, p. 147.
7. Journal, 29th Dec. 1884.
8. Corti: *The English Empress,* pp. 225-7. (Letters to the Crown Princess).

9. Ibid.
10. Connell: *Manifest Destiny*, p. 31.
11. Longford: *Victoria R.I.*, p. 481.
12. Princess Marie of Battenberg: *Reminiscences*, pp. 217–18.
13. Ibid.
14. Watson: *A Queen at Home*, p. 253.
15. Information from the Marquess of Carisbrooke.
16. *The Mountbatten Lineage*, p. 295.
17. Lowe: *Alexander III of Russia* (a quotation from Pastor Koch), p. 146.
18. Ponsonby: *Letters of the Empress Frederick*, p. 202; Busch: *Diary*.
19. McClintock: *The Queen Thanks Sir Howard*, p. 236.
20. Princess Marie of Battenberg: *Reminiscences*, pp. 242–4.
21. Ibid.
22. *Victoria, Letters*, 23rd Aug. 1886.
23. *The Mountbatten Lineage*, p. 292.
24. Lowe: *Alexander III of Russia*, p. 175.
25. Journal, 8th Dec. 1886.

CHAPTER XIX

1. Corti: *The English Empress*, p. 237.
2. Rennell Rodd: *Frederick, Crown Prince and Emperor*, p. 167.
3. *The Mountbatten Lineage*, pp. 227, 271.
4. Bolitho: *Further Letters*, p. 260, 18th March 1887.
5. Radziwill: *The Empress Frederick*, p. 174.
6. Ponsonby: *Letters of the Empress Frederick*, p. 264.
7. Ibid., p. 266.
8. Princess Victoria: *My Memoirs*, p. 85.
9. Corti: *The English Empress*, p. 242.
10. Ibid., p. 243.
11. Ibid., p. 242.
12. Princess Victoria: *My Memoirs*, p. 81.
13. Lorne: *V.R.I.*, p. 346.
14. Taylor: *Fritz of Prussia*, p. 508.
15. Ibid., p. 459.
16. Journal, 26th Aug. 1887.
17. Private information.
18. Morell Mackenzie: *Frederick the Noble*, p. 65.
19. Princess Victoria: *My Memoirs*, p. 91.
20. Legge: *The Public and Private Life of Kaiser William II*, p. 60.
21. Corti: *The English Empress*, p. 270.
22. Princess Victoria: *My Memoirs*, p. 74.
23. Corti: *The English Empress*, pp. 271–2.

24. Ponsonby: *Letters of the Empress Frederick*, p. 300.
25. Corti: *The English Empress*, p. 274.
26. *The Mountbatten Lineage*, p. 292.
27. Corti: *The English Empress*, p. 274.
28. Ponsonby: *Letters of the Empress Frederick*, p. 299.
29. Ibid., p. 296.
30. Journal, 23rd April 1888.
31. Ibid.
32. Ibid., 24th April 1888.
33. *Victoria, Letters*. Note to p. 404. 25th April 1888.
34. Bolitho: *Further Letters*, p. 268.
35. Journal, 25th April 1888.
36. Corti: *The English Empress*, p. 276.
37. Taylor: *Fritz of Prussia*, p. 492.
38. Princess Victoria: *My Memoirs*, p. 96.
39. Radziwill: *The Empress Frederick*, p. 218.
40. Corti: *The English Empress*, p. 378.
41. Ibid., p. 302. From the account written by the Empress Frederick.
42. Ponsonby: *Letters of the Empress Frederick*, p. 319.
43. Lee: *Queen Victoria*, p. 492.

CHAPTER XX

1. *The Mountbatten Lineage*.
2. *Illustrated London News*, 19th March 1892.
3. Ibid.
4. Sheppard: *George, Duke of Cambridge* (II), p. 229.
5. Journal, 13th March 1892.
6. Gould Lee: *The Empress Frederick Writes to Sophie*, p. 110.
7. *The Mountbatten Lineage*, pp. 308–10.
8. Princess Marie of Battenberg: *Reminiscences*, p. 252.
9. Journal, 23rd April 1892.
10. Buchanan: *Queen Victoria's Relations*, p. 28.
11. Buxhoeveden: *The Life and Tragedy of Alexandra Feodorovna*, p. 21.
12. Ibid., p. 23.
13. Pope-Hennessy: *Queen Mary*, p. 190.
14. Ibid., p. 191.
15. Ibid., p. 196.
16. Private information.
17. Buxhoeveden: *The Life and Tragedy of Alexandra Feodorovna*, p. 27.
18. Buchanan: *Queen Victoria's Relations*, p. 115; Pope-Hennessy: *Queen Mary*, pp. 51, 75–6.
19. Nicolson: *King George V*, p. 44.
20. Pope-Hennessy: *Queen Mary*, p. 251.

21. Buchanan: *Queen Victoria's Relations*, p. 26.
22. Crawford: *Victoria, Queen and Ruler*, p. 326.
23. Gould Lee: *The Empress Frederick Writes to Sophie*, p. 150.
24. Journal, 6th July 1893.
25. Ibid., 9th Jan. 1894.
26. Gould Lee: *The Empress Frederick Writes to Sophie*, p. 159.
27. Longford: *Victoria R.I.*, p. 531.
28. Buchanan: *Queen Victoria's Relations*, p. 30.
29. Ponsonby: *Henry Ponsonby*, p. 306.
30. Journal, 17th April 1894.
31. Gould Lee: *The Empress Frederick Writes to Sophie*, p. 170.
32. Journal, 20th April 1894.

CHAPTER XXI

1. Buxhoeveden: *The Life and Tragedy of Alexandra Feodorovna*, p. 36.
2. Ibid., p. 38.
3. Journal, 16th July 1894.
4. Grand Duke Alexander: *Once a Grand Duke*, p. 189; Lowe: *Alexander III*, p. 329.
5. Prince Nicholas: *My Fifty Years*, p. 116.
6. Ibid., p. 118.
7. Buxhoeveden: *The Life and Tragedy of Alexandra Feodorovna*, p. 41.
8. Lowe: *Alexander III*, p. 292.
9. Dangerfield: *Queen Victoria's Heir*, p. 309.
10. Pope-Hennessy: *Queen Mary*, p. 309.
11. Lowe: *Alexander III*, p. 296.
12. Pope-Hennessy: *Queen Mary*, p. 309.
13. Ibid.
14. Lowe: *Alexander III*, p. 303; *Illustrated London News*, 24th Nov. 1894.
15. Buxhoeveden: *The Life and Tragedy of Alexandra Feodorovna*, p. 43; *Illustrated London News*, 1st Dec. 1894.
16. Magnus: *King Edward the Seventh*, p. 248.

CHAPTER XXII

1. *Illustrated London News*, 1st Feb. 1896.
2. Princess Marie of Battenberg: *Reminiscences*, p. 272.
3. *The Mountbatten Lineage*.
4. Consuelo Vanderbilt Balsan: *The Glitter and the Gold*, p. 28.
5. Princess Marie of Battenberg: *Reminiscences*, p. 272.
6. Ponsonby: *Henry Ponsonby*, p. 87.

7. Ibid., p. 92.
8. *Illustrated London News.*
9. Information from the Marquess of Carisbrooke.
10. Journal, 17th Nov. 1895.
11. Ibid.
12. Barnett Smith: *Life of Queen Victoria*, p. 484.
13. Ibid.
14. Journal, 14th Dec. 1895.
15. Barnett Smith: 486–489; *Illustrated London News.*
16. Information from the Marquess of Carisbrooke.
17. Journal, 22nd Jan. 1896.
18. Longford: *Victoria R.I.*, p. 480.
19. Pope-Hennessy: *Queen Victoria at Windsor and Balmoral*, p. 33.
20. Pope-Hennessy: *Queen Mary*, p. 317.
21. Princess Marie Louise: *My Memories of Six Reigns*, p. 145; Martineau: *Roumania and Her Rulers*, p. 120.
22. Information from the Marquess of Carisbrooke.
23. Russell: *Collections and Recollections*, p. 213.
24. Journal, 22nd Jan. 1896.

CHAPTER XXIII

1. Collier: *A Victorian Diarist*, p. 16.
2. *Illustrated London News*, 26th Sept. 1896.
3. Magnus: *King Edward the Seventh*, p. 206.
4. Benson: *King Edward VII*, p. 179.
5. Journal, 28th Sept. 1896.
6. Ibid., 3rd Oct. 1896.
7. Buxhoeveden: *The Life and Tragedy of Alexandra Feodorovna*, p. 73.
8. Buchanan: *Queen Victoria's Relations*, p. 208.
9. Buxhoeveden: *The Life and Tragedy of Alexandra Feodorovna*, p. 59.
10. Grand Duke Alexander: *Once a Grand Duke*, p. 196.
11. *The Memoirs of Count Bernstorff*, p. 32.
12. Ibid.
13. Collier: *A Victorian Diarist*, p. 4.
14. *Illustrated London News*, 6th June 1896.
15. Grand Duke Alexander: *Once a Grand Duke*, p. 193.
16. Ibid.
17. Lee: *King Edward VII* (I), p. 698.
18. Cowles: *Edward VII and His Circle*, p. 342; Mossolov: *At the Court of the Last Czar.*
19. Buxhoeveden: *The Life and Tragedy of Alexandra Feodorovna*, p. 78.
20. Ibid., p. 131.

CHAPTER XXIV

1. Prince Nicholas of Greece: *My Fifty Years*, p. 178.
2. Buchanan: *Queen Victoria's Relations*, p. 38.
3. Prince Nicholas of Greece: *My Fifty Years*, p. 178.
4. Pope-Hennessy: *Queen Mary*, p. 324.
5. Chapman-Huston: *The Private Diaries of Daisy, Princess of Pless*, p. 55.
6. Ibid.
7. *The Memoirs of Count Bernstorff*, p. 34.
8. Buchanan: *Queen Victoria's Relations*, p. 32.
9. Ibid.
10. Fischer: *The Private Lives of William II and His Consort*, p. 340.
11. Gould Lee: *The Empress Frederick Writes to Sophie*, p. 221.
12. Ibid., p. 229.
13. Ibid., p. 180.
14. Buxhoeveden: *The Life and Tragedy of Alexandra Feodorovna*, p. 67.
15. Buchanan: *Queen Victoria's Relations*, p. 34.
16. Radziwill: *The Royal Marriage Mart of Europe*, p. 256.
17. Journal, 24th May 1899.
18. Buchanan: *Queen Victoria's Relations*, p. 4.
19. Buxhoeveden: *The Life and Tragedy of Alexandra Feodorovna*, p. 100.
20. *The Mountbatten Lineage*.
21. Buchanan: *Queen Victoria's Relations*, p. 196.
22. Grand Duke Alexander: *Once a Grand Duke*, p. 370.

CHAPTER XXV

1. Journal, 22nd June 1897.
2. Ibid.
3. Legge: *The Public and Private Life of Kaiser William II*, p. 67.
4. Gould Lee: *The Empress Frederick Writes to Sophie*, p. 304.
5. Longford: *Victoria, R.I.*, p. 547.
6. Connell: *Manifest Destiny*, p. 131.
7. Ibid., p. 36.
8. Journal, 31st Dec. 1900.
9. Ibid., 2nd Jan. 1901.
10. Esher: *The Girlhood of Queen Victoria* (I), p. 44.
11. Ponsonby: *Recollections of Three Reigns*, p. 87.
12. Lorne: *V.R.I.*, p. 396.
13. Ponsonby: *Recollections of Three Reigns*, p. 89; Aston: *H.R.H. The Duke of Connaught*, p. 224.
14. *Morning Post*, 4th Feb. 1901.
15. Connell: *Manifest Destiny*, p. 37.

16. Princess Marie of Battenberg: *Reminiscences*, p. 291.
17. Buchanan: *Queen Victoria's Relations*, p. 174.
18. *The Mountbatten Lineage*.
19. Ibid., p. 327.
20. Buchanan: *Queen Victoria's Relations*, p. 174.
21. *The Mountbatten Lineage*, p. 327.
22. Princess Marie of Battenberg: *Reminiscences*, p. 293.
23. Buchanan: *Queen Victoria's Relations*, p, 175.
24. Mark Kerr: *Prince Louis of Battenberg*, p. 170.
25. Princess Marie of Battenberg: *Reminiscences*, p. 294.
26. Buchanan: *Queen Victoria's Relations*, p. 176.
27. Princess Marie of Battenberg, *Reminiscences*, p. 294.
28. Mark Kerr: *Prince Louis of Battenberg*, p. 171.
29. Ibid.; *Memoirs of Prince Christopher of Greece*, p. 61.
30. Ibid.; Princess Marie of Battenberg: *Reminiscences*, p. 294.

CHAPTER XXVI

1. *Confessions of an Anarchist*, p. 64.
2. *The Fall of the Romanoffs*, p. 29.
3. Buxhoeveden: *The Life and Tragedy of Alexandra Feodorovna*, p. 110.
4. Almedingen: *An Unbroken Unity*, p. 52.
5. Ibid., p. 111; Buchanan: *Queen Victoria's Relations*, p. 105; *The Fall of the Romanoffs*, p. 33.
6. *The Fall of the Romanoffs*, p. 33.
7. Prince Nicholas of Greece: *My Fifty Years*, p. 90.
8. Almedingen: *An Unbroken Unity*, p. 54.
9. *The Fall of the Romanoffs*, p. 33; Prince Nicholas of Greece: *My Fifty Years*, p. 90.
10. Buxhoeveden: *The Life and Tragedy of Alexandra Feodorovna*, p. 111.
11. Buchanan: *Victorian Gallery*, p. 148.
12. Almedingen: *An Unbroken Unity*, p. 62.
13. *The Mountbatten Lineage*, p. 306.
14. Buchanan: *Queen Victoria's Relations*, p. 106.
15. Almedingen: *An Unbroken Unity*, p. 65.
16. Hessian Grand Ducal Archives.
17. *Confessions of an Anarchist*, p. 46.
18. Sencourt: *King Alfonso*, p. 88.
19. Information from the Marquess of Carisbrooke.
20. Princess Marie of Battenberg: *Reminiscences*, p. 306.
21. Ibid., p. 313.
22. Sencourt: *King Alfonso*, p. 94.
23. Gore: *King George V*, p. 212.
24. Collier: *A Victorian Diarist*, p. 169.

25. Ibid.
26. Princess Marie of Battenberg: *Reminiscences*, p. 321.
27. Ibid.
28. Information from the Marquess of Carisbrooke.
29. Princess Marie of Battenberg: *Reminiscences*, p. 321.
30. Ibid.
31. Information from the Marquess of Carisbrooke.

CHAPTER XXVII

1. Fischer: *The Private Lives of William II and His Consort*, p. 297.
2. Ibid.
3. Ibid., p. 347.
4. Gould Lee: *The Empress Frederick Writes to Sophie*, p. 73.
5. *The Mountbatten Lineage*, p. 308.
6. Gould Lee: *The Empress Frederick Writes to Sophie*, p. 237.
7. Princess Marie of Battenberg: *Reminiscences*, p. 294.
8. Longford: *Victoria R.I.*, p. 518.
9. Journal, 17th Sept. 1900.
10. Fischer: *The Private Lives of William II and His Consort*, p. 298.
11. Ibid., 294–9; *Illustrated London News*, 25th Dec. 1897.
12. *Illustrated London News*, 25th Dec. 1897.
13. Rennell Rodd: *Memories, 1894–1901*, p. 198.
14. Gould Lee: *The Empress Frederick Writes to Sophie*, p. 264.
15. Lee: *King Edward VII* (II), p. 140.
16. Fischer: *The Private Lives of William II and His Consort*, p. 36.
17. Daisy, Princess of Pless: *From My Private Diary*, p. 108.
18. Ibid.
19. Ponsonby: *Recollections of Three Reigns*, p. 141.
20. Lee: *King Edward VII* (II), p. 9.
21. Ibid.
22. Ibid.
23. Ponsonby: *Recollections of Three Reigns*, p. 194.
24. Ibid., pp. 264–6.
25. Nicolson: *King George V*, p. 206.
26. Duke of Windsor: *A King's Story*, p. 98.
27. Gore: *King George V*, p. 286.
28. Ibid.
29. Nicolson: *King George V*, pp. 245–6.
30. Ibid., p. 246.
31. Ibid., p. 245.
32. Ibid., p. 246.
33. Ibid., p. 245.

34. Gore: *King George V*, p. 288.
35. Ponsonby: *Recollections of Three Reigns*, p. 308.

CHAPTER XXVIII

1. *The Mountbatten Lineage*, p. 325.
2. Ibid.
3. Marden: *Fear God; Dread Naught* (II), p. 49.
4. *The Mountbatten Lineage*, p. 347.
5. Masson: *Edwina*, p. 63.
6. Connell: *Manifest Destiny*, p. 44.
7. Princess Marie of Battenberg: *Reminiscences*, p. 374.
8. Mark Kerr: *Prince Louis of Battenberg*, p. 243.
9. Ibid.
10. *The Mountbatten Lineage*, p. 326.
11. Ibid.; Connell, p. 45; Mark Kerr, p. 243; Masson, p. 63.
12. Information from the Marquess of Carisbrooke.
13. Connell: *Manifest Destiny*, p. 46.
14. Masson: *Edwina*, p. 64.
15. Mark Kerr: *Prince Louis of Battenberg*, p. 246.
16. Nicolson: *King George V*, p. 251.
17. The Duke of Windsor: *A King's Story*, p. 108.
18. Mark Kerr: *Prince Louis of Battenberg*, p. 258.
19. Murphy: *Last Viceroy*, p. 34.
20. Ibid.; Connell: *Manifest Destiny*, p. 47.
21. Hatch: *The Magnificent Mountbattens*.
22. *The Mountbatten Lineage*, p. 301.
23. French: *1914*, p. 240.
24. Arthur: *Not Worth Reading*, p. 153.
25. Ibid., p. 201.
26. Legge: *The Empress Eugenie and Her Son*, p. 157.

CHAPTER XXIX

1. Princess Marie Louise: *My Memories of Six Reigns*, pp. 186–8.
2. Ibid.
3. Buxhoeveden: *The Life and Tragedy of Alexandra Feodorovna*, p. 133.
4. Ibid.; Le Queux: *The Minister of Evil*; Liepman: *Rasputin: A New Judgement*.
5. Fischer: *The Private Lives of William II and His Consort*, p. 4.
6. Buxhoeveden: *The Life and Tragedy of Alexandra Feodorovna*, p. 133.
7. Lee: *King Edward VII* (I), p. 693.
8. Gore: *King George V*, p. 307.
9. Moorehead: *The Russian Revolution*.

10. Ibid.; Buxhoeveden, p. 241; *Memoirs of Prince Christopher of Greece*, pp. 58–60.
11. Buxhoeveden: *The Life and Tragedy of Alexandra Feodorovna*, p. 244.
12. Pridham: *Close of a Dynasty*, p. 27.
13. Moorehead: *The Russian Revolution*.
14. Pridham: *Close of a Dynasty*, p. 30; *The Fall of the Romanoffs*.
15. Nicolson: *King George V*, p. 301.
16. Buxhoeveden: *The Life and Tragedy of Alexandra Feodorovna*, p. 274.
17. Ibid., p. 299.
18. Moorehead: *The Russian Revolution*.
19. Buxhoeveden: *The Life and Tragedy of Alexandra Feodorovna*.
20. Ibid., p. 329.
21. Ibid., pp. 330–4.
22. *Illustrated London News*, 1st Jan. 1921; Gilliard: *Thirteen Years at the Russian Court*.
23. Ibid.
24. Buxhoeveden: *The Life and Tragedy of Alexandra Feodorovna*, p. 342.
25. *Illustrated London News*, 1st Jan. 1921; Gilliard: *Thirteen Years at the Russian Court*.
26. Ibid.
27. Buxhoeveden: *The Life and Tragedy of Alexandra Feodorovna*, p. 345.
28. *Illustrated London News*, 1st Jan. 1921; Gilliard,; *Thirteen Years at the Russian Court*
29. Ibid.
30. Ibid.

CHAPTER XXX

1. Buxhoeveden: *The Life and Tragedy of Alexandra Feodorovna*, p. 239.
2. Buchanan: *Queen Victoria's Relations*, p. 109.
3. Buxhoeveden: *The Life and Tragedy of Alexandra Feodorovna*, p. 110
4. Almedingen: *An Unbroken Unity*, pp. 92–100.
5. Buchanan: *Queen Victoria's Relations*, p. 110.
6. Ibid., p. 111.
7. Grand Duke Alexander: *Once a Grand Duke*, p. 372.
8. Almedingen: *An Unbroken Unity*, pp. 121–7.
9. *The Mountbatten Lineage*, p. 306.
10. *Memoirs of Prince Christopher of Greece*, p. 54; Almedingen: *An Unbroken Unity*, p. 127.
11. Ibid.; Prince Nicholas of Greece: *My Fifty Years*, p. 90.
12. Mark Kerr: *Prince Louis of Battenberg*, p. 261; Almedingen: *An Unbroken Unity*, p. 129.
13. Prince Nicholas of Greece: *My Fifty Years*, p. 90.
14. Mark Kerr: *Prince Louis of Battenberg*, p. 261.

15. *The Mountbatten Lineage*, p. 306.
16. Mark Kerr: *Prince Louis of Battenberg*, p. 262.
17. Ibid.

CHAPTER XXXI

1. Gould Lee: *The Royal House of Greece*, p. 31.
2. *Memoirs of Prince Christopher of Greece*, p. 44.
3. Ibid., p. 16.
4. Buchanan: *Queen Victoria's Relations*, p. 178.
5. Prince Nicholas of Greece: *My Fifty Years*, pp. 33–8.
6. Ibid., p. 38.
7. Martineau: *Roumania and Her Rulers*, p. 199.
8. Prince Nicholas of Greece: *My Fifty Years*, p. 83.
9. Martineau: *Roumania and Her Rulers*, p. 200.
10. Wentworth Day: *H.R.H. Princess Marina, Duchess of Kent*, p. 20.
11. Prince Nicholas of Greece: *My Fifty Years*, p. 233.
12. Gould Lee: *The Royal House of Greece*, p. 36.
13. *Memoirs of Prince Christopher of Greece*, p. 117.
14. Gould Lee: *The Royal House of Greece*, p. 31.
15. Buchanan: *Queen Victoria's Relations*, p. 183.
16. Nicolson: *King George V*, p. 281.
17. Prince Nicholas of Greece: *My Fifty Years*, p. 267.
18. *Memoirs of Prince Christopher of Greece*, p. 131–6.
19. Nicolson: *King George V*, p. 282.
20. Buchanan: *Queen Victoria's Relations*, p. 183; *Memoirs of Prince Christopher of Greece*, p. 138.
21. Queen Alexandra of Yugoslavia: *Prince Philip*, p. 29.
22. Prince Nicholas of Greece: *My Fifty Years*, p. 279.
23. Buchanan: *Queen Victoria's Relations*, p. 185.
24. Princess Marie of Battenberg: *Reminiscences*, p. 270.
25. Prince Nicholas of Greece: *My Fifty Years*, p. 289.
26. Ibid., p. 291.
27. Princess Marie of Battenberg: *Reminiscences*, p. 270.
28. *The Mountbatten Lineage*, p. 326; Mark Kerr: *Prince Louis of Battenberg*, p. 285.
29. *Memoirs of Prince Christopher of Greece*, pp. 172–3.
30. Gould Lee: *The Royal House of Greece*.
31. Prince Andrew of Greece: *Towards Disaster*.
32. Sir Leslie Hollis: *The Captain-General*.
33. Kolarz: *Myths and Realities in Eastern Europe*, p. 235.
34. Prince Andrew of Greece: *Towards Disaster*.
35. Ibid., p. 287.
36. Mark Kerr: *Prince Louis of Battenberg*, p. 291.

37. Ibid., p. 292.
38. Prince Andrew of Greece: *Towards Disaster.*
39. Ibid.
40. Gould Lee: *The Royal House of Greece*, p. 53.
41. Ibid.
42. Prince Andrew of Greece: *Towards Disaster*, Intro.
43. *Memoirs of Prince Christopher of Greece*, p. 174.
44. Prince Nicholas of Greece: *My Fifty Years*, p. 313.
45. *Memoirs of Prince Christopher of Greece*, p. 175.
46. Ibid.
47. Ibid.
48. Queen Alexandra of Yugoslavia: *Prince Philip*, p. 34.
49. Ibid.
50. *Memoirs of Prince Christopher of Greece*, p. 176.
51. Queen Alexandra of Yugoslavia: *Prince Philip*, p. 35.
52. Prince Andrew of Greece: *Towards Disaster*, Intro.
53. Nicolson: *King George V*, p. 372.
54. *The Mountbatten Lineage*, p. 330.
55. Connell: *Manifest Destiny*, p. 193.
56. Sir Leslie Hollis: *The Captain-General;* Queen Alexandra of Yugoslavia: *Prince Philip*, p. 35.

CHAPTER XXXII

1. *The Mountbatten Lineage*, p. 352.
2. *Daily Sketch; Daily Mail; Daily Mirror.*
3. Ibid., 19th July 1922.
4. *The Mountbatten Lineage*, p. 340.
5. Mark Kerr: *Prince Louis of Battenberg*, p. 290.
6. *The Mountbatten Lineage*, p. 310.
7. Buchanan: *Queen Victoria's Relations*, p. 44.
8. Ibid.
9. Ibid.
10. *The Mountbatten Lineage*, p. 310.
11. *Princess Alice, Letters.*
12. *The Mountbatten Lineage*, p. 317.
13. Buchanan: *Queen Victoria's Relations*, p. 45.
14. Private information.
15. *The Mountbatten Lineage.*
16. Private information.
17. *The Mountbatten Lineage*, p. 315.
18. *Ernest Ludwig*, p. 19.
19. Ibid., p. 25.
20. *Daily Mail; Daily Sketch*, 17th Nov. 1937.

21. *Daily Mail; Daily Mirror*, 18 Nov. 1937.
22. *Daily Express*, 20 Nov. 1937.

CHAPTER XXXIII

1. Gould Lee: *The Royal House of Greece*, p. 55.
2. Martineau: *Roumania and Her Rulers*, p. 194.
3. *Memoirs of Prince Christopher of Greece*, p. 190.
4. Martineau: *Roumania and Her Rulers*, p. 191.
5. Gould Lee: *The Royal House of Greece*, p. 59.
6. *The Mountbatten Lineage*, p. 339.
7. Ibid., p. 360.
8. Connell: *Manifest Destiny*, p. 196.
9. Ibid., p. 193; Buchanan: *Queen Victoria's Relations*, p. 189.
10. Hollis: *The Captain-General*.
11. Buchanan: *Queen Victoria's Relations*, p. 189.
12. *Memoirs of Prince Christopher of Greece*, p. 278.
13. Queen Alexandra of Yugoslavia: *Prince Philip*, p. 53.
14. *Daily Mirror*, 10th Jan. 1938; *Weekly Illustrated*, 22nd Jan. 1938.
15. *Daily Mirror*, 10th Jan. 1938.
16. Queen Alexandra of Yugoslavia: *Prince Philip*, p. 56.
17. *The Mountbatten Lineage*, p. 348.
18. Connell: *Manifest Destiny*, p. 198.
19. Wheeler-Bennett: *King George VI*, p. 396.
20. Hollis: *The Captain-General*.
21. *The Mountbatten Lineage*, p. 360.
22. Buchanan: *Queen Victoria's Relations*, p. 189; Connell: *Manifest Destiny*, p. 198.
23. *The Mountbatten Lineage*, p. 361; Connell: *Manifest Destiny*, p. 203.

INDEX

INDEX

Aberdeen, 111

Abergeldie Castle, 56, 107, 158

Acheson, Hon. Patrick, 21

Adelaide, Queen, 41

Alapaevsk, 302, 323-4

ALBANY:

Alice Mary Victoria, Princess. *See* Athlone, Princess Alice, Countess of

Helen Frederica, Duchess of, 266

Leopold, Prince, Duke of, 18, 21, 52, 63, 100, 181, 185, 197, 246

Leopold Charles. *See* Saxe-Coburg and Gotha, Duke of

Albert, Prince Consort, fondness for babies, 14-16; criticism of over alterations to Buckingham Palace, 19-20; teaches Princess Alice, 30; 1860—last visit to Germany, 44; escape in carriage accident, 45; 1861—the death of the Duchess of Kent, 50-2; visits Ireland, 54; the last great expeditions at Balmoral, 56-60; autumn worries on return to Windsor, 62-3; disturbed over behaviour of Prince of Wales, 64-7; visits Cambridge and develops fever, 67; death, 69-70; funeral, 72-3; mentioned, 18, 20, 21, 26, 32, 34, 39, 42, 48, 52, 54, 77, 98, 106, 116, 128, 154, 168, 234, 242, 246, 272

Albert Victor, Prince. *See* Clarence, Duke of

Alberta, Royal Yacht, 268

Albion Home for Girls, 178

Albrecht, Archduke, 34

Aldershot, 47, 244

Alencon, Duchess of, 266

Alexandra, Queen, 51, 54-6, 65, 97-100, 157-63, 209, 238, 261, 273, 292-3, 308

Alfred, Prince, Duke of Edinburgh. *See* Saxe-Coburg and Gotha, Duke of

Alice Bazaar, 174

Alicefrauenverein, 173-4

Alice Hospital, 150, 174

Alice, Princess of Great Britain and Ireland, Princess Louis of Hesse, Grand Duchess of Hesse and the Rhine, birth of, 13-14; as baby, 14; painted by Landseer, 16; christening, 17-18; vaccinated, 18; childhood bond with Prince of Wales, 22; present during attacks on the Queen, 22-3; plays in amateur theatricals, 23; schoolroom days, 27; at wedding of Princess Royal,

28; takes lessons from her father, 30-1; confirmation, 31; meets Prince of Orange, 34; forms unfavourable impression of him, 35; high spirits at seventeen, 38-9; 1860—meets Prince Louis of Hesse, 42; falls in love, 42; first visit to Germany, 44-5; engagement, 48; 1861—Parliament approves financial provision, 50; the death of the Duchess of Kent, 50-1; visits Ireland with parents, 54-5; accompanies her parents on the last great expeditions from Balmoral, 56-60; nurses her father, 68-9; deep bond with her father, 69; sends for the Prince of Wales, 69; at death of Prince Albert, 70; accompanies her mother to Osborne, 72; sole support of her mother, 71; 1862—strength and example, 76; *The Times* pays tribute, 77; plans for wedding, 78-81; married at Osborne, 82-5; honeymoon, 85-6; departure for Germany, 86; wedding presents, 88-9; arrival at Darmstadt, 89-90; early problems in Darmstadt court circles, 91-3; first home in Hesse, 95; meets Queen Victoria at Gotha, 97; 1863—at wedding of Prince of Wales, 100; birth of first child, Victoria, 101; christening, 101-2; resists mother's efforts to persuade her to live in England, 103; moves into new summer home of Kranichstein, 105; autumn holiday at Balmoral, 107; fortunate escape in carriage accident, 108-11; 1864—the Schleswig-Holstein war, 111-12; problems over her mother's loneliness, 113; birth of daughter, Elizabeth, 114; 1865—differences of opinion with the Queen, 116-17; at meeting of Queen Victoria and King of Prussia, 120; 1866—the building of the New Palace in Darmstadt, 120; the Seven Weeks War, 121-5; birth of third daughter, Irene, 123; nurses in the hospitals, 122; pleads for agreement with Prussia, 125; hardships in impoverished Hesse, 125; war experiences increase her interest in nursing, 126; 1867—seeks financial aid from her mother, 128-9; rift with Queen, 130-1; entertained by Napoleon in Paris, 133; entertains